Professional Learning Communities
Divergence, Depth and Dilemmas

Professional Learning

Series Editors: Ivor Goodson and Andy Hargreaves

The work of teachers has changed significantly in recent years and now, more than ever, there is a pressing need for high-quality professional development. This timely new series examines the actual and possible forms of professional learning, professional knowledge, professional development and professional standards that are beginning to emerge and be debated at the beginning of the twenty-first century. The series will be important reading for teachers, teacher educators, staff developers and policy makers throughout the English-speaking world.

Professional Learning Communities
Divergence, Depth and Dilemmas

Louise Stoll and Karen Seashore Louis

Open University Press

Open University Press
McGraw-Hill Education
McGraw-Hill House
Shoppenhangers Road
Maidenhead
Berkshire
England
SL6 2QL

email: enquiries@openup.co.uk
world wide web: www.openup.co.uk

and Two Penn Plaza, New York, NY 10121-2289, USA

First published 2007

A catalogue record of this book is available from the British Library

ISBN-10: 0 335 22030 4 (pb) 0 335 22031 2 (hb)
ISBN-13: 978 0 335 22030 4 (pb) 978 0 335 22031 1 (hb)

Library of Congress Cataloging-in-Publication Data
CIP data applied for

Typeset by YHT Ltd
Printed in Poland EU by OZGraf S.A. *www.polskabook.pl*

The *McGraw·Hill* Companies

Dedication

To friends and colleagues in our own national and international professional learning communities, and with special memories of Ray

Contents

List of figures and tables

Figures

Tables

List of contributors

Dr Dorothy Andrews is the Director of the Leadership Research Institute (LRI) and the National Director of IDEAS in the Faculty of Education, University of Southern Queensland. Dorothy teaches in the areas of curriculum and pedagogy, leadership and organizational theory. Her current field of research is in the area of school improvement. Within the LRI, she is a member of the IDEAS Core Team which was awarded the Gold Medal of the Australian Council for Educational Leaders (ACEL) in 2003.

Ray Bolam was Emeritus Professor of Education in the School of Social Sciences at Cardiff University. He was a co-director of the Effective Professional Learning Communities (EPLC) Project. Before his untimely death in August 2006, he had recently co-written, for the General Teaching Council in England, a policy-oriented research synthesis on continuing professional development for capacity building.

Lynn Butler-Kisber is an Associate Professor in the Department of Integrated Studies in Education at McGill University in Montreal. She is Director of the Centre for Educational Leadership, and of the Graduate Certificate Programs in Educational Leadership. She teaches courses on language arts, qualitative research, and teacher education. Her research and development activities have focused on classroom processes, literacy learning, student engagement, educational leadership, professional development, and qualitative methodologies.

Angela Greenwood is a primary school headteacher. She has taught in both primary and secondary education and has worked in initial teacher education. Angela was seconded to the Effective Professional Learning Communities (EPLC) Project as a headteacher researcher. Her particular interest has been in the international dimension in education as a school improvement tool, having researched this area for her doctorate.

Richard Halverson is an Assistant Professor in Educational Leadership and Policy Analysis at the University of Wisconsin-Madison. His research develops conceptual frameworks based on cognitive psychology and classical philosophy to capture the complexity, expertise and situated nature of instructional leadership practice in schools and seeks to communicate findings to researchers and practitioners through developing online, multimedia cases of practice.

Andy Hargreaves is the Thomas More Brennan Chair in Education at Boston College, USA. With a background of teaching and lecturing in the UK, then co-founding the International Center for Educational Change in Toronto, Canada, Professor Hargreaves has written or edited 25 books in education. His book *Teaching in the Knowledge Society* (2003) received an Outstanding Book Award in Curriculum Studies from the American Educational Research Association. His most recent book, co-authored with Dean Fink, is *Sustainable Leadership*.

Kristine Kiefer Hipp is an Associate Professor in Leadership Studies at Cardinal Stritch University in Milwaukee, Wisconsin. She consults widely, facilitating organizational change in school districts related to her research on leadership and professional learning communities. Dr Hipp regularly presents at the regional, nation, and international levels, and publishes in refereed journals and book chapters. Recently she co-authored *Reculturing Schools as Professional Learning Communities*.

Ilana S. Horn is Assistant Professor of Mathematics Education at the University of Washington. Her specialization is secondary mathematics, with a focus on issues of classroom teaching and learning, the influence of departmental organization on both students' and teachers' learning and identities, teacher communities, and equity-geared reforms.

Jane Bumpers Huffman is an Associate Professor in Educational Administration at the University of North Texas, Denton, Texas. She teaches masters and doctoral level courses in leadership, theory, and organizational change. Dr Huffman presents regionally and nationally, and publishes in peer reviewed journals and book chapters. In 2003, she co-authored *Reculturing Schools as Professional Learning Communities* with Kristine Kiefer Hipp and other contributing authors.

David Jackson led England's National College for School Leadership's Networked Learning Communities (NLC) programme – the world's largest network-based school reform initiative, involving 130 NLCs (1500 schools). Previously, he was a headteacher for 14 years. He has taught at the University of Cambridge and has published on a range of topics – including leadership, school improvement, knowledge management, student voice, and networked learning.

Dr Sharon D. Kruse is a Professor in the Department of Educational Foundations and Leadership at the University of Akron. Among her publications are two co-authored books on school change and improvement, the first with Karen Seashore Louis, *Professionalism and Community: Perspective on Reforming Urban Schools* (Corwin Press, 1995), and the second with Jason Earle, *Organizational Literacy for Educators* (Lawrence Erlbaum, 1999).

Dr Marian Lewis is a Senior Lecturer in the Faculty of Education and member of the Leadership Research Institute (LRI) of the University of Southern Queensland. Within the LRI, Marian is a member of the IDEAS Core Team which was awarded the Gold Medal of the Australian Council for Educational Leaders (ACEL) in 2003. Her research is in the area of knowledge creation – more specifically, how contextualized professional knowledge may be created by the professional community within schools.

Ann Lieberman, an Emeritus Professor from Teachers College, Columbia University is now a senior scholar at the Carnegie Foundation for the Advancement of Teaching. She is widely known for her work in the areas of teacher leadership and development, networks, teacher learning communities and the prospects and problems of school improvement. Her unique contribution has been that she has been able to go between school and university – embracing the dualities of our field – theory/practice; process/content; intellectual/social learning; and policy and practice.

Judith W. Little is Professor of Education at the University of California, Berkeley. Her research interests centre on the workplace contexts of teaching, teachers' careers and collegial relationships, and policies and practices of professional development. In her most recent research, she has delved into the nature of teachers' professional community and its relationship to teacher development and school reform.

Karen Seashore Louis is Rodney S. Wallace Professor of Educational Policy and Administration at the University of Minnesota. Her primary research interests focus on school improvement and school reform, especially improvement in K-12 leadership and policy over the last 30 years, particularly in urban secondary schools. She is the author of many books, the most recent of which are *Organizing for School Change* (2006) and *Aligning Student Support with Achievement Goals: The Secondary Principal's Guide* (2006) (with Molly F. Gordon).

Milbrey W. McLaughlin is the David Jacks Professor of Education and Public Policy at Stanford University. Professor McLaughlin is Co-Director of the Center for Research on the Context of Teaching, and Executive Director of the John W. Gardner Center for Youth and Their Communities, a partnership between Stanford University and Bay Area communities to build new practices, knowledge and capacity for youth development and learning. She is widely published in education policy issues, contexts for teaching and learning, productive environments for youth, and community-based organizations.

Dr Coral Mitchell is an Associate Professor in the Faculty of Education at Brock University, St Catharines, Ontario. Her areas of research are the development of extended learning communities in schools and the educational roles of school principals. She uses these investigations to inform her teaching of graduate-level courses in educational change, ethics in educational leadership, group dynamics, and school organization.

Bill Mulford is the Professor and Director of the Leadership for Learning Research Group in Faculty of Education at the University of Tasmania. He has been a teacher, principal, assistant director of education and past president of the Australian Council for Educational Administration (ACEA) and the Commonwealth Council for Educational Administration (CCEAM). He acts as an advisor to state and national departments of education and consultant to international organizations such as the Organization for Economic Co-operation and Development (OECD) and the United Nations Educational, Scientific, and Cultural Organization (UNESCO). He continues to research and publish extensively in the areas of educational leadership, organizational learning and student outcomes.

Jan Robertson is an Associate Professor and Assistant Dean in the School of Education, the University of Waikato, Hamilton, New Zealand. She is Director of the Educational Leadership Centre and teaches in the leadership programme. Her research and development interests are leadership coaching, higher education leadership programmes and action research with practitioners. Jan is also a member of ILERN – an international leadership in education research network funded by the National College for School Leadership in the United Kingdom.

Dr Larry Sackney is a Professor of Educational Administration at the University of Saskatchewan. His areas of research include institutional capacity building, school effectiveness and school improvement, planning and leadership. His current research is focused on capacity building and knowledge management in the learning community. He was a founding member of the International Congress for School Effectiveness and Improvement (ICSEI) and served as its third president.

Sylvia Sklar, Associate Director at the Centre for Educational Leadership (CEL), McGill University, has more than 25 years of experience in designing and managing a wide variety of non-credit professional development programmes for all stakeholders in education. She has also presented workshops for educators in Europe, the Caribbean and North America. She is currently Assistant Professor in the Department of Integrated Studies in Education (DISE) at McGill.

Louise Stoll is Past President of the International Congress for School Effectiveness and Improvement and Visiting Professor at the London Centre for Leadership in Learning, Institute of Education, University of London, and University of Bath. She was a co-director of the Effective Professional Learning Communities (EPLC) Project. Her current research, development work and writing focuses on capacity building and professional learning communities within and between schools nationally and internationally.

Joan E. Talbert is Senior Research Scholar and Co-director of the Center for Research on the Context of Teaching at Stanford University. She is author or co-author of books, articles, and chapters on teacher professional communities and careers, school organization and policy contexts, math education reform, research methods for studying embedded contexts of teaching, and district system reform. Recent publications include *Professional Communities and the Work of High School Teaching* (with Milbrey W. McLaughlin).

Julie Temperley is Director of Temperley Research Limited, designing and delivering development and research projects that yield useful outcomes for practitioners and policy makers. She helped develop the research and knowledge management strands of the National College for School Leadership's (NCSL's) Networked Learning Communities programme. Recent publications include NCSL's *Network Leadership in Action* series, and *Improving Schools through Collaborative Enquiry* (Continuum Press, 2005), co-edited with Hilary Street.

Tom Whittingham is Leadership, Management and Governance Strategy Manager in South Gloucestershire Local Authority in England. He has taught in both primary and secondary schools, and was headteacher of two primary schools. He leads international learning in South Gloucestershire and was instrumental in creating a Leadership Academy across the Children and Young People's Service in 2004. He is particularly interested in developing international professional learning communities to extend learning opportunities built on innovative international leadership partnerships.

Series editors' preface

Teaching today is increasingly complex work, requiring the highest standards of professional practice to perform it well (Hargreaves and Goodson 1996). It is the core profession, the key agent of change in today's knowledge society. Teachers are the midwives of that knowledge society. Without them, or their competence, the future will be malformed and stillborn. In the United States, George W. Bush's educational slogan has been to leave no child behind. What is clear today in general, and in this book in particular, is that leaving no child behind means leaving no teacher or leader behind either. Yet, teaching too is also in crisis, staring tragedy in the face. There is a demographic exodus occurring in the profession as many teachers in the ageing cohort of the Boomer generation are retiring early because of stress, burnout or disillusionment with the impact of years of mandated reform on their lives and work. After a decade of relentless reform in a climate of shaming and blaming teachers for perpetuating poor standards, the attractiveness of teaching as a profession has faded fast among potential new recruits.

Teaching has to compete much harder against other professions for high calibre candidates than it did in the last period of mass recruitment – when able women were led to feel that only nursing and secretarial work were viable options. Teaching may not yet have reverted to being an occupation for 'unmarriageable women and unsaleable men' as Willard Waller described it in 1932, but many American inner cities now run their school systems on high numbers of uncertified teachers. The teacher recruitment crisis in England has led some schools to move to a four-day week; more and more schools are run on the increasingly casualized labour of temporary teachers from overseas, or endless supply teachers whose quality busy administrators do not always have time to monitor (Townsend 2001). Meanwhile in the Canadian province of Ontario, in 2001, hard-nosed and hard-headed reform strategies led in a single year to a decrease in applications to teacher education programmes in faculties of education by 20–25 per cent, and a drop in a whole grade level of accepted applicants.

Amid all this despair and danger though, there remains great hope and some reasons for optimism about a future of learning that is tied in its vision to an empowering, imaginative and inclusive vision for teaching as well. The educational standards movement is showing visible signs of over-reaching itself as people are starting to complain about teacher shortages in schools, and the loss of creativity and inspiration in classrooms (Hargreaves *et al.* 2001). There is growing international support for the resumption of more humane middle years philosophies in the early years of secondary school that put priority on community and engagement, alongside curriculum content and academic achievement. School districts in the United States are increasingly seeing that high quality professional development for teachers is absolutely indispensable to bringing about deep changes in student achievement (Fullan 2001). In England and Wales, policy documents and White Papers are similarly advocating for more 'earned autonomy', and schools and teachers are performing well (e.g. DfES 2001). Governments almost everywhere are beginning to speak more positively about teachers and teaching – bestowing honour and respect where blame and contempt had prevailed in the recent past.

The time has rarely been more opportune or more pressing to think more deeply about what professional learning, professional knowledge and professional status should look like for the new generation of teachers who will shape the next three decades of public education. Should professional learning accompany increased autonomy for teachers, or should its provision be linked to the evidence of demonstrated improvements in pupil achievement results? Do successful schools do better when the professional learning is self-guided, discretionary and intellectually challenging, while failing schools or schools in trouble benefit from required training in the skills that evidence shows can raise classroom achievement quickly? And does accommodating professional learning to the needs of different schools and their staffs constitute administrative sensitivity and flexibility (Hopkins *et al.* 1997), or a kind of professional development apartheid (Hargreaves 2003)? These are the kinds of questions and issues which this series on professional learning sets out to address.

This book addresses one of the most promising and widely adopted initiatives to improve the quality of professional learning and knowledge in schools – *professional learning communities*. Professional learning grew out of the knowledge and experience that had been gained over many years from encouraging teachers to work together more collaboratively. It was informed by a deeply rooted tradition of how to convert organizations in general into learning organizations or learning communities – which could access, circulate and distribute knowledge and evidence as a way to achieve continuous improvement. And it was certainly propelled forward by the increasing availability of bodies of statistical evidence about student achievement, school by school, as a result of the ascent of the accountability movement. This provided communities of learners with increased and improved evidence to inform their judgements about what improvements needed to be made in their schools, and about the impact of these improvement efforts.

Foundational work on professional learning communities by Karen Seashore Louis, Shirley Hord, Milbrey McLaughlin, Joan Talbert and others highlighted how schools could achieve better results in student learning if the adults in the school were learning and working well together for students' benefit, and using evidence to inform their judgements. As the results of this pioneering work proliferated, professional learning communities became a subject of energetic advocacy by high-profile consultants, and a central feature of administrative policy in many nations, states and school districts.

After all the intensive activity and implementation efforts surrounding professional learning communities, it is now time to take stock, to have a research-based appraisal of what they have achieved, of where and why they have fallen short, and of the kinds of challenges and further opportunities that remain. From the United States and United Kingdom, this book's editors bring together leading researchers from their respective countries and other parts of the world to explore the problems as well as the possibilities of professional learning communities; the dilemmas in, the depth of and the divergent ways in which members of these communities can and do work together; the linking of professional learning communities to assessment, evidence and results; and the extension of these communities across entire school systems and networks of fellow professionals and improving schools.

The case has been established for some time as to why professional learning communities are important. The strategy has been adopted and implemented on an increasingly wide scale. This book brings together the best expertise in the area to appraise this innovation's progress, question some of the more dubious ways in which it has been interpreted and implemented, and push it further forward to increase its effectiveness. If you work in a professional learning community, are considering becoming so, or are experiencing difficulties and frustrations in the process, this book provides powerful insights that will help you move ahead.

Among the contributing authors to this volume is the late Ray Bolam who sadly passed away as the book was going to press. In Britain and beyond, Ray Bolam was a pioneer of so much of the scholarship and development work that preceded professional learning communities and laid the foundation for them. In school-based professional development, whole-school curriculum change, educational evaluation and educational change, his work carved out distinctive paths that many others would follow. Ray Bolam was an impressive and iconic, yet also a generous and genial, figure in the world of professional development and school change, and his sudden loss is a great one to the family who loved him and the field he profoundly influenced.

Andy Hargreaves
Ivor Goodson

References

Department for Education and Skills (DfES) (2001) *Achieving Success*. London: HMSO.

Fullan, M. (2001) *Leading in a Culture of Change*. San Francisco, CA: Jossey-Bass/Wiley.

Hargreaves, A. (2003) *Teaching in the Knowledge Society*. New York: Teachers College Press.

Hargreaves, A. and Goodson, I. (1996) Teachers' professional lives: aspirations and actualities, in I. Goodson and A. Hargreaves (eds) *Teachers' Professional Lives*. New York: Falmer Press.

Hargreaves, A., Earl, L., Moore, S. and Manning, S. (2001) *Learning to Change: Beyond Teaching Subjects and Standards*. San Francisco, CA: Jossey-Bass/Wiley.

Hopkins, D., Harris, A. and Jackson, D. (1997) Understanding the school's capacity for development: growth states and strategies, *School Leadership and Management*, 17(3): 401–11.

Townsend, J. (2001) It's bad – trust me, I teach there, *Sunday Times*, 2 December.

Waller, W. (1932) *The Sociology of Teaching*. New York: Russell and Russell.

Acknowledgements

This book would not have been possible without the involvement and contribution of a large number of people. First, we would like to acknowledge all the staff in the professional learning communities we have studied and worked with and all of the colleagues we have worked with on projects to study professional learning communities. We also want to thank the contributors to the book, for their insights, and their passion about making a difference that leads to them focusing their attention on professional learning communities. Thanks to these and other friends and colleagues who are studying and working to create, develop and sustain professional learning communities in different countries around the world. There is now a core of people internationally who operate as a professional learning community, sharing, critiquing and building on each other's ideas. We value their critical friendship. The publishing and production team, led by Fiona Richman, our commissioning editor, and including Katie Metzler and Jennifer Rotherham, editorial assistants, have kept us on track at all stages of the process and provided us with helpful guidance and feedback when requested – many thanks. To the series editors, Andy Hargreaves and Ivor Goodson, we are grateful that you included this book in what we think is an important series. Our special thanks to Sherry Morris for her administrative support in pulling together the manuscript. We greatly appreciate her good humour and her attention to detail at the editorial stage. Last, but by no means least, we want to thank each other! We have enjoyed co-editing the book with each other. It has been stimulating, fun, collegial, supportive and mentally challenging, everything we believe professional learning communities should be.

one

Professional learning communities: elaborating new approaches

Louise Stoll and Karen Seashore Louis

You can't be growing all the time. There are ebbs and flows: when you get into a new school year; after a few weeks; the beginning of a new term; the end of term tidying up and rewards and satisfaction. No document you can produce will ever show us all those layers.

(Headteacher, quoted in Stoll *et al.* 2006b, booklet 12: 2)

We take this headteacher's (principal's) challenge seriously. She is almost certainly right that it is impossible to capture fully all the nuances of what makes professional communities work. Nevertheless, we approached this book with the belief that it is worth subjecting the popular ideal of professional learning communities (PLCs) to greater scrutiny. After all, many proponents eulogize its potential power to build capacity and transform schools, but there are still too few schools that know how to start – or, if they are already well along the road to developing professional learning communities, how to inject further energy into their efforts. In the light of significant efforts in many countries in the last few years to personalize learning and involve a wider range of stakeholders in school improvement, it is timely to subject the concept to greater analysis and see whether there are any new perspectives on professional learning communities that can help enrich our understanding of what they are, how to develop them, and what they do for teachers, students, and parents.

In this chapter, we start this search by exploring five questions:

- How are professional learning communities currently defined?
- Do existing definitions capture the full extent of professional learning communities?

- Does the existing knowledge base lead us to deep understanding of how to develop professional learning communities?
- Does the existing knowledge base draw sufficient attention to the challenges of professional learning communities and how they might be addressed?
- Do existing collections pay sufficient attention to varying national contexts?

How are professional learning communities currently defined?

There is no universal definition of a professional learning community, but there is a consensus that you will know that one exists when you can see a group of teachers sharing and critically interrogating their practice in an ongoing, reflective, collaborative, inclusive, learning-oriented, growth-promoting way (Mitchell and Sackney 2000; Toole and Louis 2002). An underlying assumption is that the teachers involved see the group as a serious collective enterprise (King and Newmann 2001). It is also generally agreed that effective professional learning communities have the capacity to promote and sustain the learning of professionals in a school with the collective purpose of enhancing student learning (Louis *et al.* 1995; Bolam *et al.* 2005).

Each of the words making up the phrase 'professional learning communities' brings its own important meaning. The word *professional* suggests that the community's work is underpinned by: a specialized and technical knowledge base; a service ethic orienting members to meet client needs; strong collective identity through professional commitment; and professional autonomy through collegial control over practice and professional standards (Talbert and McLaughlin 1994). Although teachers have limited control over professional standards, historically they have been able to exert discretionary judgement in the classroom (Day 1999), and in many countries they have a strong (although not exclusive) influence on curriculum standards.

During the 1990s, much of the emphasis was on 'professional community'. It is not insignificant that the word 'learning' now appears between 'professional' and 'communities', because it connotes a shift in the emphasis away from a focus on process towards the objective of improvement. Although some early research on teachers' workplace focused specifically on learning – Rosenholtz (1989) distinguished between 'learning enriched' and 'learning impoverished' schools – others pointed out that cohesive groups often have limited interest in changing their current practice. Little (1999), for example, distinguished between schools with strong teacher communities in which the professional culture is either that of 'traditional community' (where work is co-ordinated to reinforce traditions) and 'teacher learning community' (where teachers collaborate to reinvent practice and share professional growth). Collective learning departs from traditional forms of professional development, which emphasize opportunities for individuals to hone their knowledge and skills in and out of their school settings. Learning in the context of professional communities involves working together towards a common understanding of concepts and practices (Bryk *et al.* 1999; Marks *et al.* 2002; Stoll *et al.* 2006a). What is held in common supplements, but does not supplant, what teachers learn individually and bring to their classrooms?

Underlying the earliest discussions of professional community was the core assumption that the group's objective is not to improve teacher morale or technical skills, but to make a difference for students (pupils). Building on the arguments for the importance of *caring* as a component of school cultures (Noddings 1992; Beck 1994; Sergiovanni 1994; Hargreaves with Giles 2003), the professional community literature assumes that teachers always need to focus on the relationship between their practice and their students. However, a focus on caring without a clear link to support for student learning is regarded as meaningless and counterproductive, particularly for disadvantaged students (Louis *et al.* 1995). Subsequent analyses of student achievement in schools indicated that the presence of professional community that is centred on student learning makes a significant difference to measurable student achievement (e.g. Louis and Marks 1998; Bolam *et al.* 2005). This is what gives the concept the 'legs' to stand among other proposals for reform (Louis 2006).

In sum, the term 'professional learning community' suggests that focus is not just on individual teachers' learning but on (1) professional learning; (2) within the context of a cohesive group; (3) that focuses on collective knowledge, and (4) occurs within an ethic of interpersonal caring that permeates the life of teachers, students and school leaders.

Do existing definitions capture the full extent of PLCs?

Professional learning communities have largely been interpreted as referring to groups of teachers supported by leaders. Is this group of 'stakeholders', however, now sufficient to serve the needs of *all* students in diverse contexts, as well as bringing about the kind of change needed in a complex and fast changing world? We think it is time for an expanded approach to the concept of professional learning communities to include both a broader membership and involving divergent knowledge bases.

An enlarged framework for professional learning communities forces those within schools to consider who has a valid stake in making a difference to students' learning and life chances. The saying 'it takes a whole village to raise a child' has particular resonance in relation to professional learning communities: can and should teachers go it alone? Schools exist within a wider social context. Disadvantage within the community has a significant impact on schools beyond its effects on individual students (Mortimore and Whitty 1997; Ainsworth 2002), and it is well established that parents are co-educators with teachers (McNeal Jr 1999). While school effectiveness research demonstrates that schools can make an important difference, this must not be construed to mean that teachers can be held entirely responsible for the success or otherwise of their students (Reynolds 1996). Others have vital roles to play too.

Teachers' knowledge base also traditionally encompasses subject knowledge, pedagogical knowledge, and that relating to child or adolescent development. Is this knowledge base truly broad enough to encompass all of the challenges that face children and young people in a diverse and changing society? There are other relevant and essential knowledge bases – some but not all of which may be professional knowledge – that are likely to be critical in helping improve schools. This may also mean challenging the status system of whose knowledge counts most – and the difficulty of doing this should not be underestimated.

In Table 1.1 we lay out some newer approaches to membership of PLCs that extend the available knowledge bases.

In addition to these alternative ways of construing potential PLC membership, there are other external stakeholders with specific expert knowledge that schools either call on or who, through critical friendship or creating 'urgency' (Earl and Lee 2000), may generate the impetus for developing PLCs. Such examples include staff in school districts and higher education institutions, external consultants and policy makers. Broadening perceptions of professional learning communities means rethinking notions of specific 'location' for professional learning community. Professional learning communities can cross boundaries, both the fuzzy social differentiations that develop between groups within the school, and the clearer borders that separate the school's members from those in the community and in other schools. As with any boundary crossing, expanding our ideas about 'who belongs' presents challenges to the existing culture.

Taking a more inclusive perspective on membership in professional learning communities also raises a key question: are there developmental pathways in terms of increasing involvement? Do you have to start with teachers before you can involve support staff? We currently have more questions than answers. For example, if a staff member is supporting a special needs student in the classroom, but is not involved as an equal in a PLC's development, how will this affect consideration of how to manage inclusion effectively? Similarly, if a school's students have social care needs

Table 1.1 Membership and knowledge bases of new professional learning communities

Systemic extensions to PLC membership	Knowledge bases available to the PLC
PLC as group(s) of teachers (original definition of PLC)	Pedagogical and other related
Extended across the school to include support staff, governing bodies/ members of school councils and students	Other professional knowledge, e.g. knowledge of specific learning needs Student knowledge External knowledge, e.g. financial acumen
Extended among schools, to include networks of schools, often within school districts/local authorities, e.g. network or district as PLC, and sometimes including district personnel as members	Access to greater amounts of the same knowledge bases
Extended beyond schools to include parents	Local knowledge and intimate knowledge of individual children
Extended beyond schools with the wider community and other services	Other professional knowledge, e.g. health, social care, business, etc.
Extended beyond country borders to include participants in different cultural contexts	Intercultural knowledge

that affect their learning and development but social workers play no part in developing the professional learning community, what are the effects on developing collective responsibility for student learning? Also, is it important or essential to have a thriving within-school professional learning community before you focus on developing external networks or do you start with multiple pathways? The jury is still out on many of these questions, which provides scope for further research.

While these examples suggest the need to broaden our understanding about what constitutes a professional learning community and who might qualify as a legitimate member, it is essential to emphasize that the purpose always remains the same – to enhance student learning. The desire to make schools more responsive to stakeholders may be an admirable goal in itself, but lies outside of the primary purpose of professional learning communities. Adding stakeholders to a PLC must not dilute or deflect its purpose, but augment its capacities and what it can achieve. In this sense, a recent definition of a professional learning community explains the extended professional learning community that we have described here: 'an inclusive group of people, motivated by a shared learning vision, who support and work with each other, finding ways, inside and outside their immediate community, to enquire on their practice and together learn new and better approaches that will enhance all pupils' learning' (Stoll *et al.* 2006a: 5).

Does existing knowledge lead us to deep understanding of how to develop PLCs?

There is a considerable amount of writing on professional learning communities, their characteristics and development processes, and yet it is extremely difficult to develop professional learning communities. This is at least partly due to the 'layers' described by the headteacher; the subtle nuances of communication, relationship building, collaboration and collective learning. Judith Warren Little (2002: 944) posed a challenge a few years ago to those who offer simplistic solutions or recipes:

> if we are to theorize about the significance of professional community, we must be able to demonstrate how communities achieve their effects ... The urgency associated with contemporary reform movements, especially those targeted at persistent achievement disparities, has intensified pressures on teachers and fueled policy interest in the collective capacity of schools for improvement. This is a timely moment to unpack the meaning and consequences of professional community at the level of practice.

We need better understanding of the collaborative processes in schools that lead to desirable outcomes for schools and those they serve. To do this, we need to go deeper in looking at concepts such as dialogue. While the idea of members of a team being able 'to suspend assumptions and enter into a genuine "thinking together"' (Senge 1990: 10) may be extremely appealing, what does this mean when colleagues actually get together? What is it that opens up the 'thinking together' and, indeed, 'learning together' rather than 'this is how you could do it better'? It is the subtle nuances that we need to understand. The same kinds of questions can be asked about aspects of professional learning community such as the role of culture and distributed leadership. What is it that makes these concepts 'tick'?

To go deeper, we will also need more sophisticated processes and tools that can be used by professional learning communities or those supporting them; not well intentioned but mechanical tools, but more sophisticated processes and tools based on research that both helps promote understanding of and engagement with the idea and practice of professional learning communities with particular reference to people's own contexts, as well as stimulating professional learning communities by promoting self-evaluation, reflective enquiry, dialogue, collaborative learning and problem solving (Stoll *et al.* 2006b).

Does the existing knowledge base draw sufficient attention to the challenges of PLCs and how they might be addressed?

The difficulty of developing professional learning communities should not be underestimated. In addition to the usual daily implementation issues associated with any change process, there are bigger hurdles that, as yet, remain unresolved in many places. Of these challenges, we have chosen to highlight several in this book, although we recognize there are other important ones. The first challenge is the endemic difficulty of creating PLCs in secondary schools, where size and structure militate again school-wide collaboration, and where, specific disciplinary knowledge takes priority over shared knowledge about pedagogy and adolescent development needs. This is why secondary school studies of professional learning communities often focus on subject departments, and why professional community is usually lower among secondary school teachers (Louis and Marks 1998). A deputy head (assistant principal) in a secondary school in one of our research projects (Bolam *et al.* 2005) described his school's professional learning community using a metaphor of a lava lamp with moving oil blobs, illustrating challenges of developing professional learning communities in secondary schools: 'The learning community is the lamp but different things move around. At the moment the [specific subject] department is rising and is near the top of the lamp, but in three years' time ... it may look different' (Stoll *et al.* 2006b, booklet 6: 3).

A second challenge within professional learning communities is brought into even sharper focus when their membership is extended beyond classroom teachers; that is the nurturing of social capital. Social capital is based on the quality of relationships among members of a social group and is facilitated by the extent and quality of internal and external networks. As Hargreaves (2003: 5) notes: 'As a shorthand, intellectual capital is about know-what and know-how and social capital is about know-who.' Social capital is often taken for granted in tightly knit communities. However, the more cohesive the internal ties are within a group, the less likely the members are to be densely networked with people in other groups. As those who study social networks have found, it is ties among groups that foster the most rapid spread of information (Granovetter 1973). Without due attention to fostering ties outside the school, strong professional communities can, paradoxically, become a barrier to change. If we take seriously the call to extend professional learning communities, going beyond schools as individual units of change, the situation becomes even more complex and the need to address social capital even more imperative, finding ways to help people engage with each other, and remain engaged, in 'relationships that have high degrees of satisfaction and achievement' (West-Burnham and Otero 2004: 9).

Another key challenge, also explored in this book, is sustainability, described by Hargreaves and Fink (2006: 17) as being 'basically concerned with developing and preserving what matters, spreads, and lasts and ways that create positive connections and development among people and do no harm to others in the present or in the future'. Sustainable development in all organizations, including schools, is premised on a number of principles, including inclusiveness, connectivity, equity, prudence, and consistent attention to the needs of human beings (Gladwin *et al.* 1995). What matters most in PLCs, however, is learning in the broadest sense (Delors *et al.* 1996); learning that is for all and is continuous (Stoll *et al.* 2003). For Hargreaves and Fink (2006: 17), and for us, sustainable improvement 'preserves and develops deep learning for all that spreads and lasts'. This raises tensions between the inevitable and necessary flexibility and moving, energized set of relationships and stability, because it is extremely hard to learn in unstable settings. Instability is a serious problem for schools which, as public institutions, have a limited ability to manage their own policies, even under school-based leadership and management. Instability that comes from outside the school is currently confounded by turnover among teachers and school leaders in many countries. Rather than worrying about lack of new blood, many school systems worry about how to create social connections and community under conditions in which every year brings a large number of new staff members, many of whom have little experience. Rapid changes in personnel may reinforce the experienced educators' belief that they need to be self-reliant rather than counting on support from peers and school leaders (administrators).

Sustaining connections and community is made more complex by the explosion of technology, which permits the development of online groups that provide stimulating sources of information and safe, neutral arenas for support, but may also be unstable, more likely to involve imbalanced participation, and less amenable to the sustained, deep, reflective engagement that most of us associate with face-to-face relationships that endure over time (Trauth and Jessup 2000).

Do existing collections pay sufficient attention to varying national contexts?

For a number of years, the most widely cited research about professional community and how to develop professional learning communities emerged from North America and, particularly, the USA. Professional learning communities, however, have been explored by colleagues in other countries for some time. As interest in PLCs' potential grows internationally, it is important both to acknowledge the work coming out of other countries as well as attending to the nuances of different cultural contexts.

This collection pulls together people from different countries in the English-speaking world, many of whom have spent significant periods of time exploring professional learning communities. The book grew out of initial informal meetings among a group of colleagues involved in the International Congress for School Effectiveness and Improvement (www.icsei.net) who have been exchanging findings and insights for several years. As we found commonalities in our data that were reassuring, we also confronted similarities in the challenges that we face. As we began to organize the book, we also felt that it was important to include several of our North American colleagues whose recent work seemed central to addressing the common themes and challenges that emerged in ICSEI. Thus, we hope that the contributions in this book will be of value to readers in many countries, who seek to understand and develop professional learning communities without reverting to simplistic recipes. Our contributors are not papering over real differences in the educational systems and roles that characterize their different national contexts, but we have asked each of them to emphasize those findings that reflect what is shared rather than distinct. Furthermore, we wish to acknowledge colleagues in countries not represented in this volume who are making valuable headway in the development of understanding and critical, reflective and contextualized use of findings about professional learning communities. Space constraints have limited our ability to present a comprehensive overview of the state of the art.

Conclusion

We see professional learning communities as an integral part of today's educational world – a world of greater connections – and planned this volume as a step in the direction of more divergent thinking. We therefore choose to include issues ranging from 'who belongs' in PLCs, to how to stimulate them in authentic rather than technocratic ways, to how to create meaningful connections within large, unwieldy networks of people who can meet face to face relatively rarely. We also probe the nuances of what is discussed in professional learning communities, and how it is discussed, because until we know how people work together in these unfamiliar contexts, it is hard to make recommendations about how to expand them. Getting deeper into the subtleties of translating the rhetoric of professional learning communities into reality is also going to be critical to ensuring effective professional learning communities in a complex and changing world, as is really getting to grips with serious challenges that have the potential to derail the whole process.

The remainder of the book is divided into parts where the contributors tackle aspects of these three issues: divergence, depth and dilemmas. There is a short introduction to the contributions at the start of each part, and the book concludes with a short invited reflection on professional learning communities.

In the spirit of promoting professional learning communities, we conclude with four questions that you and fellow members of your professional learning community (or each of your professional learning communities) may wish to consider before you read the contributions and four to consider after your reading.

Questions for reflection and dialogue before reading the book

- What is your interpretation of the expression 'professional learning community'?
- Who do you think of when you say 'our professional learning community'?
- What are the two or three aspects of developing your professional learning community or of professional learning communities you know that you would like to explore in more depth?
- What are the key challenges as you see them in developing professional learning communities?

Questions for reflection and dialogue after reading the book

- Has your interpretation of the expression 'professional learning community' changed? If so, why? Which author(s) challenged you most?
- Who do you now think of when you say 'our professional learning community'?
- Have contributions in the book provided any insights into the aspects of developing your professional learning community or of professional learning communities you know you want to explore? If so, how might you use these insights? If no, where might you go to seek out further knowledge?
- Have contributions in the book identified ways in which some of your challenges might be resolved? Where else might you seek further knowledge?

References

Ainsworth, J. (2002) Why does it take a village? The mediation of neighborhood effects on educational achievement, *Social Forces*, 81(1): 117–52.

Beck, L.G. (1994) *Reclaiming Educational Administration as a Caring Profession*. New York: Teachers College Press.

Bolam, R., McMahon, A., Stoll, L., Thomas, S., Wallace, M., Greenwood, A., Hawkey, K., Ingram, M., Atkinson, A. and Smith, M. (2005) *Creating and Sustaining Effective Professional Learning Communities*. DfES Research Report RR637. University of Bristol. www.dfes.gov.uk/research/data/uploadfiles/RR637.pdf, accessed 12 March 2006.

Bryk, A., Camburn, E. and Louis, K.S. (1999) Professional community in Chicago elementary schools: facilitating factors and organizational consequences, *Educational Administration Quarterly*, 35: 751–81.

Day, C. (1999) *Developing Teachers: The Challenges of Lifelong Learning*. London: Falmer Press.

Delors, J., Al Mufti, I., Amagi, A., Carneiro, R., Chung, F., Geremek, B., Gorham, W., Kornhauser, A., Manley, M., Padrón Quero, M., Savané, M.-A., Singh, K., Stavenhagen, R., Suhr, M.W. and Nanzhao, Z. (1996) *Learning: The Treasure Within – Report to UNESCO of the International Commission on Education for the Twenty-first Century*. Paris: UNESCO.

Earl, L. and Lee, L. (2000) Learning, for a change: school improvement as capacity building, *Improving Schools*, 3(1): 30–8.

Gladwin, T.N., Kennelly, J.J. and Krause, T.S. (1995) Shifting paradigms for sustainable development: implications for management theory and research, *Academy of Management Review*, 20(4): 874–907.

Granovetter, M. (1973) The strength of weak ties, *American Journal of Sociology*, 6(6): 1360–80.

Hargreaves, A. and Fink, D. (2006) *Sustainable Leadership*. San Francisco, CA: Jossey-Bass; and Chichester: John Wiley and Sons.

Hargreaves, A. with Giles, C. (2003) The knowledge society school: an endangered entity, in A. Hargreaves (ed.) *Teaching in the Knowledge Society: Education in the Age of Insecurity*. Maidenhead and Philadelphia, PA: Open University Press.

Hargreaves, D.H. (2003) From improvement to transformation. Keynote presentation to the Sixteenth International Congress for School Effectiveness and Improvement, Sydney, January.

King, M.B. and Newmann, F.M. (2001) Building school capacity through professional development: conceptual and empirical considerations, *International Journal of Educational Management*, 15(2): 86–93.

Little, J.W. (1999) Teachers' professional development in the context of high school reform: findings from a three-year study of restructuring schools. Paper presented at the Annual Meeting of the American Educational Research Association, Montreal, April.

Little, J.W. (2002) Locating learning in teachers' communities of practice: opening up problems of analysis in records of everyday work, *Teaching and Teacher Education*, 18(8): 917–46.

Louis, K.S. (2006) Changing the culture of schools: professional community, organizational learning and trust, *Journal of School Leadership*, 16(4): 477–89.

Louis, K.S. and Marks, H. (1998) Does professional community affect the classroom? Teacher work and student work in restructuring schools, *American Journal of Education*, 106(4): 532–75.

Louis, K.S., Kruse, S.D. and Associates (1995) *Professionalism and Community: Perspectives on Reforming Urban Schools*. Thousand Oaks, CA: Corwin Press.

Marks, H., Louis, K.S. and Printy, S. (2002) The capacity for organizational learning: implications for pedagogy and student achievement, in K. Leithwood (ed.) *Organizational Learning and School Improvement*. Greenwich, CT: JAI.

McNeal Jr, R.B. (1999) Parental involvement as social capital: differential effectiveness on science achievement, truancy, and dropping out, *Social Forces*, 78(1): 117–44.

Mitchell, C. and Sackney, L. (2000) *Profound Improvement: Building Capacity for a Learning Community*. Lisse: Swets and Zeitlinger.

Mortimore, P. and Whitty, G. (1997) *Can School Improvement Overcome the Effects of Disadvantage?* Institute of Education Occasional Paper. London: Institute of Education.

Noddings, N. (1992) *The Challenge to Care in Schools: An Alternative Approach to Education*. New York: Teachers College Press.

Reynolds, D. (1996) The problem of the ineffective school: some evidence and some speculations, in J. Gray, D. Reynolds, C. Fitz-Gibbon and D. Jesson (eds) *Merging Traditions: the Future of Research on School Effectiveness and School Improvement*. London: Cassell.

Rosenholtz, S.J. (1989) *Teachers' Workplace: The Social Organization of Schools*. New York: Longman.

Senge, P.M. (1990) *The Fifth Discipline: The Art and Practice of the Learning Organization*. New York: Doubleday.

Sergiovanni, T.J. (1994) *Building Community in Schools* (reissued edn). San Francisco, CA: Jossey-Bass.

Stoll, L., Bolam, R., McMahon, A., Wallace, M. and Thomas, S. (2006a) Professional learning communities: a review of the literature, *Journal of Educational Change*, 7(4): 1–38.

Stoll, L., Bolam, R., McMahon, A., Thomas, S., Wallace, M., Greenwood, A. and Hawkey, K. (2006b) *Professional Learning Communities: Source Materials for School Leaders and Other Leaders of Professional Learning*. London: Innovation Unit, DfES, NCSL and GTCe. www.standards.dfes.gov.uk/innovation-unit/collaboration/2127523/?version=1, accessed 4 June 2006.

Stoll, L., Fink, D. and Earl, L. (2003) *It's About Learning (and It's About Time)*. London: RoutledgeFalmer.

Talbert, J.E. and McLaughlin, M. (1994) Teacher professionalism in local school contexts, *American Journal of Education*, 102: 123–53.

Toole, J.C. and Louis, K.S. (2002) The role of professional learning communities in international education, in K. Leithwood and P. Hallinger (eds) *Second International Handbook of Educational Leadership and Administration*. Dordrecht: Kluwer.

Trauth, E.M. and Jessup, L.M. (2000) Understanding computer-mediated discussions: positivist and interpretive analyses of group support system use, *MIS Quarterly*, 24(1): 43–79.

West-Burnham, J. and Otero, G. (2004) *Educational Leadership and Social Capital.* IARTV Seminar Series No. 136. Jolimont, Victoria: IARTV.

Part 1

Divergence

Authors of chapters in this part explore the purpose of professional learning communities from a range of different perspectives and interpretations. While traditional conceptions of professional learning communities have focused exclusively on teachers and school leaders, these chapters broaden the frame of reference to include a larger group of core participants.

Ray Bolam, Louise Stoll and Angela Greenwood (Chapter 2) argue that support staff have been neglected partners within professional learning communities. Based on their research in England, they describe how support staff can be involved and the positive impact this can have, as well as issues and implications of involving support staff.

Extending the learning community to involve students, parents and the wider community is the focus of Coral Mitchell and Larry Sackney (Chapter 3), who describe a provincial initiative in Saskatchewan, Canada that reflects the principles of inclusiveness, wholeness, and connection that Mitchell and Sackney believe are critical to the success of any learning community.

David Jackson and Julie Temperley (Chapter 4) argue that the school as a unit is now too small scale and isolated to offer adequate scope for the professional learning of all of its adult members in a knowledge-rich and networked world. Drawing on the experience of the Networked Learning Communities initiative in England, they make a powerful case for school-to-school learning collaborations.

Louise Stoll, Jan Robertson, Lynn Butler-Kisber, Sylvia Sklar and Tom Whittingham (Chapter 5) draw on the experiences of one English local authority and its international partners in Australia, New Zealand and Canada to demonstrate the potential for international networks to promote professional learning community within and between schools and a school district in an increasingly interconnected world.

two

The involvement of support staff in professional learning communities

Ray Bolam, Louise Stoll and
Angela Greenwood[1]

Introduction

A professional learning community is characterized by the commitment and involvement of *all* staff in the community, not just teaching staff. People work together across the school, not just in groupings of particular subjects, phases or roles. Staff feel collectively responsible for the learning and development of all pupils, and everyone plays a part in this and is valued for their experience and expertise. These are some of the conclusions about the involvement of support staff in professional learning communities (PLCs) from a study of PLCs in English primary, secondary, nursery and special schools – *Creating and Sustaining Effective Professional Learning Communities*[2] – which took place from January 2002 to October 2004 (Bolam *et al.* 2005).

These findings and, indeed, the decision to include support staff within the scope of a study of PLCs, demonstrate how thinking and practice has been shifting about the key players in promoting pupils' learning. Support staff have an important role to play in helping to enhance pupils' learning and promote school improvement, for example through supporting pupils with special educational needs and very young children. Their development and involvement as key members of the school's learning community is essential. In England, a national agreement between the government, employees and, originally, all but one of the school workforce unions that was related to raising standards and tackling workload 'acknowledges the vital role played by school support staff' (ATL *et al.* 2003). Traditionally, however, those exploring PLCs have focused only on teachers and school leaders. As Louis and Gordon (2006: 2) point out, this 'ignores critical resources that lie fallow in most schools'.

With this wider agenda in mind, the project definition we adopted was: 'An effective professional learning community has the capacity to promote and sustain the learning *of all professionals in the school community* with the collective purpose of enhancing pupil learning' (italics added for emphasis). As a result of the study we elaborated the definition, as follows:

> A professional learning community *is an inclusive group of people*, motivated by a shared learning vision, who support and work with each other, finding ways, inside and outside their immediate community, to enquire on their practice and together learn new and better approaches that will enhance all pupils' learning. (Stoll *et al.* 2006: 5; italics added for emphasis)

The project's overall purpose was to draw out credible, accessible and practically useful findings – for policy makers, coordinators/providers of professional development and school leaders – about schools as professional learning communities; and for teachers and other adults working in schools about the cultures, behaviours and structures that enable them to play an active role in creating and sustaining PLCs.

To achieve this purpose, we adopted several research methods:

- a literature review;
- a questionnaire survey of headteachers (principals), or continuing professional development (CPD) coordinators, from a national sample of almost 400 schools of all types – nursery, primary (elementary), secondary and special – drawn from local authorities across England;
- examining links between characteristics of effective professional learning communities and pupil progress through factor analysis and multilevel models;
- case studies in 16 schools around the country – three nursery (preschool), five primary, five secondary, three special – at different stages of development as a PLC;
- bringing representatives from the case study schools together for workshops to validate and extend the research findings.

In summary, the project's overall findings were:

- Pupil learning was the foremost concern of people working in PLCs and, the more developed a PLC appeared to be, the more positive was the association with two key measures of effectiveness: pupil achievement and staff professional learning.
- Effective PLCs in all school phases fully exhibit eight key characteristics: shared values and vision; collective responsibility for pupils' learning;

collaboration focused on learning; individual and collective professional learning; reflective professional enquiry; openness, networks and partnerships; inclusive membership, including support staff; and mutual trust, respect and support.

- Professional learning communities are created, managed and sustained through four key processes: optimizing resources and structures; promoting individual and collective professional learning; explicit promotion, evaluation and sustaining of an effective PLC; and leadership and management supporting PLC development. Furthermore, the extent to which these four processes are carried out effectively is a third measure of overall PLC effectiveness.

In this chapter, we consider key aspects of the findings as they relate to the involvement of all staff in four ways: membership; roles; impact; and how school leaders promote involvement. Finally, issues and implications are discussed in light of the continuing changing context for schools in relation to support staff.

Who is a member of the PLC?

From the outset, a key issue was to do with who was, or should be, considered as a member of a PLC. Much of the reviewed international literature tended to assume that only teachers are members. This was always unlikely to be true in England, especially in nursery and special schools where teaching assistants and support staff are, more often than not, integral to teaching and learning. In addition, a widely adopted approach to human resource development in schools – 'Investors in People' – included support staff in its definitions and standards. Finally, the introduction of the national workforce agreement made it essential that support staff be considered directly as potential PLC members.

Who are we talking about when we refer to 'support staff'? Nomenclature and roles of support staff differ across countries and even within the English education system itself there is often inconsistency. First, we should make clear that in England, unlike in some countries, certain functions – for example, pastoral care and counselling – are carried out by teachers, and are not included in our definition of support staff. In the study, and this chapter, we use the term *support staff* for two groups of employed staff in schools:

- *teaching assistants* (TAs) are those staff – learning support assistants, special needs assistants, nursery nurses, assistants and officers, general assistants, technicians and child care staff – who contribute directly to pupils' education, often playing a significant role in classrooms and working directly with teachers;

- *non-teaching support staff* (NTSS) are those staff – secretaries, office administrators, cleaning staff, site caretakers (janitors), nurses and school meals supervisors – who make a less direct contribution to classroom learning but can play an important role in pupils' education, including their behaviour and general welfare, outside the classroom.

However, as indicated below in the discussion of workforce remodelling this terminology no longer reflects the new situation in England and, of course, the position in each country varies considerably.

In the survey, respondents overall felt that their PLCs involved and valued TAs more than NTSS, and those from schools with primary and nursery aged pupils seemed more likely than secondary schools to involve both TAs and NTSS. In addition, 47 per cent of primary and 35 per cent of secondary respondents said support staff were involved in reviewing pupil outcome and progress data, while more than three-quarters of all respondents reported that temporary and supply staff were included in continuing professional development (CPD) activities.

Survey respondents identified their school as either 'starting out' on a journey of developing a PLC, being a 'developer' or already at a stage of 'maturity' (these self-ratings were validated for the 16 case study schools). We separated out the responses of the three groups to different survey items and factors derived from factor analysis. In the secondary schools, we found statistically significant differences (at the 0.05 level) between all three stages and the factor representing the participation of support staff in the PLC. For primary schools, a statistically significant difference was found only between those reporting themselves at the mature or developer stages and those reporting themselves as starting out. In other words, PLCs at a further stage of development appeared more likely to include support staff in their PLC. Perhaps not surprisingly, in both primary and secondary schools, correlational evidence suggested that support staff involvement in the PLC was greater in smaller schools.

The 16 case-study schools helped us to put flesh on these bare survey findings. In all 16 schools, the PLC appeared to include teaching staff and TAs. But responses from support staff themselves varied across different schools, depending partly on the extent of their contribution to educational activity. In all three nursery schools, the PLC was considered to include all staff working in the school and, in some cases, beyond the school boundaries. For example, one headteacher commented that everyone connected with the school was a member of the learning community, although she drew a distinction between the teaching team, 'in which I include the nursery nurses', and the extended staff team, 'which includes cleaners, caretakers, dinner ladies and governors as well'. This distinction related to specific tasks and responsibilities, for example, only the teaching team were involved in the daily meetings before school but the extended team were often involved in school functions. Lunchtimes and break times were seen as part of the children's learning experience and support staff were making an active contribution to learning at these times.

Without exception, support staff were included as members of the PLC in the five primary schools but here, too, there was a distinction between those staff involved in the 'inner core' of the PLC and those in more peripheral positions. Who was 'inside' and who was 'outside' the core also varied between schools. Common to all was the potential for supporting teachers in delivering a positive impact on pupil learning, whether directly by working in class or indirectly by, for example, ensuring lunchtimes ran smoothly or the school building was kept in good order. Non-teaching support staff, who included lunchtime supervisors, administrative staff and caretakers, tended to make up this peripheral group.

In a primary school facing closure, despite many staff changes and the unusual number of supply teachers, all interviewees felt they were members of the PLC. One teacher said: 'there's no real pecking order. The beauty of this place is that everybody works as a team. There is no one who would say "this job is far superior to that one", whether it be the headteacher or the cleaner. They are all part of the same team and it is a quality team'. This was echoed by another primary school headteacher:

> Everyone, including the caretaker. It's the whole school staff; we all do our bit. The caretaker is brilliant; he goes on school visits with the children and gets involved. We have two cleaners; they are here one hour a day. It's difficult for them, the children are gone, but they are always invited to anything that we arrange, staff parties – they are seen as part of the community but it's difficult for them, I appreciate that.

In the five secondary schools, the PLC was reported to involve all teaching and support staff, although there was variation about the extent to which others were included. Comments from staff in the different schools give a flavour of their approach: 'it is a very strong team of staff and that's everyone: the support staff, caretaker, kitchen staff. Everyone works together; it's a very good community and the students are fabulous and the relationship between the teachers, all the staff and the children is really good, very strong' (secondary deputy head). In another school all staff were regarded as PLC members and parents and students were also included. The head said: 'We've always worked with parents and children as an extended family. We talk about the family and the extended family and we talk about family values ... Respect is given to all colleagues, right through to our six-hours a week cleaners. They feel very proud.'

In special schools, support staff can outnumber teachers. At the special secondary school, everyone was seen as a member of the wider PLC – teachers, special needs assistants (SNAs), caretaker, lunchtime support assistants, nurses as well as staff on the buses bringing the children to school. Core members were the teaching and classroom SNA staff, and two of the senior SNAs were also members of the senior management team. Teachers and SNAs had developed a very close working partnership.

At the special nursery school, which saw itself as a 'mature' PLC, all staff were seen as core. There were four classes with three staff in each team (one teacher with two TAs). Teams met to debrief at the end of each day, each week for a planning lunchtime, and each month with the speech and language therapist. The outreach team met together about once a month. External inspectors had commented very favourably upon the good working relationships between staff. There appeared to be a single PLC despite the fact that the nursery was involved in a variety of activities – some nursery based, others outreach. However, the head recognized that the 'Saturday staff' felt less involved.

How do support staff contribute to the PLC?

The differences between the classroom roles of teacher and TA tended to be blurred in nursery schools. For example, in one nursery school, TAs were referred to as 'nursery officers'. Not only did they share the role of leading pupil learning as key workers for individual children, alongside the teachers, but they were also responsible for an area of curriculum management in the same way as teachers. Individual support staff could be integrally involved: for example, the 'projects' coordinator' at one nursery school wrote proposals to secure funding for education projects as well as initiating the family programmes to be offered in the school.

In the primary schools, TAs played a significant classroom role, although their actual contributions were influenced by their qualifications and, as mainly part-time employees, their daily working patterns. There was generally a close working relationship between them and teachers. They frequently shared responsibility for pupil learning. The teacher normally planned the work and the TA worked with individual pupils or a small group, alongside the teacher or in a group room. There were instances where TAs had received specific training to enable them to carry out tasks such as reading assessments. In one school the TA was involved in team teaching Spanish to a class of Key Stage 2 pupils.[3]

Secondary support staff sometimes worked across subject departments, especially when supporting a child on a one-to-one basis. In one school, teachers and TAs worked together closely, with TAs taking a support role but with a working agreement that they were partners, not afraid to take certain initiatives within their role. However, the main initiative for teaching development came from the teachers. This relationship arose from individual professional values, expertise and skills, rather than explicit policy. One TA described the work of the support staff: 'Five of us are doing one-to-one pupil mentoring ... In maths, P works more with the maths teacher in the bottom set. He is very good with the pupils. He knows the sort of work we do ... He differentiates the work; he knows the children.'

Of course, it was not all plain sailing. In one school, staff rarely came together in the staffroom, apart from a briefing at the start of each day, due to time constraints. Furthermore, the situation often varied between departments. In the same school, the Modern Foreign Languages teachers did not appear to work together with the TAs, who also did not attend departmental meetings. The TAs all met up to share, but at the same time as departmental meetings, so they felt excluded. One, who worked in the department, said: 'The teachers do not discuss plans with me, or explain what they are doing, so I feel in a subordinate role here.'

Also, it was often difficult for NTSS staff to be centrally involved due to issues to do with time and their employment contracts. For example, lunchtime supervisors played an important role in one school and received specific training about feeding and behaviour management relevant to the pupils' needs, but they were only in school for the lunchtime period, while the school nurse was employed by the local health authority rather than the school and was also less connected.

In the special schools, support staff outnumbered teachers and played a very large part in the PLC. The secondary special school had an SNA as part of its senior management team and there was a very close working partnership between SNAs and teachers. Several teaching staff commented that SNAs made a key contribution to planning:

> All my teaching colleagues I suspect would agree with this ... they are a very valuable resource. Not in the old terms as they used to say, they're just there to wipe noses and comfort us; they make a very real contribution to students' learning. They have insights and experience and knowledge that can be of great benefit. And I certainly value them when I plan. (Deputy headteacher)

An SNA said: 'I think if anybody walked into the majority of classrooms that I go into and support, they would find it difficult at times to see who was the teacher and who was the SNA because we work so closely together that I hope that it would be difficult to distinguish.'

The organizational arrangements could have positive and negative consequences. In the residential school, the TAs followed the classes of children, not the subject. One teacher said: 'so I work with five TAs. This makes it very hard to work as a team ... [but] ... the TAs have a critical role because they follow the student round and they know them better than me'.

What is the impact of involving support staff?

The project identified two substantive measures of PLC effectiveness: impact on pupils' learning, academic progress and engagement; and impact on the morale and practice of staff and of the school as an organization (Bolam *et al.* 2005). Support staff contributed to both of these, and the PLC also impacted on them.

Where there was close cooperation and sharing of responsibility for pupils' learning, there appeared to be increased understanding of the needs of the child/young person and pupils' achievement and learning activities were reviewed with these needs in mind (cf. Newmann and Wehlage 1995). Where teachers and TAs planned together, and where there was a clear understanding of the objectives through a shared vision, TAs tended to take the initiative and devise their own strategies (cf. Huffman 2001).

One nursery teacher described her professional learning from TAs when she was a student teacher at the school: 'I had all the theory. It's not the same. They had lots of time for me. I was nervous. I was a teacher and they were nursery officers. I was afraid of what they would think. They supported me with planning materials. They helped me with the way to do things. They were encouraging.'

In schools where the timetable was organized into subject lessons, the TA who stayed with the class often had a deeper knowledge of the pupils than did the teachers. So, in addition to the TAs' contribution to planning and pupils' individual learning targets, as they moved from class to class with the children they often also provided information and advice to teachers arising from the immediately preceding classes. This could be of considerable value, particularly in special schools.

The impact on support staff's professional practice and confidence was clear. For example, one nursery school TA thought that: 'You get a lot of encouragement here to keep learning. Morale and motivation are very good here, we're a team', while a nursery nurse elsewhere commented: 'The staff meetings are important for sharing the experiences from training, and I feel we all have something to offer. And when you see the commitment of all around you ... it all adds to your own commitment.'

One primary school demonstrated how, by developing expertise of lunchtime school meal supervisory assistants (SMSAs), children's behaviour and attitude to learning could be positively affected. For two SMSAs, a training course had impacted on their professional practice, causing them to reflect on their interactions with children. They now looked for less confrontational ways of interacting, and the children had reacted positively. An SMSA explained:

> Being head supervisor, I have to deal with the discipline before it moves on to teachers and headmistress and where I used to shout or raise my voice before, now I don't. I stop, think and think 'No, we shouldn't do this' and my whole approach to the children and to my job itself has changed and we're only a few weeks into the course. It really has changed and S said it's affected her that way as well. It makes you think, and after all is said and done that's what it is about isn't it?

In one secondary school, the head's administrative assistant also thought the work of her and her colleagues was having a positive effect on pupils: 'Everyone is working towards better attendance. Children work in the school office. That encourages attendance. There are many other things going on other than in the classroom – for example achievement days – that encourages them to learn.'

Leading and managing a professionally inclusive PLC

Headteachers and other school leaders were crucial in promoting a learning-focused collaborative culture, characterized by mutual trust, respect and support. Their methods for involving support staff were largely an extension of those for teachers: optimizing the use of resources and structures, such as time, space and communication mechanisms; promoting individual and collective learning; explicitly promoting, evaluating and sustaining the PLC; vision building and trust building, distributing leadership, hiring to the vision, and coordinating professional learning and performance development.

There was no single pathway for increasing the involvement of support staff, nor did heads have a blueprint for doing so. They did it pragmatically, because it made sense to make the best use of *everybody*'s time and skills to promote pupils' learning. It seemed more straightforward in nursery and special schools and with the younger classes in primary schools, where the numbers of support staff were greatest. Secondary schools varied across departments.

Nevertheless there were some typical features. Thus, one of the facilitators most frequently mentioned by survey respondents was a supportive culture with an ethos of valuing all individuals and learning. As one primary school respondent wrote: 'Giving everyone status – making them feel valued by giving them confidence to take responsibility and act independently – but knowing that they will always be supported when necessary.'

A key strategic mechanism was to engage in the rigorous process of acquiring Investors in People (IiP) accreditation, the national standard of good practice for the training, development and motivation of *everyone* employed in an organization including non-professional staff (www. iipuk.co.uk). More specific methods included:

- encouraging support staff to participate in staff meetings, staff development days and activities – and publicly valuing their contributions;
- allocating time and funds for their specific professional development;
- providing joint staffrooms and facilities;
- defining their roles as active contributors in classroom, planning and related activities, like parent evenings;
- including staff – teachers and TAs – on the panels for the appointment of new staff.

The leader's style and personality were, of course, critical. One primary school secretary said:

> The head is a very good boss. She's very fair, not just in your professional life but also in your personal life. She's always there whatever the crisis. It could be something quite outside the school but she will do her utmost helping to get you where you want to be. She doesn't take sides. If two people have a problem she'll get them together and say 'Let's sort this out'. Staff are not afraid to come forward and say things like 'I've made a mistake'. That's when the quality comes through because people feel comfortable. Yes she is the boss and she is the head. But you can also say 'Can I come in and shut the door and speak off the record?' and you can. And I don't think there is a member of staff who wouldn't knock at her door and say this. Everybody is very open.

Modelling valued behaviour was also used frequently. One nursery school head was convinced of the importance of creating a staff culture in which staff felt valued:

> I suppose I am modelling – partly things I do believe strongly in, like the fact that morale is paramount, staff morale. I just think having a positive feeling staff and a place where people actually enjoy coming to work just counts for so much in a school, not just for the children but for staff commitment and everything else. I want staff to want to work here really. I want them not to resent the fact that it's the end of the holidays ... when people actually come back they say 'Oh it's good to be back' and that's really nice and I'm so pleased people say that because they like to be back together ...

Issues arising and conclusion

Greater involvement of support staff clearly has considerable potential for the development of PLCs, but it is not without its challenges, as our research and the changing policy context highlight. These relate to differential pay, status and working hours.

The recent workforce remodelling legislation has the potential to disrupt and change the collaborative working partnerships between support staff and teachers as, in the attempt to reduce teachers' workload, distinctive hierarchies are being highlighted. There is also a possible threat to teachers' professionalism as support staff take on functions that were formerly the preserve of teachers. A further agenda which may change the nature of support staff status and working practices is the 'single status agreement' in relation to career and pay structure. This is being implemented in varying stages throughout England and will have cost implications of varying degrees for schools. Together, these national agendas could change the nature of collaborative working between teachers and support staff, and highlight existing friction regarding status and pay and conditions.

At the time of our project, a large part of the professional learning of support staff took place on a day-to-day basis. This needs to be supported by appropriate professional development opportunities such as including support staff in professional development interviews, in-service training (INSET) and access to training opportunities. These appear to enhance the way through increased confidence and skills, in which they can subsequently support teachers. While the Teacher Development Agency (formerly the Teacher Training Agency) has plans for continuing professional development of support staff (TTA 2005), there are major inhibitory factors. The often part-time working hours of TAs and SMSAs can be a barrier to them participating in training and meetings which often take place outside their working hours, although we found evidence of more flexibility in secondary schools. Budgetary constraints of schools also often lead to support staff training taking second place to teachers' opportunities. Where support staff were able to access these opportunities they were invariably valued.

If the examples of best practice are to be translated to other schools, certain issues need to be addressed by policy makers and schools. Support staff need dedicated access to appropriate professional development as a right and schools need to be allocated financial resources to deliver this in a flexible way. Teaching assistants need to be part of the planning and evaluation process in all schools. The central role of the teacher should, however, under no circumstances be lost or diluted.

This again raises the question: who counts as a *professional* and by what criteria? We took it as axiomatic that teachers and headteachers are trained, qualified, paid and held accountable for the standards of teaching and learning in a school, and that support staff are entirely legitimate members of a professional learning community. We were advised on several occasions that it was more productive to focus on people 'being *professional*' rather than 'being *a* professional'. We agree and believe that a way forward may involve adopting professional standards as a basis for deciding what counts as professional behaviour by any and all members of a PLC. Teachers and headteachers now have professional standards in the form of draft professional standards for teachers, the General Teaching Council of England's (GTC 2002) *Statement of Professional Values and Practice for Teachers* and the Department for Education and Skills' (DfES 2004) *National Standards for Headteachers*, revised by the National College for School Leadership (NCSL). These sets of standards could be used to inform the work of a school staff seeing themselves as a *professional* learning community. The recent establishment of higher level teaching assistant (HLTA) standards signals movement in the direction of including support staff as recognized members of a *professional* learning community. Once appropriate professional standards are developed for all support staff, it will be important for each school staff to ensure that all their professional standards are mutually consistent.

A professional learning community is an inclusive one in which support staff have a critical role. In a rapidly changing policy environment, however, where it is finally being recognized that schools cannot improve on their own, and that the full support of parents and the community is essential, we are left with a final question: does the term 'professional learning community' sufficiently capture the contribution of the full range of possible members who need to be committed to and involved in promoting and sustaining their own learning with the collective purpose of enhancing pupil learning?

Notes

1   We would like to acknowledge all our fellow team members. Furthermore, as this book went to press, Ray Bolam died very suddenly. This was a huge and very sad loss to all of the team. He was a great leader and champion of professional learning communities.
2   The project was funded by the Department for Education and Skills (DfES), the General Teaching Council for England (GTCe) and the National College for School Leadership (NCSL).
3   There are four key stages in England. Pupils aged 7–11 are in Key Stage 2.

References

Association of Teachers and Lecturers (ATL), Department for Education and Skills (DfES), GMB, National Association of Headteachers (NAHT), National Association of Schoolmasters Union of Women Teachers (NASUWT), National Employers' Organization for School Teachers (NEOST), Professional Association of Teachers (PAT), Secondary Heads Association (SHA), Transport and General Workers' Union (TGWU), UNISON and Welsh Assembly Government (WAG) (2003) *Raising Standards and Tackling Workload: A National Agreement.* www.remodelling.org, accessed 11 December 2005.

Bolam, R., McMahon, A., Stoll, L., Thomas, S., Wallace, M., Hawkey, K. and Greenwood, A. (2005) *Creating and Sustaining Effective Professional Learning Communities.* DfES Research Report RR637. University of Bristol. www.dfes. gov.uk/research/data/uploadfiles/RR637.pdf, accessed 11 December 2005.

Department for Education and Skills (DfES) (2004) *National Standards for Headteachers.* Nottingham: DfES Publications. http://publications.teachernet.gov.uk/, accessed 3 February 2006.

General Teaching Council (GTC) (2002) *Statement of Professional Values and Practice for Teachers.* London: GTC. www.gtce.org.uk/standards/disc/, accessed 3 February 2006.

Huffman, J.B. (2001) The role of shared values and vision in creating professional learning communities. Paper presented to the Annual Meeting of the American Educational Research Association, Seattle, April.

Louis, K.S. and Gordon, M.F. (2006) *Aligning Student Support with Achievement Goals: The Secondary Principal's Guide.* Thousand Oaks, CA: Corwin Press.

Newmann, F.M. and Wehlage, G.G. (1995) *Successful School Restructuring: A Report to the Public and Educators by the Center on Organization and Restructuring of Schools.* Madison, WI: CORS.

Stoll, L., Bolam, R., McMahon, A., Thomas, S., Wallace, M., Greenwood, A. and Hawkey, K. (2006) *Professional Learning Communities: Source Materials for School Leaders and Other Leaders of Professional Learning. Booklet 1: User Guide: Getting Started and Thinking about Your Journey.* London: DfES Innovation Unit, NCSL and GTC.

Teacher Training Agency (TTA) (2005) *Building the School Team: Our Plans for Support Staff Training and Development.* London: TTA.

three

Extending the learning community: a broader perspective embedded in policy

Coral Mitchell and Larry Sackney

Nineteenth-century teachers dropped into a twenty-first-century classroom would probably recognize the room as a classroom and the building as a school. English teachers dropped into a Canadian classroom would probably experience the same sense of familiarity. In other words, schools tend to be similar across time and place, as do the experiences of students and teachers who work within them. This persistence is not necessarily a problem, but it raises the question of the extent to which institutions established in a nineteenth-century context continue to deal appropriately with the mysteries, challenges, and interests of twenty-first-century learners. This question lies at the heart of our explorations into the character of a professional learning community.

Our quest has taken us into schools of many different sizes, shapes, and localities, as we have asked people to tell us about their schools and their experiences therein. Their responses, and our observations, have convinced us that the notion of a professional learning community is deeply inclusive and broadly connected. It extends well beyond the professional cadre, and it is concerned with far more than what happens within the school walls. These notions of inclusiveness, wholeness, and connection serve as the cornerstone for the ideas we share in this chapter. We begin by defining some concepts of community and by outlining some principles of engagement in a learning community. This foundation sets the stage for a description of an inclusive learning community in action. We conclude by presenting some benefits of this extended perspective on learning communities.

Concepts of community

Our view of a learning community is embedded in a perspective shaped by the work of David Bohm (1980; 1985), a theoretical physicist who wrote a series of critiques on the fragmented view of the world that was the legacy of Newtonian physics. Bohm argued that, at a fundamental level, the physical world is not separated into distinct parts that retain their individuality when they come together to form a new unit. Rather, he saw the parts as emerging from a unified whole that continued to connect and integrate the pieces even when they moved some distance from the centre. This world perspective informs our understanding of a professional learning community: that it is fundamentally a place of and for connections, relationships, reciprocity, and mutuality.

From this standpoint, a learning community is always and only about people, their lives, and their experiences. As Starratt (2003) has advocated, it positions a learning community in human terms: human thought and action, human drives and desires, human interests and purposes, and human growth and learning. This perspective sharpens our focus when we enter schools, for even when we ask about rules, roles, procedures, and structures, we are concerned with the ways in which these elements inform, shape, and/or burden learning – not just for students, but also for teachers, administrators, parents, and other members of the educational community.

The wholeness concept immerses teaching and learning in a wide array of learning events, experiences, activities, and interests. Some of these show up in the places where curriculum is developed: state and district educational agencies, support agencies, curriculum writing groups, and the like. Other learning opportunities come from emerging events on the local, national, and world stages. Still others are made visible in the personal interests of the students and teachers within the classroom, as well as from the expertise of parents and other community members. Some of the learning opportunities look much like regular school curriculum, but others are more organic and process-oriented. In some cases, learning is apparent through written, oral, and other modes of communication, but some learning situations yield no observable learning product. What links all the learning moments is that there is a change in understanding, a shift in awareness, a movement in the soul: someone is different in some way because learning has taken place. Without some sort of shift, learning cannot be said to have happened, and without learning, teaching cannot be said to have happened.

Our understanding of a *professional* learning community is that teachers, too, are learners who are taught important and interesting lessons by their students, by the broader community, by each other, and by the parents of their students. We have noticed that teachers who are active learners have new and exciting ideas to share, and the excitement of their professional learning breathes life and energy into their classrooms. We have also observed teachers who perpetuate standard practices, who bring few new ideas or practices into their instruction. These classrooms lack the spontaneity, excitement, and enthusiasm of the classrooms where teachers share their own learning with their students. This is perhaps the most important concept of a learning community: that all members of the community are energized by learning from and with one another.

Principles of engagement

A deep level of engagement and connection among various stakeholder groups is not typical of most schools, and there is limited literature that describes how people other than teachers and students become valued members of the learning community. This gap led us into schools to explore how educators invite and encourage participation within and beyond the school walls. Our investigations have uncovered five key principles that underlie successful development and effective extension of learning communities.

The first principle, *deep respect*, is the foundation for all engagement and for all other principles. In following this principle, individuals give personal and professional care and concern to children and adults alike. Parents and community members are welcomed into the school and the classroom, and doors between colleagues and classes remain open. Deep respect positions each student, teacher, staff member, administrator, parent, and community member as a valued participant in the life of the school, someone with ideas and thoughts to share and with an important role to play. Teachers are freed to operate with professional autonomy and integrity, students are supported to be active learners, and parents are invited to be partners in the education of their children. When people hold deep respect, they speak respectfully not just *to* people but also *about* people. This principle does not imply that conflicts and differences never emerge, but it means that, when they do, issues are raised appropriately, and the partners in the disagreement assume good intentions, invite voice, test assumptions and attributions, and protect the dignity and self-respect of the other.

Collective responsibility, the second principle of engagement, is the one we have found to be the most common in our research schools. This principle encourages all staff members to assume responsibility for all children in the school. Instead of taking ownership only for the students in their own classroom or professional assignment, teachers feel a sense of commitment to all children. Collective responsibility also extends to parents and community members, who are seen as having responsibility for the educational experience of the children in the school and who are encouraged to be directly involved in school and classroom matters. These are the individuals who shed light on the history, background, interests, and lives of the students, and their role in informing educational decisions and directions should not be underestimated. Collective responsibility is also the principle that nudges teachers to collaborate with their colleagues, to stay involved and informed, and to contribute effectively to school functioning. It is the principle that compels individuals to acknowledge their own mistakes, to take corrective steps, and to learn from the event.

Engagement is energized and enriched by the third principle, *appreciation of diversity*. This principle does not speak to a *tolerance* of difference. Instead, it positions difference as a *core value* of the school. People celebrate difference because it serves as the spark for new learning, growth, and development. When diverse teaching styles and knowledge bases are highlighted and encouraged in the school, it pushes people into avenues of growth that had never before been contemplated, thereby stretching the professional repertoire beyond usual, habitual, or comfortable practice. This principle allows students, as well, to shine in their own way, on their own terms, and in their own areas of ability, even those who do not typically shine in educational circles. One of the most gratifying outcomes of this principle is that we have seen it generate understanding and acceptance of extreme characteristics in students, such as autism, Down syndrome, or other physical or cognitive challenges. This outcome has emerged from two sources: first, teachers and staff members recognize and praise these children for their unique gifts, which signals to their classmates that they can learn something quite interesting and unusual from these children. Second, teachers and staff members have no tolerance for abuse, criticism, teasing, gossiping, or complaining, and when extreme behaviours emerge, classmates are encouraged to see the person behind the behaviour. We have also seen this approach to diversity to be important at the staff level, where people tolerate no complaining, gossiping, criticism, or abuse of colleagues.

A *problem-solving orientation* is the fourth principle used to shape engagement. Acting upon this principle helps people to remain flexible and to tolerate the ambiguity and uncertainty that accompany active experimentation and ongoing change, both of which are essential aspects of a learning community. This is the principle that encourages school people to ask questions about the nature of their practice (professional practice, learning practice, administrative practice, and so on) and about the effects of their practice on colleagues, classmates, students, parents, and others. It is the principle that stimulates people to seek out a wide array of data, to solicit feedback from a variety of sources, and to ask probing questions about how the data and feedback can inform and transform their practice. These are the questions that serve to maintain a spirit of continuous improvement in the school and in classrooms. When a school is oriented toward problem-solving, we do not hear complaints, criticism, blame, or attack. Instead, we hear people acknowledging errors, differences, and uncertainties, and taking the initiative to deal directly with them. We hear questions around what could be done differently, who needs to be involved in the shift, and how the process might unfold to protect the interests of the students and of learning. This approach positions issues as challenges and mysteries rather than as problems, and it shines the spotlight on what people do know and can do rather than on any imputed deficits.

The fifth and final principle of engagement is *positive role modeling*. This principle raises awareness about the ubiquity of role modeling, with the important question not being: 'Will I be a role model today?' Instead, the key question is: 'What kind of a role model am I being today?' Each moment is seen as a teaching moment, and all members of the school community (including students) are encouraged to think about what they are teaching and what others might be learning from their actions and speech. Each moment is also seen as a learning moment, and all members of the community (including teachers) are encouraged to think about what they are learning in that moment. Because this principle positions all community members as both teachers and learners, it encourages the generation of a wide array of teaching and learning options, and it supports the development of distributed leadership, where individuals from all stakeholder groups seek out opportunities both to learn and to lead.

We want to emphasize that, in our school observations, we have not always found the five principles to be evident, nor have we found all individuals living the principles at all times. People are people, and even in a highly evolved learning community some less admirable human behaviours appear. We have, however, found that, even when the principles are violated, they serve as a rallying point around which individuals gather their thoughts and realign their actions. In a learning community, these are the principles that bring people back to a sense of the whole and a reminder of their purpose; they are the principles that offer safety and support as individuals step forward to engage with other members of the school community. In the next section, we provide an example of what these principles of engagement looked like in one innovative provincial program designed specifically to improve student learning.

Community in context

Although Saskatchewan's School^{PLUS} initiative was not designed explicitly around the principles of engagement described above, they can be detected in the practices that were used to generate a more inclusive learning community across the province. The School^{PLUS} reform is unique in its attempt to transform schools by directly involving diverse groups and external agencies in school activities. Our description of this reform demonstrates the ways in which the principles of engagement can shape community-wide commitment to education and contribute to improved teaching and learning in schools.

In 1999 the Saskatchewan government established the Task Force on the Role of the School. The review was conducted because of the changing social and economic influences, the emergence of a knowledge-based society, advances in technology to support learning, and new knowledge about how learning occurs. The Task Force met from 1999 to 2001 and submitted its *Final Report* in 2001. In February 2002, the Government of Saskatchewan responded to the Task Force with an endorsement of a new vision for schools and affirmed that schools today serve two primary functions:

- *To educate children and youth* – developing the whole child, intellectually, socially, emotionally, spiritually and physically;
- *To support service delivery* – serving as centres at the community level for the delivery of appropriate social, health, recreation, justice and other services for children, youth and their families (Saskatchewan Education 2002).

School[PLUS] was a term coined by the Task Force to describe a new vision of schools as centres of learning, support, and community for the children, youth, and families they serve. The School[PLUS] concept stressed learning excellence for all students and for active involvement with families and support from human service providers and community members (ibid.: 2). It called for all schools to adopt the philosophy and practices of the learning community.

Saskatchewan's Effective Practices Framework

In order to implement the School[PLUS] philosophy, an Effective Practices Framework (see Figure 3.1) was developed to provide schools, school divisions, and communities with key practices and resources to support local initiatives. The Effective Practices Framework is premised on the development of children and youth intellectually, personally, socially, physically, and culturally/spiritually. The development is based on the creation of learning communities that involve school staff, families, human service providers, and the community. At each school a Needs Assessment Committee is to be formed comprising of the various stakeholder groups to assess the extent to which needs exist at each dimension on the Effective

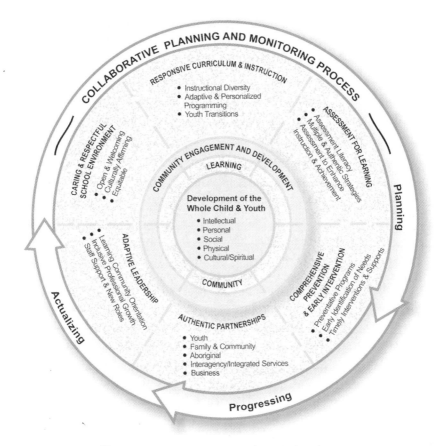

Figure 3.1   Effective Practices Framework – Saskatchewan Learning

Practices Framework. Once the needs have been identified, the various stakeholders develop action plans to rectify the concerns.

The framework identified six effective practices and critical elements of each practice and provided print, web-based, and human resources to support their use. The areas of effective practices include:

- caring and respectful school environment;
- responsive curriculum and instruction;
- assessment for learning;
- comprehensive prevention and early intervention;
- authentic partnerships;
- adaptive leadership.

Caring and respectful school environment

Caring and respectful schools are 'open, inclusive and culturally affirming centres of learning, support and community' (Saskatchewan Learning 2004a: 6). Understanding schools as learning communities sees schools as places where staff, families, and community members are committed to creating environments that 'support healthy development and learning success for children and youth' (ibid.: 6). To develop the learning community, quality relationships, characterized by genuineness, caring, unconditional acceptance, and inclusiveness, are crucial. They are committed to the shared belief that all students have unique abilities and needs, learn in a variety of ways, and can be successful. They are also places of collaboration that 'link people at the classroom, the school and community level to a shared vision and a common purpose' (ibid.: 11). As such, caring and respectful schools are places where people work together to improve learning outcomes for students and families.

Responsive curriculum and instruction

The School[PLUS] framework calls for a rethinking of teaching and learning. It calls for reflective practice among students, teachers, and others involved in the education system; it calls for teachers to learn new teaching strategies and approaches; it asks that teaching and learning be culturally affirming and appropriate; and it asks schools to create support systems for all students, especially when students are vulnerable or facing challenges in their lives (Saskatchewan Learning 2004b).

Responsive curriculum and instruction is flexible and adaptable, and provides all students with a variety of developmental and learning experiences. Providing such an experience means that teachers need to know their students. For those students who require individualized programs, a Personal Program Plan (PPP) is developed that can involve many different human service providers.

Responsive curriculum and instruction is influenced by the learning environment; the curriculum topics and materials; instruction; the quality of relationships among and between teachers, students, parents, and community members; and the values and needs of the community (Saskatchewan Learning 2003). Teaching is key to improving student learning, and communities of practice (Wenger 1998) are expected to emerge through a process of collaborative critical reflection.

Assessment for learning

Saskatchewan Learning (2004a: 21) views educational assessment and evaluation practices as contributing to the delivery of quality education for children and youth. To do so, teachers need to ensure that their assessment and evaluation practices are varied, unbiased, and appropriate to meet the diverse learning needs of students. Assessment for learning is a continual process involving a variety of approaches linked to curriculum objectives, student abilities, and teacher practices.

Saskatchewan Learning is concerned that schools use data-based decision making and learning standards using continuous improvement processes. Teachers are expected to develop learning rubrics for the various subject areas and to collect data for the purposes of assessment, and the authors of this chapter have conducted numerous workshops on setting standards and using data to inform educational decisions. Victoria Bernhardt's (1998) work on data bases and Jan O'Neil's (2000) work on SMART (specific and strategic, measurable, attainable, results-oriented, and timebound) goals have been used. The Saskatchewan Educational Leadership Unit (SELU) has also sponsored workshops by the DuFours, who advocate for the development of professional learning communities using SMART goals (e.g. DuFour and Eaker 1998).

Comprehensive prevention and early intervention

Saskatchewan Learning (2004b), based on a review of the literature, sees timely action in young people's lives as a way of supporting student engagement in learning. Comprehensive prevention and early intervention involving the student, the family, other human service providers, and the community, is intended to manage conditions, reduce vulnerabilities, and support success. A number of strategies are identified to engage all youth within schools:

- to think differently about how students, educators, and other adults work together;
- to plan course content with students and support self-directed learning;
- to increase the voice and role of students;
- to assess current practices of youth engagement as a school learning community and to identify areas for growth (Saskatchewan Learning 2004b).

Authentic partnerships

The intent of developing partnerships with human service providers and the community is to bring resources to bear directly on the family. The focus of

School^PLUS is on the child and the family, and authentic, collaborative partnerships promote the values of mutual care and respect (Saskatchewan Education 2001). In an attempt to meet the diverse needs of students, schools are expected to partner with the community and other agencies in new ways. Caring and respectful schools bring educators, students, families, community members, and human service providers together in order to maximize student learning. 'Such partnerships grow from the commitment to a common purpose, develop over time and are nurtured by mutual trust and respect' (Saskatchewan Learning 2004a: 44). Authentic partnerships are characterized by:

- openness to share information;
- willingness to contribute to planning, decision making and pursuit of mutual goals;
- agreements on working relationships, policy and program objectives;
- commitment to sharing responsibility, resources, risks and benefits (ibid.: 44–5).

Adaptive leadership

According to Saskatchewan Learning (2004a: 9), schools require a leadership approach characterized by adaptability and the ability to respond nimbly to challenges and issues. Such an approach to leadership:

- is collaborative and values teamwork;
- actively engages parents as partners;
- seeks student participation and involvement in decision making;
- utilizes community resources and expertise (ibid.: 9).

The school leadership team's mandate is to create the conditions for growth and change to occur. In order to do so, they must develop the culture, structures, and processes to support, facilitate, and lead vibrant learning communities that 'take an active, reflective, collaborative, learning-oriented, and growth promoting approach toward the mysteries, problems, and perplexities of teaching and learning' (Mitchell and Sackney 2000: 9). Leaders are expected to take 'an active role in shaping people's beliefs and values by creating a broader reference for their learning community' (Saskatchewan Learning 2004b: 19). In order to do so, they must ensure that:

- every member of the community is a learner;
- the learning community has a clear purpose, vision, and goals;
- the learning community values a collaborative culture and nurtures strong, meaningful relationships;
- leadership is shared among participants;
- structural conditions support members as a learning community.

Adaptive leadership (Heifetz and Linsky 2002) is required to build a vibrant learning community. Adaptive leaders do not believe in maintaining control but rather in building capacity and leadership among learning community members. According to Heifetz and Linsky, adaptive leaders do not erect walls; they replace walls with bridges.

Connecting School^PLUS practice with the principles of engagement

The framework that guided the development of the School^PLUS reforms has implicitly accommodated the principles of deep respect, collective responsibility, problem-solving orientation, appreciation of diversity, and positive role modeling that we described at the beginning of this chapter. For example, deep respect, appreciation of diversity, and positive role modeling are fundamental pathways to creating a caring and respectful school environment, developing responsive curriculum and instruction, and providing adaptive leadership. Collective responsibility, deep respect, and problem-solving orientation are centrally involved in authentic partnerships and comprehensive prevention and early intervention strategies. Appreciation of diversity and problem-solving orientations generate effective assessment for learning. At a comprehensive level, the practices through which the model is enacted develop from a process of collaborative problem-solving and program planning that includes all the partners in the learning community: parents, teachers, other professionals, administrators, and students. In these ways, the practical model is an exemplar of the five principles for participation in a learning community.

Bringing School^PLUS to life required change in all sectors. The initiative's website states, 'What is required is nothing short of a new social institution' (Saskatchewan School^PLUS 2005). As part of the government's implementation plan, three foundational strategies have been developed:

- the community-engagement and action planning strategy;
- the enhancing integrated school-linked services strategy;
- the strengthening educational capacity strategy.

This restructuring represents a major effort at establishing an integrated learning community that will serve the needs of children and youth. This is an interesting effort that needs to be studied closely over the intervening years. It is a major paradigm shift in the way schools operate and represents a more integrated approach to building learning community capacity.

Benefits of an extended learning community

In this chapter, we have presented concepts, principles, expressions, and a provincial model of and for an extended notion of a professional learning community. Our observations indicate that, when all members of the school community train their thoughts and actions on teaching and learning, exciting things happen. The learning environment in such schools supports UNESCO's (1996) four pillars of knowledge, 'learning to know, learning to do, learning to live, and learning to be' (cited in Stoll *et al.* 2002: 47) for students, teachers, administrators, support personnel, and other members of the school community. The active engagement of many different community members raises the professional bar for staff and the academic bar for students, and it does so in a respectful and supportive fashion.

The student experience in this kind of environment is rich, multifaceted, and respectful. Students receive a lavish choice of curricular, co-curricular, extra-curricular, and out-of-classroom experiences; they have opportunities to focus their learning on areas of personal interest; and they have strong supports for building capacity in areas of personal challenge. Students are seen as individuals; each child is known by name, and every child has a place in the school. Students are treated with respect and consideration, and no child is made to lose face or to be embarrassed in front of peers. When their behaviour or performance does not meet the standards, they are reminded of the school principles and supported in their attempts to reach the bar. Because their unique contributions and achievements are celebrated, they grow in confidence and self-esteem, and they serve as positive role models for their classmates and school mates.

The experience of staff members in this kind of environment is also rich, multifaceted, and respectful. The shared commitment to learning releases professional energy, distributes professional knowledge, engages professional commitment, and unleashes creative forces. It keeps issues and challenges from escalating to extreme levels, and it promotes school-wide ownership of decisions, directions, and outcomes. Expanded opportunities for professional growth and development increase the chances of success and raise professional confidence and competence. Staff members of all work categories are encouraged to take initiative, to take risks, and to make autonomous decisions, and they are supported as they move forward into new and challenging territory. The excitement of their own learning energizes their work with students and parents and provides positive role models for students and colleagues.

The Saskatchewan School[PLUS] model described in this chapter is not yet typical of most schools or of what happens in most provinces. It grounds education in the belief that 'it takes a whole village to raise a child'. This conception of schools is similar to that advocated by Hartle and Hobby (2003: 388), where: 'parents and teachers, educators and local businesses, students and adults – people inside and outside the school walls – work together to build a learning community'. We acknowledge, however, that the construction of an inclusive learning community is not easy. We agree with Toole and Louis (2002: 257) that: 'professional learning communities have often not seemed "actionable" [because] they contain a set of inherent tensions that must be identified and managed'. We have found that, when school people rely on procedures and structures to build the learning community, it often falls apart when the person driving the initiative leaves the school or loses heart. By contrast, when the community is built on principles and when the principles become the driving structure and cohering force for the school, then people are equipped to identify and resolve the tensions that emerge in their own contexts. When the principles drive professional practice, the learning environment can continue to be enriching, engaging, and energizing even in the face of changes to staff or leadership (Mitchell and Sackney 2005; Sackney *et al.* 2005).

This concept is particularly interesting because almost every province in Canada has pegged its school improvement policies on the notion of the learning community. The Province of Alberta, for example, has budgeted $80 million for school improvement projects based on the learning community idea, and several other jurisdictions have launched similar initiatives. This focus provides a rich ground for researchers to study how learning communities develop and sustain themselves, and we believe that we are entering an exciting era in the development of learning community theory and practice.

We also believe that we are entering a new world order grounded in metaphors of wholeness and connections, diversity and complexity, relationships and meanings, reflection and inquiry, and collaboration and collegiality. We contend that, if teaching and learning are to move into these realms, educators need to learn from and with a variety of partners, to analyse and reflect on many forms and sources of data, and to use the extended perspectives to inform educational decisions. Professional practice of this nature can provide students with rich, exciting, creative learning opportunities that push them past their comfort level and that engage them in thinking about some of the mysteries, perplexities, and deep questions of the twenty-first century. These are the kinds of school experiences that can support a knowledge society, that can encourage democratic participation, and that can yield more equitable access to the goods of society.

References

Bernhardt, V.L. (1998) *Data Analysis: For Comprehensive Schoolwide Improvement*. Larchmont, NY: Eye on Education.

Bohm, D. (1980) *Wholeness and the Implicate Order*. London: Routledge and Kegan Paul.

Bohm, D. (1985) *Unfolding Meaning: A Weekend of Dialogue with David Bohm*. London: Routledge and Kegan Paul.

DuFour, R. and Eaker, R. (1998) *Professional Learning Communities at Work*. Alexandria, VA: ASCD.

Hartle, F. and Hobby, R. (2003) Leadership in a learning community: your job will never be the same again, in B. Davies and J. West-Burnham (eds) *Handbook of Educational Leadership and Management*. London: Pearson-Longman.

Heifetz, R. and Linsky, M. (2002) *Leadership on the Line*. Boston, MA: Harvard Business School Press.

Mitchell, C. and Sackney, L. (2000) *Profound Improvement: Building Capacity for a Learning Community*. Lisse: Swets and Zeitlinger.

Mitchell, C. and Sackney, L. (2005) Learning community lighthouse schools. Paper presented at the Canadian Society for the Study of Education Annual Conference, May, London, Ontario.

O'Neill, J. (2000) SMART goals, SMART schools, *Educational Leadership*, 57(5): 46–50.

Sackney, L., Mitchell, C. and Walker, K. (2005) Building capacity for learning communities: a case study of fifteen schools. Paper presented at the American Educational Research Association Annual Conference, April, Montreal, Canada.

Saskatchewan Education (2001) *Task Force and Public Dialogue on the Role of the School: Final Report*. Regina, SK: Saskatchewan Education.

Saskatchewan Education (2002) *Working Together Toward School^{PLUS}: Parent and Community Partnerships in Education*. Regina, SK: Saskatchewan Education.

Saskatchewan Learning (2003) *Effective Practices Toward School^{PLUS}: Responsive Curriculum and Instruction*. www.sasked.gov.sk.ca/branches/cap_building_acct/school_plus/rci/index.shtml, accessed 25 June 2004.

Saskatchewan Learning (2004a) *Caring and Respectful Schools: Ensuring Student Well-Being and Educational Success*. Regina, SK: Saskatchewan Learning.

Saskatchewan Learning (2004b) *Toward School^{PLUS}: Empowering High Schools as Communities of Learning and Support*. Regina, SK: Saskatchewan Learning.

Saskatchewan School^{PLUS} (2005) *Giving Saskatchewan Students What They Need to Succeed*. www.schoolplus.gov.sk.ca/pe/main/about, accessed 9 June 2005.

Starratt, R.J. (2003) *Centering Educational Administration: Cultivating Meaning, Community, Responsibility*. Mahwah, NJ: Lawrence Erlbaum.

Stoll, L., Bolam, R. and Collarbone, P. (2002) Leading for change: building capacity for learning, in K. Leithwood and P. Hallinger (eds) *International Handbook of Educational Leadership and Administration* (2nd edn). Dordrecht: Kluwer.

Task Force and Public Dialogue on the Role of the School (2001) *School^{PLUS} A Vision for Children and Youth: Final Report*. Regina, SK: Saskatchewan Instructional Development and Research Unit.

Toole, J.C. and Louis, K.S. (2002) The role of professional learning communities in international education, in K. Leithwood and P. Hallinger (eds) *International Handbook of Educational Leadership and Administration* (2nd edn). Dordrecht: Kluwer.

Wenger, E. (1998) *Communities of Practice: Learning, Meaning and Identity.* Cambridge, MA: Cambridge University Press.

four

From professional learning community to networked learning community

David Jackson and Julie Temperley

Introduction

The world is becoming profoundly more knowledge-rich, and networks, in response, are now an increasingly significant organizational form. Characteristics of network-based knowledge and learning systems are paradigmatically different from the prevailing orthodoxies of the past. In this chapter we argue that the school system, long separated, fragmented and resistant to lateral learning, is beginning to demonstrate the potential of school-to-school collaboration and is generating evidence that enables us to understand how to do this in a disciplined way – and with a focus upon both raising the bar and closing the gap.

The case being made here is not for beyond school collaboration and enquiry *as opposed to* internal professional learning. It is not networked learning community *instead of* professional learning community (PLC) – quite the reverse. Both are necessary for rich professional learning for adult members of school communities. Instead we argue that the school as a unit has become too small scale and isolated to provide scope for professional learning for its adult members in a knowledge-rich and networked world. A new unit of meaning, belonging and engagement – the network – is required. In fact, the collaborative learning and enquiry norms of PLC actually *require* openness to learning sources from outside the community (Bolam *et al.* 2005). This permeability to external learning, from other schools and from the public knowledge base, is crucial to informed organizational learning.

School networks are almost certainly a key part of the answer. The problem is that we currently still know too little about the dynamics and relationships between professional learning and networked learning. That makes networked learning vulnerable to accusations of being too 'social', or of lacking discipline and focus. There is a very real concern about 'cost benefit' (both transaction cost and opportunity cost) in networks. As Little (2005) has argued, this is fresh ground and, as yet, much under-researched.

Expanding the paradigm

Across the English-speaking world, dominant school improvement models have similar characteristics: schools are designed on factory production principles; the profession is layered and structured; the system is tiered – a hierarchy of school, school district, state and national agency. Policy is mandated, practices are prescribed, outcome targets specified. The logical route to improvement appears to be to strengthen delivery mechanisms and tighten accountabilities through targets, inspection, financial incentives and consumer choice.

Such 'top-down', outside-in change approaches that apply existing knowledge across the system work well in the short term, but then stall. Medium- to long-term improvement requires a shift to capacity building for sustainability. Change needs are too rapid, knowledge is too ubiquitous, contexts of knowledge application are too diverse. Centrally coordinated strategies are unlikely to be sensitive to unique challenges of diverse contexts. They neither stimulate nor use practitioner innovation and ownership. Most important, although this reform model has been shown to raise general levels of attainment, it has failed to close the gap in educational achievement between the most and least advantaged (Bentley 2003; Hargreaves 2003).

On the other hand, the same history of reform would indicate that random, unstructured and unconnected distributed learning patterns do not serve the system well either. Experience would suggest they are unlikely ever to achieve the common purpose and connectivity required to bring coherence and alignment to organizational efforts.

An alternative way of providing the connection and alignment to address these concerns is offered by networks of schools that engage in orchestrated 'networked learning'. Both logic and evidence from practice tell us that purposeful collaboration is more fruitful to learning than competition. In fact, we argue that what we are calling 'networked learning' – joint work founded upon learning principles, that enables effective practice to be developed and tested within context through collaboration between institutions – appears to offer a highly effective method of adaptation and integration. It was this approach that lay at the heart of what England's National College for School Leadership (NCSL) set out to achieve in the Networked Learning Communities (NLC) programme.

Networked learning communities

The NLC programme was a large-scale 'development and enquiry' initiative involving 137 networks (1500 schools) between 2002 and 2006. It was specifically designed to provide national policy and system learning (as well as practice evidence) about network design and implementation issues, network size and type, facilitation and leadership, formation processes and growth states, brokerage, system support and incentivization. It was charged with generating evidence about how and under what conditions networks can make a contribution to raising student achievement, about the leadership practices that prove to hold most potential for school-to-school learning and about the new relationships emerging between networks as a 'unit of engagement' and their local authority (school district) partners.

There were six strands to the basic framework of the NLC design:

- *pupil learning* (a pedagogic focus);
- *adult learning* (professional learning communities a key aspiration);
- *leadership learning* (at all levels);
- *organizational learning* (new organizational learning norms);
- *school-to-school learning* (networked learning);
- *network-to-network learning* (lateral system learning).

Each network additionally elected to have at least one external partner, usually a higher education institution (HEI) or local authority (LA/school district) – or both. There were also four non-negotiable principles:

- *moral purpose* – a commitment to success for *all* children ('raising the bar and closing the gap' is a social justice representation of the same theme);
- *shared leadership* (for example, co-leadership);
- *enquiry-based practice* (evidence and data-driven learning);
- adherence to a *model of learning*.

Networks were supported to co-construct learning and engage in enquiry relevant for their context. However, there was one model of learning that provided a programme-wide discipline and analytical template for what we are calling 'networked learning' (see Figure 4.1). Utilization of this model of learning in support of collaborative working disciplines (networked learning) proved to be very powerful for networks of schools within the NLC programme (Jackson 2003).

'Networked learning' is at the heart of the relationship between school networks and the professional learning community. The next section explores what was learned from NLCs about the concept of networked learning. We will then go on to illustrate the links between networked

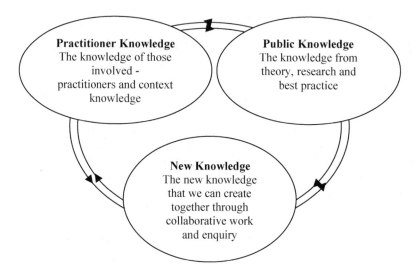

Figure 4.1   Three fields of knowledge

learning communities and professional learning communities by drawing from research evidence gathered during the programme.

Networked learning as a part of a changed paradigm

First a few words about what networked learning is not. Within schools and between schools, adults are involved in multiple random 'networking' relationships, some with strong ties, others arising from weak ties (Granovetter 1973; Watts 2003). These connections offer rich opportunities for learning and make up an unpredictable tapestry of interpersonal connections. They are not, though, 'networked learning' – they are 'networking'.

Networked learning takes place when individuals from different schools in a network come together in groups to engage in purposeful and sustained developmental activity informed by the public knowledge base, using their own know-how and co-constructing knowledge together, as described in the 'three fields' learning model. In doing so, they are involved in four distinct learning processes:

- *Learning from one another*: where groups capitalize on their individual differences and diversity through sharing their knowledge, experience, expertise, practices, and know-how.
- *Learning with one another*: where individuals learn together, notice that they are learning together, co-construct learning and make meaning

together. Collaborative practitioner enquiry, and collaborative learning about recent research are good examples of this activity.

- *Learning on behalf of*: where learning between individuals from different schools is also done on behalf of other individuals within their school and network – or the wider system.
- *Meta-learning*: where individuals are additionally learning about the processes of their own learning.

Learning 'on behalf of' others is particularly important to the concept of networked learning. It means that 'networked learning', as it relates to schools, is the interaction of two types of learning: learning that takes place between individuals from different schools, and subsequent transfer of learning that takes place to other individuals within participants' schools.

Thus networked learning has the potential to expand professional identity from the school as a unit of community to the locality (the network) as a unit of educational community. Participants across schools agree a shared purpose and content focus for their learning, they use evidence-based models and protocols for professional development and their learning has practical relevance to the context and aspirations of their local network of schools.

This contextual relevance focuses activity on some sort of change. Within NLCs this means changes in teachers' knowledge and understanding and changes in their school-level behaviour and classroom practice are an intermediary outcome. The ultimate purpose of networked learning is to improve student learning, achievement and attainment. Wider benefits also include improved confidence and self–esteem amongst participants, enhanced motivation and a greater sense of professional efficacy and identity.

These outcomes begin to answer questions about cost benefit. When practitioners within a network come together, it takes an effort of will. They need no persuading that the effort has to be made worthwhile in terms of learning gains and changed practices. That is the first thing they problem-solve. In contrast, despite what is known about high-quality continuing professional development (CPD) activities, all too often teachers' experience within their own schools has been that learning does not start with the knowledge that they bring; often it does not connect with the publicly available knowledge base; and rarely is new knowledge created and captured through collaborative processes on behalf of a wider constituency. In this respect, for those practitioners whose host school has poor internal learning cultures, participation in a network offers a liberation from context (Hargreaves 2003).

A working model or metaphor may help to illuminate and make practical the networked learning concept.

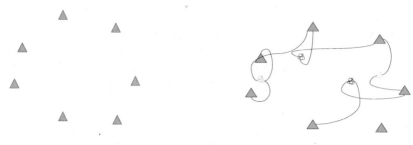

1. Network partner schools   2. The growth of threads and knots

3. The net - working!

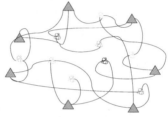

Figure 4.2   Threads, knots and nets

A model for 'networked learning'

Church and colleagues (2002) alighted upon the 'net' metaphor as a way of accessing and illustrating the distinctiveness of key components of network activity. In Figure 4.2, the triangles represent the network units (in this case, member schools). The threads between them stand for the necessary relationships, communication and trust. They represent relationships with a purpose or what Kanter (1994: 97) calls 'the collective and collaborative optimistic ambitions of the participants'. The knots represent what participants do together, networked learning groups undertaking activity on behalf of themselves *and* the whole. It is these knots that provide a learning network with its internal architecture, a flexible 'structure' that only exists to achieve benefit for members – primarily the children within schools, but also the adults and the community served by the network.

Network members seek to effect purposeful change together – on behalf of the network. And when they create collaborative groups to work and learn together, they are engaging in an effort to contribute to that shared goal. This joint activity gives the network focus, strength and purpose. It adds value.

Without trust and high levels of communication there are no networked learning relationships. In this way, the threads operate as a 'sub-structure' – the cultural norms of networked learning. They link the participants through communication, shared ideas, information, relational processes – even problem and conflict resolution. The participants spin these threads themselves; they voluntarily participate and connect – networked learning is founded upon discretionary effort. These 'threads' and 'knots' together provide the tensile strength of the network and need to be tended, stretched and played in just the same way that fishermen artisans will tend and play a conventional net.

The 'networked learning' knots are key points of dynamic learning, with potential for wider resonance (Little 2003). They represent the network's meaningful work. From our study of NLCs there seem to be five types of knots that enhance professional learning:

- *joint work groups* (e.g. project teams, curriculum development groups);
- *collective planning* (e.g. steering groups, professional development groups);
- *mutual problem-solving teams* (e.g. focus groups);
- *collaborative enquiry groups* (e.g. enquiry teams);
- *shared professional development activities* (e.g. learning forums/joint staff days).

Some of these might be seen as being 'architectural' to the network (such as steering groups and learning forums), whilst others are more fluid and adaptive (such as enquiry teams and project teams). The most effective learning knots tend to involve active and sustained enquiry and problem-solving activities between network members from participant schools.

Good knots have strong threads, and joint work arrangements between staff from network schools foster threads. Which comes first? From the NLC programme, the answer is almost certainly that development is iterative, but it is equally true that 'threads' will not precede 'knots'. We need to do good work together to develop strong threads – and there is strong theory and evidence of the potential dysfunctionality of trying to spin threads as ends in themselves.

So, the net metaphor represents the overarching 'structure' or 'fabric' created through the stays (the partners), the relationships (threads) and the 'networked learning' activities (knots). Participants design and re-create structures which are flexible and adaptive, not fixed and constraining. It is an expanded 'professional learning community'; a structure that exists outside normal institutional parameters, that offers freedoms unencumbered by institutional role or status parameters and perceptions. Within the NLC programme, there are many examples of joint work groups containing very mixed membership, including adults other than teachers (assistants and support staff; non-educational professionals, parents, governors – school council members) and pupils. Usually the leadership of these groups is determined by purpose rather than 'rank'.

To conclude the metaphor, network architecture, like any other organizational structure, needs to be tended by someone in a leadership role whose professional identity makes that task a priority (Wohlstetter *et al.* 2003). You also have to work the net (Lieberman and Grolnick 1996; Lieberman 2006). A networked learning community, just like a professional learning community, needs appropriate leadership and facilitation. This relationship will be explored in the next section.

The journey of networks within the NLCs programme was a hard one. If the representations and claims in this chapter appear at times to suggest that the answers are easy, be assured that it was never like that. Instead, the development of school networks for those leading them was complex, challenging and important. Each network was different. Local context posed its own particular set of challenges. Developmental and collaborative histories were unique; variously expanded by external support possibilities and constrained by past relationships. Network leaders worked against the grain of the system and made meaning from their experience as they went along.

PLC and NLC – could there be a relationship?

In this section we make five claims about the relationship between networked learning community (as designed in the NLC programme) and professional learning community. Together, they build a powerful argument for the need to ensure that PLCs and NLCs are connected, rather than viewed as alternative sources of professional learning.

Claim 1: Networks both build from and contribute to professional learning community in respective schools

The definition below, derived from the work of the Southwest Educational Development Laboratory, suggests that a PLC is:

> a school committed to achieving a culture of collective learning and creativity that is characterized by: shared values and vision; supportive and distributed leadership; collaborative professional norms; an enquiry orientation; and facilitative organizational conditions. (Pankake and Moller 2002: 2)

A networked learning community is a cluster of schools working in partnership to enhance the quality of pupil learning, professional development, and school-to-school learning. The programme design drew from an OECD seminar in defining networks as follows:

> Networks are purposefully led social entities that are characterized by a commitment to quality, rigour and a focus on outcomes ... They promote the dissemination of good practice, enhance the professional development of teachers, support capacity building in schools, mediate between centralized and decentralized structures, and assist in the process of re-structuring and re-culturing educational organizational systems. (OECD 2000: 4)

There is a clear synergy between the two definitions.

There are three ways in which school networks appear to strengthen or extend professional learning community:

1. In a network of schools the strength of some schools' internal learning culture enables other schools to learn from that through network activity.
2. A school's own professional learning culture is enhanced by 'networked learning'. In other words, schools learn to collaborate more effectively internally by collaborating externally. The benefits are recursive.
3. Permeability to learning from the external knowledge-base (theory, research and the practice of other schools) is necessary to avoid stagnation and constant recycling of a school's existing knowledge-base.

It was a specific element of the NLC design to support the development of schools as professional learning communities. Networked learning communities placed teachers, leaders and groups of schools at the heart of innovation and knowledge creation, enabling the development of context-specific practices and problem-solving solutions. The design built from what was known in other sectors (Kanter 1994; OECD 2000; Lank 2005).

The evidence from the Networked Learning Communities initiative appears to suggest that *between* school networks may, in fact, be both the catalyst and context for the internal redesign required to generate professional learning networks *within* some schools.

Claim 2: Networks have the potential to take professional learning community to scale

Returning to the two definitions, one notable difference is that the second expands the 'unit of meaning' to a group of schools and also embeds its purposes within wider system influence. The network is viewed as a mediating unit between tiers of the educational structure, and it is seen as having the potential to re-culture local systems.

One reason for this is that networks have the potential to harness the energies of practitioner members. This may be critical to moving beyond the standards plateau across the system (Fullan 2005). Despite the obvious challenges and the discretionary effort required to establish and sustain networks, around 7000 schools, one-quarter of the total number of schools in England, volunteered to participate in learning networks between 2002 and 2006. Interestingly, finance was not their incentive. Critical drivers included the orientation towards learning, the sense of local control, the potential for local innovation and the compelling nature of the networks' aspirations. In England, networks have already moved to scale.

Claim 3: Networks offer a more efficient unit of engagement for intermediate system personnel, such as school districts and universities, and make it easier for those organizations to contribute external knowledge

There is a strong evidence-base that school development benefits from external facilitation (e.g. Fullan and Miles 1992; Stringfield 1998). Having adapted over the past decade or more to the expectations and demands of the delivery and accountability system, current intermediate institutions (local authorities and universities, primarily) are not well geared to the new task of brokering and facilitating networks. Turn the challenge around, though, and self-supporting networks can increasingly be seen as a means of facilitating innovation and change from the ground, as well as con-tributing to a progressive restructuring of support systems (Demos/NCSL 2002; Hopkins 2003). The system emphasis then becomes less about exercising control (both impossible in an increasingly autonomous context and antithetical to creativity and innovation), and more about harnessing the interactive and creative capability of system-wide forces.

Critical to understanding the conceptual step-change that can help to achieve this are two frames of thinking. The first is to begin to see the network as the 'unit of meaning' (so that a district with 100 schools and 14 networks would move from having 100 units to 14 units of engagement). The second is to understand the changed nature of the relationship itself.

Our evidence on university partners (Campbell *et al.* 2005) and district involvement with school networks (NCSL 2004) indicates that external partners can foster network growth through a range of practical partner-ship activities:

- supporting school group self-review and peer review – using data to enable the choice of a learning focus that will raise standards;
- facilitating relationships and activity between participant schools;
- encouraging commitment from headteachers – and involvement of the best school leaders beyond their own school on behalf of the network;

- advising on the use of funding and critical friends;
- brokering links with HEIs, other LA staff and consultancy support – brokering partnerships;
- connecting groups of schools with existing network practice and knowledge, both within the LA and beyond.

These are very different roles – more enabling, more capacity-building – than those of recent history, and involve different skill sets. The most helpful characterization is that the district or university moves from being the expert to being a learner about, and co-designer of, network activity.

Claim 4: Networks foster effective collaborative professional learning

Two substantial research projects have verified the power of school networks in fostering effective collaborative professional learning. The NLC external evaluation study (Earl and Katz 2005) identified 'professional knowledge creation and sharing' as an *interim outcome* of NLCs, with impact on pupil learning, engagement and success as the *ultimate outcome*. They also identified seven 'key features' of learning networks. The first five are: purpose and focus, relationships, leadership, accountability, capacity building and support. The other two, collaboration and enquiry, are worth considering in a little more detail.

Collaboration allows for sharing *both* within schools *and* across systems; it spreads innovations beyond discrete sites; it creates a dynamic process of interpretation and evaluation of practice between colleagues; and fosters identification with the larger group, extending commitment beyond the single classroom or school.

Enquiry is a fundamental tenet of learning networks – a 'non-negotiable' design feature of the NLC programme. It is the process through which practitioners are able systematically and intentionally to explore information from research, experts and each other in support of local decision-making and problem-solving. Collaborative enquiry also involves thinking about, reflecting on and challenging individual and collective experiences to come to a deepened understanding of shared beliefs and practices.

What the external evaluation data make clear is the added dimension that working on behalf of a wider group – the school, community, profession, all children – brings to our understanding of what motivates network leaders and participants to invest in the collaboration and enquiry. The evaluation offers a theory of action that draws on beliefs and values – on the moral purpose at the heart of the professional learning community.

This resonates with the findings of the NLC programme research team. In 2004–05 the team studied the relationship between networked learning and collaborative CPD for adults[1] in schools in 85 networks, exploring three specific questions:

- How do NLCs improve the quality of adult learning and CPD?
- How do NLCs improve the quality of classroom practice?
- How do NLCs improve school-to-school learning?

They found that, whilst at one level collaboration was a means by which networks secured buy-in from a wide range of partners, most effectively it was built into professional learning and enquiry as the principle means by which networks achieved depth – through the effective transfer of knowledge and skill. Significantly, peer-to-peer collaboration was the dominant model, mostly combined with specialist expertise provided through partnership with universities and district personnel.

Examples of effective collaborative activities included:

- teachers teaching teachers across a network;
- participation in collaborative work groups;
- action research-based professional development involving a commitment to reciprocity and the creation of structures for sharing learning;
- collaborative teams working with district partners;
- peer-support teams receiving further mentoring from university staff.

To discover the focus of practitioner learning in the network the enquiry looked at seven areas of teachers' professional knowledge (see Figure 4.3). Figure 4.3 clearly indicates that the top two reported areas of focus for professional learning in networks were pedagogical knowledge and knowledge of learners (e.g. learning to learn). They were also interested in the collaborative processes within the CPD.

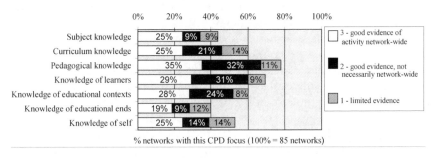

Figure 4.3   The focus of adult learning within NLCs (Shulman grid)

The most commonly used CPD processes highlighted within NLCs (see Figure 4.4) were the 'use of external expertise' and the 'individualized nature of the activity', both cited by over 80 per cent of the networks, and the 'use of peer support', and 'professional dialogue'. These also showed the most evidence of being widely networked.

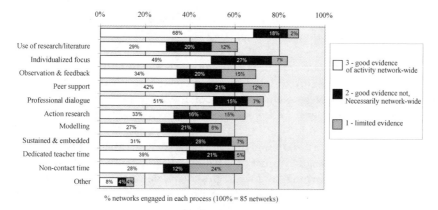

% networks engaged in each process (100% = 85 networks)

Figure 4.4 Adult learning processes undertaken within NLC (EPPI grid)

The evidence reinforces the earlier point that networks provide a more effective 'unit of engagement' for external support than the individual school. By their very nature, networks offer more sustained avenues for adult learning than the traditional 'in-house activity' or 'one-day course'. A key ingredient of effective CPD from a systematic review of research evidence on collaborative CPD (CUREE 2004: 6) is the development of 'processes to encourage, extend and structure professional dialogue'. Almost by definition, NLCs fit this requirement – they are designed to engender dialogue between practitioners.

Claim 5: Networks have as their intermediate aim improving teaching practices and as their key outcome, raising pupil achievement

A critical question is what difference do networks make? Here we highlight two important outcomes of NLCs.

Improving teaching practices

From the programme research, perceptions about impact in relation to NLC school-to-school activity included:

- an enhanced understanding and perception of pupils' capabilities;
- changes in teachers' skills and competence;
- enhanced self-esteem (e.g. through experience of leading staff meetings in other schools, opening network events and addressing LA colleagues).

Some NLCs also noted the effect of changing practices and collaborative learning on staff retention and recruitment.

The research also asked the question: *is adult learning in NLCs improving the quality of classroom practice?* Networks reported ways in which they believed they were impacting on classrooms.

- Network activity was seen as encouraging schools to take a fresh look at their understanding of and approaches to lesson and learning design.
- Many networks were committed to collaborative planning at an individual or subject level and were focused on practical, classroom-based activity.
- NLCs were seen as enabling practitioners to gain first-hand practical experience of a broader range of learning environments, issues involved in personalized learning, and strategies available to deal with them.
- Practitioners in networks felt able to use membership to enhance their understanding and use of externally generated programmes and strategies (e.g. assessment for learning, learning styles, thinking skills).
- Engagement with enquiry activity was significant in changing teachers' views of their pupils and their capabilities.

Improving pupil achievement

In a systematic review of network evaluations (CUREE and NCSL 2005), the review question was: *What is the impact on pupils of networks that include at least three schools?* Networked professional learning emerged as being at the heart of the majority of the effective networks – those making clear differences for pupils. This methodology effectively 'backward mapped' from evaluations showing pupil gains to the practices generating those gains.

The ultimate test of pupil gains in the UK lies with attainment data. In England, GCSE results at age 16 (Key Stage 4) have long been the currency of choice. Whilst there are multiple graphs that could be displayed (Key Stage 2 assessment data for 11-year-olds, individual network growth patterns, data sets by local authority) two data sets reporting Key Stage 4 outcomes for Networked Learning Communities schools compared with non-Networked Learning Communities schools demonstrate significant improvement in pupil achievement.

Key Stage 4 data for 2005 supplied by England's Department for Education and Skills (DfES) shows NLC schools rose more than non-NLC schools in the percentage of pupils achieving five or more A* to C grades between 2004 and 2005. In terms of average point score across all grades, the results again show that NLC schools rose more than non-NLC schools (see Figure 4.5).

When comparing Key Stage 4 for 2005 with the results from 2003 (see Figure 4.6), again NLC schools rose more than non-NLC schools in the percentage of pupils achieving five or more A* to C grades.[2]

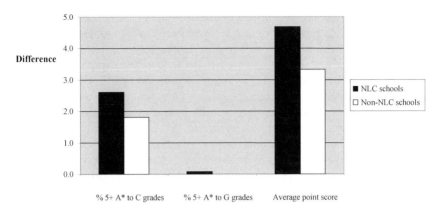

Figure 4.5 Difference between 2004 and 2005 at Key Stage 4

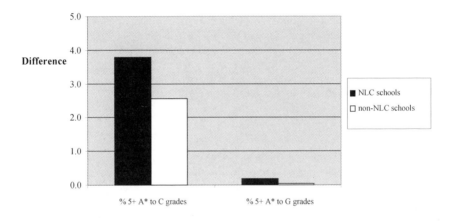

Figure 4.6 Difference between 2003 and 2005 at Key Stage 4

Conclusion

The key word in all the above analyses is *learning*. Effective networks promote 'networked learning' – and that is a step on the road towards a learning system. What both grounded theory and research from the NLC programme tell us emphatically is that by *aligning* networked learning processes for adults and pupils, and having leadership that promotes and supports that learning, there is evidence that networks appear to succeed in their twin objectives of fostering learning community and raising pupil achievement.

The achievement data presented above are both a validation and a bonus. It could be argued that finding a way of working which gives control back to the profession, fosters professional learning, stimulates innovation, energizes and enthuses teachers, distributes and grows leadership, and balances central accountability with peer responsibility would be the way to go, even if results only stayed the same. Generating the conditions that enable all that and do no harm to results would be quite an achievement. However, those who sculpt their craft in the forms of professional and networked learning community are motivated by how their changed practices improve learning and close the achievement gaps for young people. Being at the heart of their core purpose, it is unsurprising that evidence of improved results follow.

Notes

1 NLCs used the term 'adults' to include all practitioners, e.g. learning support and classroom assistants as well as teachers in schools. However, the vast majority of participants in collaborative CPD in network schools were teachers and school leaders.
2 No comparison in terms of average point score is possible, as the method of calculating the score was changed between 2003 and 2005.

References

Bentley, T. (2003) The purposes of networks and their contribution to collaborative capacity. Unpublished policy discussion paper, Demos, London.

Bolam, R., McMahon, A., Stoll, L., Thomas, S. and Wallace, M. (2005) *Creating and Sustaining Effective Professional Learning Communities*. DfES Research Report RR637. University of Bristol. www.dfes.gov.uk/research/data/uploadfiles/RR637.pdf, accessed 13 March 2006.

Campbell, A., Kane, I., Keating, I., Cockett, K., McConell, A. and Baxter, C. (2005) *Networked Learning Communities and Higher Education Links*. NCSL/Liverpool Hope University research report. www.NCSL.org.uk, accessed 13 March 2006.

Church, M., Bitel, M., Armstrong, K., Fernando, P., Gould, H., Joss, S., Marwaha-Diedrich, M., De La Torre, A.-L. and Vouhe, C. (2002) *Participation, Relationships and Dynamic Change: New Thinking on Evaluating the Work of International Networks*. London: University College London.

Centre for the Use of Research and Evidence in Education (CUREE) (2004) How does collaborative continuing professional development (CPD) for teachers of the 5–16 age range affect teaching and learning? www.curree-paccts.com/dynamic/curree40.jsp, accessed 13 March 2006.

Centre for the Use of Research and Evidence in Education and National College for

School Leadership (CUREE and NCSL) (2005) Systematic research review: the impact of networks on pupils, practitioners and the communities they serve. www.ncsl.org.uk.

Demos/National College for School Leadership (NCSL) (2002) Learning from experience: a literature review designed to help those establishing and running Networked Learning Communities. Paper presented at the Networked Learning Communities Launch Conference, Nottingham, June.

Earl, L. and Katz, S. (2005) *Learning from Networked Learning Communities (Phase 2) – Key Features and Inevitable Tensions.* Phase 2 Report of the Networked Learning Communities External Evaluation. London: DfES.

Fullan, M. (2005) *System Thinkers in Action: Moving Beyond the Standards Plateau.* London: DfES Innovation Unit and National College for School Leadership.

Fullan, M. and Miles, M.B. (1992) Getting reform right: what works and what doesn't, *Phi Delta Kappan,* 73(10): 745–52.

Granovetter, M. (1973) The strength of weak ties, *American Journal of Sociology,* 78(6): 1360–80.

Hargreaves, D. (2003) *Learning Laterally: How Innovation Networks Make an Education Epidemic.* London: Demos, DfES Innovation Unit and NCSL.

Hopkins, D. (2003) Understanding networks for innovation in policy and practice, in D. Istance (ed.) *Networks of Innovation: Towards New Models for Managing Schools and Systems.* Paris: OECD.

Jackson, D. (2003) What is networked learning? Paper presented to the American Educational Research Association Annual Meeting, Chicago, April.

Kanter, R. (1994) Collaborative advantage: the art of alliances, *Harvard Business Review,* July–August: 96–108.

Lank, E. (2005) *Collaborative Advantage: How Organizations Win by Working Together.* London: Palgrave Macmillan.

Lieberman, A. (2006) Where do system leaders come from? Tracing the development of new patterns and practices of leadership in school-to-school networks. Unpublished introduction to NCSL research report.

Lieberman, A. and Grolnick, M. (1996) Networks and reform in American education, *Teachers College Record,* 98(1): 7–45.

Little, J. (2003) Unpublished contribution to Networked Learning Communities Research Seminar, National College for School Leadership, Cranfield, May.

Little, J. (2005) Nodes and nets: investigating resources for professional learning in schools and networks. Unpublished paper written for the NLC programme, February.

National College for School Leadership (NCSL) (2004) *What Are We Learning About: LEA Involvement in School Networks?* www.ncsl.org.uk, accessed 13 March 2006.

Organization for Economic Co-operation and Development (OECD) (2000) *Knowledge Management in the Learning Society.* Paris: OECD.

Pankake, A. and Moller, G. (2002) Professional learning communities: a synthesis of a five-year study. Paper presented to the American Educational Research Association Annual Meeting, New Orleans, April.

Stringfield, S. (1998) External support systems in the school transformation process.

Research report for the Center for Research on the Education of Students Placed at Risk, Johns Hopkins and Howard Universities.

Watts, D.J. (2003) *Six Degrees: The Science of a Connected Age*. New York: W.W. Norton.

Wohlstetter, P., Malloy, C.L., Chau, D. and Polhemus, J. (2003) Improving schools through networks: a new approach to urban school reform, *Educational Policy*, 17(4): 399–430.

five

Beyond borders: can international networks deepen professional learning community?

Louise Stoll, Jan Robertson, Lynn Butler-Kisber, Sylvia Sklar and Tom Whittingham

Introduction

There is increasing consensus that professional learning communities (PLCs) play a key role in building individuals' and schools' capacities for continuous and sustainable learning in a rapidly changing world. Leaders have a major responsibility for facilitating the development of PLCs (Stoll and Bolam 2005), but where can they turn for their own learning to support them in this? We would argue that this necessitates going beyond their schools.

The importance of school leaders looking beyond their schools for ideas and support has long been recognized in the school improvement and educational change literature (e.g. Fullan 1993). Many educators have developed valuable professional relationships with colleagues in other schools (see Jackson and Temperley, Chapter 4, and Lieberman, Chapter 14, in this book). Networking between educators enables them to share and tease out principles of good practice, engage in in-depth dialogue across schools, create knowledge to respond to particular challenges that any one school might find hard to resolve, observe colleagues elsewhere, experience fresh perspectives, reduce isolation, and see their own school through a different lens. As such, as well as for its potential in spreading policy, networking is becoming well established in many countries (OECD 2003; Veugelers and O'Hair 2005).

As school boundaries become less fixed through networking initiatives, educators worldwide also find themselves brought much closer, dealing with similar learning challenges resulting from social, technological, economic and other global change forces. Over the past decade, Robertson and

Webber (2002) have conducted research on leadership programmes to understand more fully the impact of experiences on leaders' development. We also believe that it is vital that leaders have 'boundary breaking' authentic community learning experiences across contexts to challenge them to reflect on their values, assumptions about learning and beliefs about pedagogy and policies.

In this chapter, we explore the development of international networks of school leaders promoted by an English local authority (school district) and international partners which appears to be both helping to deepen PLCs within the leaders' schools as well as developing and extending the local authority's own PLC. First, we describe how the international networks initiative was established. We tell the stories of two international networks, and then describe their impact, before identifying emerging issues that appear to be important to the development of networks that can deepen and extend PLC. We also describe how sustainability is being approached through a third international network. Our data sources are diverse. We draw on questionnaire and interview data from visit participants; interviews of and reflections from facilitators, as well as data gathered by them, including videotaped discussions; and notes taken by all of us at meetings.

The origins of the international networks

The seeds of international networks were planted in South Gloucestershire, a local authority (LA) with 114 schools in south-west England where Tom, as an LA officer, was responsible for promoting both international learning and leadership. He observed that leaders experience constant challenge with daily leadership dilemmas whilst frequently working in isolation, often leading to declining confidence. Prior experience taught him that mentoring, coaching or having informal peer networks made a difference. Participants on a teacher visit to Toronto he had coordinated described how it 'encouraged innovative out-of-the-box thinking' and developed and supported a network extending beyond their local cluster of schools, right across the local authority. He and headteacher colleagues perceived a need after international visits to create a forum within which learners could reflect in a planned manner, and the idea of ongoing enquiry groups was born.

A recently established initiative by the British Council in partnership with the National College for School Leadership (NCSL) – the International Placements for Headteachers (IPH) – offered headteachers 'opportunities to not only learn from best leadership practices worldwide but also to reflect upon their own practices', through 'quality professional leadership dialogue with their colleagues globally' in different cultures and contexts. This provided the funding for South Gloucestershire's international visits.

Tom also felt that if the international learning perspective was to continue to grow, it would benefit from engaging a 'critical friend', so he contacted Louise, a researcher, thinking her research on building professional learning communities might be 'galvanized' into exploring the progress and impact of the international initiatives as well as helping to sustain momentum. He thought her connections with the international partners and knowledge of the cultural contexts where South Gloucestershire had planned headteacher visits would prove invaluable. In addition, he was personally interested in getting a critical friendship perspective on the way South Gloucestershire was attempting to use international visits and other leadership learning initiatives to build professional learning community within and between schools and among local authority advisers.

The Australian experience

In the first international network experience we describe, ten South Gloucestershire headteachers from primary, secondary and special schools went to Victoria in May 2003. The visit stemmed from interests in international education, innovative approaches to teaching and learning and continuity across the school phases, networks, education of 14–19-year-olds, and models of leadership development that might result in the development of enquiry groups and partnerships to support headteachers as learners across the authority. The headteachers read preparatory readings, meeting to explore aspirations for their international learning experience. A common interest emerged in teaching and learning styles that enable more effective pupil learning.

On arrival, an evening at an Australian principal's home promoted informal contact with hosting principals, helping to start forming working relationships. Inputs from experts 'of world renown' on the second day explored implications of future thinking for education and transformation. During the rest of their stay, the headteachers visited nine schools matched to individual school phases, focusing on: understanding how 'learning how to learn' was being developed; effective leadership styles to transform practice; networked learning community development, impact and implications; and ICT use to support learning. The approach taken was coordinated so that colleagues from both countries presented ideas and strategies, and the English headteachers shared their learning at the end of each working day.

The headteachers described their experience as extremely enriching: 'the most profound professional development exercise and the most profound personal development'; 'It called into question my culture, my assumptions that you have to have an education system like this'; and 'I'm a conformist and I came back a rebel! It's driven me to address fundamental issues.' They believed this was because the visit powerfully emphasized learning and schools creating their own future, as well as mixing theoretical models against which they could reflect on their practice with valuable examples of practice. Social bonding within a larger educational context also led to a more equal relationship between headteachers in all phases, and productive professional exchange. They came back with greater confidence 'to step out of the here and now', 'with permission and passion, and prepared to take risks' to ensure they were able to focus on what matters: learning and teaching. In September 2003, the Director of England's National Remodelling Team wrote in a national newspaper:

> I recently met a group of heads from South Gloucestershire who had been working with heads in Melbourne, Australia. They had come back from a placement and were exploring how they could continue to share information. I have never seen a group of Heads more animated about what the experience had done for their learning because they'd had their horizons opened and they could think of things in a different way. (Smithers 2003)

The New Zealand experience

Four South Gloucestershire headteachers visited New Zealand with eight colleagues from two other south-west England local authorities to study and learn more about coaching leadership (Robertson 2005) with Jan at the University of Waikato, Hamilton. This visit originated at a coaching workshop Jan led in England where Tom observed its potential for leadership development throughout the authority.

The headteachers completed questionnaires prior to their visit to explore expectations. Reasons for going to New Zealand were varied. The specific focus on coaching attracted some, as one wrote: 'To have new ideas on how to motivate teachers who want to take on new ideas, but don't embed these ideas into practice'. Some reasons related to the country's education context, for example: 'New Zealand has a worldwide reputation for aspects of effective learning and teaching ... I would like to see effective NZ practice in schools.' Others thought that it was an exciting professional opportunity to broaden their experience and for rejuvenation: 'it seemed like an ideal opportunity to widen my horizons and experience other people's vision – indeed, other nation's vision. Personally, I hope to be revitalized and inspired as well as learning new strategies'.

The visitors were welcomed with a 'kiwi-BBQ dinner'. Many commented that experiencing the country immediately through the hospitality in someone's home, and getting to know each other informally, set the scene and collegiality which was evident throughout the next fortnight. During the visit, the leaders studied the theory of coaching through the practice of coaching, working in coaching partnerships. The first day and a half was spent practising and reflecting upon the skills of active listening, reflective questioning, context interviewing, self-assessment, and goal-setting. During two days in schools chosen for their focus on leadership coaching and building learning communities, they watched leaders coaching, talked with teachers, and spent time in classrooms. The bicultural experience of being welcomed formally by one school within the local Maori community challenged many to reflect on beliefs and assumptions valued in their own schools. Finally, they joined other New Zealand leaders at an international leadership institute focusing on learning-centred leadership. During these days, they sat together to debate issues and plan change in their authorities, and met their coaching partners every day to continue practising coaching skills and set individual goals and action plans for student achievement. At the end, each participant wrote Jan a letter of reflection on their New Zealand experiences, setting out their next year's goals for their school and/ or career.

In their post-visit surveys, all reported that their expectations had been met. The purpose and uses of coaching had a profound impact on many:

the realization that talking through an issue with a colleague who is really listening and concentrating can be illuminating. The conversation you have with yourself inside your own head is somehow not at all comparable. In talking about an issue with my coach, and through his focused questioning, I realized that the underlying factors were not those I had believed them to be. The coaching arrangement provided the scaffold that extended my thinking beyond the point where it normally would have rested ... Coaching has enabled me to distinguish clearly between leadership and management.

Maori culture had an equally significant impact:

For me, it was an understanding of culture and what it was possible for this to mean in schools. I feel I, and probably many others, have talked glibly about school culture and then wondered why, within wider communities, our values and culture have felt isolated. The integration and respect given to Maori rituals and culture and the valuing of parents as part of the process was enlightening and 'real'.

For one, a significant learning occurred at home during the visit: 'allowing myself time to let go of the school and allowing my deputy to manage the school successfully ... This has enabled me to reflect on my changing leadership style'.

The visit clearly affected them profoundly, as one wrote: 'The importance of the international dimension in enabling a sense of perspective on your personal and professional life – gaining a glimpse of another culture always adds an immeasurable depth to one's thinking.'

The impact

While the leaders' feedback after their visits is encouraging, a key question is to what extent their visits made a difference to PLC back in South Gloucestershire. As we have been following the story, we have observed two levels of PLC impact: deepening the learning of individuals over time and their work within their school PLCs; and extending the learning more broadly throughout South Gloucestershire.

Deepening the learning within school PLCs

Learning depends on making connections (Bransford *et al.* 1999). Too frequently, learning experiences are 'one-offs', forgotten in the pressures of daily life. A core aim of international visits is that they will lead to benefits for the schools of those who have the experience. We have been interested to understand how international networks can help school leaders develop their own school PLCs. On their return, the headteachers visiting New Zealand, for example, described their plans to continue with a pre-established coaching partnership, one established in New Zealand, or establish one with another head or their deputy head. Some also set themselves coaching goals, for example to 'ensure that the focus of staff meetings is firmly on learning and teaching rather than daily minutiae. This is an area where my coach could help'.

When Jan visited England in July 2005, the leaders had implemented some of their ideas about promoting coaching throughout the school to develop staff and encourage them to take more professional ownership and responsibility to consolidate their in-school PLC. In particular, three aspects of the New Zealand experience appeared to have assisted with connections and transfer back to individual school PLCs. One was the coaching partner, established to support the leaders' initiatives; the second was setting clear goals and actions; and, finally, the later visit and correspondence with Jan, the New Zealand facilitator, kept the connections and personalized learning component of the tour at the forefront of the leaders' minds.

In some schools staff also experienced similar learning opportunities. In one school, where the head had been to New Zealand and had 'gained more than I thought from the outset; it's still reverberating', two members of staff had been to another country to explore coaching and they were combining their learning to feedback to staff. Elsewhere, to spread the ideas and language more widely across their schools, in six schools a group of teachers visited the Melbourne schools previously visited by their headteacher and were subsequently feeding back their learning throughout their schools. As one headteacher whose colleagues had gone to Melbourne noted: 'They were empowered. I saw them doing things they haven't done before.'

Extending the learning across the local authority

A particularly interesting feature has been the ways that learning from the international visits have been extended both between participants visiting each country and beyond them to other headteacher and local authority adviser colleagues. For example, the Melbourne group returned enthused and resolved to 'Shape the Future'. It had became clear to them in Melbourne that 'if the future is collaborative, we need to understand this and what it means for people's entitlements'. Supported by Tom and a small grant from England's Innovation Unit within the Department for Education and Skills, they continued to meet, evolving their shared experience even further and starting to develop a common language. Using an idea they picked up in Victoria, they prepared an accord – a commitment to one another, defining the purpose of their network and their relationship – *Towards a Preferred Future for Learning and Education* (Casson *et al.* 2004), to guide their own further work and be used as a basis for discussion with colleagues or to be 'adopted, adapted, revised, borrowed from or discarded' by others. One explained how: 'thinking about futures [in Melbourne] got us thinking out of the box ... out of our own context and comfort zone. It got us thinking "What are we doing?" and also led to the accord and getting more involved in leadership in South Gloucestershire'. Another commented: 'the work of this learning group has given me a new "lens" through which to consider aspects of my work. It has allowed me to deepen and diversify my perceptions of all aspects of my working context from the "micro" to the "big picture" '. Developing the accord appeared to be particularly important in signifying the way these headteachers wanted to work together and was instrumental in helping to build enquiry networks and establish the Leaders of Learning meetings in the authority.

The visitors to New Zealand planned to share information about the visit throughout the local authority, to officers, advisers and fellow headteachers, including lobbying where appropriate. In their action plan, they outlined intentions to promote existing leadership development of new heads and experienced leaders through coaching. This plan was elaborated collaboratively with local authority (LA) advisers when Jan visited England in July 2005. The focus was on extending the coaching programme, but also an opportunity for LA officers to hear more about the experiences and experience coaching, working in LA pairs and then groups to discuss implications for further development in the LA and plan ahead.

This and other international activity is being extended through the authority's Leadership Academy as a trigger to develop a wider PLC of school and local authority leaders across South Gloucestershire, trying to ensure that quality learning is shared across the whole Department for Children and Young People in South Gloucestershire. Participants are bringing their learning into other Leadership Academy programmes as well as working in local cluster groups, and have established learning sets across a group of schools with a programme of self-evaluation intervisitations between school leaders. The Leadership Academy is also currently working to create a partnership of school leaders and local authority leaders. Developments in different international networking initiatives have informed the Academy that educational leaders' main function is to focus on improving learning and leadership opportunities, to develop their own leadership capacity and that of their institution.

Learning thus far

As we reflect on the learning journeys stimulated by these visits, themes are emerging about issues to consider and fruitful avenues to explore when trying to develop international networks that can deepen and extend professional learning community: the importance of the learning mode and theme; the role of change agents; and sustainability. These themes are now described, with illustrations from the international experiences.

Learning modes and themes

Key features of the experiences described here have been modes of collaborative learning and enquiry to promote deeper engagement in the experience. These learning processes have also been blended with the visits' theme. This appears to have been powerful in deepening and extending participants' learning experience.

The Melbourne group explored futures thinking and transformation of learning and teaching with targeted inputs, two-way dialogue, school visits and focused group meetings at the end of the day, emphasizing 'learning how to learn'. Most important in the New Zealand experience has been that leadership coaching was both the learning mode and study tour focus. Leaders critiqued principles and theory behind the coaching model, then practised the skills of coaching, while developing their professional relationship. They were always working on three levels: on one, they were learning the skills; on the next, they were reflecting on and critiquing processes of coaching, their own ability and the facilitation of such processes and impact on leadership development; and on the third level was their own reflection around their leadership practice as they worked with their coach, focusing on their professional practice and their schools and communities. This is a powerful learning mode, as the necessary support and challenge is provided to ensure change actually occurs during and after the professional development (Robertson 2005). The participants also carried out professional goal-setting in relation to what they had been learning and thinking about on the study tour, making an overt commitment to these changes in practice that they wanted to occur on return to England.

Change agents

International networks that help promote professional learning community do not just happen. They need to be nurtured and supported. Our experience and data gathered thus far suggest that there have been different kinds of change agents.

Ideas champion

A most important part of the process of support is individuals who will champion the cause at all ends of the communities, who have the energy and commitment, as well as the innovation to try out new ideas and take risks and leaps into an unknown but exciting future (Webber and Robertson 2004). From the perspective of the other authors and head-teachers involved, Tom has been a champion through drive, commitment and energy, and promoting links and connections with other change agents and funders within England, nationally and internationally resulting in all the visits taking place, as well as contracting an external evaluator/critical friend to support the endeavour. The British Council's Leadership Team Leader spoke of 'Tom's ability to see the "big picture". He has a clearly expressed vision, which he is putting into practice through assessing innovative and creative opportunities through the British Council programmes and opportunities'. Creating the environment in which international networks can develop to a point at which they coalesce to deepen and extend professional learning community has taken time, and Tom's contribution in preparing the groundwork has been critical.

He also went to New Zealand. Those he accompanied were unanimously positive about his role, viewing him as astute, warm, inclusive, and quietly and sensitively guiding and focusing colleagues to go deeper and further in their thinking, as one wrote:

He has the natural ability to lead in a very quiet and unassuming way but with a very strong presence. He always makes you feel that your contributions are valuable which gives you that confidence to carry on with your reflective thinking. He is always just behind you, nudging you gently forward. He can summarise very eloquently and reflectively the learning that has taken place, his questioning is not threatening but makes you think ... I came away from New Zealand a very different person due to Tom's skills as a facilitator and his role model on how to lead people.

External experts

The role of external experts has been very important in these two experiences. For those visiting Melbourne, the key stimulus for the accord and the futures focus on their return to England came from a day spent with world-renowned experts in this area. For the headteachers who went to New Zealand, Jan's expert knowledge and continued involvement through her return visits to South Gloucestershire and ongoing online communication has added significantly to the knowledge base of leaders and, already in some cases teachers, about a reflective collaborative learning strategy that can help promote professional learning community.

External facilitators

The principal of one of the Melbourne schools acted as a key link in the planning of that experience. Headteachers were also accompanied by a consultant headteacher from another part of England, assigned by NCSL and the British Council. One explained this facilitator's role, although we have not specifically evaluated it, as: 'to encourage reflection and maximize learning. Not through being an "expert" but by insightful questioning and reflective conversation. The coach to the team'. In a third experience we describe later in this chapter Lynn and Sylvia, collaborating with school board partners in Montreal, and working with partners in England, have been responsible for ensuring visits were planned and structured a powerful learning experience as well as promoting and participating in follow-up activities to help to sustain momentum and ensure the learning continues.

External critical friend

With an innovative activity such as this, it is easy to become too attached and close to evaluate impact. Having a 'critical friend' can provide support and challenge. While we have all charted the networks' progress, we have also all been active participants in developing them, except for Louise who was officially contracted to collect and feedback data. Nonetheless, she has taken an 'evaluation for learning' orientation as well as connecting colleagues in the different countries. From the perspective of other colleagues, this role should not be underestimated.

Sustainability: from international networks to international professional learning communities

Achieving sustainability – preserving and developing deep learning for all that spreads and lasts in ways that also creates benefits for others around you (Hargreaves and Fink 2006) – is complex. Existing evidence on the sustainability of PLCs is limited but indicates that sustaining a thriving PLC is not easy (see Hargreaves, Chapter 13 in this book). This is likely to be all the more true across borders with international networks. There is potential for international networks such as those described to develop into international professional learning communities, but at the moment they are still nascent, with ongoing links between individual members.

To illustrate the potential of developing an international PLC with members in two countries, we turn to the story of a third international network in which South Gloucestershire has participated. With a focus on social inclusion in England and Quebec, Canada, 12 headteachers from the South West Affiliated Centre (SWAC) of NCSL visited Montreal. Lynn and Sylvia from McGill University collaboratively designed an intense, multi-faceted learning experience with SWAC's leadership strategy adviser, the McGill team and the leaders of two greater Montreal school boards, another example of districts supporting international networks. Tom was also involved in early discussions.

Each headteacher and principal was assigned to a learning pod (group) with six members (including leaders from both countries). A 'flying pod' (an international team of the visit's facilitators) was also formed to support the school leaders. The schedule included attending a provincial teachers' convention together, visiting at least three schools and the two school boards, and engaging in daily debriefings and local cultural activities and receptions. At a closing symposium, each pod presented lessons learned. Presentations were videotaped on a live video feed and posted on the McGill website (http://mediasite.campus.mcgill.ca) for sharing with other school leaders. School board members, school commissioners and government officials attended the symposium. A brochure describing the project was produced and proposals were made for funds to build sustainability of the network and for sharing effective professional development for leaders at international conferences.

Community leadership is being explored and developed in this international group through learning pods that build on models of cooperative/collaborative learning. They are self-directed, small and intimate professional groups made up of participants from multiple contexts that appear to provide a space for safe exchanges and reflection and an opportunity for experiencing one another's contexts with a lens for juxtaposing contexts to explore problems from different perspectives.

Since the Montreal visit, participants have continued learning collaboratively through email exchanges, live video conferencing, written reflections, and meetings to strengthen and sustain the connections. In November 2005, the Canadian principals and members of the flying pod paid a return visit. The school leaders greeted each other like old friends after a year of exchanging personal and professional emails and video conference meetings. Pods spent three days in school visits, home hospitality and heart-to-heart dialogue, while the flying pod visited schools and local authorities. Finally, each pod shared their learning in presentations videotaped in front of a live audience at the University of Exeter. Ideas for the future include a joint writing retreat, Quebec/UK student leadership conference and exchange, a two-week trading places project between pod schools involving a head/principal and a teacher, and twinning classrooms within the pods using technology for collaborative projects.

A question arises about the appropriate length of a network's life. While there is now, appropriately, significant attention being paid to sustainability of improvement, evidence on networks highlights that these are much more fluid organizational forms, fit for a certain purpose, and that people may come together for this and then move on. It is the commitment to networking for the purpose of learning, rather than a particular networking topic that requires sustaining. As one South Gloucestershire headteacher explained about the Melbourne network and other South Gloucestershire leadership learning networks in which he had been involved, they were 'continually evolving and developing as members of groups develop themselves and deepen their understanding. It's a learning curve for us'. Only time will tell whether the international PLCs are sustainable, but the Canadian experience shows promising beginnings.

Conclusion

At one level, the purpose of offering international leadership experiences is to build educational networks and partnerships between colleagues and schools in different countries, ensuring that school leaders are aware and taking account of global trends. At a deeper level, another purpose for these learning networks, rather than those focusing on connecting schools or school leaders within one country, is taking a group of leaders away from their familiar contexts and introducing a radically different cultural experience linked to a substantive focus on learning that can help them break boundaries in their own thinking as they work to enhance learning and teaching for everyone in their schools. This journey is also just beginning in South Gloucestershire. The process is generative and dynamic in that none of the participants know exactly where it will take them, but our experience thus far suggests that these international networks have helped school leaders promote their own PLCs through a process of continual learning in a no-risk environment, as well as connecting the leaders as a group and between the groups to deepen, extend and enrich the learning community throughout the local authority, thus helping to develop other leaders across schools and the authority. The power of what is happening came through at a 12-hour Leadership Academy day in South Gloucestershire in November 2005, where leaders from all of the international networks shared their experiences along with participants in all of the other Leadership Academy enquiry groups. Many teachers from study tour schools came to hear the messages their headteachers had heard during their visits. Members from all parts of an evolving international professional learning community came together in person, via teleconference (Montreal), through prepared DVD presentations (New Zealand principal), and from presentations of those who had been to Melbourne. As one headteacher said: 'The day was superb. It's the most amazing thing I've ever been to ... people will talk about it for a long time.'

References

Brandsford, J.D., Brown, A.L. and Cocking, R.R. (1999) *How People Learn: Brain, Mind, Experience, and School*. Washington, DC: National Academy Press.

Casson, P., Cooper, C., Davey, W., Gibson, R., Isaac, J., McArthur, C., Sibley, D., Spenceley, B. and Wilkinson, A. (2004) *Towards a Preferred Future for Learning and Education: An Accord Prepared by a South Gloucestershire Leadership Enquiry Group*. Chipping Sodbury: South Gloucestershire Council.

Fullan, M. (1993) *Change Forces: Probing the Depths of Educational Reform*. London: Falmer Press.

Hargreaves, A. and Fink, D. (2006) *Sustainable Leadership*. London: John Wiley & Sons; and San Francisco, CA: Jossey-Bass.

Organization for Economic Co-operation and Development (OECD) (2003) *Networks of Innovation: Towards New Models for Managing Schools and Systems*. Paris: OECD.

Robertson, J.M. (2005) *Coaching Leadership: Building Educational Leadership Capacity Through Coaching Partnerships*. Wellington: New Zealand Council for Educational Research.

Robertson, J.M. and Webber, C.F. (2002) Boundary-breaking leadership: a must for tomorrow's learning communities, in K. Leithwood and P. Hallinger (eds) *Second International Handbook of Educational Leadership and Administration*. Dordrecht: Kluwer.

Smithers, R. (2003) That dreadful business, *Guardian*, 23 September, http://education.guardian.co.uk/egweekly/story/0,,1047272,00.html, accessed 24 October 2006.

Stoll, L. and Bolam, R. (2005) Developing leadership for learning communities, in M. Coles and G. Southworth (eds) *Developing Leadership: Creating the Schools of Tomorrow*. Maidenhead: Open University Press.

Veugelers, W. and O'Hair, J. (2005) *Network Learning for Educational Change*. Maidenhead: Open University Press/McGraw-Hill Education.

Webber, C.F. and Robertson, J.M. (2004) Internationalization and educators' understanding of issues in educational leadership, *The Educational Forum*, 68(3): 264–75.

Part 2

Depth

If professional learning communities are to realize their potential, more finely nuanced understanding is needed of the development processes. The authors of the chapters in this part take different approaches to the subject of 'depth', either by adding more detail to an element of professional learning communities or going deeper into the change process. All of the chapters are underpinned by a sense of collective responsibility.

Judith Warren Little and Ilana Horn (Chapter 6) subject teachers' conversation to micro-analysis. Using one example from a group of American teachers they have often studied, they demonstrate how commonplace conversational practice, 'normalizing problems of classroom practice', can function either to open up or close off generative dialogue that promotes teacher learning.

In his chapter, Rich Halverson (Chapter 7) takes a penetrative look at the intentional ways leaders build tools to shape instructional and other professional practices. Using three case studies in the USA, he highlights how artefacts create the sense of agency leaders and teachers use to design structures to help shape the practices of others, and create the conditions under which leadership can be distributed more widely in professional learning communities.

Cultural change is the focus of Sharon Kruse and Karen Seashore Louis's chapter (Chapter 8). Reflecting on a case study of an American school district, they explore the social dynamics within which learning occurs in professional learning communities, highlighting the development of collective understanding which leads to collective responsibility. This chapter also highlights that the development process takes time and also, frequently, external impetus.

A recent development has been the emergence of research-based professional learning community processes and tools. In Chapter 9, Kristine Kiefer Hipp and Jane Bumpers Huffman explain how they have developed and used a number of assessment instruments in the USA to create supportive conditions for developing professional learning communities by promoting dialogue. They conclude that such tools can facilitate deeper ongoing communication about PLC assessment and progress.

Based on their research and development in the IDEAS project in Australia, Dorothy Andrews and Marian Lewis (Chapter 10) demonstrate how it is not only possible to create professional learning community in a system that already has favourable conditions, but also working on professional learning community driven by values can both help schools in an early stage of school development as well as move more confident schools to a new level of excitement.

six

'Normalizing' problems of practice: converting routine conversation into a resource for learning in professional communities

Judith W. Little and Ilana S. Horn

> I started the geoboards today and it – it felt like mayhem. Like, it felt like no one kind of understood. I just had a vision of what it – I *thought* it should look like and it didn't look anything like that. (Alice March, 9th grade algebra teacher)

Alice's account of mayhem opens the weekly meeting of the Algebra Group, nine teachers in an urban, working-class school who have succeeded, through their collective activity, in fostering a higher-than-predicted level of student participation and achievement in mathematics. Alice's words may strike many as typical of those spoken by beginning teachers, or perhaps by more experienced teachers attempting something new. What is *not* typical is the way the conversation subsequently unfolds as she and her colleagues work to understand what happened in Alice's classroom that day and what it might mean for their teaching. That exchange, one of many recorded in this group, provides the starting point for an analysis of generative conversation among teaching colleagues.

Our analysis is motivated by a practical dilemma: deep, sustained conversations among teachers about matters of teaching and learning remain uncommon, even among groups that might reasonably be seen as professional communities committed to instructional improvement (McLaughlin and Talbert 2001). Unpacking such conversations in detail may contribute to making them a more widespread feature of teachers' professional experience. Yet only in a few cases, and relatively recently, have researchers begun to look at the actual dialogue among teachers to locate evidence that will help us understand why some kinds of conversation prove powerful in pushing the boundaries of teaching and teacher learning while others prove less generative. Most of this development results from research in the context of organized professional development activity (Grossman *et al.* 2001; Kazemi and Franke 2004; Sherin and Han 2004), with a smaller body of work emerging from research on more informal workplace interactions (Little 2002; 2003; Horn 2005; Khorsheed 2005).

This chapter devotes close attention to the details of dialogue as teachers talk with one another about teaching and learning. We have examined recorded talk among teachers in small working groups within two schools to suggest how and under what conditions such dialogue might generate professional learning, bolster professional community, and strengthen classroom practice. Each of these groups – some organized within subject departments, others at the grade (year) or school level – embraces a collective identity (like the 'Algebra Group' in which Alice participates) and each sees itself as engaged in improvement-oriented professional work. Although these interactions arise in ordinary workplace contexts, our broader aim is to contribute to a framework of more general utility in characterizing professional learning opportunity as an avenue for both individual learning and collective capacity. That is, we see this analysis as part of a larger program of research that permits us to understand the possibilities for school reform that reside in professional communities and in other contexts with the potential to stimulate and support professional learning.

Locating problems of practice in the flow of teacher talk

Teacher talk may be productive in many respects. However, we argue that for talk to be generative of professional learning and robust professional community, teachers must develop both the inclination and the resources for learning in and from teaching practice (Ball and Cohen 1999). For that reason, we focus specifically on conversational moments that entail accounts of classroom experience and that signal problems of teaching practice, treating the frequency and nature of such moments as indicators of the generative power of a teacher community. What part do such problems of teaching and learning play in teachers' recorded talk? How often do they arise, with regard to what aspects of teaching, and with what degree of specificity and transparency? How do they get taken up, or not?

We locate relevant conversational moments by systematically mapping episodes of talk marked by shifts in topic and/or participation structures. We identify 'problems of practice' through linguistic and paralinguistic cues that signal classroom interactions experienced as troublesome, challenging, confusing, unexpectedly interesting, or otherwise worthy of comment. Such cues may include explicit references to trouble ('mayhem'), expressions of emotional distress ('frustration'), and direct appeals for feedback or assistance ('what am I doing wrong?'), many of them accompanied by changes in intonation and emphasis.

To establish that a conversation is conducive to professional learning, we seek evidence that the dialogue does more than simply report on or point to problems of practice, but supplies specific means for identifying, elaborating and reconceptualizing the problems that teachers encounter and for exposing or generating principles of practice. By doing so, we find that the groups differ with regard to both the incidence of problems of practice – how densely they populate the conversation in any given group – and the way in which they are taken up or not.

In this chapter, we highlight one extended episode of talk – the 'Alice's Mayhem' episode – to show how specific discourse practices characterize a teacher group in which professional learning opportunities are plentiful. In 17 meetings of the Algebra Group recorded over a four-month span, we found a high proportion of sustained talk about problems of practice and thus see this group as a useful case in working toward a conceptual model of generative dialogue. By comparison, in meetings among other collaborative groups spanning the same period, we located substantially fewer such episodes and fewer instances in which expressed problems of practice were taken up at any length.

In the space available, we cannot detail all the nuanced ways in which learning opportunities were created and professional relationships formed through conversation in the selected episodes and in the larger corpus of data. Nor can we lay out in full detail the ways in which talk among Alice and her colleagues proved distinctive and unusually powerful in the professional learning opportunity it presented. Therefore, in the remainder of this discussion we highlight the way in which these teachers build on one widespread conversational practice in ways that systematically differentiate this group from the other collaborative groups we studied. Specifically, we posit that the way in which teachers enact and build on routine ways of 'normalizing problems of practice' opens up opportunities for learning in, from, and for practice.

Normalizing problems of practice

In all of the groups, we repeatedly see exchanges in which teachers' expressed problems are met with *normalizing* responses – that is, moves that define a problem as normal, an expected part of classroom work and teacher experience. Normalizing moves supply reassurance ('you'll be fine, don't worry') and establish solidarity ('it happens to all of us'). Yet we also see systematic, patterned differences in the way such practices function in interaction across groups. Specifically, we see differences in whether the teachers' moves to normalize a problem result in turning a conversation *away from the teaching or toward the teaching as an object of collective attention.* In the former case, teachers convey reassurance, sometimes adding specific bits of advice or familiar aphorisms, before turning away from the problem and moving on to other instrumental tasks. In the latter case, teachers treat the shared and expected (normal) character of a problem as the starting point for detailed discussion of specific classroom instances and as a means to help anchor emergent advice to more general problems and principles of teaching.

We acknowledge that teachers have much to accomplish in their work together, and the time devoted to unpacking problems of practice varies in relationship to the priorities at hand. Yet we also argue that the foundation for individual professional learning and collective capacity for improvement is more surely supplied where problems of practice stimulate in-depth discussions of the sort outlined in the second scenario. To illuminate the nature of such discussions, we examine the normalizing practices made visible in the 'Alice's Mayhem' episode and the way they function to open up opportunities for learning.

Normalizing the problem of 'mayhem' and opening opportunities for learning

The episode we call 'Alice's Mayhem' takes place on a Tuesday afternoon early in the school year, at the beginning of the weekly meeting of the Algebra Group. Alice, a new teacher, has arrived to the meeting drying her tears, accompanied by Jill, the co-chair (head) of the department. The other teachers delay the start of the meeting to await their arrival and encourage Alice to share her account of what had happened ('put it out there'). Alice and her colleagues then devote about 15 minutes to elaborating and probing the rather daunting image of mayhem, successively posing and evaluating three possible explanations for the troubles that developed in Alice's classroom. Over the course of the conversation, 'mayhem' is made accessible to reflection and remedy. The talk exposes interpretive resources by which these teachers routinely make sense of their experience, along with strategies for anticipating and curtailing the inevitable instances of mayhem when they occur.

In the following excerpt, Alice's colleagues respond to her account of mayhem first by assuring her that the disconnect between vision and reality is an enduring dilemma in teaching for both novice and experienced teachers.[1]

1	Alice:	Uh, well my frustration, I think, was just, I started the
2		geoboards today and it, it *felt* like mayhem. Like, it felt
3		like no one kind of understood – I just had a *vision* of
4		what it – I thought it should look like and it didn't look
5		anything like that and then ... I was trying to keep
6		students together in their groups, but they, they weren't
7		staying together. And then ... What was happening? So
8		then I wanted to communicate the whole putting the
9		rectangle around the triangle but it's like, if I do it in
10		front of class, no one's paying attention but if I go
11		around to groups, I felt like I wasn't communicating it to
12		all the students. So I think that – and after processing it
13		with Jill, I think they were getting stuff done. It's just
14		that I have a vision of what group work should look like,
15		and it's not looking anything like that. And I just feel
16		like they're getting more and more unfocused in class.
17	Guillermo:	That would be my fourth block [class].
18		*[laughter]*
19	Female:	And mine!
20	Jill:	But a reality right?
21	Guillermo:	Yeah.
22	Jill:	Reality check, is that we all know what it *can* look like,
23		we all know what we're *striving* for. But my God – we're
24		just like this *all* the time. After 10 years, after 2 years,
25		after 5 years, everyday is like that because we don't
26		know what's walking into our classroom. On a daily
27		basis.
28	Howard:	I'll tell you Alice, I mean I've been here a long time.
29		<unclear> This was the first time I ever used geoboards
30		with an Algebra *One* class because I was so afraid of
31		how easily they would just go off and play. And the only
32		reason that I attempted it *this* time was this was our time
33		to do it. And as much as it wasn't meeting like a *vis*ion I
34		was putting out that might have just been low
35		expectations.
36	Alice:	Yes.
37	Howard:	I mean, you put something like that in their hands for the
38		first time and there's a certain level of, play with it,
39		<unclear> but whether they're focusing on <unclear>.

As in other groups we observed, the algebra teachers quickly normalize Alice's story through reassurances about her problem: her class is likened to other unruly classes (ll. 17 and 19); the experience is portrayed as endemic to the work of teaching, no matter what the teacher's level of experience (ll. 20–27); and a possible consequence of using a potentially distracting manipulative (ll. 28–39), something that can even happen to teachers who have been here 'a long time.'

One might imagine the conversation stopping here, with someone saying 'So, really, don't let it upset you,' or 'It's just a matter of experience – it will get better.' Indeed, this is one of two main patterns we observe in other groups, the second being to conclude that the problem is outside the control of the teacher.[2] However, normalizing practices in the Algebra Group do not merely preface a pat explanation ('it's just classroom culture') or quick aphorism ('don't smile until Christmas'). Rather, the normalizing moves are joined to questions that provide a starting place for a deeper discussion by explicitly eliciting more detail and inviting analysis. Such questions activate a crucial transition to focused reflection on a problem of practice. In this instance, after Guillermo, Jill and Howard have rushed to assure Alice that her problem is normal ('reality check!'), Guillermo asks: 'Alice, can you identify the source of the squirreliness? Like <unclear> they, they wanted to play with the geoboards but didn't have time to do it?' (ll. 40–41).

The discussion that ensues is extensive and complicated, lasting 11 more minutes and including statements by eight of the ten teachers present. Two experienced teachers, orienting to the problem of 'starting geoboards,' speculate that the squirreliness arises from a familiar kind of teaching challenge: introducing 9th graders to math manipulatives (geoboards), which naturally lend themselves to playing. But as Alice considers Guillermo's question, she recalls that the trouble did not originate with the geoboard exercise. Over the next three minutes, she re-frames the problem twice. First, she posits that students' understanding of area (or more precisely, lack of it) was at the root of the mayhem problem.

> Yeah. I'm not sure, I think it even – it felt like it kind of even started with the warm-up like they weren't – I don't know. Maybe it was a sense of – it's like, they don't really have a concept of area *at all*. So maybe it was a sense, maybe they're afraid of the – of not being able to do these ideas. No it was like they were just counting the squares the whole time. I kept saying, 'Okay, well is there a rectangle there?' and it was like – that was going *beyond* for them. Um. So maybe it's just that the concepts are challenging for them. I don't know. (ll. 45–53)

This reformulation has a provisional sense to it. There are a couple of pauses, several unfinished sentences, and expressions of uncertainty ('I don't know'), and explicit revisions ('No it was ...'), all of which indicate that this is an emerging version of what happened in the classroom that has not yet been closely considered. Alice's new account considers the students' mathematical understanding: they were just counting the squares to figure out area, while she wanted them to find rectangles that would allow them to calculate area more efficiently.

Alice then proposes a second revision by introducing an element that had been missing in the original formulation – her own anger with the students:

> Yeah. I guess there was that sense that by the end? I was like – it was like the first time that I just felt *angry* with them like/because it felt so – like I wasn't in control? that I started to get angry. And part of that is my control issues. And so, I didn't even know – like by the end I was like, 'I want you guys to stay after.' And I didn't know if I felt *good* about having them stay after or if that was a good way to handle it, but it was like – I just wanted them to know I mean *business* and we needed to get *work* done and – you know? (*2 second pause*) So. (ll. 75–83)

Again, a colleague's question ('Were they receptive to that?') invites further elaboration. Accompanied by much laughter, Alice re-plays the classroom scene and the students' response:

Alice:	Yeah, I mean, they were like (*exhales indignantly*), 'This is not fair!'
Jill:	*laughs*
Alice:	I'm like (*2 second pause*)
Jill, Guillermo:	*laughing*
Alice:	I mean like.
Guillermo:	Perfect.
Alice:	So they stayed after 2 minutes, you know. And I mean that was. It was fine.
Jill:	*Snorting, like holding back a laugh.*
Guillermo:	Yeah, but they're like *dying* for those two minutes, right? Like two minutes=
Alice:	Yeah I mean, it's like, 'Two minutes? Come on!'
Charlie, others:	*laughing*
Alice:	So. (85–99)

Alice's admission of anger and her humorous replay of the students' response prompt another set of normalizing moves, these focused on the pervasively emotional nature of teaching experience. Guillermo links her experience to his own experience of becoming angry in his fourth period class: 'You really are describing my fourth block. Minus the staying after for 2 minutes. (*Alice, others laugh.*) Because at some point I'm angry enough that I don't want to SEE them for 2 more minutes! (*others laughing*) (ll. 100–104). He points in passing to a lesson from experience ('I also don't want to try to enforce two minutes of silence or whatever') and goes on to talk through what he realized through his struggles with his own class:

So I got angry too at what they wouldn't do. I think a large part of that is inevitable first-time-through things. For me, it's first-time-through like fall Math 2, given what they had last semester for Math 1 and some of those frustrations and um – I just don't know what's reasonable for them in terms of expectations. (ll. 140–146)

Here, he invokes a teaching principle that has been suggested by earlier comments: the first time through something (be it a curriculum, an activity, or, in his case, a class with a particular history), it is difficult to know what is reasonable to expect of and from students – and anger interferes with one's ability to gauge realistic expectations.

Of course, broad statements of principle do not provide much leverage for changing practice; there is no obvious action to be taken by the teacher. However, Guillermo's next move is to apply his principle back to Alice's experience of mayhem and, in doing so, provide a substantively different interpretation. In her emergent account of the mayhem, Alice bemoaned that students were counting squares to calculate area. She has cast this as evidence that the students did not 'have a concept' of what was going on mathematically. Having had experience with the curriculum these students would have encountered in the eighth grade, he explicates for her what might be reasonable to expect. He says: 'So I would have thought that given the unit that they do in 8th grade, that a sense of area would not be an issue. But some of them think that area's length times width. So in some sense, their counting squares is the *right* thing' (ll. 146–152). Applying his own principle about what is reasonable to expect, Guillermo counters Alice's earlier explanation: their counting squares is the right thing because it is more on target with the idea of area than the formulaic length times width version that many students have. It is not clear from this interaction whether this bit of pedagogical content knowledge was incorporated into Alice's understanding of the mayhem, but it certainly was made available to her and others at the table.

Others' contributions also display this pattern of linking Alice's problem of mayhem to their own experience, and building on the link to articulate principles of teaching and the gradual, uneven process of learning to teach. For example, Jill recounts the 'chaos' that ensued the first two times she used a particular activity to introduce area: 'And I remember thinking, "*What* did I *not* get the first time around?" You know?' Carrie picks up the example, having taught the same activity, and uses it to state a more general principle for interpreting and responding to 'mayhem' or 'chaos':

Carrie: When, when they get upset and they seem to be off task and
          acting goofy, it usually is motivated by 'I'm so confused and
          the *last* thing I want to do is *admit* I'm confused
Alice: Mhm.

Carrie:	So I'm instead I'm going to find a way to distract myself or distract others so that I don't have to *face* the *fact* that
Alice:	Mhm.
Carrie:	I don't know how to do something.' Um. So I always try to sympathize. Like, I'll feel/feel myself being *mad*, like 'You guys aren't working! What are you doing?' And then I like try to take a step back and say, 'Okay. *What* are they afraid of?
Alice:	Mhm.
Carrie:	How can I make them feel comfortable with that fear?
Alice:	Mhm.
Carrie:	What can I say to them or what can I do for them to make them feel (.) like, this is a safe place.' And that usually takes me somewhere where – it never is *fully* successful, but I see some successes and then that translates into other days that become more successful. (ll. 196–214)

Carrie's contribution illustrates characteristic features of the 'principled' talk in this group: principles for teaching are cast not as aphorisms or behavioral tips, but as ways of interpreting students' responses. This principled or generalized talk gains specification through what Horn (2005) has termed 'rehearsals' and 'replays,' or narrations that enact the principle in anticipated or past practice. In this instance, Carrie narrates her own thinking as she helps assuage her students' fears about failing in a mathematics task, which she sees as underlying their rowdy behavior. Over the 15 minutes of talk, the teachers build at least three such principles for interpreting the case of mayhem by attending closely to what students do and say:

Interpretive principle 1 (Guillermo, Jill, Charlie): When teaching any activity, content or group the first time, you can't anticipate what students will do, but whatever you learn from paying attention to students will help you in the future.
Interpretive principle 2 (Howard and Judy): When kids act out in this context, it may be because you've underestimated the novelty of the task or materials – e.g., kids want to play with manipulatives at first.
Interpretive principle 3 (Carrie): When kids act out in this context, it may be because they're confused or fearful about the content you're teaching and trying to hide their confusion or fear.

The teachers explicitly relieve one another from *blame* but not from *responsibility* for problems of practice, conveying the expectation that they will all consistently learn in and from their teaching practice. Thus, Jill ends her account of 'chaos' by saying: 'And so you, you *can't* blame yourself for something that there's *no* way you could know. And you'll take that knowledge and you'll do something with it the *next* time around.'

Normalizing, specifying, and generalizing in talk about problems of practice

As the conversation develops, certain dynamics emerge that we posit are, in combination, importantly constitutive of professional learning opportunity within robust professional community. First and most central, teachers in the Algebra Group normalize problems in ways that legitimate such problems as deserving of sustained attention. By routinely asking questions and eliciting additional information, they communicate the inherent complexity and ambiguity of teaching while supplying themselves with the specifics needed to introduce and evaluate multiple explanations for the problems that surface. That is, normalizing practices function here not as a means for providing reassurance and moving on to other tasks, but as a means for digging into problems of practice.

Second, the teachers' conversation moves constantly between specific accounts of classroom practice and general lessons from experience. If only tales of woe had been shared with Alice, the conversation might have proved rich in detail, comforting or even cathartic, but not necessarily generative for the teachers' learning. If only general principles of teaching had been shared, unattached to specific examples, the work of applying these principles to actual practice would have remained opaque, left to the individual teacher to imagine. The work of recontextualizing such generic teaching principles or unspecified images of classroom practice is a central challenge of teacher learning. The linking work that happens in this conversation helps the group collectively construct a class of instances and narrated responses that are clustered around defining and explaining a common teaching problem and a set of principles for responding to it.

Generative dialogue as routine practice

Analysis of the full array of Algebra Group meetings convinces us that the 'Alice's Mayhem' episode is typical in two respects. First, it typifies the way that the group spends its time together, structuring talk and activity in ways that make classroom practice visible and available for consideration. There was little or no talk of mundane administrative business in any meeting we observed. A weekly 'check-in' routine balances the need for coordination (what mathematics topics and tasks each teacher is working on this week) with the opportunity to take up problems or pursue new ideas. At the end of the 'Alice's Mayhem' episode, Jill asks, 'Does anyone else want to check in?' thus confirming the status of the 'Alice's Mayhem' exchange as normatively within the expected bounds of the weekly check-in routine.

Across the meetings we recorded, the teachers also work on the mathematics that they teach, doing math problems together to unpack the nature of the cognitive demands on students or predict what will be difficult to learn. They work on designing or revising mathematics tasks so that they build students' conceptual understanding and confidence, or talk about using groups effectively so that students' contribute to each other's success. And throughout, the group takes a stance of learning in and from the classroom practice of its members. References to 'struggles' appear repeatedly in the group's meetings, individual interviews, and email messages. Struggle, as employed in this group, signals intellectual and emotional engagement in learning, whether by students or teachers.

Second, our highlighted episode typifies the group's conversational practices as they take up expressed problems of classroom practice. Although problems of practice surface in every collaborative group we studied, and although teachers in every group responded by 'normalizing' those problems in some fashion, this group consistently employed normalizing moves in ways that highlighted the complex, ambiguous nature of teaching and opened up problems for analysis and reflection. Problems expressed by experienced teachers elicited fewer overt reassurances than novice teacher Alice received, but they otherwise prompted the same kinds of questions and reflection evident in the 'Alice's Mayhem' episode. Through the interplay of normalizing, specifying, and generalizing, often seamlessly interwoven in specific utterances, teachers make their pedagogical reasoning transparent. By embracing problems of practice within the scope of the group's shared purposes and tasks, and by cultivating conversational practices that open up and sustain attention to problems of practice when they surface, the Algebra Group goes some considerable distance toward creating opportunity for professional learning and the collective pursuit of ambitious teaching and learning.

One might reasonably ask what enables the Algebra Group to locate professional learning at the center of workplace professional community in a way that other committed, energetic groups do not. What supports the generative dialogue so consistently and routinely in evidence? In this analysis, we have focused on specific conversational practices, but it is *through* those practices that the members of the group marshal other intellectual, social and material resources.

Central to these resources are those focused on knowledge of mathematics and on shared commitments to expanding students' access to mathematics. The Algebra Group teachers have taken steps to deepen their expertise in mathematics teaching through collective participation in high-quality professional development and through strong network ties with individuals and groups invested in mathematics teaching reform. References to ideas and practices derived from those individuals and groups occur frequently in meetings and interviews, and outside colleagues periodically attend the group's weekly meetings or in its more intensive 'Algebra Week' event in the summer. By contrast, the other collaborative groups we studied were more dependent on their own internal resources and more tenuously connected to external sources of expertise or encouragement, especially in the subject domains in which they taught (see also Little 2003).

In addition, the Algebra Group teachers consistently make use of an extensive, shared set of curricular resources (the 'Algebra Binder', together with a bookshelf of related texts, notebooks and folders) that they have located, selected, revised, or designed in their efforts to make mathematics more accessible to all their students. As Ball and Cohen (1996: 8) anticipated, these materials constitute important 'terrain for teachers' learning.' By contrast, other collaborative groups had fewer shared curricular resources on which they could draw, either because they were in an early stage of collaborative curriculum development, or because they did not conceive of curriculum as a public resource for their own learning (or both).

Finally, demonstrated patterns of initiative and leadership sustain the group's attention to problems of practice. Building on the record of a former chair who was described as 'remarkable at building community,' the current co-chairs see themselves as responsible for maintaining the ethos of professional learning in the Algebra Group. They take a visible role in posing questions, eliciting accounts of classroom practice, preserving a focus on teaching and learning – and encouraging initiative of these sorts by others. Such leadership practice proved less visible, ambitious, or consistent in other groups we studied.

Conclusion

Each of the groups we investigated is populated by energetic, competent, thoughtful teachers who take responsibility for students' success; in this respect, they meet an accepted threshold of professional learning community. Yet the groups demonstrated quite different orientations toward problems of practice and commanded quite different resources for engaging such problems when they arose. In part, they differ in the room they make for problems of practice in the first place, which is itself a function of the purposes and tasks that bring them together. But given the disclosure of problems of practice, they also differ in the familiar practice of rendering problems as normal and expected aspects of teaching – and thus in the generative potential of their talk together.

We contend that talk within teacher communities is likely to be generative of professional learning and instructional improvement to the extent that it invites disclosure of and reflection on problems of practice. In the analysis developed here, we identify one commonplace conversational practice – normalizing problems of classroom practice – that routinely functions either to open up or close off generative dialogue. When linked closely to questions that invite disclosure and reflection, the practice of 'normalizing problems of practice' functions as a bridge to a more probing investigation of teaching and learning. We portray variation in this practice as one crucial indicator of the generative potential of teacher talk, but certainly not the only one. By paying close attention to this and other details of dialogue, we propose to make headway on a conceptual model of professional learning opportunity, one that specifies the nature of robust, public pedagogical reasoning, together with the cognitive, social, material, organizational and normative resources that enable it.

Notes

1   For purposes of this narrative, we have eliminated or modified most of the detailed transcription conventions that aid a more fine-grained analysis of the data.
2   For one example in which both of these patterns are evident, see Little (2003: 933–5).

References

Ball, D.L. and Cohen, D.K. (1996) Reform by the book: What is – or might be – the role of curriculum materials in teacher learning and instructional reform? *Educational Researcher*, 25(9): 6–8, 14.

Ball, D.L. and Cohen, D.K. (1999) Developing practice, developing practitioners: toward a practice-based theory of professional education, in L. Darling-Hammond and G. Sykes (eds) *Teaching as the Learning Profession: Handbook of Policy and Practice*. San Francisco, CA: Jossey-Bass.

Grossman, P., Wineburg, S. and Woolworth, S. (2001) Toward a theory of teacher community, *Teachers College Record*, 103(6): 942–1012.

Horn, I.S. (2005) Learning on the job: a situated account of teacher learning in high school mathematics departments, *Cognition & Instruction*, 23(2): 207–36.

Kazemi, E. and Franke, M.L. (2004) Teacher learning in mathematics: using student work to promote collective inquiry, *Journal of Mathematics Teacher Education*, 7: 203–35.

Khorsheed, K.R. (2005) Knowledge resources at work for improving instruction. Unpublished PhD dissertation, University of Michigan.

Little, J.W. (2002) Locating learning in teachers' communities of practice: opening up problems of analysis in records of everyday work, *Teaching and Teacher Education*, 18(8): 917–46.

Little, J.W. (2003) Inside teacher community: representations of classroom practice, *Teachers College Record*, 105(6): 913–45.

McLaughlin, M.W. and Talbert, J.E. (2001) *Professional Communities and the Work of High School Teaching*. Chicago, IL: University of Chicago Press.

Sherin, M.G. and Han, S.Y. (2004) Teacher learning in the context of a video club, *Teaching and Teacher Education*, 20: 163–83.

seven

How leaders use artifacts to structure professional community in schools

Richard Halverson[1]

Why does professional community play an important role in school reform? The key to understanding how schools engage in and, more importantly, resist change is found in the organizational structure of schooling. During the 1970s and 1980s, organizational theorists applied the concept of *loose coupling* to understand schools' structures. Weick (1976; 1996) and Meyer and Rowan (1983) traced how schools' structures evolved to allow considerable autonomy for teachers and specialists. The result was that teachers were assigned responsibility for practices within the classroom and administrators (school leaders) worked on school maintenance, such as controlling the entrance and exit conditions for students and staff and buffering teachers from external interference (and inspection). School cultures evolved to cement the loose-coupling between administrative and instructional practice into place, both formally (through collective bargaining agreements that preserved teacher autonomy), and informally (through resistance to intrusions by leaders into classroom instructional practice).

In the 1990s, professional community emerged as a central topic for reforming the cultures of loosely coupled systems. Professional communities reflect a school's ability to develop and act upon a shared understanding of practice. Strong professional communities in schools that promote collective responsibility for student learning and norms of collegiality among teachers are associated with higher levels of student achievement (Little 1982; Newmann and Wehlage 1995; Lee and Smith 1996; Louis *et al.* 1996). Through developing a shared understanding of the benefits and constraints of existing instructional practices, a school's professional community provides the capacity for collective action. Most important, however, professional communities reflect the levels of trust around instructional practices among the adults in schools (Bryk and Schneider 2002; Halverson 2003). Trust is a critical resource for change in loosely coupled systems. Leaders and teachers must establish considerable levels of trust to set aside traditional protective behaviors in order to work together to build toward alternatives. Establishing professional community helps build the kinds of relational trust in schools that helps teachers set aside structures that protect their autonomy and relax the cultural barriers for collaborative action.

Halverson (2003) suggests that leaders create professional community by employing structures to facilitate certain kinds of social interaction in schools. Coleman (1988) describes the stages of trust development: first, actors need to *interact* around common interests, second, these interactions lead to the development of *obligations* between actors; and third, actors have the opportunity to *fulfill* their obligations. Professional community is then a form of organizational trust that results from structuring interaction through which professionals incur and satisfy obligations to improve student learning. The role of school leaders in stimulating professional community is to create structures for building and fulfilling obligations around issues vital to instructional improvement. In this chapter I argue that leaders create the conditions for strong professional communities by sequencing structures to: initiate interaction; facilitate the development of obligations; and provide systemic feedback on the degree to which mutual obligations have been met. If professional community is the path for tightening the coupling between leadership and instruction in schools, then this research aims to provide leaders and teachers with a vocabulary for understanding the tools necessary for making the transition from our current schools to the next generation of schooling.

Exploring how artifacts influence practice

A key function of school leadership is to influence the local practices of teaching and learning (Spillane *et al.* 2004). In part, leaders seek to influence the practice of others through the *artifacts*, or programs, policies and procedures they develop and deploy (Halverson 2002). The concept of an artifact as an intervention designed to shape the actions of others is rooted in human-computer interaction and activity theory research (cf. Norman 1991; Engeström 1993). In schools, artifacts include any entities designed to influence others' practice. Leaders build and adapt artifacts such as role positions, daily schedules, faculty meetings, and meeting agendas to shape instructional practices. The analysis of artifact features provides an occasion to examine how designers thought about the practices they intended to effect (Halverson 2003; 2004).

The argument developed here examines artifacts to trace how leaders think about how they spark and direct relational trust-building efforts in schools. The argument relies on several recent ethnographic research studies including: a three-year study of how leaders in an urban preK-8 school created the conditions to improve student learning; a two-year study of how an urban school leader created conditions to improve learning for students who traditionally struggled; and a year-long investigation of how school principals developed and adapted teacher evaluation tools to improve teaching and shape professional norms. Each study included extensive interviews, observation and document collection. All data were coded to identify the artifacts involved in school leaders' work, the degree to which leaders adapted existing artifacts to new and emergent purposes, and the degree to which artifacts interacted with each other and with social norms to create emergent forms of interaction.

The studies suggest that leaders sequence different kinds of artifacts to create and maintain professional community. To identify the different kinds of artifacts involved, I first provide a brief description of leadership practices at work in the three school cases. Then I offer a typology of different kinds of artifacts to describe three stages of tools leaders use to shape social interaction.

Case 1: Adams School – instructional leadership in an urban school

When Principal Therese Williams became principal in the late 1980s, Adams School (pseudonym) had one of the worst student achievement records in Chicago. Williams faced considerable challenges reshaping instructional practices at Adams over her 12 years as the school's principal. Adams was a K-8 school with over 1200 students (98 per cent free and reduced lunch; 99 per cent African-American) spread across two buildings. In the beginning, staff in the two buildings barely tolerated each other, and Williams saw her initial task as building a shared sense of purpose. She began by enforcing common student behavioral standards within the buildings and creating social opportunities for staff to interact across buildings.

Williams and her staff recognized that collegiality needed to pay off in terms of improved student learning. Their analysis of test scores from the early 1990s led to a general agreement that early literacy provided the critical instructional gateway that rippled across subsequent grade levels. Instead of mandating a curriculum that teachers could subvert or ignore, Williams and her literacy coordinator sought to help staff recognize the nature of the problem in literacy instruction and to take ownership of the design for a solution.

Their first initiative, Breakfast Club, was designed as a monthly opportunity structured to allow teachers time to discuss recent research in early childhood literacy. Williams provided a hot breakfast for teachers, staying in the background as teachers struggled to understand research articles in terms of their own practice. The Breakfast Club was a poorly attended voluntary program in its first year, but attendance increased regularly after word got out that discussions included valuable organizational information. Breakfast Club blossomed into a key organizational resource. As one Adams teacher remarked: 'We found out that we enjoyed talking with one another, that it was a benefit. Because we don't have a chance to talk with one another – if you leave your class and start talking to one another, teachers don't have that luxury. So this gave them a chance to talk with one another.' In the second and third year, Breakfast Club discussions began to turn more toward teachers volunteering to try the research-based practices in their classrooms and report back to the group, providing a valuable form of real-world feedback on the research. The literacy coordinator and teachers ended up designing a balanced literacy approach for the school.

The most important outgrowth of Breakfast Club, however, was realization that the school needed structures to provide internal feedback for their program design. The standardized test scores provided neither sufficient nor timely information for program refinement. As the Adams Literacy Coordinator noted:

> We realized that the tests themselves didn't give us much information about what we could do to improve our scores – mainly because we received the results well after we could do anything about it. We thought about a more frequent assessment program ... that would help us tell where the children were.

Several teachers worked with the Literacy Coordinator to develop a series of Five-Week Assessments to provide performance benchmarks for teachers. Initially, teachers ignored the results of the Five-Week Assessments because the first benchmark tests did not obviously relate to their curriculum or the standardized test. Teachers then reverse engineered the standardized test to construct examinations that provided increasingly accurate predictions about how students would fare on the language arts aspects of the examination. After three years of development, the Five-Week Assessments were recognized by Adams teachers as important sources of feedback for instruction.

Principal Williams fought against developing too many programs or policies that would spread valuable resources across too many instructional goals. She was committed to letting the school's chosen artifacts mature. Her main tool against program bloat was her use of the district-mandated School Improvement Plan (SIP). The district required an SIP that linked discretionary budgetary resources to explicit instructional goals. Williams used the planning process as a framing tool for reform within the school. Teachers were required to argue for the need for new initiatives or continuing support for existing activities, and these public discussions served to inform the school community about the instructional priorities. Williams designed the SIP to link artifacts to outcomes so that teachers, parents, the district and the local school board understood the school's rationale for instructional investments. The professional community developed at Adams supported efforts to build new artifacts at the point where the previous structures left off, and ended up improving language arts learning for students across the school (Halverson 2003).

Case 2: Franklin School – leadership for social justice

Many obstacles for improving learning for all students are tacitly embedded in existing service delivery systems. Principal Deb Hoffman recognized that traditional service delivery models often served to perpetuate the very obstacles to learning they were originally designed to overcome. Her development of an Integrated Service Delivery model (Frattura and Capper in press) in Franklin Elementary School demonstrated how she used a variety of artifacts to challenge and reshape existing practices at multiple levels in her school. Integrated service delivery (ISD) presented an organizational approach to reshaping traditional 'pull-out' strategies for special education, English as a second language, and speech and language pathology students. The central strategy of ISD was to reduce class size by pairing special education and classroom teachers to provide mainstreamed services. Principal Hoffman commented: 'If somebody said "cite the three things that changed Franklin school," I would say reallocating resources to reduce class size, professional development and building the capacity of the staff.' In addition, Principal Hoffman acquired additional resources, redesigned hiring and student assignment, and managed the interface with an initially skeptical community.

Franklin was a K-2 school located in a small city with about 360 students (60 per cent white; 25 per cent free and reduced lunch) and 60 staff members. It also had a significant immigrant population requiring bilingual support. Shortly after Principal Hoffman arrived as a first year administrator in 1997, she realized that the very students with most trouble reading and writing were also being pulled out of the classroom for support services. These students, Hoffman reasoned, needed the regular classroom context experience more than children who remained in the classroom. Why not, then, reverse service delivery to bring specialist to students rather than students to the specialists?

Sparked by a district strategic planning report, Principal Hoffman gathered a team of interested teachers in early 1998 to craft a successful Comprehensive School Reform (CSR) grant to restructure service delivery. Hoffman used the master schedule to reassign teachers, specialists and students to smaller class sizes, worked with her staff to build a professional development program focused on differentiated instruction, and focused new hiring practices on acquiring a bilingual resource specialist and dual-certified teachers to fill the expanded classroom sections. Many teachers, parents and specialists struggled initially. One teacher wrote: 'instead of a kinder, gentler and more open school, the situation here is more volatile than ever. Do you think this atmosphere is best for kids?' After initial resistance, however, most Franklin parents and teachers began to realize the value of ISD, and student achievement scores for all students improved.

Integrated service delivery represents a comprehensive school reform plan as a series of artifacts that reshaped how staff can engage children in reformed teaching and learning practices. Principal Hoffman's work illustrated how artifacts already in use could be repurposed to structure changes in the school's professional community. She realized that the changes in practice would go as far as the teachers allowed, and followed a strategy to help teachers learn new practices, hired new teachers who could work together in classroom teams, and used the student assignment process to create optimal matches of teachers, specialists and students (Halverson 2004).

Case 3: Structuring formative feedback to improve reading

Rural and small-town school districts across the USA have been faced with a recent history of downsizing, diminishing resources and lower enrollments. Pearson Elementary School (pseudonym), in a rural Midwestern district, was opened as a K-6 school in a building formerly occupied by a junior high school. Principal Stein led the Pearson teachers and staff to assemble a powerful configuration of artifacts for generating and using achievement data to improve reading scores across her schools:

> The thing I love about data is that it helps me be more of an instructional leader. If I do focus on it, it helps me be very intentional about what I expect in an observation, what my expectations are for my school. I can get data on just about anything we want to talk about, but then it becomes weeding through it, and what's the important data. What is it – some data we'll get and it doesn't give us a picture of anything and we kind of start to create a picture.

Principal Stein integrated the use of data across her work as a school leader, and worked with teachers to repurposing in-house expertise to develop their data-based literacy program.

Like Principal Hoffman at Franklin, Pearson's Principal Stein worked with her staff to acquire a CSR grant that led to staff capacity to collectively engage in instructional improvement. During the latter stages of the Pearson CSR grant, the staff targeted literacy skill development as the focus of their instructional design efforts. The Principal and the Title 1^2 teacher led the development of a sophisticated, locally designed process for measuring the effects of literacy program design on student learning. The Title I teacher, a veteran reading specialist with training in Reading Recovery, worked with teachers for six years to reconfigure the K-2 reading program. The effort's cornerstone was Guided Reading (GR), a program that develops student strategies for processing text at increasing levels of difficulty (Fountas and Pinnell 1996). The Pearson program relied on running records – individualized, ongoing formative student assessments – to help teachers organize groups for reading activities. The Title I teacher organized her schedule to spend time working with groups of students and teachers in each classroom in order to get a sense of teachers' practice and student performance. She assembled binders of running records information to track student progress over time, and she worked with teachers to supplement the GR assessments with formative feedback tools from Reading Recovery and other district assessments.

Taken together, these data provided a powerful resource for measuring program quality. Still, the data would have little effect until teachers used it to inform instruction. Pearson's leaders realized the value of structured opportunities for reflection in making formative data useful. The Title I teacher met weekly with every teacher and monthly with the K-4 and special education teachers to discuss and disaggregate the data. When teachers began to realize that GR was not addressing the needs of several students, one teacher shared her experience at an Orton-Gillingham phonics-based program workshop. After several other teachers attended the workshop, the Pearson team began to integrate Orton-Gillingham activities and assessments into the literacy program for selected students. The formative assessment program helped staff anticipate the results of the state examination. The Title I teacher described how she was 'rarely surprised, because the running records help to determine where the children should be on the [district assessments], which predict the [state exams] well.'

How leaders sequence instructional improvement

These abbreviated case histories show the wide-ranging ways that school leaders spark instructional changes. In prior work (Halverson 2003) I proposed a typology for categorizing these efforts according to their origins. *Locally designed artifacts* are created by leaders and teachers to shape local practices; *received artifacts* come into the school community already developed by identifiable sources (e.g. through districts or curriculum developers) and are adapted by leaders and teachers to local uses; and *inherited artifacts*, such as the academic calendar and the disciplinary organization of the curriculum, predate the work of teachers and leaders and provide the context for the local system of practice. Building professional community requires leaders to both develop new artifacts and use received artifacts against the inherited context to create legitimate occasions for staff interaction.

However, analysing how leaders build on the emergent trust and capacity for collective problem-solving and knit instructional improvement programs into a whole cloth requires another set of distinctions between artifacts. Here I propose the sequence of *Stage 1*, *Stage 2* and *Stage 3* artifacts to capture how leaders sequence instructional improvement activities that, in the end, develop professional community.

Stage 1 artifacts

Stage 1 artifacts are used to spark the initial conversations in school communities reluctant to engage in professional community and catalyse opportunities that overcome the isolating effects of loose coupling in schools. At Adams, developing the capacity for collective change first required that teachers could stand to be in the same room together. Breakfast Club legitimated time for teachers to discuss instructional issues and collectively reflect upon the changes necessary to improve teaching and learning. This need to establish basic social norms for interaction was not as pressing at either Franklin or Pearson. Still, both Principals Hoffman and Stein used trust-building activities to launch their CSR development and implementation in their schools by relying on existing cultures of teacher interaction to establish the capacity for collective action in new areas.

Received artifacts can also act as catalysts for sparking professional community. High-stakes accountability policies sparked Adams School, and to a lesser extent both Franklin and Pearson schools, to constructive action. Similarly, CSR grants acted as a Stage 1 artifact that provided a focus for instructional improvement at Franklin and Pearson. The grant development process created opportunities for teachers to come to a common understanding of the change process; assembling the different pieces of the grants gave design team members chances to fulfill obligations to participate successfully in a common endeavor. Once awarded, the trust developed through the grant writing process and structures provided by the CSR extended this initial capacity development into the ability to make real changes in student learning.

Received artifacts differ from locally designed artifacts as catalysing agents. While the features of locally designed artifacts are built by the people who will use them to catalyse change, received artifacts are built by others to spark change from a distance. The use of a received artifact depends upon how local users make sense of artifact features in terms of local priorities. The ability of local leaders to allow received artifacts to have local effects shows why implementation can also be considered as a form of design.

The reception of high-stakes accountability policies presents an instructive case. Principal Williams emphasized accountability to show her staff that the need for change was coming from outside the school, and not solely from the school administration. As the Adams Literacy Coach explained: 'I think with the onset of (State test), it did something very interesting that almost forced us to work as a team.' This shift stemmed from Williams' ability to appropriate accountability policies to bolster existing instructional initiatives while at the same time allowing her to establish an organizational rhetoric that the leadership team were on the same side as her staff – both groups could be united in a common effort to improve teaching and learning for students.

Stage 2 artifacts

Leaders used Stage 2 artifacts to focus newly formed professional communities on making problems tractable and solvable. Data reflection retreats and collaborative curriculum design efforts built on the prior efforts of Stage 1 artifacts, converting emergent professional trust into authentic professional interaction. Breakfast Club discussions at Adams encouraged teachers to experiment with new literacy practices in their classrooms, but they were uncertain about how to proceed. Teachers and leaders began talking about developing an assessment, based in the teaching standards, to test the degree to which new practices were helping teachers reach their instructional goals. The Five-Week Assessment built on and focused the insights of the Breakfast Club into a process that helped refine the scope of the Adams professional community into the ability to make instructional problems tractable.

Leaders use Stage 2 artifacts to focus in on certain aspects of a domain in order to allow the details of specific problems to stand out and become more manageable. Pearson's leaders, for example, assembled a series of Stage 2 artifacts to focus attention on what the school perceived as the key instructional problem in the school: early childhood reading. Pearson leaders constructed Stage 2 artifacts that transformed the problem space from the vague challenge of 'teaching children to read better,' to 'using what we already know about reading to build a more effective learning environment for K-2 children.' The formative student achievement information also allowed the staff to tweak the instruction program as it unfolded in order to improve learning opportunities. The Pearson staff used the process of developing a collaborative approach to reading instruction as an occasion to assemble a locally designed (the teaching schedule and assessment binders) and received artifacts (formative assessments, redefining the responsibilities for Title 1 and Special Education positions) into a complex system of practice that focused their existing instructional expertise.

Stage 2 artifacts can also redirect instructional capacity to new uses. Franklin's veteran teaching staff had wide experience in posing and solving a variety of instructional problems, but these had led to divisions between classroom teachers and specialists. Principal Hoffman used integrated service delivery as an opportunity to help teachers 'bridge' their expertise into the new domains of differentiated instruction and collaborative teaching. Hoffman used the redesigned professional development program and dual certification of new faculty positions to build collaborative expertise that enabled the school to engage in a deeper understanding of integrated service delivery.

Stage 3 artifacts

Finally, leaders use Stage 3 artifacts to link disparate initiatives and reinforce instructional program coherence (Newmann *et al.* 2001). Developing Stage 3 artifacts, such as school improvement plans, CSRs and annual budgets, requires leaders and teachers to commit to a common instructional framework and to use this framework to guide innovation and professional development. This, in turn, reinforces professional community, symbolically demonstrating the importance of core innovations to the wider school community.

Leaders use Stage 3 artifacts to rein in the divergent initiatives at work in most schools. Stage 3 artifacts produce (and reflect) a publicly available plan of action that shows how individual artifacts are sequenced to produce intended effects. For example, after developing and sequencing a series of Stage 1 and Stage 2 artifacts to enhance her school's capacity for integrated service delivery, Principal Hoffman used Franklin's master schedule as a core process to match teachers and students together in effective instructional combinations. The master schedule reflected her commitment to integrating the principles of ISD into the core instructional practices, as well as to limit special needs population of any classroom to 30. Once constructed, the master schedule serves as a public enactment of how the Franklin priorities play out in everyday practice.

School improvement planning provides a Key Stage 3 artifact in many schools. However, loose coupling often insulates classrooms from group discussions of change. These school leaders recognized the role of improvement plans in moving talk into practice. The Adams School, for example, used a year-long process of agenda-setting, gathering data on effectiveness, review and new plan development that asked teachers to consider what was worth supporting in the school, and teachers were called on to become advocates:

> People need to stand up for themselves at the meetings, I can't stand for them. After many of the meetings people would come up to (the Literacy Coordinator) and let her know things they wanted but didn't bring up, and (she) would say how they needed to step up and speak their minds at the meetings ... Everything is tied into the SIP somehow, that's what gives it credibility in the school. The budget, and the initiatives are all tied in, if you want to participate, you have to come early and stay late.

The Adams SIP development process provided an umbrella for organizing the array of instructional programs while at the same time acting as a symbolic representation for what the school felt to be their working instructional vision.

Conclusion

Over the course of their reform efforts, we observed how each school demonstrated strong professional communities in action. The principals did not begin with the intention of developing professional community, but communities resulted from their efforts to address the key problems of instruction. Each leader recognized the importance of collaborative action in creating systemic change in their schools. Their goal was to improve student learning, and their means were varied. The lesson is that professional community is a valuable by-product of efforts designed to engage staff in resolving the chronic problems of teaching and learning. As Adams' Principal Williams explained: 'We began to believe in the importance of professional community when we realized that, it wasn't taking classes, but that it was when teachers started talking about their teaching that the scores started improving.' Their goal was to improve student learning, and their means were varied. The lesson is that professional community is a valuable by-product of efforts designed to engage staff in resolving the chronic problems of teaching and learning. The artifacts themselves prove to have little power other than their potential to communicate intent. Actualizing the potential of artifacts requires leaders to work with teachers to create a receptive culture for implementation, and artifacts that served to catalyse professional development in one school could be dismissed as irrelevant or resisted in another. The idea of staging artifacts is important. If successful systemic change depends on tighter coupling of administrative and instructional practice, and if professional community is key to linking leadership and teaching, then leaders need to sequence activities to help teachers toward more collaborative forms of work. Artifacts provide a window on how leaders think and act about this dual process of developing structures and cultures. They are not ends in themselves: the tools of a master craftsman can simply be doorstops in the hands of a dolt.

In *Learning Policy*, David Cohen and Heather Hill (2001) argue the obvious point that policies intended to influence complex instructional practices stand a better chance of implementation when they allow opportunities for practitioners to learn the requirements of the new policies. Understanding how good school leaders use artifacts to develop and marshal the capacity for systemic change by increasing collective understanding could help on both ends of the policy spectrum: policy makers could use this knowledge to build better tools for local use, and leaders and teachers interested in improving their practice could use this research to guide their own development efforts.

Notes

1   The research reported in this chapter was supported by the National Science Foundation, the DeWitt Wallace Foundation, the Spencer Foundation, the Northwestern University School of Education and Social Policy, the Wisconsin Center for Education Research (WCER), and the University of Wisconsin–Madison School of Education. Any opinions, findings, or conclusions expressed in this chapter are those of the author and do not necessarily reflect the views of the funding agencies, WCER, or cooperating institutions.
2   Title 1 is a US Federal Education program designed to provide supplemental instructional services for disadvantaged students.

References

Bryk, A. and Schneider, B. (2002) *Trust in Schools: A Core Resource for Improvement*. New York: Russell Sage Foundation.
Cohen, D.K. and Hill, H. (2001) *Learning Policy: When State Education Reform Works*. New Haven, CT: Yale University Press.
Coleman, J.S. (1988) Social capital in the creation of human capital, *American Journal of Sociology*, 94: 95–120.
Engeström, Y. (1993) Developmental studies of work as a testbench of activity theory: analyzing the work of general practitioners, in S. Chaiklin and J. Lave (eds) *Understanding Practice: Perspectives on Activity and Context*. Cambridge: Cambridge University Press.

Fountas, J. and Pinnell, G. (1996) *Guided Reading: Good First Teaching for All Children*. Portsmouth, NH: Heinemann.

Frattura, E. and Capper, C. (in press) *Leading Beyond Compliance: Integrated Comprehensive Services for All Learners*. Thousand Oaks, CA: Corwin Press.

Halverson, R. (2002) Representing phronesis: supporting instructional leadership practice in schools. Unpublished doctoral dissertation, Northwestern University, Evanston, IL.

Halverson, R. (2003) Systems of practice: how leaders use artifacts to create professional community in schools, *Educational Policy and Analysis Archives*, 11(37). http://epaa.asu.edu/epaa/v11n37/, accessed 7 September 2005.

Halverson, R. (2004) Accessing, documenting and communicating the *phronesis* of school leadership practice, *American Journal of Education*, 111(1): 90–122.

Lee, V.E. and Smith, J.B. (1996) Collective responsibility for learning and its effects on gains in achievement for early secondary school students, *American Journal of Education*, 104(2): 103–47.

Little, J.W. (1982) Norms of collegiality and experimentation, *American Educational Research Journal*, 19(3): 325–40.

Louis, K.S., Marks, H. and Kruse, S.D. (1996) Teachers' professional community in restructuring schools, *American Educational Research Journal*, 33(4): 757–98.

Meyer, J.W. and Rowan, B. (1983) The structure of educational organizations, in M. Meyer and W.R. Scott (eds) *Organizational Environments: Ritual and Rationality*. San Francisco, CA: Jossey-Bass.

Newmann, F.M. and Wehlage, G.G. (1995) *Successful School Restructuring: A Report to the Public and Educators*. Madison, WI: University of Wisconsin, Center on Organization and Restructuring of Schools.

Newmann, F.M., Smith, B., Allensworth, E. and Bryk, A.S. (2001) *School Instructional Program Coherence: Benefits and Challenges*. Chicago: Consortium on Chicago School Research. www.consortium-chicago.org/publications/pdfs/p0d02.pdf, accessed 17 July 2003.

Norman, D.A. (1991) Cognitive artifacts, in J.M. Carroll (ed.) *Diagnosing Interaction: Psychology at the Human–Computer Interface*. New York: Cambridge University Press.

Spillane, J.P., Halverson, R. and Diamond, J.B. (2004) Towards a theory of leadership practice: implications of a distributed perspective, *Journal of Curriculum Studies*, 36(1): 3–34.

Weick, K. (1996) *Sensemaking in Organizations*. London: Sage Publications.

Weick, K.E. (1976) Educational organizations as loosely coupled systems, *Administrative Science Quarterly*, 21(1): 1–19.

eight

Developing collective understanding over time: reflections on building professional community

Sharon D. Kruse and Karen Seashore Louis

Introduction

We have been investigating and writing about professional community and organizational learning since the early 1990s, along with other colleagues whose chapters appear in this volume. During the last few years, we have been heartened by the increasing attention paid to the importance of professional learning communities (PLCs) as a major lever for improving teachers' work lives and student experiences. We are, however, also discouraged by the transformation of the concept from a basis in deep, cultural understanding of how schools function to produce effective instructional settings to a 'program' that can be implemented in a relatively short period of time (Louis 2006). We are also drawn to recent studies that have traced the effects of change over time – real historical investigations rather than longitudinal studies that look at two- or three-year time slices (Brouillette 1996; Hargreaves 2006). This chapter explores the importance of time – and the collective understandings that develop over time – on the slow development of a professional learning community in a single setting.

A note on naturalistic inquiry and collaboration

Our work interweaves case materials, initially developed by the first author as part of a running set of notes related to her role in providing support to the district in the case, and our reflections on them. In the early part of the 2000–01 school year, Sharon Kruse was asked to assist a district in developing a year-long set of workshops and in-service offerings to acquaint district teachers with the continuous improvement planning model adopted by the state. As the initiative moved into its second and subsequent years, Kruse remained associated with the initiative in a technical assistance and documentation role.

Throughout this period, informal field notes were collected (Lincoln and Guba 1985; Merriam 1990). Initially these notes were a reflection on process, serving to inform the up-coming in-services rather than as a research record. During the first six months it became evident that this district was not typical in either its approach to developing teachers or in its approach to change. At this juncture, the field notes became more structured and a series of semi-formal, open-ended interviews with district leadership were completed. Over the course of the next five years Kruse served as a critical friend and provided occasional in-service. In keeping with Josselson and Lieblich (1995), the goal was to make sense of the change effort in the context of the lived experience, crossing the boundaries of consultant, trusted colleague and critical friend.

As readers familiar with the field of professional community will note, the authors of this chapter have enjoyed a long professional relationship, so it was only natural that we would discuss Kruse's experiences as a participant observer in a change process. Through these conversations we began to develop a clear narrative related to the events and experiences of this district. Our collaborative thinking crystallized one afternoon when our conversation took a more didactic turn. As we discussed the collected data, we began to align the Spencer City Schools' experiences with those aspects of our prior thinking about professional communities and organizational learning, and began to discuss new ideas about external and internal stimuli for change. In the tradition of naturalistic data collection and analysis, we examined the data and developed the findings presented in this chapter in tandem, resulting in the analysis that follows.

A sense of well-being and accomplishment

The Spencer City Schools[1] are considered, both by themselves and others, as excellent and consistently high performing. Located in a conservative state with a long-standing focus on testing and proficiency, Spencer schools consistently performed well, achieving all 23 of the state-set performance goals. The high school bragged about the number of national merit scholars and admissions to prestigious universities. Other indicators of excellence abound. Annual per pupil expenditures average $7505.00 per student, about $500.00 more than other similar districts.[2] District attendance averages 96.7 per cent, it graduates 97.4 per cent of its students within four years, and 77.3 per cent of the teachers hold a master's degree. The district enrolls approximately 5250 students in four elementary (primary) schools, two middle (junior secondary) schools and one high school (upper secondary), and serves families that are largely solid working and middle class.

Thus, in the early years of the accountability movement, Spencer City Schools enjoyed a sense of well-being. Families believed the schools were doing well and teachers benefited from a strong professionalized culture. District-sponsored staff development was a regular event and teachers knew they could count on several yearly opportunities to have time to meet with colleagues to learn about current classroom practices and curriculum trends. With a long-standing focus on school-level innovation, Spencer responded like many other high-performing districts in the early years of restructuring with more attention to new reading and math programs during day-long in-services sessions and follow-up training.

Comprehensive, coordinated reforms simply were not on anyone's agenda for the district, however. In fact, the superintendent[3] embraced the ideal of a 'centralized mission and decentralized practices.' In his words, 'I believed that if I hired good people, and I did, they would know what was best for their students in their school, anything else would just be insulting,' a perspective that was reinforced by strong parent support for the schools and teachers.

Perturbation in a stable system

In our experience, many schools demonstrate some visible signs of professional community, but these typically reflect 'fragmented' relationships among teachers. Within a reasonably well-functioning school, groups of teachers band together informally because they long for real discussions about instruction and improvement. Sometimes these correspond to subject matter interests (McLaughlin and Talbert 2001) or teams (Kruse and Louis 1997), but they often involve subsets of teachers who have become passionate about one innovation or another – the infusion of the arts and humanities into regular classroom, interdisciplinary curriculum, using learning styles as a basis for instruction – and they may not involve most teachers. This web of professional relationships binds many teachers to their work setting (Hausman and Goldring 2001), although most find that the greatest source of continuous practice improvement derives from reflection on their own practice (Kruse 1997). This stable pattern of fragmented professional community can either be reinforced or undermined when schools come under pressure to change. Some schools may become more cohesive, while in others, poorly managed conflict over reform may undermine existing community (Achinstein 2002; Rousseau 2004).

Spencer schools in a process of change

In the mid-1990s, the state imposed a series of proficiency tests for the fourth, sixth and ninth grades.[4] While Spencer fourth graders did well, results for the sixth and ninth graders were mixed. Analysis revealed differences in racial achievement and between boys and girls. In addition, there were significant differences among elementary (primary) schools. The state challenged schools to take on increased responsibility for the academic performance of students and the Spencer district began to look at test items to determine areas of content knowledge on which students tested well or poorly.

New state accountability efforts led to a significant shift in how the district thought about autonomy at the school level as well as their own role in curriculum planning and implementation. The superintendent and the curriculum director focused their attention on what teachers taught, how they taught and how teachers knew that students were learning the material. After lengthy discussion during the 1999–2000 school year, the curriculum director said that, 'unless this was a district wide effort we stood no chance in making real changes in what teachers did with kids so we decided to think big – everything we would do we would do with everyone … if we wanted systemic change we would need to work systemically. Nothing less.' This stood in sharp contrast to teachers' assumption that the district would focus on those teachers in the 'testing years.' In the year following the first testing cycle, teachers of the fourth and sixth grades requested transfers to other grades. The district granted none of the requests. The district's leaders began to send out the message that, 'we are all responsible for student achievement – no one would be exempt from that responsibility.'

District leadership and culture change

In general, educational researchers have seen top-down change as antithetical to the development of strong professional community (Poole 1995), and have viewed the development of professional community as stemming from teacher leadership (Andrews and Lewis 2002). At the very least, it is assumed that great performance in schools will depend on making influence between administrators (school leaders) and teachers more reciprocal (Anderson 2004). Case studies of top-down comprehensive change often emphasize its potential for dividing teachers, even driving some to leave (Bueker 2005). If teachers are not angered or dispirited, it is because they are able to resist district initiatives by creating their own interpretations of how they will work (Honig and Hatch 2004). But even under the best of circumstances – where teachers initiate an effort to create common teaching standards – differences in norms and assumptions about professional prerogatives can erode efforts to create common instruction (Achinstein 2002; Pomson 2005). In contrast to these images about how best to create professional consensus around new instructional practices, there is little question that Spencer teachers were looking at a top-down effort to change.

Wearing down resistance and distractions: year 1 activity

Although the Spencer leadership team was clear about the direction they believed the district should take, teachers were less convinced. Some believed that the state initiatives would fade away, others were convinced that they were doing the best they could, while resisters believed that their view of curriculum and instructional standards would prevail. Nevertheless, the superintendent and curriculum director began to consider district-wide strategies for improving student achievement. They began by holding required, day-long meetings of teachers, organized by grade level and content area, to involve them in understanding the content knowledge, practices and skills contained in the draft state standards. In these sessions data from the state tests was examined, as were the new standards for alignment with the tests and the current district curriculum.

The results were stunning. Teachers soon absorbed two disheartening facts. First, teachers, all licensed and with many master's degrees, often did not have a comprehensive understanding of the content required to teach the new standards at the level to which they were written. The most startling example was the mathematics curriculum. Although teachers had enjoyed in-service workshops on problem-solving and inquiry-based mathematics, they were astonished by the complexity of material they would need to know to teach the new standard well. Second, the pace at which they had been teaching the curriculum was well behind that which they would need to employ if they were to address both the depth and breath of the new standards.

District leadership, including the superintendent, curriculum director and school principals, decided that the best way to address the issue of content knowledge was to build from the expertise of district teachers. Common subject area meetings were held with all teachers coming together to discuss the treatment of standards through the grades. This at times required that an entire middle school or high school content area would be absent for a whole day as they met to discuss how specific themes were addressed, starting in kindergarten and working up through the high school curriculum.

The curriculum director began to develop poster-sized graphic organizers of the standards by theme and content, replacing the state's organization by grade level and course formats. Participating teachers worked together to understand how the ideas fit together and where the curriculum spiraled. These linkages were underscored and color coded – when content needed to be discussed it was with teachers of more advanced content explaining the more advanced aspects of the concept or skill, and teachers with more skill with certain pedagogical forms – cooperative grouping or writing across the curriculum – teaching others to understand how they might be of use in another's classroom.

The meetings were long, contentious and intellectually grueling. As the graphic organizers multiplied, teachers became frustrated with the amount of content to be addressed, and the curriculum director developed several mantras that she used with regularity – teachers who complained about limited time to address a concept in a unit or grade level were reminded that, 'we're after real learning that sticks' and that they could 'trust the [curriculum] spiral.' Her words conveyed her conviction that a student's full understanding of a difficult concept would take repeated efforts by teacher after teacher, learning event after learning event. She reminded teachers that, 'We can't work any harder than we already are so we have to work smarter': new ideas could be incorporated into the existing schedule if teachers were reflective about how they used their time. To help address the need to cover the state content, pacing guides were developed in most subject areas. These were not imposed as universal lesson plans but rather as aids for teachers to ensure that all standards would be addressed.

The first year of the effort closed with cautious optimism. New bridges had been built between teachers both within schools and grade levels but also across long-held traditional boundaries of grade level and school. Teacher surveys indicated that they believed that the sessions had made them 'more aware' of the state standards and they 'strongly agreed' that the sessions were worthwhile. The more positive teachers looked forward to the next year's activities and offered to assist in the planning as part of a paid team over the summer, while others held out hope that 'this too will pass.'

Rethinking the role of the district

In contrast to the predominant assumption that bottom-up change will lead to a more professionally focused school culture, an emerging literature emphasizes the role of the district. District culture affects students' per-ceptions of their school's culture (Pritchard *et al.* 2005), teachers' will-ingness to change their practices and engage in organizational learning (Koschoreck 2001), and principal leadership during change processes (Johnson 1998). Student achievement is higher in districts with a strong continuous improvement focus (Marshall *et al.* 2004), and when districts emphasize capacity for change among teachers, district-mandated initiatives can be more successful (Togneri and Anderson 2003). While the Spencer district staff was not familiar with these findings, they moved ahead under the assumption that they could change school culture while cultivating teacher professionalism.

The emergence of a key change agent in year 2

The 2001–02 school year began with renewed focus on working on the development of meaningful learning experiences for students who attended schools in the Spencer City School District. The curriculum director used testing results as a vehicle for celebration – students had scored modestly better in all areas, and particular improvement was observed in mathematics. But the summer planning teams returned to work with a new agenda: they wanted more opportunity to work on instruction with teachers in their own schools. The curriculum director, on the other hand, wanted to shift the attention of all teachers from classroom instructional practices to that of assessment. A compromise was struck: meetings would be cross-district by grade level at the elementary grades and by teaching area at the middle and high school levels. When teachers met they would be allowed a half day to focus on the pacing guides and a discussion of 'hard to teach, hard to learn' standards, but the other half day would be focused on formative and summative assessment pedagogies.

As the first meetings took place, common complaints began to emerge – the pacing guides were too ambitious; the resources the district provided teachers did not provide much needed materials to address a significant portion of the standards as written; and teachers were experiencing difficulty explaining the district's new focus to parents who wanted to know what had happened to activities and units that had been removed from the curriculum when it was discovered that they no longer aligned with the standards at a particular grade level.

The curriculum director stepped forward to address each concern. She noted that the need to inform the community was important and that she would personally address this matter with school leadership. Subsequently, she spoke at a parent meeting at every school across the district to explain the new professional development initiatives and why they were important to student learning. Publicly, she also noted that, 'we have done the best we could do with what we knew at the time' and vowed that the district would 'learn from our mistakes.' She would go on to say that, 'things will change as we learn more about all of this' and teachers could expect a 'cycle of changes as we get better at this effort.' Privately, she worried about her ability to convince the faculty that, 'a continuous improvement effort is by its very nature, continuous.' She decided that she would maintain the messages of the first year, stressing the focus on student learning for all kids and the long-term nature of real teacher learning.

As she worked at maintaining a consistent message with all the groups of teachers, administrators and parents, she also struggled with continuing to move the teaching staff toward even more challenging goals. By taking on assessment as the year 2 goal, she had purposely and deliberately moved still further into areas of practice that teachers had long held within their private domain. The in-service and discussion in year 2 made public the very private practices of grading and reporting student progress.

In introducing these ideas she merged the slogans and mantras of the first year into a saga that focused on teachers' efforts to learn and change – how teachers had come together to develop the pacing guides, how they had worked together to begin to understand how the new standards-based curriculum might be addressed across the district and how she had been willing to put her resources forward to help teachers improve student learning. She openly asked what could be taken from those learning experiences and used for these new challenges. Incorporated into the emerging saga was a story about year 2, which emphasized how hard implementing a standards-based curriculum was and about how difficult truly knowing what students were learning and how well they were learning it could be. The saga became a defining element for the district – significant messages were sent about expectations of and support for teachers' class-room practice and student learning over the long haul.

Beyond the hero's journey

Up to now our story has emphasized the role of a single person – the Spencer District curriculum coordinator – in pushing for significant changes in instructional practice. The educational and business literature is full of stories of transformational leadership, which often follow Burn's seminal study of the character and quality of political leaders who changed the world (Burns 1978). In contrast, the emerging literature on the district's role in changing school and teacher culture emphasizes the fact that it is largely indirect. Effective districts should focus on the broad tasks of leadership – goals, instructional focus, leadership development, teacher recruitment and retention, and professional development – and leave the details of instruction to the school (Leithwood *et al.* 1998; Harris 2001). Studies of the major reform initiatives in Chicago argue that districts influence professional community by hewing to a strong human resource development strategy: increasing in knowledge, skills, dispositions, and social resources of adults in schools (Smylie 1996; Smylie and Wenzel 2003). If we look at what happened in the third and fourth years of change

in the Spencer District, we can see how these two stories – direct transformational leadership and supportive leadership that promotes teachers'
professional learning communities – become consistent.

Years 3 and 4: teachers begin to take charge

On the surface the year 3 activities were much like those of year 2. Grade
and content specific meetings continued, and although many of the prior
year's concerns were addressed (new mathematics materials were researched and purchased) new concerns surfaced. The issue of the 'racing
guides' still rankled as did concerns about the implementation of common
assessments. Teachers began to raise questions about what the goals really
meant. As one teacher asked: 'If we expect all kids to learn at high levels,
how many times can they re-take the test to prove that they have?'

Not surprisingly, this question resonated with teachers across the district.
It also raised more questions about the pacing/racing guides, as another
teacher asked: 'How can we re-teach and still stay on target to complete the
content by when we are supposed to?' Still other teachers asked: 'Aren't
these two goals working at odds with each other?' The curriculum director
responded with her usual message of continuous learning, adding that she
hoped that teachers would 'get more focused on which standards matter
more and where we really want kids to know things deeply and where a less
thorough understanding is acceptable.' In other words, she asked teachers
to develop consensus around what matters most, boring down from the
surface of the state curriculum to their own professional wisdom.

Teachers were clear that along with these challenges, they faced the
routine disappointments of the profession – some students came unengaged,
parents were becoming more demanding and also more removed. Discipline
was a constant struggle and the increased demands of achieving at high
levels had, in some cases, really challenged teachers to discover new ways of
addressing reluctant and resistant students. Not all felt it could be done.

Rather than simply complaining, teachers returned to studying the
standards, learning the content more deeply themselves and further refining
the assessments they had developed. Year 3 ended with a sense that
everyone finally understood how hard this work was and how long it would
take, and with a sense of shared direction for the work and, perhaps, its
ultimate reward.

Year 4 is less than halfway through at the time of writing. In an early
interview with the curriculum director she shared that plans for this year
are still emerging, and that these reflect the priorities that are developing
among groups of teachers. Most teachers are asking for more time to
develop and refine assessments – both the summative common assessments
as well as those daily assessments used as formative feedback for

instructional decision making. Other teachers suggest that they want to spend time looking at student responses to the items already written and to determine which assessment items are best at determining what students have learned and how well they have learned it. Still other teachers are looking to address the issues of classroom management that plague even the best teachers among us. The summer team met again in July 2005 and worked to develop a format that provided teachers opportunity to reflectively consider those items of concern. The curriculum director's final comment on the matter was, 'no matter what we do the focus is still on student learning and that's no small victory.'

Reflections on creating PLCs

Everyone who writes about PLCs is concerned with the question of how to promote and extend them to include larger numbers of teachers. As we considered the case, several issues emerged.

First, the importance of *extended time* appears critical. Popular writing about PLCs seems to regard them as an innovation that can be initiated in one year, and institutionalized in the next. In contrast, the Spencer City Schools case suggests that even under positive conditions – good schools, strong community support, a generally positive relationship between the district and teachers, and significant resources for professional development – helping teachers beyond comfortable positions in 'fragmented communities' is a long-term proposition. The relevance of time is related to the usual litany of factors that are hard to remove: a preference for small group discussions of curriculum and instruction with trusted colleagues in the same school and discipline/grade, an attachment to practices that have been honed over the course of a career, the 'never enough time' problem that occurs even when more time is allocated, and the sheer complexity of considering the intersection between scope and sequence of content, assessment of student learning, and instructional strategies. These factors undermine many efforts to create school-wide, deep conversations about teaching and learning, much less the effort to initiate cross-school conversations.

Second, the core principle of developing PLCs is to keep *all eyes on teaching and learning*. If the district had started with an emphasis on PLCs, it seems very unlikely that a sustained four- to five-year initiative that cost the district its entire professional development budget and required countless hours of teacher volunteer time could have been sustained. The focus was not just on raising test scores, but on increasing teachers' ability to think about how their collective work affected student learning. Because of the deep uncertainties involved in 'trusting the spiral' and waiting for results over a period of years, it was important for all involved to believe that they were making real changes for real students.

Third, the case suggests that there is an important place for *top-down initiatives* to create PLCs, which challenges a deep-seated belief that PLCs emerge organically in schools with effective principal and teacher leadership. The Spencer school initiative was clearly developed and directed (at least initially) by district staff members. We highlight the role of the curriculum director as change agent, but she, of course, required strong backing from the superintendent and the school board – particularly since the initiative was extended and expensive. But we have also noted that the initiative was not a program with accountability for centrally designed goals. Instead, particularly beginning in the second year, there was significant effort to locate and nurture smaller PLCs that grew up around issues that evoked teachers' passions. Although the district provided a framework and a sense of persistence, the energy and intellectual contributions of the group were recognized, built in, and rewarded.

Fourth, there is an associated principle of innovation *resilience* that appears strongly in the field notes. While most teachers look at district initiatives with the assumption that 'this too shall pass,' it was clear after the first year in Spencer that there was seriousness of purpose that would persist. Many have pointed to the 'implementation dip' that accompanies change – although this was not a program being implemented, the frustrations of grappling with such a complex effort often outweighed the perceived benefits for much of the first and second year. Districts need the willingness to let other initiatives go if they wish to create meaningful conversations across schools and grade levels about teaching and learning.

Finally, this case represents another *challenge to the simplistic notion that the school is the primary unit of effective change.* While we do not believe that district-wide PLCs are the only or even the most important strategy for increasing PLCs, the Spencer case calls into question the assumptions that professional learning will occur primarily within the school for elementary teachers, within teams for middle school teachers, and within disciplinary groups for high school teachers. While the Spencer City Schools are not a perfect example of building a district-wide culture of professional community, they demonstrate its potential.

Notes

1   A pseudonym.
2   Like many states in the USA, schools are funded by a combination of state and local taxes.
3   In the USA, the superintendent is the chief director of education of a local district, and reports to an elected school board.
4   In the USA, 'grades' refer to the students' year level, and not their academic marks.

References

Achinstein, B. (2002) Conflict amid community: the micro-politics of teacher collaboration, *Teachers College Record*, 104(3): 421–55.

Anderson, K.D. (2004) The nature of teacher leadership in schools as reciprocal influences between teacher leaders and principals, *School Effectiveness and School Improvement*, 15(1): 97–113.

Andrews, D. and Lewis, M. (2002) The experience of a professional community: teachers developing a new image of themselves and their workplace, *Educational Research*, 44(3): 237–54.

Brouillette, L. (1996) *A Geology of School Reform: The Successive Restructurings of a School District*. Albany, NY: SUNY Press.

Bueker, C.S. (2005) Teachers' reports of the effects of a whole-school literacy reform model on teacher turnover, *Elementary School Journal*, 105(4): 395.

Burns, J.M. (1978) *Leadership*. New York: Harper Torchbooks.

Hargreaves, A. (2006) Educational change over time? The sustainability and non-sustainability of three decades of secondary school change and continuity, *Education Administration Quarterly*, 41(3): 3–41.

Harris, A. (2001) Building the capacity for school improvement, *School Leadership and Management*, 21(3): 261–70.

Hausman, C.S. and Goldring, E.B. (2001) Sustaining teacher commitment: the role of professional communities, *Peabody Journal of Education*, 76(2): 30–51.

Honig, M. and Hatch, T. (2004) Crafting coherence: how schools strategically manage multiple, conflicting demands, *Educational Researcher*, 33(8): 16–30.

Johnson, A.M. (1998) A response to restructuring: the dilemmas of school principals in a process of change, *Urban Review*, 30(4): 309–32.

Josselson, R. and Lieblich, A. (1995) *Interpreting Experience: The Narrative Study of Lives*. Newbury Park, CA: Sage.

Koschoreck, J.W. (2001) Accountability and educational equity in the transformation of an urban district, *Education and Urban Society*, 33(3): 284–304.

Kruse, S.D. (1997) Reflective activity in practice: vignettes of teachers' deliberative work, *Journal of Research and Development in Education*, 31(1): 46–60.

Kruse, S.D. and Louis, K.S. (1997) Teacher teaming in middle schools: dilemmas for a schoolwide community, *Educational Administration Quarterly*, 33(3): 261–89.

Leithwood, K., Leonard, L. and Sharratt, L. (1998) Conditions fostering organizational learning in schools, *Educational Administration Quarterly*, 34(2): 243–76.

Lincoln, Y.S. and Guba, E.G. (1985) *Naturalistic Inquiry*. London: Sage Publications.

Louis, K.S. (2006) Changing the culture of schools: professional community, organizational learning and trust, *Journal of School Leadership*, 41(1): 165–73.

Marshall, J., Pritchard, R. and Gunderson, B. (2004) The relation among school district health, total quality principles for school organization and student achievement, *School Leadership and Management*, 24(2): 175–90.

McLaughlin, M.W. and Talbert, J.E. (2001) *Professional Communities and the Work of High School Teaching*. Chicago, IL: University of Chicago Press.

Merriam, S. (1990) *Case Study Research in Education: A Qualitative Approach*. San Francisco, CA: Jossey-Bass.

Pomson, A.D.M. (2005) One classroom at a time? Teacher isolation and community viewed through the prism of the particular, *Teachers College Record*, 107(4): 783–802.

Poole, W. (1995) Reconstructing the teacher-administrator relationship to achieve systemic change, *Journal of School Leadership*, 5(6): 565–96.

Pritchard, R.J., Morrow, D. and Marshall, J.C. (2005) School and district culture as reflected in student voices and student achievement, *School Effectiveness and School Improvement*, 16(2): 153–77.

Rousseau, C.K. (2004) Shared beliefs, conflict, and a retreat from reform: the story of a professional community of high school mathematics teachers, *Teaching and Teacher Education: An International Journal of Research and Studies*, 20(8): 783–96.

Smylie, M.A. (1996) From bureaucratic control to building human capital: the importance of teacher learning in education reform, *Educational Researcher*, 25(9): 9–11.

Smylie, M.A. and Wenzel, S.A. (2003) *The Chicago Annenberg Challenge: Successes, Failures, and Lessons for the Future. Final Technical Report of the Chicago Annenberg Research Project*. Access ERIC: Full Text (142 Reports – Evaluative). Chicago, IL: Consortium on Chicago School Research.

Togneri, W. and Anderson, S.E. (2003) How high poverty districts improve, *Leadership*, 33(1): 12–16.

nine

Using assessment tools as frames for dialogue to create and sustain professional learning communities

Kristine Kiefer Hipp and Jane Bumpers Huffman

As schools and districts struggle with initiating and implementing school reform measures that target student achievement, research informs us of strategies that promote dialogue in assessing schools as professional learning communities (PLCs). In work with schools, we find Argyris's (1990: 242) advice to be pertinent and important. Educators must suspend judgment, listen on multiple levels, and eliminate the arrogance in thinking, 'Our beliefs are *the* truth. The truth is obvious. Our beliefs are based on real data. The data we select are the real data.' It is clear to us that in schools thinking and dialogue should be more reflective. Unfortunately, the lack of supportive structures in schools including lack of time, fear of risk, and lack of trust perpetuate independent rather than interdependent thought. Hipp *et al.* (2004: 32) reveal that teachers in more advanced PLC schools 'are more than pleased to be there, have respect for their peers, and trust in their formal leaders.' School reform is more apt to occur if educators engage less in following outdated rules and in making quick decisions, and more in finding and using time to question current practices and create shared meaning about what is worth doing. This chapter illuminates recent efforts in schools using specific tools to increase the dialogue across teachers and school leaders as they prepare to embark on the challenging work of creating supportive conditions for student learning.

To accomplish this purpose, first we begin with a brief overview of a long-term study that provided the content of our assessment tools. Second, we present the assessment tools as *frames* to stimulate conversations related to creating and sustaining PLCs. Third, considering theory, frameworks, and expertise in the field, we illuminate the importance of dialogue as an ongoing conversation among school staff. In conclusion we remain convinced these initial efforts in dialogue set the stage for school communities to promote reflection, build relationships, address critical issues, guide decisions, and advance unity of purpose, commitment and accountability – all leading to change in instructional practices that affect student learning.

As we work with schools in the administration of our assessment tools, the Professional Learning Community Assessment (PLCA), and the Professional Learning Community Development Rubric (PLCDR) we find that schools have difficulty initiating PLCs. For educators, new innovations only seem to add to the overload, fragmentation, and incoherency of tasks aimed at school reform. They both fear and reject new fads and add-ons that further disconnect and distract them from issues of greatest importance – teaching and learning (Fullan 2000). Thus it is important for purposeful dialogue to occur that invites conversation about what people care about; what they perceive as strengths, discrepancies and frustrations; and, most importantly, what needs to be changed. This sets the stage for educators to use these tools to identify issues and take action related to school reform.

Wheatley (2002: 15) gives us pause to reflect on what too often exists: 'There is no continuity between actions, there are no pauses, no paths, no pattern, no past and no future. There is only the clamor of the ... fragmentary present. Everywhere there are surprises and sensations, yet nowhere is there any outcome. Nothing flows through; everything interrupts.' How will schools build the capacity to create learning communities that enhance student learning? Perhaps the answer lies in deep and enduring conversations that inform and stimulate reflection and action toward the achievement of a common purpose.

A long-term study of schools purposefully creating PLCs

The research that undergirds the content of these tools emerged from a multiple methods study surrounding PLCs that took place over a five-year period (1995–2000). Creating Communities of Continuous Inquiry and Improvement was a federally funded project directed by Shirley M. Hord at the Southwest Educational Development Laboratory (SEDL) in Austin, Texas. The project began with Hord's (1997) review of both educational and corporate literature culminating in an emergent conceptualization of five related dimensions that defined the essence of a PLC (see Table 9.1).

Next, she invited educators of all educational backgrounds to serve as co-developers, or external change agents in project schools. Co-developers joined principals and teachers in these schools to create PLC schools by sharing resources and expertise, and consistently focusing on the dimensions of PLCs. These schools included rural, urban, suburban, private and

Table 9.1 Dimensions of a professional learning community

Shared and supportive leadership	School administrators participate democratically with teachers by sharing power, authority, and decision-making, and promoting and nurturing leadership among staff
Shared values and vision	Staff shares visions for school improvement that have an undeviating focus on student learning. Shared values support norms of behavior that guide decisions about teaching and learning
Collective learning and application	Staff at all levels of the school share information and work collaboratively to plan, solve problems and improve learning opportunities. Together they seek knowledge, skills and strategies and apply this new learning to their work.
Shared personal practice	Peers visit with and observe one another to offer encouragement and to provide feedback on instructional practices to assist in student achievement and increase individual and organizational capacity
Supportive conditions • relationships • structures	*Collegial relationships* include respect, trust, norms of critical inquiry and improvement, and positive, caring relationships among students, teachers and administrators *Structures* include a variety of conditions such as size of the school, proximity of staff to one another, communication systems, and the time and space for staff to meet and examine current practices

public K-12 schools and represented all socioeconomic backgrounds. In community, co-developers were challenged by the undertaking and committed to support one another – to create schools that continuously inquire and seek to foster both student and adult learning. The following section briefly describes the data collection processes in *phases* over seven years (1998–2005) that ultimately provided the data from which the PLCA and PLCDR were developed.

In *Phase 1* of our study, researchers (including us) conducted phone interviews with principals and lead teachers in 19 schools across six states to gather baseline data, and then conducted additional face-to-face interviews with the same teams. Our purpose was to gather perceptions as to how their schools were progressing as PLCs defined by the five dimensions they were purposefully trying to understand and integrate. Data were again collected in *Phase 2*, when SEDL staff and co-developers interviewed a greater representative sample of staff from 12 remaining schools, to gain further insights beyond the principal and lead teacher who were most committed to the PLC project.

Finally, in 2003, *Phase 3* picked up where the SEDL project ended. A team of researchers re-entered the two most advanced PLCs on three different occasions to collect both qualitative and quantitative data using these tools. The intent was to discover what made these schools different than others in the project and determine how they could use the tools for continuous improvement. What made these schools sustain their focus and alignment of efforts when others did not? Research in these two schools, and other schools and districts in which we work, is ongoing and serves to further inform findings and the use of these tools for assessment purposes.

Use of tools to initiate and deepen conversation

Schools that are operating as professional learning communities must foster a culture in which learning by all is valued, encouraged, and supported. These communities should reveal a culture in which 'the staff, intentionally and collectively, engage in learning and work on issues directly related to classroom practice that positively impacts student learning' (Cowan and Hord 1999: 4). In practice, structures are often provided that bring people together to learn, but what are teachers and principals actually learning? Do we ask what is worth doing? And, is what we are doing impacting on student achievement? These questions provide the impetus for initiating conversations.

In 2000 and 2001 the research team continued to analyse data over time, and illuminate practices through exemplars and non-exemplars that either promoted or hindered school efforts and progress (Hipp and Huffman 2002). The success of any innovation and change in schools is dependent on how well staff can sustain their efforts and embed them into the culture of their school. If new approaches are viewed as short term or quick fixes to perceived problems, the impact will be superficial, confined to a few, select participants, and generally ineffective. Thus the question remains, *how do schools develop and maintain momentum and long-term success in the change process?*

We selected Fullan's (1985) three phases of change – initiation, implementation and institutionalization – as providing a structure for lasting change. Staffs that prevail and provide opportunities for students to improve, move through these phases to institutionalization, where the change initiative becomes embedded into the culture of the school. Guided by supportive leadership and a shared vision, these school communities are committed and hold themselves accountable for student learning. These leaders identify and solve problems amid a climate that invites risk, which requires continual refocusing. A lead teacher at one of our more advanced schools stated: 'The goal is to produce a lifelong commitment to learning, success in both academic, technological and other fields ... basically every decision that we made focuses on student learning.' Institutionalization is the phase of change that is least reflected, or even addressed, in the vast majority of school improvement efforts. Nonetheless, institutionalization of all five related PLC dimensions is essential for schools to engage in sustained improvement and for continuous learning and renewal to occur.

From the data analysis, themes were identified that led to the development of a visual organizer (Huffman and Hipp 2003) and two assessment tools: (a) the Professional Learning Community Assessment (Olivier *et al.* 2003), and (b) the Professional Learning Community Development Rubric (Hipp *et al.* 2004). The value in these tools has been their potential to serve as *frames* to help educators in schools and districts initiate and implement PLCs by engaging in conversations around teaching and learning, and further examine *what* they are learning that is most critical to success. Prior to developing these PLC tools, the researchers linked Fullan's change model with Hord's dimensions to provide a framework that describes practices at various levels. Each phase, through which an innovation moves to reach desired outcomes, is briefly described in Table 9.2.

Table 9.2   Fullan's phases of change model

Initiation	Staff adopt an innovation by making the decision to proceed with the change
Implementation	Staff begin to operationalize the innovation into practice
Institutionalization	The innovation is recognized as an ongoing part of the system or the 'way things are done around here'

Both tools demonstrate the use of these emergent and integrated frameworks. In reality, change is complicated and does not always follow a forward progression. This is often due to external factors such as those posed by standardized school reform mandates that significantly influence the work of schools and hinder progress and sustainability. Depending on each school's resiliency and strategy in addressing new challenges, some schools remain revitalized and continually renew themselves, while others grow passive and reactive. In schools, educators are challenged to use the organizer and the two tools to frame ongoing conversations to address important issues related to student achievement.

Professional Learning Community Assessment

The PLCA was designed as a diagnostic tool to assess perceptions about the school's principal, staff, and stakeholders (parents and community members) based on the five dimensions of a professional learning community and the critical attributes (Olivier *et al.* 2003). This 45-item assessment includes practices observed at the school level that occur more ideally at Fullan's implementation and institutionalization levels of change that are aligned with Hord's dimensions of shared and supportive leadership, shared values and vision, collective learning and application, shared personal practice, and supportive conditions – relationships and structures (see Figure 9.1 for the first ten items). Construct validity was established and the PLCA was field-tested. As educators use this tool over time, they can measure continual progress and use dimensions and even specific items to guide their practices as they develop plans to meet their goals.

The PLCA has been most successfully used when staff members rate each item and provide specific evidence for their rating. The dialogue begins and typically discrepancies surface rather quickly. It is most effective when dialogue takes place in mixed groups rather than job-alike, subject area, or grade level (year) groups, so staff can look beyond their individual units to consider and relate their actions across the system. In turn, teachers and administrators are privy to impressions that often reveal varying beliefs and assumptions across the organization. As ratings vary, continued discussion is warranted to clarify discrepant perceptions and move staff to a common understanding of their current reality as they create their PLC organically.

The tool has also been used to align the dimensions with school goals in order to develop initial plans and help work teams to accomplish stated goals. A common language begins to emerge as plans become focused and purposeful and manifest themselves in action. Moreover, when external factors are added to the mix, the notion of a PLC moves to that of a purposive working *system*. Fullan (2005) reveals the realities that adversely affect the implementation and sustainability of large-scale reform, and consequently advocates for partnerships across *the whole system*. He asserts: 'if you want to change systems you need to increase the amount of purposeful interaction between and among individuals within and across ... systems' (ibid.: 17). We recognize the value in districts using this tool as well – thus educators throughout the district become resources for each other in varied and reinforcing relationships, thereby expanding the notion of a learning community.

Professional Learning Communities Assessment

Directions:
This questionnaire assesses your perceptions about your principal, staff, and stakeholders based on the five dimensions of a professional learning community (PLC) and related attributes. There are no right or wrong responses. This questionnaire contains a number of statements about practices, which occur in some schools. Read each statement and then use the scale below to select the scale point that best reflects your personal degree of agreement with the statement. Shade the appropriate oval provided to the right of each statement. Be certain to select only one response for each statement.

Key Terms:
Principal = Principal, not Associate or Assistant Principal
Staff = All adult staff directly associated with curriculum, instruction, and assessment of students
Stakeholders = Parents and community members

Scale:
   1 = Strongly Disagree (SD)
   2 = Disagree (D)
   3 = Agree (A)
   4 = Strongly Agree (SA)

STATEMENTS		SCALE			
	Shared and Supportive Leadership	SD	D	A	SA
1.	The staff is consistently involved in discussing and making decisions about most school issues.	0	0	0	0
2.	The principal incorporates advice from staff to make decisions.	0	0	0	0
3.	The staff have accessibility to key information.	0	0	0	0
4.	The principal is proactive and addresses areas where support is needed.	0	0	0	0
5.	Opportunities are provided for staff to initiate change.	0	0	0	0
6.	The principal shares responsibility and rewards for innovative actions.	0	0	0	0
7.	The principal participates democratically with staff sharing power and authority.	0	0	0	0
8.	Leadership is promoted and nurtured among staff.	0	0	0	0
9.	Decision-making takes place through committees and communication across grade and subject areas.	0	0	0	0
10.	Stakeholders assume shared responsibility and accountability for student learning without evidence of imposed power and authority.	0	0	0	0

Figure 9.1   The Professional Learning Community Assessment (PLCA) – first page only

In practice the PLCA serves as a *frame* through which staff, through dialogue, assess their school culture reflective of:

- sharing power, authority and decision-making around issues of teaching and learning;
- the alignment of values and vision and related behaviors that demonstrate an undeviating focus on student achievement;
- seeking and applying new knowledge, skills and strategies that respond to diverse student needs;
- regularly reviewing student work, sharing personal practice, and problem solving critical issues to improve student learning;
- the presence of effective systems, structures, and resources that reveal current practices supporting student learning;
- understanding cultures that involve the entire school community in promoting continuous, unified efforts to embed change in the culture of the school.

Principals, other school leaders, and central office staff in our schools have used the PLCA to become more resourceful and share leadership around issues of teaching and learning. In many ways leaders can provide facilitation and develop the supportive conditions necessary to address issues around student achievement and sustaining a positive school culture. We have found that one of the most critical actions in reculturing focuses on building and reinforcing relationships.

In *Schools That Learn*, Senge *et al.* (2000: 326) asserted: 'a nurturing professional community seems to be the container that holds the culture. Teachers feel invigorated, challenged, professionally engaged, and empowered, just because they teach there.' As we studied one advanced PLC, one teacher remarked: 'I think the morale has gotten better over the years. I think that everyone is seen as important – an important part of the puzzle, that everyone contributes regardless of your role or your title. And I think what everyone realizes is that what they do matters and counts.' It appears that educators listen to one another and recognize the value of broad-based stakeholder involvement and ownership. Thus, through dialogue, staff can articulate the standards they will live by and put into action (Pankake 1998).

The PLCA has allowed us and users alike to discover that some schools are more advanced in their progression; others are not even at the point of initiation. As a result, the PLCDR, designed as an informal instrument, was developed to not only add another phase, *not initiated*, to the three existing phases: initiation (*starting*), implementation (*doing*), and institutionalization (*embedding*), but to allow staff to relate the PLC dimensions to their school cultures. This tool can either be used in tandem with the PLCA or it can stand alone and invite additional meaningful conversations.

Professional Learning Community Development Rubric

The PLCA provided the content for the development of the PLCDR, designed for use by school staff to reflect on the school's culture and to delineate the progression of specific school level practices that reflect each dimension through each level of change. To date, the PLCDR has been used informally with schools and districts, not as a standardized assessment tool to be used for diagnostic purposes like the PLCA (see Figure 9.2 for shared and supportive leadership section). As we use the PLCDR in schools and districts, we ask staff to reveal their perceptions by checking the boxes that most reflect each dimension along the continuum. Next, we follow a similar process to that which was described in the PLCA section. Staff share individual ratings in small groups by providing evidence related to their practices and culture, and then engage in dialogue that focuses on discrepant viewpoints. This moves the dialogue to identifying next steps in addressing issues, problems, concerns and specifically how to meet school or district goals. These conversations are not to be seen as a single event, but invite staff to engage in ongoing conversations in a variety of situations and venues, such as at the team, department, school, and district levels.

Dimensions	Not Initiated (stifled)	Initiation (starting)	Implementation (doing)	Institutionalization (embedding)
Shared and Supportive Leadership Administrators share power, authority, and decision-making, while promoting and nurturing leadership.	Leadership is held by school administrators; staff are not empowered around issues of teaching and learning. ☐	Pockets of leadership exist beyond school administrators; staff are nurtured and encouraged to take leadership roles. ☐	Leadership is prevalent across the school; staff share power, authority, and responsibility around issues of teaching and learning. ☐	Leadership and decision-making are broad-based; empowerment exists around issues of teaching and learning; staff are committed and accountable. ☐

Figure 9.2 Professional Learning Community Development Rubric (PLCDR) – Shared and Supportive Leadership (Hipp *et al.* 2004)

We offer these tools to engage school and district staff in dialogue, specifically around PLCs – focusing on beliefs, practices and reculturing. Additional sources provide insight into the skill of dialogue, and how to facilitate even deeper conversation, stronger relationships, and more effective practices illuminating diverse ways of thinking.

Additional sources supporting dialogue in school reform

Numerous sources provide direction for engaging others in the skill of dialogue for the purpose of reculturing in the work of creating PLCs. These sources provide theory, frameworks for exploring varying mental models, and expertise discovered from initiatives implemented in education and in the corporate world that affect organizational learning and growth (Senge *et al.* 1994; 2000; Patterson *et al.* 2002; Wheatley 2002).

Bohm (1996) proposes that breakdowns in effectiveness of team and organizational learning are fueled by how we see the world in categories and distinction of thoughts that perpetuate rigid ways of thinking. This is common in the beliefs and assumptions educators initially bring to the table. Until dialogue skills are practiced in schools, mental models will remain firmly established and restrict an openness to learn. When we work in schools to promote open dialogue, teachers and principals work in pairs or triads creating Venn diagrams, depicting two to three overlapping circles, to identify their commonalities and commitments to move toward some agreed action. We see this strategy improves communication, links conception and implementation, and serves to solve problems that culminate in shared meaning and purposeful action.

In Senge *et al.* (1994), contributors offer insights into the variety of skills that comprise effective dialogue. Ross and Roberts draw on Argyris's (1990) work to balance inquiry and advocacy, which is simply presenting one's thinking and inviting others to challenge ideas and thinking to arrive at new insights and, ultimately, deepen one's sense of practice. They speak to the challenge in letting go of cherished beliefs and assumptions and changing from the inside out by establishing relationships that promote integrity.

While reflecting on responses from the PLCA and the PLCDR, staff often see the gap between their current reality and where they want to be. This ideally serves to ignite passion and creativity to align action with shared purpose. Teachers and administrators find insight not in mean scores, but within conversations about the descriptors and where they want to direct their efforts. Finally, to promote trust and respectful interactions, inclusive schools must develop a culture that is dynamic and based on the values, beliefs, and assumptions of the people within. In *Schools That Learn* (Senge *et al.* 2000: 325) Margaret Arbuckle expressed:

> As educators – designers for learning – we have come to understand that some school cultures stimulate and promote learning. Others stifle it. You can feel the difference as soon as you walk into a school. Culture is rooted deeply in people. It is embodied in their attitudes, values, and skills, which in turn stem from their personal backgrounds, from their life experiences, and from the communities they belong to.

How then can people influence the culture of a school in any sustainable way? It is clear that the value of ongoing dialogue that shapes a culture of professional learning is absolutely essential in school reculturing. The principal at one of our advancing PLCs explained how the school culture is developed in relation to meeting student and staff needs: 'In the summer ... or at the beginning of the year we sit down and look at the needs of the teachers ... and the students. So we tailor our beginning of the year staff development to meet those needs.'

It is therefore important to read the culture and move forward when facilitating dialogue using these tools to assess the culture and current practices in schools. In one school, while examining the results of the assessment, teachers explained that they had 75 minutes of planning time each day, which allowed for more opportunities to share than is found in many schools. However, the teachers continue to point out that even this amount of time is not enough to engage in conversations that lead to the difficult work of reculturing. They further explain the many activities conducted during these planning and team times may include curriculum mapping, lesson/unit planning; sharing information; instructional strategy demonstrations from central office; parent and student conferences; problem-solving; and diverse ways of thinking.

Addressing conversations on a global front, as in *Turning to One Another: Simple Conversations Restore Hope to the Future*, Wheatley's (2002: 3) message easily transfers to hope for school reform as she asserts: 'I believe we can change the world if we start listening to one another again ... Simple, truthful conversation where we each have a chance to speak, we each feel heard, and we each listen well ... Human conversation is the most ancient and easiest way to cultivate the conditions for change.'

We find this quote compelling due to the perception that the values and actions in today's schools are often unhealthy and hinder student learning. Typical interactions seldom move beyond being cordial to one another. In contrast, at one institutionalized school, Olivier *et al.* (2005: 33) report that: 'Everyone in the school is necessary for creating the school's accomplishment. We use terms such as "we work as a team," "this school is like family," and "everyone here cares." This shows that ... regarding problem solving – it is basically everyone's responsibility.'

Creating the supportive conditions for dialogue is the most critical piece in developing a collaborative culture – a culture where an exchange of ideas flourish – a place where everyone can make a difference thereby fostering the capacity needed to build mature and sustainable learning communities. Change in self, and ultimately organizational change, comes as a result of knowing our beliefs and assumptions and inviting others to challenge our thoughts. If we do not turn to one another now, little will be achieved to accomplish our moral purpose: 'We cannot be truly human apart from communication ... to impede communication is to reduce people to the status of things' (Freire 1970: 123).

Conclusion

Schools involved in sincere efforts to broaden the base of leadership to include teachers and administrators, to define shared vision based on student learning, and to provide a culture of continual support, are much more likely to make great strides in becoming learning organizations and addressing critical student needs. Creating and sustaining PLCs is a journey as evidenced by the time and energy exerted to move schools from one phase to the next. The PLC tools facilitate an ongoing communication process of assessment and progress toward goals, fueled by supportive conditions that promote healthy conversations about teaching and learning. To reculture our schools, change cannot be separate and fragmented, but must be collaborative and embedded within the daily work to address the needs of students. To meet the diverse needs of students requires a change of attitudes and habits of action; thus change involves learning – learning through dialogue. Davis (2002) maintains the notion that community development is not an achievement or event, it is an *undertaking*. This undertaking requires resources, leadership, and continuous support to succeed as an inclusive school community. Learning evolves and must engage and nurture interdependent thinking in an environment where all people are connected and valued. People must be able to disclose their assumptions and viewpoints openly, without fear of sanctions and retribution. Thus, the development of a positive school culture is imperative. Without a doubt, learning communities centered around productive dialogue about student learning hold the key for student success.

References

Argyris, C. (1990) *Overcoming Organizational Defenses*. Needham, MS: Allyn and Bacon.
Bohm, D. (1996) *On Dialogue*. London: Routledge.
Cowan, D. and Hord, S. (1999) Reflections on school renewal and communities of continuous inquiry and improvement. Paper presented at the American Educational Research Association Annual Meeting, Montreal, Canada, April.
Davis Jr, O.L. (2002) Editorial on community, *Journal of Curriculum and Supervision*, 18(1): 1–3.
Freire, P. (1970) *Pedagogy of the Oppressed*. New York: Herder and Herder.
Fullan, M. (1985) Change processes and strategies at the local level, *Elementary School Journal*, 84(3): 391–420.

Fullan, M. (2000) The three stories of education reform, *Phi Delta Kappan*, 81(8): 581–4.

Fullan, M. (2005) *Leadership & Sustainability: System Thinkers in Action*. Thousand Oaks, CA: Corwin Press.

Hipp, K.A. and Huffman, J.B. (2002) Documenting and examining practices in creating learning communities: exemplars and non-exemplars. Paper presented at the American Educational Research Association Annual Conference, New Orleans, LA, April.

Hipp, K.K., Pankake, A.M., Olivier, D.F. and Huffman, J.B. (2004) Case studies: institutionalizing professional learning communities. Paper presented at the American Educational Research Association Annual Meeting, San Diego, California, April.

Hord, S.M. (1997) Professional learning communities: what are they are and why are they important? *Issues About Change*, 6(1): 1–8. Austin, TX: Southwest Educational Development Laboratory.

Huffman, J.B. and Hipp, K.K. (2003) Professional learning community organizer, in J.B. Huffman and K.K. Hipp (eds) *Reculturing Schools as Professional Learning Communities*. Lanham, MD: Scarecrow Press.

Olivier, D.F., Hipp, K.K. and Huffman, J.B. (2003) Professional learning community assessment, in J.B. Huffman and K.K. Hipp (eds) *Reculturing Schools as Professional Learning Communities*. Lanham, MD: Scarecrow Press.

Olivier, D.F., Pankake, A.M., Hipp, K.K., Cowan, D.F. and Huffman, J.B. (2005) Longitudinal study of two institutionalized PLCs: analyses of multiple variables within learning communities. Paper presented at the American Educational Research Association Annual Conference, Montreal, Canada, April.

Pankake, A.M. (1998) *Implementation: Making Things Happen*. Larchmont, NY: Eye on Education.

Patterson, K., Grenny, J., McMillan, R. and Switzler, A. (2002) *Crucial Conversations: Tools for Talking When Stakes are High*. New York: McGraw-Hill.

Senge, P., Cambron-McCabe, N., Lucas, T., Smith, B., Dutton, J. and Kleiner A. (2000) *Schools That Learn*. New York: Doubleday.

Senge, P., Kleiner, L., Roberts, C., Ross, R. and Smith, B. (1994) *The Fifth Discipline Fieldbook*. New York: Doubleday.

Wheatley, M.J. (2002) *Turning to One Another: Simple Conversations to Restore Hope to the Future*. San Francisco, CA: Berrett-Koehler.

ten

Transforming practice from within: the power of the professional learning community

Dorothy Andrews and Marian Lewis

Our fundamental challenges in Education ... involve ... cultural changes, and that will require collective learning. They involve people at multiple levels thinking together about significant and enduring solutions ... and then helping those solutions come about. (Senge, quoted in O'Neil 1995: 21)

Senge's quote captures the essence of current research on school improvement, namely, that whole-school approaches enhance school outcomes and the solutions to challenges for the future must be centered on dialogue and collective action by the professional community (Kruse *et al.* 1995; Louis and Marks 1998; Hipp 2004). Newmann *et al.* (2000) reported that the schools which demonstrated the highest student learning outcomes, even in areas of disadvantage, were those that were more focused in terms of their activities, where staff worked collaboratively sharing common goals and where staff had significant input into decision-making about their work.

This chapter reports on the experiences of Australian schools engaging with a process of school-wide revitalization known as Innovative Designs for Enhancing Achievement in Schools (IDEAS) (Crowther *et al.* 2002a) which centers on the work of teachers. The IDEAS process engages teachers in sharing purpose and developing identity. Teachers undertake a process of professional enquiry that enables them, through language and metaphor, to create systems of meaning which impact on their classroom practice and professional relationships. The professional capacity of teachers to improve school outcomes (such as student learning, relationships with the community, and the coherence of school operation) is enhanced.

Innovation Designs for Enhancing Achievement in Schools uses organization-wide processes to engage teachers in futuristic thinking and the creation of a shared approach to pedagogy, linking their personal pedagogical work with the work of the whole school (Andrews and Lewis 2004). The organization-wide processes enable groups of professionals to create understandings that could not easily be created by individuals. The process is managed by a school-based IDEAS management team and school-based facilitator/s. The school staff engages in collaborative learning in order to enhance the school's approach to teaching and learning, and to heighten the integration of teaching and learning with the school's vision, values and infrastructures.

The IDEAS process also recognizes the fundamental importance of teacher leadership in successful school revitalization (Crowther *et al.* 2002b). Teachers within the professional learning community are able to lead and mobilize their colleagues, engaging and influencing people throughout the organization. These processes of thinking and working together build the capacity of the professional community to add value to classroom and school-wide practices (Katzenmeyer and Moller 1996; Smylie and Hart 1999), improving teaching and learning as a result.

Teacher leaders in IDEAS schools engage with administrator leaders in collaborative action based on 'parallelism' that is characterized by a sense of shared purpose, mutualism and allowance for individual expression (Crowther *et al.* 2002b). Parallelism leads to alignment between the school's vision and teaching and learning practices, facilitating the development of a professional learning community, culture building and school-wide approaches to teaching and learning. It makes possible the enhancement of school identity, teachers' professional esteem, community support and students' achievements (Andrews and Crowther 2002).

As a result of their engagement in the organization-wide processes, teachers are actively involved in studying professional problems, making decisions about what to do, and committed to achieving results in implementing those decisions (Owens 2004). The professional community develops a school-wide pedagogy (SWP) that is: 'Agreed principles of teaching, learning and assessment that derive from highly successful classroom practices, take into account the distinctive needs of students and are grounded in authoritative educational theory' (Crowther *et al.* 2002a: 39). This focuses the work of teachers, and provides guidance for the development of the infrastructure and professional development that supports their work.

The research

Drawing on research by the University of Southern Queensland Leadership Research Institute research team[1] we illustrate the links between personal and school-wide pedagogical aspirations and illuminate the creation of shared meaning within the organization. It is this shared meaning that provides a foundation for culture building and the creation of an image of a preferred future. It is the shared purpose and focused pedagogical approach that results in enhanced student outcomes.

The two cases reported in this chapter have been selected from larger qualitative multi-case studies (Crowther and Andrews 2003; Lewis 2005) and draw on data from in-depth interviews with the principal and IDEAS team members, focus group sessions with other teachers and students, as well as documentation and data collected during their IDEAS involvement.

Newlyn Public School: professional learning community in challenging circumstances

Newlyn, a suburb of Sydney, Australia, is part of an area recognized for its high levels of disadvantage. Teachers' accounts of their experiences revealed a school with low achievement levels and significant behaviour issues in this 464 student school, particularly in upper primary. Some teachers had low expectations of what *these students* could achieve. There was little support for teachers, relationships were poor and staff turnover high. The enthusiasm of new teachers was dampened by these difficult conditions and their lack of voice. 'When I first came here, there was very much a deficit view of well we can't achieve anything with these kids. It was absolutely survival mode through the day' (Nina, Associate Principal, IDEAS Facilitator).

The process of change began with the appointment of a new principal who was prepared to confront the situation he found. Committed middle managers worked with the principal, united in the belief that the Newlyn students were capable of achieving better educational outcomes, despite their disadvantage. As an initial, short-term, response, the administration (school leaders) introduced a daily literacy block, imposing strict guidelines on literacy teaching. A required daily numeracy block subsequently followed. While these initial steps resulted in positive change, the administration team recognized that effective school-wide change needed to be owned and driven by teachers.

Coincidentally, the school was given the opportunity to participate in IDEAS. Two middle managers, Julia (the deputy principal) and Nina (an associate principal) seized the opportunity, seeing IDEAS as a vehicle for achieving broad-based change. The shift in leadership relationships, from top-down imposition to mutualism, began with the formation of the IDEAS team, a group of classroom teachers who worked with Julia and Nina (the designated IDEAS facilitators) to manage the change process in the school. Starting out as a small group, the IDEAS team grew. Attendance at IDEAS meetings was voluntary and while there was stable core of members, the group was fluid, involving close to half of the 38 teachers in the school.

Developing a framework for action

The facilitators, working with the teachers in the IDEAS team, engaged the staff in the processes of inquiry that lead to the creation of the Newlyn pedagogical framework: a shared vision, underpinned by shared teacher, student and parent values, and a schoolwide pedagogy (Figure 10.1). The vision is full of meaning for the school, capturing the future the Newlyn school community collectively aspires to create. The underpinning values work with the vision to set the direction while the school-wide pedagogy provides the way for the school to build the future that has been envisaged.

Teachers talk of this framework as providing a clear direction and sense of common purpose, 'allowing us to have our own way of teaching but we

Vision:	Making Connections: Learning for Life
Underpinning values	Lifelong learning Respect Individual needs Care Connecting Fun
Schoolwide pedagogy (extract)	■ Be consistent with common routines and practices that span grades and stages so that students know what to expect and how to participate ■ Acknowledge and build on language and literature as the fundamental tools for learning ■ Hold high expectations of students and teachers ■ Encompass explicit teaching of social skills and problem solving ■ Ensure that teaching and learning is enjoyable for all participants ■ Facilitate the development of positive, caring relationships ■ Promote student engagement through providing opportunities for meaningful negotiation and student choice ■ Provide a relevant and inclusive curriculum with explicit links to real-life contexts

Figure 10.1 Newlyn Public School pedagogical framework

are all going in the one direction' (Ben, teacher, IDEAS team). It constitutes the 'Newlyn way': 'It's something that is pervasive … it is a way of thinking' (Peter, teacher, IDEAS team).

The SWP principles listed in Figure 10.1 are extracted from a longer list, the level of detail reflecting the importance the IDEAS team placed on keeping the meaning of the agreed pedagogical principles explicit. The imposition of the literacy block in 2002 had begun the key process of *embedding explicit teaching* and *common routines* across the school. Building on this, the IDEAS team developed a common planning format, giving greater consistency to programming across the school (Nina) and a sense of common expectations (Peter).

An important group of pedagogical principles address student engagement in their learning. Disengagement, especially at the upper primary level, was reflected in poor behaviour. The SWP recognized that teaching and learning needed to be enjoyable, have explicit links to real-life contexts and provide for student negotiation and choice. Some principles, for example those relating to high expectations and the development of caring and positive relationships, were being addressed simultaneously, as part of the whole thrust of pedagogical change and working towards the vision. The IDEAS team planned to address all the principles over time.

New ways of working

The pedagogical framework gave the school a new purpose and direction. Its development and implementation engaged teachers in inquiry processes that impacted on how they worked together and on their classroom practice. The experience and success of their collective endeavors also significantly increased teacher confidence and shared commitment to whole school change. Working with these processes, teachers embraced pedagogic leadership, having their say and making decisions about teaching and learning (Susie, teacher, IDEAS team). The IDEAS team gained in confidence to the extent that they began to solve problems and were trusted by the principal to make decisions about how to move forward with the process (Petrea, teacher, IDEAS team). This represented a significant shift from 'the top telling us what to do' to being 'a classroom teacher in a position where you can have an influence on what the whole school is doing' (Susie). Increased teacher confidence extended beyond the IDEAS team – as the collective development of the pedagogical framework and ongoing implementation of the SWP meant that there was a broad based understanding of 'the Newlyn way' (IDEAS focus group). This allowed teachers to talk about their pedagogy from a basis of shared understanding.

Through inquiring into and making decisions about their practice, teachers developed a sense of shared responsibility for bringing about change and were as committed as the administration to having a good school, with good results. As Peter noted: 'I think we are all empowered ... all leaders ... we are all stakeholders.' The IDEAS team meetings, open to all staff, provided a forum for professional dialogue where everyone could speak freely (John, teacher, IDEAS team). This model of teacher-driven change in classroom practice was quite different from the earlier administrator driven change, and, as Julia reflected, more likely to succeed.

Changes to classroom practice

The development of a school-wide pedagogy and the ongoing in-depth discussions about teaching and learning, impacted on individual teacher practice in a range of ways. The SWP prompted teachers to question the effectiveness of their classroom practice (John). Recently graduated teachers seemed comfortable with the pedagogical principles, seeing 'the things we learned about at university really do get put into practice' (Lorraine, teacher). Another said she was really inspired – and 'this stuff is what I personally believe anyway' (Georgie, teacher, IDEAS team). Some more experienced teachers felt affirmed (Debbie, teacher, IDEAS team) and some talked about their reflections on classroom practice: 'I do believe that kids need to take responsibility for their own learning but I hadn't gone that next step to actually implement it into the classroom ... I'm doing that now' (Ben).

Teachers linked their greater awareness of classroom practices to improved student behaviour, with more productive activities and greater focus on learning reducing student frustration levels. 'We had kids on ledges, jumping off roofs, stuck in trees and all sorts of stuff. Since we changed our approach to learning, they are more interested in staying in the classroom' (Georgie). 'Teachers are questioning their own pedagogy ... [and] the spill over effect is that behaviour problems have decreased significantly' (Debbie).

The SWP did not necessarily reflect everyone's personal pedagogy – but the recognition that previous practice was not working motivated change and the explicit pedagogical principles provided a basis for moving forward. The SWP highlighted practice that worked at Newlyn (John) and while some teachers felt uneasy changing their classroom practice: 'the fact that our whole school has adopted this has made them feel more comfortable in taking risks to actually try it ... I think they are actually getting better results and feeling more and more comfortable in doing it' (Georgie).

Better relationships with increased collegiality and high levels of trust occurred as a result of the types and level of engagement in the processes of change. Some teachers, however, were not prepared to adopt the Newlyn vision and pedagogy, and a number of teachers opted to transfer to other schools rather than change in this way.

Early indications of positive change

Newlyn tracked individual student progress in literacy and numeracy, keeping a centralized record of achievement. Data from the Basic Skills Test (BST), administered to students in Year 3 and Year 5, had shown some improvement over the years, but the school was only matching the general improvements across the state. Newlyn needed 'not only to improve but ... to improve at an accelerated rate' (Julia). The most recent results indicated that Newlyn student were catching up with other students across the state – a change which the principal linked to pedagogical change: 'We have had huge growth ... especially in the last 12 months in regards to our teaching and learning practices ... The staff are ... making decisions that affect teaching and learning. They are realizing that they have a huge impact on children's learning.'

A re-administration of the IDEAS teacher survey at the end of 2003 indicated significant improvements in every area, particularly better relationships and improved pedagogy. Significant changes in classroom practice impacted on student behaviour, their enjoyment of learning and learning achievements. As Nina reflected 'it is a totally different school'.

Despite all that has been achieved, Newlyn remains a very challenging environment. 'This is a tough school ... but ... now we are making a difference and we are getting results. Our kids are improving, the behaviour is improving and our results are improving' (Julia).

Sustaining the changes

At the end of 2003, a number of teachers had decided to move on. The 2004 school year begin with 14 new classroom teachers. Systems were in place, however, to share the meaning embedded in the pedagogical framework with these new teachers, bringing them into the 'Newlyn way'. These included a thorough initial orientation and ongoing professional development, mentoring, collegial planning and mutual support – strategies all supported by the coherence across school structures. The IDEAS team, renamed the Teaching and Learning Committee, began to coordinate curriculum and professional development activities, guided by their vision of Making Connections: Learning for Life, and keeping 'the bigger picture' in mind (IDEAS focus group).

Laurelvale State Primary School: building on success

> We have chosen to work this way, we feel empowered and we have confidence in our own practice. We work together – we plan, test children, organise class groups, use focused teaching and teach across grades. (IDEAS focus group)

Laurelvale State Primary School caters for 600 students and has 33 long-serving and experienced teachers. Located in regional Queensland, the school has a proud history of achievements in academic, sporting and cultural spheres. According to state-wide data this was ranked as a successful school. However, all was not well as recent changes in local demographics were beginning to have an impact and as Steven, the principal, reflected that it was 'time to renew'. Deciding that IDEAS was to be the vehicle for renewal, the school began its journey in March, 2001, led by a school-based facilitator (Patricia), and managed by an IDEAS team of 12 self-nominated staff, including the principal.

In 2003, the IDEAS team reported on what they had achieved over the period by building a journey board to highlight the important stages in their 'journey to revitalization' (see Figure 10.2). They had also developed a vision and schoolwide pedagogy (see Figure 10.3), then used these artifacts to take informed action. The capacity developed within the professional community during the process of creating the vision and SWP enabled the teachers to build on their existing practices, add in new ways of working and develop focused action to enhance student learning outcomes in writing

Figure 10.2 The Laurelvale journey

Vision Statement	*Together we achieve the extraordinary*
Together	We … co-operate, communicate, support
We Achieve	We … are all learners, are responsible, are adaptable
the Extraordinary	We … take risks, celebrate success, strive for excellence

Figure 10.3   The vision and school-wide pedagogy

The school survey results indicated strong support by all staff, parents and students. In essence, Laurelvale was a very good school by any standards. But concerns were also identified, namely:

- The lack of a vision that provided the school community with inspiration and direction.
- Teachers' concern that school planning processes were not sufficiently inclusive.
- A shared concern of students and teachers that physical infrastructures were inhibiting effective teaching and learning.
- The lack of a shared approach to teaching and learning – a schoolwide pedagogy.
- Concern over some students' achievement and engagement in learning.

Exploration of school systemic data also provided challenges, in particular, writing literacy and use of computers across the curriculum.

Figure 10.4   The school report

literacy. 'This sense of shared purpose has been enabled by a process that has given us the opportunity and capacity to talk together' (Patricia). The 2001 school's survey results (see Figure 10.4) confirmed the situation at that time and action was taken to address the concerns that were raised.

However, by 2003 the school survey results for staff items indicated a significant improvement in all these concerns. These results, along with other evidence, indicated that both the principal and the professional community had addressed the survey challenges. In addition, staff interviewed reported that involvement in IDEAS had resulted in the development of a cohesive and dynamic professional community, focused on professional inquiry to resolve issues and solve problems. As the teacher focus group commented: 'we were able to identify the sorts of things that were important to us as a school community, including the importance of working together, achievement for all students and the importance of building a culture that strives for *excellence*'.

They also reported significant improvement in student outcomes and motivation. The teachers agreed to focus their action on writing literacy and in particular, boys' writing literacy. As they reflected: 'Writing had been an area of concern for the school community for several years. This, combined with the systems requirement that every school develop a literacy strategy, prompted us to continue the search for literacy solutions.'

The initiatives were developed and implemented by teachers in consultation with outside experts who were invited into the school to work with the professional community through shared action. Patricia reflected:

> We implemented a series of strategies to measure the effects of the pedagogical practices that we had generated through our SWP in relation to the introduced literacy program. We had people come along that could help us with skills and knowledge that we needed and as the literacy initiative unfolded the teachers began keeping work samples to show growth of children's writing. This practice has been continued to this day.

Evidence of improved student involvement and achievements appear in the statistics on writing that show significant improvement in participation, with 38 published and winning articles in 2003 compared to ten in 2001 as well as winning awards for writing at a national level. The 2003 state-wide standardized testing also demonstrated significant improvement in writing in students from Year 3 to Year 5. This was most notable for students in the lower 25 per cent of the state and particularly the results for boys. However, as Patricia pointed out: '[the] ... current data indicate that the more gifted have not enhanced their outcomes to the same extent. Other challenges are improvement in higher order thinking skills and integration of computers across the curriculum'.

Factors contributing to success

Successful change in the school could be attributed to a number of factors, including the development of clear strategic intent, use of professional conversation strategies and embedding the vision and SWP into practice. Through their conversations about the vision, the teachers developed a shared commitment to the future direction of the school: 'we argued about words, we struggled to reach consensus. We spent a great deal of time on the necessity for the vision statement to relate to teaching and learning. This reinforced the need for the vision statement to have meaning for students, for parents and for school staff' (Patricia).

Once the vision statement was developed it was used to build an understanding of the meaning of *together*, *achieve* and *excellence* in classrooms. 'The words were important as they identified the sorts of things that were important to us as a school community' (John, IDEAS team). In

2003 both teachers and students reflected on what it feels like to teach and learn 'extraordinary things together':

> It creates an environment that is exciting and diverse. We believe in what we do and we find that kids respond to the new teaching and learning principles. We need a plan together and we are drawing on experts to help us ... it takes us out of our comfort zone and we want to improve our skills as a teacher. This is having an impact on kids. (Mary, teacher)

> Some people are good at some things and some at others – when you put it all together we achieve great things. (Year 5 student focus group)

Developing a focus around pedagogy required a high level of engagement and commitment to resolving differences through dialogue. The IDEAS team used skilful discussion and focused conversation to build teacher capacity to have these important discussions: 'It would also hopefully encourage openness and teamwork, build trust, and help us move in a positive direction' (Sally, IDEAS team).

The IDEAS team also found ways to embed the vision and SWP principles into the practice of individual teachers. This required time and allowance for experimentation as well as ongoing collegial and expert support:

> The IDEAS Team ran meetings focusing on what SWP meant and how it related to teachers' beliefs about teaching – their own personal pedagogy ... We discussed possible ways to mentor and to share information. We also undertook a focused conversation on linking school-wide pedagogy to personal pedagogy. (Patricia)

Once the vision and SWP were created, the professional community, led by the facilitator and several IDEAS team members worked with the staff to develop a literacy strategy to improve writing literacy. When they needed to draw on external expertise they negotiated with the literacy expert about how their 'package' might enhance current teaching practice and meet the needs of the Laurelvale students. The IDEAS team also developed strategies to keep all staff informed: 'we also sought feedback at staff meetings from teachers who were trialling the literacy initiative in their classrooms. These early discussions would lead to what we call "staff meeting snapshots" providing teachers with an opportunity to share what was working in their rooms' (Sally).

Other factors also influenced these positive changes in the school. A new-found confidence was noticeable in the school, along with a growing awareness that practice was improving.

> We realize now that we can do it ourselves ... we have the confidence in the staff that we can do it together. (Rebecca, IDEAS team)

> People have come to accept that you can do extraordinary things without anxiety if you go about it the right way. The professional development activities, the conferences and breakfasts show teachers that developmental work can be fun, can be relaxing, not tedious. Also, as a school we are now able to say, 'If a new imperative from outside doesn't fit, abandon it'. That has helped us get a sense of ownership. (Steven, principal)

An indication of changing practice is provided by the following quotes from a range of teachers who participated in a focus group discussion:

> I am a traditional teacher and still am. I have been prepared to have a go at the literacy initiative and I have made more changes to my teaching in the last two years than I have for the whole of my career. We share, get expert support and work and plan together. [We] see other people's strengths that add value to our work.

> Teaching has changed, just the way you work with kids. Negotiating and listening, they are coming up with the ideas, working with kids in a different way.

> The use of data (student literacy achievement) has enabled the teachers to search for enhanced coherence in the school and to speak with authority about their work.

As teachers' ways of working changed, demands developed for the principal to address another issue, originally raised in the 2001 survey: the need for refurbishment of the physical environment. Coincidentally, the principal had received refurbishment funding but had held off making a decision to use these funds until the professional community was clear about what was needed to support new classroom practice. It was now time to act. This time, decision-making about refurbishment became a collaborative effort with decisions readily reached about what was needed.

This reflects the kind of parallel leadership that has been a constant feature of the Laurelvale journey. The principal, after initially providing the opportunity to become involved in IDEAS, stepped back and enabled others to take the lead in the areas of literacy and subsequent professional development. He engaged the broader community in the visioning dialogue and has communicated ongoing successes. In 2003 the school gained national recognition of its substantial success by winning one of the Australian school excellence awards. Teacher leadership has taken a range of forms, but has featured the facilitator and IDEAS team members most particularly. The change from 'within' has been the result of the principal and the professional community taking on responsibility to: 'build on what already were the school strengths ... [and go] from good to great'.

Conclusion

The two cases illustrate the power of the professional community to transform their school from within. These primary schools are dissimilar in many ways, yet both are examples of how the professional community of a school can come together to create an image of their desired future and share the responsibility for working towards its realization. In both of the schools, the professional community created a pedagogical framework that provided sense of purpose, a clear direction for the future and shared understanding of the kinds of pedagogical practice that would lead to success. In both, there was broad-based commitment to change and shared responsibility for action. Both schools used the organizational change processes embedded in IDEAS as a vehicle for achieving outcomes that grew out of their collective aspirations. At Newlyn Public School the aspiration was to lift learning levels and improve their life chances of their students. At Laurelvale State Primary School, in a context of high achievement, the focus was more specifically improving literacy outcomes, in particular for the lower achieving boys.

While Newlyn and Laurelvale had different reasons for engaging in processes of whole-school revitalization and, in a sense, made different journeys, their experiences illustrate important aspects of these change processes. Both of the cases indicate the power of school-wide change from within the organization, through engagement in processes that:

- motivate teachers, inspiring them to change, and provide a vehicle for that change regardless of the school's starting point and aspiration;
- take a whole-school view of change, both in organization-wide processes and in shared responsibility for school improvement;
- are non-threatening and add value to existing successful practice;
- allow for the collective development of a system of shared meaning, using a 'language' that everyone understands. This both allows everyone to enter into the conversation and provides an explicit guide to action;
- connect teachers in deep conversations about pedagogy – exploring successful personal and shared (schoolwide) pedagogy that is contextualized and leads to ongoing inquiry into different dimensions of pedagogy;
- involve teachers in professional inquiry into practice;
- change the leadership dynamics in the school, with teachers taking on pedagogical leadership roles within the professional community;

- build the confidence and the capacity of the professional community to take responsibility for school improvement, to engage in probing conversations about practice, solve problems and make decisions.

A reading of this list clearly indicates the central role played by the professional community in these change processes. In IDEAS, while there is no expectation that all teachers will be leaders, people are encouraged to step forward, volunteering to take leadership roles. The IDEAS team, grounded in the broader professional community of the school, works with the in-school facilitator/s to manage the change process, motivating others and using professional conversations to engage colleagues in dialogue about their practice. In both the cases the previous ways of working were proving ineffective (for different reasons and to different degrees). Working with IDEAS, the teacher leaders were able to mobilize the professional community to create and work with new practice in the classroom.

In both cases the principal took on a metastrategic role. The principals assessed the situation they found and took decisive action to begin the process of change. Both then stepped back and allowed the IDEAS team, with the facilitator/s, to manage the process. At Newlyn, the principal was kept informed of the developments and fully supported the direction and nature of the change; he worked with his leadership team to make infrastructural changes that embedded the new vision and SWP. Similarly, at Laurelvale, the school did not rely on the principal to lead pedagogical reforms. In both schools, but particularly at Laurelvale, the principal had a significant role in communicating the new identity being generated within the school, to the school community. In both schools, the principal remained connected with the process of change but did not control it. This is a way of working that can be very challenging to a principal.

In both schools, the professional community was concerned with improving student learning. The pedagogical changes were grounded in an understanding of the students' needs, and a recognition that previous pedagogical approaches are no longer effective. The issues, once identified, were addressed by developing new approaches in classrooms, the outcomes of which are reflected in current student data. This data indicates improvement in student engagement and in learning outcomes.

The responsibility for change was school-wide in both schools. Challenges have been faced by the whole community and a way forward created – built on success. At Newlyn, the transformation is easy to discern with teachers themselves reporting that the school is 'a totally different place'. The transformation at Laurelvale is more subtle. In both schools, however, teachers have changed the way they view their work and have gained in confidence. Teachers work together in new ways, responding to challenges by collectively seeking solutions and developing new approaches that better meet the needs of their students. Significantly, both have reported impact on student engagement and learning.

Note

1   The Leadership Research Institute team consists of Professor Frank Crowther, Dr Dorothy Andrews, Dr Marian Lewis, and associates Allan Morgan, Mark Dawson and Joan Conway.

References

Andrews, D. and Crowther, F. (2002) Parallel leadership: a clue to the contents of the 'black box' of school reform, *International Journal of Educational Management*, 15(4): 152–9.

Andrews, D. and Lewis, M. (2004) Building sustainable futures: emerging understandings of the significant contribution of the professional learning community, *Improving Schools*, 7(2): 129–50.

Crowther, F. and Andrews, D. (2003) *From Conceptual Frameworks to Improved School Practice: Exploring DETYA's Innovation and Best Practice Project Outcomes in Queensland Schools*. ARC SPIRT Grant Report to Australian Government Department of Education Science and Training, Canberra. www.dest.gov.au/highered/respub.htm, accessed 5 July 2005.

Crowther, F., Andrews, D., Dawson, M. and Lewis, M. (2002a) *IDEAS Facilitation Folder*. Leadership Research Institute, University of Southern Queensland. Brisbane: Education Queensland.

Crowther, F., Kaagan, S., Ferguson, M. and Hann, L. (2002b) *Developing Teacher Leaders: How Teacher Leadership Enhances School Success*. CA: Corwin Press.

Hipp, K. (2004) Teacher leadership: illustrating practices reflective of schools engaged in purposeful efforts to create and sustain learning communities, *Leading & Managing*, 10(2): 54–69.

Katzenmeyer, M. and Moller, G. (1996) *Awakening the Sleeping Giant: Leadership Development for Teachers*. Thousand Oaks, CA: Corwin Press.

Kruse, S., Louis, K. and Bryk, K. (1995) Analysing school-based professional community, in Karen S. Louis and Sharon D. Kruse (eds) *Professionalism and Community: Perspectives on Reforming Urban Schools*. Thousand Oaks, CA: Corwin.

Lewis, M. (2005) Teachers reimaging their professional practice: the implementation of school-based pedagogical frameworks. *Early Career Research Project: Final Report*. Toowoomba: University of Southern Queensland.

Louis, K.S. and Marks, H. (1998) Does professional community affect the classroom? Teachers' work and student experiences in restructuring schools, *American Journal of Education*, 106(4): 532–75.

Newmann, F., King, M.B. and Youngs, P. (2000) *Professional Development to*

Build Organizational Capacity in Low Achieving Schools: Promising Strategies and Future Challenges. Madison, WI: University of Wisconsin-Madison, Center on Organization and Restructuring of Schools.

O'Neil, J. (1995) On schools as learning organizations: a conversation with Peter Senge, *Educational Leadership*, 52(7): 20–2.

Owens, R.G. (2004) *Organizational Behaviour in Education*. 8th edn. Boston, MA: Pearson.

Smylie, M. and Hart, A. (1999) School leadership for teacher learning and change – a human and social capital development perspective, in J. Murphy and K. Seashore Louis (eds) *Handbook on Research on Educational Administration*. San Francisco, CA: Jossey-Bass, pp. 421–41.

Part 3

Dilemmas

Developing professional learning communities, like any serious change effort, is beset with dilemmas. The authors of the chapters in this section describe three particularly pressing challenges, offering rays of hope for addressing these dilemmas.

It is well charted that school improvement is much more complex for secondary schools. Milbrey McLaughlin and Joan Talbert (Chapter 11), from their extensive experience of studying professional learning communities in American high schools, explain the particular challenges they face as well as highlighting a number of practices that support professional learning communities.

The issue of social capital underpins successful collaborations and partnerships. Bill Mulford (Chapter 12) reviews the literature on bonding social capital within schools, bridging social capital between schools and linking social capital between schools and their communities, concluding that there is a developmental sequence to building what he describes as 'social professional learning communities'.

Andy Hargreaves (Chapter 13) cautions that the sustainability of 'professional learning communities' is in danger because of distortion of their original meaning. Drawing on findings of his research in the USA and Canada, he sets out seven principles of more sustainable learning communities, challenging readers to revisit the principles that underlie their own professional learning communities.

eleven

Building professional learning communities in high schools: challenges and promising practices

Milbrey W. McLaughlin and Joan E. Talbert

A decade ago, the National Association of Secondary School Principals (NASSP 1996) issued an influential report on the status of America's high schools, *Breaking Ranks: Changing an American Institution*. Professional learning communities (PLCs) formed the heart of the NASSP blueprint for high school reform: 'every high school will be a learning community for teachers and the other professionals it employs' and 'each educator will create a personal learning plan' (ibid.: 63).

Yet, despite compelling evidence about the value of a PLC, communities of practice of the stripe imagined by this blue ribbon panel remain exceptions in the landscape of American high schools – be they large, small, wealthy, poor, culturally diverse or homogeneous. For example, a survey conducted by Public Agenda in 2002 found that only one in five high school teachers said that they 'regularly meet to share ideas about lesson plans and methods of instruction' (Public Agenda 2002: 23). Such professional practices to support teachers' ongoing learning and instructional improvement are rare.

At the most general level, the tasks of building and sustaining high school professional learning communities are no different from those for elementary and middle schools: creating a culture that prompts teachers to critically reflect on their practice and the infrastructure necessary to support their collective use of data to improve teaching and learning. However, high schools present particular, interrelated challenges to building and sustaining professional learning communities.

Challenges to developing high school professional learning communities

Structural impediments to teachers' professional learning communities have received the most attention from reformers and researchers. The complex organizational structure of comprehensive high schools and subject department boundaries mitigate efforts to build whole-school learning communities (Fullan and Hargreaves 1991; Siskin and Little 1995). High school teachers' work structure – five classes of 50 minutes and around 130 students each day – means that time for collaboration is in short supply. Paperwork, classroom management tasks, and multiple course preparations draw teachers' time and energy away from getting to know students personally and working with colleagues on instruction. The anomic environment found in most large, comprehensive high schools undermines motivation and support for a professional learning community devoted to improving all students' learning.

High school leadership differs in critical ways from conditions in most elementary and many middle schools. Functioning as what one high school principal dubbed 'the mayor of a small city,' secondary school administrators (leaders) are hard pressed to provide instructional leadership across myriad subjects of the high school curriculum or to serve as a model for inquiry, risk-taking and professional learning.

The *professional culture* of high schools presents the most difficult challenge of all. Traditional norms of high school teaching – teaching subjects rather than students – shape teachers' conceptions of their professional responsibilities and attitudes toward students. In one high school we studied, for example, when commenting on the high failure rate of their students in math, teachers consistently responded with some version of 'I've got my standards' and little empathy or sense of responsibility for students who were not successful. To this point, Public Agenda (2002: 23) found that only two in five high school teachers had 'high expectations for the students and (push) them to do their very best.' Most respondents said that teachers just pass on marginal students, and one in three teachers in large high schools and one in five in small high schools said: 'too many teachers are just going through the motions.'

A pervasive *culture of student disrespect for teachers* in America's high schools breeds violence, cheating and discipline problems. For example, only 16 per cent of students in large high schools and 22 per cent in small high schools said students treat teachers with respect (Public Agenda 2002: 19). Student attitudes, combined with perceived lack of supports and resources for teaching their diverse students, depress teachers' professional commitment and spirit: four out of five high school teachers across high schools of all types say morale is low (ibid.: 23). The benefits of a PLC comprise a hard sell in such an institutional context. Lacking the experience of working in a strong school community, most high school teachers do not see student respect and motivation as tied to the professional culture of the school.[1]

External contexts also influence professional community. High stakes accountability systems that press for immediate test score gains in literacy and mathematics affect high school teachers' choices as they do their colleagues at elementary and middle school levels. For high school teachers, though, this policy context often fosters competition among departments and exacerbates performance issues associated with students who enter high schools lacking basic literacy skills. These factors, too, create disincentives for teachers to spend time critically reflecting on practice, collaborating with colleagues across the school, or investing in professional growth. While such challenges for change are quite well understood, the literature offers few examples of strategies and practices effective in building high school learning communities. Studies of PLC in high schools typically feature extraordinary subject departments with strong teacher leaders (McLaughlin and Talbert 2001), yet knowledge about how to develop such communities on a larger scale – across units within a school and across schools – requires studies of the rare high schools that have built school-wide learning community. Our research on reforming high schools identified a few such schools that are the focus of this chapter. Their experiences offer evidence of practices that can change the professional culture of American high schools.

Evidence to support case studies of high school learning communities

We draw upon ten years of research on high schools involved in the Bay Area School Reform Collaborative (BASRC), a reform initiative focused on building school-wide professional communities that use data to guide continuous improvement efforts.[2] Our primary data source was a two-year intensive study of reforming Bay Area high schools conducted from 1999 to 2001. Here we report teacher survey data for a broad sample of 27 BASRC schools to locate high schools in relation to other grade levels on several measures of professional community and culture.

For our study of reforming high schools, we selected case study sites that had a reputation for engaging in whole-school reform; all are distinguished by their commitment to building school-wide learning community to improve student outcomes. From a pool of Bay Area high schools that met this criterion, we selected ten schools that represented a range of student demographics and organization designs and that worked with a variety of the external reform support organizations. During the two years of our research in the ten schools, we used multiple research methods: interviews, observations, student and teacher focus groups, and a teacher survey and student record data. Based on initial data collected in all ten schools, we identified three high schools with strong learning communities for more intensive case studies.

Locating high schools on professional community indicators

Consistent with broader literature, high schools involved in BASRC were weaker than elementary schools on all measures of reform culture used in our study – teacher learning community, inquiry practices, and use of nontraditional student assessment instruments (see Figure 11.1). High schools were also weaker than middle schools on two of these measures, while teachers in all grade levels showed low levels of collaboration inside their classrooms.

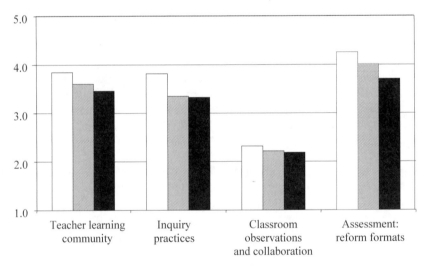

□ Elementary schools (243 teachers in 13 schools)
▨ Middle schools (86 teachers in 5 schools)
■ High schools (375 teachers in 9 schools)

Figure 11.1   School reform culture and instruction: grade level differences

Although high schools are generally weak on measures of teacher learning community, our research on reforming high schools challenges the contention that high schools are intractable structures and fundamentally inhospitable environments for building professional learning communities. We found examples of vibrant professional learning communities, and positive responses to the institutional and normative challenges sketched

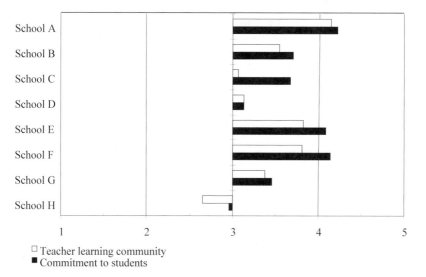

Figure 11.2 Case study school differences: teacher learning community and commitment to students

above. We also saw that professional learning communities sat at the heart of high school reform and that they go hand in hand with teachers' commitment to students.

Teacher surveys revealed considerable variation in strength of learning communities across the reforming high schools in our sample. Schools A, E, and F stand out as particularly strong teacher learning communities, on the basis of our field observations as well as survey data (see Figure 11.2). In these schools, teachers felt supported and encouraged to take risks. Teachers learned new practices, tried them in their classroom, reflected on their successes and challenges, and then shared their reflections with other teachers. Teachers also observed one another and offered feedback. They collaborated with colleagues both within and across departments and grade (year) levels. As a teacher in one school explained: 'I'm watching people who've taught for years and years and years suddenly experience change – see things differently, see it in a new light, work differently, collaborate in a way that I've never seen work before.'

However, in schools with weaker communities, notably Schools C, D, and H, professional learning was not a collective endeavor, but rather was viewed as an individual responsibility. In turn, commitment to students was relatively weak and variable across the faculty. The school-wide community was a place where announcements were made and administrative issues were addressed. Attempts to create a stronger professional community through required activities, like mandated use of BASRC's cycle of inquiry protocol, resulted in 'contrived collegiality' instead of genuine collaboration (Hargreaves 1994). Leadership strategies and professional practices in these schools contrasted sharply with those in Schools A, E, and F and helped to illuminate the effective community-building practices we describe here.

Locating reforming high schools on student outcome trends

The three high schools strongest in professional learning community showed steady improvement on the state's SAT-9 assessments over a three-year period, exceeding the slight growth trend for Bay Area high schools. Notably, all of the reforming high schools we studied outperformed the typical high school in the region, except for the school weakest in professional learning community (School D). These data suggest that, despite the considerable range of professional cultures represented in our sample, reforming high schools' efforts to increase collaboration and reflective practice were paying off in improved student achievement. The high schools most advanced in developing learning communities had been changing their professional cultures long before 1998 and most likely would show stronger gains if prior data points for SAT-9 assessments were available.[3]

Practices that support professional learning communities in high schools

The high school professional learning communities in our study stood out for their commitment to use evidence of student learning and achievement gaps to focus instructional improvement efforts. Teachers in these schools shared responsibility for ensuring that all students met grade level standards in subject areas, and they worked together to design strategies, materials, and practices to achieve this goal.

Through collaboration on common work, teachers in these high schools developed new knowledge to improve their instruction and were strategic about bringing in expert support from outside the school. They reflected on their practice, individually and together, and used evidence of student learning to design and evaluate interventions to address learning differentials among student groups. Through this process, teachers created shared language and standards for their practice, within and across subjects. They sustained the evolving school culture and communities of practice by recruiting and mentoring new teachers with a focus on the school norms of learning, collaboration, and collective responsibility.

How did these school communities overcome the significant obstacles to building PLCs in high schools? Our analysis of community building in these schools highlights organizational strategies and practices that brought about change in professional culture over time.

Developing broad leadership

Redesigning leadership to promote PLC meant not only changing the role of the principal from business manager to instructional leader, but it also meant distributing the leadership across multiple units and actors. As one principal commented: 'The day of principal control is gone.' Principals effective in building and sustaining PLCs capitalized on teachers' knowledge and expertise and were strategic about building teacher leadership. As one principal explained: 'You have to be intuitive enough to recognize the right strengths in people and in figuring out ways to place them where they can impact whole-school change and not just classroom change.' For example, one principal asked an experienced English teacher, who had received a great deal of literacy training and had an excellent rapport with the staff, to fill the newly created role of a school-wide literacy coach. The principal of another school set up mini-grants that allowed teachers to be in charge of projects. In another high school, the principal tapped teachers for a planning team that was responsible for designing and conducting teaching and learning study groups. In a high school structured according to a house system, the principal created 'house leaders' as new leadership opportunities for teachers. These strategies for expanding teacher leadership hooked teachers into reform and professional learning; they also established a leadership pipeline that supported PLCs in the face of staff or administrative turnover.

Engaging student voices

Expanded leadership also included students in diverse roles – as part of governing committees, as part of the school's inquiry process, as collaborators with teacher communities working to develop reform solutions. Where student voice was more than pro forma, teachers found student perceptions and insight invaluable to their own learning and reflection. Resulting change in school culture was significant. For example, one educator told us: 'it seemed like this kind of wildfire thing happened where the kids who were involved started just dropping by to give opinions and were pushing to get the next meeting happening.' Students subsequently created a formal student team and students assisted in creating a bilingual tutoring and translation service that assists teachers and students during the school day. Students comment positively on their new relationships with teachers. For instance, students at one school reported feeling more connected to both adults and fellow students and felt that their involvement helped them to work better with others. Teachers also have seen changes in school culture and morale. One said:

> I think it makes me a much better teacher. They echo absolutely everything that [we] have talked about in terms of in dismay at different situations, staff wise, and resource wise, and everything else wise ... It's always wonderful to see them be caring too because sometimes the sense of apathy can be overwhelming ... their keen awareness, as well as their excitement and willingness and desire to make things better, is a good shot in the arm.

Developing communication and collaboration across department boundaries

In our sample of reforming high schools, departments were the primary focus of reform work, as might be expected in contemporary high schools. Teachers' survey reports on teacher learning community, inquiry practices, classroom observations and collaboration, and use of reform assessments vary more between departments within school than between schools (see Table 11.1). This is particularly the case for instructional reform practices and teacher collaboration in classrooms. The data also indicate that schools vary in the extent to which they set conditions for learning community development both within and across departments, seen earlier in Figure 11.1 as school differences in overall strength of community.

Schools that developed broad teacher learning community did so in part by engendering cross-department communication and teacher collaboration

Table 11.1   Locus of differences in teaching practice

	School effect	Subject effect*	Department effect**
School reform culture			
Teacher learning community	+		+
Commitment to students	+		+
Classroom observations and collaboration		+	+
Reform instruction			
Student discourse and reflection		+	+
Reform assessments format		+	+
Reform outcomes		+	+

Notes:
* Mathematics (−)
** Controlling for school and subject

around school reform work. They created mutually supportive relationships between the interdisciplinary school community and individual department professional communities. One reform coordinator in a weak school community described how the *absence* of this sense of school-wide purpose undermined reform progress: 'It's like somebody trying to put together a recipe, and a bunch of people adding in all their stuff and the meal stinks because everybody's putting in their own two cents.' A school-wide professional community eliminates the myriad unconnected activities typical of comprehensive high schools and aligns the efforts of the entire school community to improve student engagement and achievement.

Several factors enabled teachers to move beyond their department's work to see reform as 'our work, the whole school's.' One school designed their instructional and advising system to cut across department boundaries – a structural response most possible in a smaller high school. The large comprehensive high schools in our sample also managed to develop community at the school level, however. Critical was an expressed, common mission and faculty commitment to it. One school's faculty was animated by their passion to 'disprove conventional wisdom' about the potential and achievement of poor youth of color. They joined the school because of this mission and devoted long hours to addressing its challenges. Other reforming high schools' faculties were united by a focus on literacy. In these schools, the English department led the reform that engaged teachers from several departments as they began to see how students' literacy affected outcomes in their subject area.

Aligning and creating standards offered opportunities for meaningful collaboration within and across departments. Standards work served as 'text' for school-level PLCs; reform coordinators and literacy coaches facilitated work across departments. Literacy coaches worked with all departments, facilitating the teaching of reading and writing. Teachers presented student work and standards-based units they had developed. For example, at one high school's staff training a teacher shared her standards-based unit on the French revolution. At another school, teachers completed a 'jigsaw' exercise wherein teachers in each department shared their progress on aligning standards and curricula with colleagues in other departments. Although groups were comprised of members from different disciplines, standards provided them with a common reference point.

The resulting cross-department talk afforded occasion both for collegial exchange and for calibration of expectations across subject areas. These sessions turned teachers toward constructive conversation, or what Little and Horn (Chapter 6 in this book) term 'consequential talk.' One teacher explained the importance of joint work to changing the nature of cross-discipline dialogue: 'Once we've done some work together then we have something to talk about and something to communicate about, rather than to gripe about something that is going wrong.' These conversations also led teachers to see themselves as responsible for *all* of the school's students. As a teacher described the change at her school: 'People aren't just competing for their departments, they're competing for the kids. It's like "our kids," it's not like "my department's kids."'

Teacher presentations boosted teachers' sense of professionalism and community:

> We actually had teachers from this campus give small seminars … that's really validating for teachers in general because we pay lots of money for these people to come in and talk at us when we have a lot of people on campus who are doing [great] things that they can share them with us … that makes more of a teaching community.

A teacher in another high school likewise described the contributions of internally led professional development: 'One of the ways I've seen growth in this school is simply in the in-service. I've noticed that the best presentations that I've been to and the things I've learned the most from … it's been the people that we already have here, it's no longer the people outside that I'm learning from.' A focus on developing teacher expertise within the school bolstered teachers' sense of professionalism, pride in their school, while also helping the school create a sustainable school-wide professional learning community.

Developing common language and purpose through inquiry

When teachers from different departments are brought together, they often think that they have little, if anything, to talk about. With different textbooks, assessments, and curricula, the language of one department can be completely foreign to another. For schools making progress in whole-school reform, a structured process of inquiry created a bridge and professional community among the different disciplines. As one reform coordinator stated: 'Why collect data? Because you get information about (our school's) skills and because it binds us together as a whole staff. It gives us a common language and experience. I hear teachers say: "I have a way to talk to people now."'

In addition to providing teachers with a common language, inquiry also helped teachers understand how school-wide reform work pertains to their discipline and how they could benefit from being part of a school-wide professional community. For example, several high schools chose a school-wide effort focused around literacy. At first, disciplines other than English struggled to understand how this focus pertained to their work. By correlating test scores and grades, teachers realized that literacy affected student achievement across disciplines. One science teacher told us how his attitudes toward students and his instruction were transformed by learning that the disappointing student performance he attributed to student apathy instead reflected the fact that many could not read the 10th grade science material. Math teachers also saw that students with low literacy skills performed poorly in their classes. As the reform coordinator explained: 'I heard the math chair say something to the effect that their reading scores had a lot to do with performance in math. And I think they're convinced of that.' This common language and purpose laid the groundwork for growing a school-level PLC.

Finding time

Joint work takes time. Faculty in reforming high schools found time by changing their work structure and dedicating time for collaboration. One school received a state waiver to make Wednesday a half day so they could spend a block of time focused on creating a new curriculum. Another high school used a delayed Friday schedule – also by state permission – to pursue their work on standards. Yet another moved to a block schedule as a way to support student learning and their PLC. The BASRC Summer Institute provided time that teachers considered essential for their work around standards, inquiry into student learning and curriculum revision – the 'stuff' of a professional learning community. As one teacher described the benefits of the Summer Institute:

> When you're teaching through the week, you're just scrambling with courses, grading – and then you have an after school meeting. It's not the time to say "here's some really new concepts that you're going to have time to talk out, reflect on, think about and start implementing".
>
> [In the Summer Institute] we're free of the stresses of teaching; we don't have the students for those four weeks. And so the structure of having it in summer time, the relaxation, the collegiality all work together to form a real positive experience for us. We're more willing to accept each other then if we had an after school meeting and had to get ready for tomorrow's classes.

Basing school decisions on evidence

If a shared mission and common vision for student learning brought teachers together in a PLC, evidence-based inquiry into connections between practices and student learning provided the engine that motivated and deepened teachers' reform work and community. High schools dee-pening reform through their PLCs became sophisticated about using data to evaluate practice and focus improvement efforts. One teacher community narrowed its focus to Latino males, for example, in an effort to better understand the disturbing trends in achievement and retention their data revealed.

In several schools, inquiry work resulted in accountability being expressed *within* the school and PLCs – not just in external measures such as the SAT-9. Teachers used disaggregated data and their own local measures such as writing assessments to set performance benchmarks for specific groups of students; instruction in key subjects formed the basis for internal standards accepted by both high school teachers and students. The result, according to one teacher: 'is it's focusing them [students] more and they're seeing more work and doing better work. And if they're not able to do it, they go back and do it again because there's no way around it.' In these instances, standards built a strong and new culture of accountability among high school students.

Internal standards also fostered greater accountability among teachers. As one department chair explained:

> Having the benchmarks that students have to meet in order to go on to the next grade changes the way students view assignments as well as how I view an assignment. It's changed the way things are working in my classroom as far as student work and how I'm able to make the curriculum. I think this has improved things in both directions – from the teachers' and the students' perspective.

Another teacher expressed a similar message: 'I think that makes you think about what you're teaching. Instead of just handing out the same things year after year, you're saying: "that's not going to work real well with that benchmark, so what do I need to do to be more successful?"' In this sense, internal accountability and the situated professional learning it promoted reinforced one another through connections to teachers' day-to-day work. Internal standards were both the product of professional learning community and the basis for its critical reflection.

Using external resources and supports

Each of these reforming high schools took direction and momentum from an outside support provider – the Coalition of Essential Schools, the Bay Area School Reform Collaborative, Joint Ventures of Silicon Valley. One had consent decree money in addition to BASRC resources to support their professional learning community. Teachers and leaders at each school asserted that their reform efforts and professional learning communities could not have got underway or achieved what they did without an external agent and these extra funds. This was particularly true in large high schools where professional politics were rampant and teacher reform support uneven. A school-site reform coordinator highlighted the importance of an outside perspective:

> Because our support providers are from the outside, they can say things we can't say. They don't have an agenda other than getting the work done and doing what's best for kids. They know where the school needs to go; they are personable and non-threatening people and such good facilitators that everybody knows and likes them. They have just been able to get in here and push and do things that people involved here couldn't do.

However, we also saw that identifying and engaging quality support providers presented a particularly acute problem for high schools. In the Bay Area, there was no 'directory' they could consult to identify support providers to meet their needs. Further, all high schools struggled to locate effective content support providers; their needs far outstripped supply.

Dollars associated with these outside reform initiatives paid for supports vital to the development and functioning of professional learning communities: Summer Institutes, support providers, reform coordinators, and assistance with inquiry. Teacher time made available with these funds was, in the view of most faculties, the most important resource of all. The principal of a high school whose strong teacher community reform successfully spearheaded its reform effort said:

> The main ingredient in school reform, in my opinion, is being able to buy teacher time to actually do the processing, to do the work. The funding from BASRC allows us to do that. At first, I was kind of concerned about how much money we were spending on people. Now, I don't think we spend enough on people. That's where it is, where it happens. This allows us to have summer planning, to do the retreats, to buy release periods. The kinds of things that get people really engaged. I tell schools who come to visit us, 'If you guys are really interested in change, talk to your superintendent and your Board about finding the funding to buy time. Because without time, it isn't going to happen.'

Managing turnover to sustain professional learning communities

Teacher and administrator turnover presents huge difficulties at all school levels in terms of consistency of practice, school environment and supports for instruction. This study of reforming high schools shows how a strong professional learning community can provide a rudder in turbulent times and that turnover is not necessarily a bad thing. In reforming high schools with a strong sense of mission and culture, turnover often signified the 'pushing out' of people opposed to change. It also presented opportunities to hire people who supported the school's vision and were both willing and able to participate in the reform work. One principal explained that he wanted to hire people who: 'are used to this introspection, sharing, what have you, and so, the majority of the people that I've hired are people who are by very nature collaborative.' A reform coordinator explained: 'When people get hired right now, he's [principal] telling them, "If you don't want to collaborate, and if you don't want to work on standards-based work, this is not the place for you."' Thus, for several of our case study schools, turnover provided the opportunity to build and sustain a stronger professional learning community.

Conclusion

This research provides evidence that comprehensive high schools are not intractable and that the kinds of change imagined by National Association of Secondary School Principals can occur in 'typical' high schools. The high school learning communities we studied were not merely 'doing reform'; they were 'doing high school differently.' Department boundaries softened or disappeared; teachers' practice became more student centered – teaching something to somebody. Inquiry and evidence about practice grounded discussions about student learning and needed change. For these high schools, broadening leadership, situating professional learning within the school community, and developing improved uses of data and internal accountability systems were a product of, as well as necessary conditions for, changing the school's culture in ways that motivated and enabled professional learning communities to thrive.

Notes

1   We find that students' school experiences and attitudes mirror their teachers' professional culture. In one study, we observed a correlation of 0.8 between student ratings of teacher-student respect in the school and teacher ratings on measures of teacher learning community (CRCT 2002).
2   The Bay Area School Reform Collaborative (BASRC) was founded in 1996 with an Annenberg Challenge Grant and matching funds from the Hewlett Foundation. During its first five years, BASRC supported the reform work of 86 schools spread across the region's five counties; since 2001 it has focused on district system reform, working with 26 Bay Area districts, with funding from the Hewlett Foundation and several other local foundations. In 2005 BASRC changed its name to Springboard Schools and began to work with districts across the state on a fee-for-service basis.
3   California's assessment system changed several times during the period 1993–

2005, and reliable SAT-9 data are available only for the 1998–2001 period. Prior to and after this period different state tests were in use, thus limiting opportunity for longitudinal analysis of school performance.

References

Center for Research on the Context of Teaching (CRCT) (2002) *Bay Area School Reform Collaborative: Phase One (1996–2001) Evaluation.* Stanford University, Stanford, CA: CRCT.

Fullan, M. and Hargreaves, A. (1991) *What's Worth Fighting For? Working Together for Your School.* Milton Keynes: Open University Press.

Hargreaves, A. (1994) *Changing Teachers, Changing Times: Teachers' Work and Culture in the Postmodern Age.* London: Cassell; New York: Teachers College Press.

McLaughlin, M.W. and Talbert, J.E. (2001) *Professional Communities and the Work of High School Teaching.* Chicago, IL: University of Chicago Press.

National Association of Secondary School Principals (NASSP) (1996) *Breaking Ranks: Changing an American Institution.* Reston, VA: NASSP.

Public Agenda (2002) *Sizing Things Up: What Parents, Teachers and Students Think about Large and Small High Schools.* Washington, DC: Public Agenda.

Siskin, L.S. and Little, J.W. (1995) *The Subjects in Question: Departmental Organization and the High School.* New York: Teachers College Press.

twelve

Building social capital in professional learning communities: importance, challenges and a way forward

Bill Mulford

Introduction: what is social capital?

The idea of social capital has enjoyed a remarkable rise to prominence. By treating social relationships as a form of capital, it proposes that they are a resource which people can draw on to achieve their goals. It joins other forms of capital (economic, human, cultural, identity, and intellectual) as a resource and accepted contributor to our individual, community and national well-being. International bodies such as United Nations Educational, Scientific, and Cultural Organization (UNESCO), Organization for Economic Co-operation and Development (OECD) and the World Bank have engaged in extensive conceptual, empirical and policy related work in the area and a number of websites are devoted entirely to the area.[1]

What do we mean by 'social capital'? In a recent analysis of contemporary academic literature in the area, the World Bank (Grootaert *et al.* 2004) found that it has been discussed in two related but different ways. The first is subjective or cognitive in nature and refers to resources (such as information, ideas, support) that individuals are able to procure by virtue of their relationships with other people. The second is structural in nature and refers to the individual's involvement in informal networks and formal civic organizations. Despite these differences, the World Bank (Grootaert *et al.* 2004: 3) concludes that social capital 'is most frequently defined in terms of the groups, networks, norms, and trust that people have available to them for productive purposes'.

As well as this generally accepted definition, Grootaert *et al.* (2004: 4) point out that common distinctions are made among 'bonding', 'bridging' and 'linking' forms of social capital. 'Bonding' social capital refers to 'ties to people who are similar in terms of their demographic characteristics, such as family members, neighbours, close friends and work colleagues'. 'Bridging' social capital is also horizontal in nature but refers to 'ties to people who do not share many of these characteristics'. However, it continues to connect 'people with more or less equal social standing'. 'Linking' social capital operates across power differentials and thus is seen vertical in nature. It refers to 'one's ties to people in positions of authority such as representatives of public (police, political parties) and private (banks) institutions'.

Knowing the definition of social capital and its different forms is helpful, but does little to assist in building social capital in professional learning communities in schools. In addressing this gap, this chapter concentrates on the three different forms of social capital, their importance and the challenges involved in achieving each. Bonding social capital occurs among work colleagues within schools, and is the most researched area. Bridging social capital is found between schools. This area is a recent but growing one in the research literature, especially in the area of networking. Linking social capital is found between a school and its community. While there is a long research tradition in this area it tends to be unidirectional, concentrating on what the community can do for the school, but recent research presents a multidirectional perspective. The chapter concludes with a summary of the importance of, and challenges in developing, the three forms of social capital and, arising from this material, a way forward. This way forward involves those in schools seeing their task as developmental, *starting* with the building of social capital.

Three forms of social capital in schools: their importance and challenges

Bonding social capital: within schools

Being a valued part of a group is important for all those in schools. In what follows, the importance and challenges of bonding social capital for students, teachers and school leaders are examined.

Students

The OECD (2004: 127) has recently affirmed the well-established conclusion that a general sense of belonging at school is so important for students' life chances and success that it should be given equal indicator status with academic results. Recent research supports this argument. In a large-scale longitudinal study, Feinstein (2000: 20) found that pupil peer relations, locus of control and self-concept were related to later life successes, such as employment and earnings. At a more general level, Field (2005) found that people's social relationships play a vital role in their capacity for learning. Within-school social capital is also linked to student academic results. The OECD's (2004) PISA study, for example, shows a relationship between student–teacher relations and performance in mathematics; Beatty and Brew (2005) found students' sense of relatedness with school mediated their academic engagement; and Hogan and Donovan (2005) found significant relationships between students' subjective agency and academic outcomes, and a range of social capital outcomes such as sociability, trust in others, collaboration, being a good student, and participation in community groups.

However, Beatty and Brew (2005) worry that, despite its importance, student sense of connectedness with school can easily be eclipsed by a preoccupation with performance outcomes and test-focused teaching. Like the OECD, Hogan and Donovan (2005: 100) believe that inattention to broader outcomes of schooling 'underestimates the net contribution that schools make to individual wellbeing and aggregate social utility ... and conclude that this situation is neither sensible, efficient nor defensible on social justice grounds'.

In brief, then, research makes clear how important groups, networks, norms, and trust (in other words, bonding social capital) can be, not only for student feelings of self worth, day-by-day enjoyment of school and academic results, but also for their later life chances. The research identifies ways in which this might be achieved encouraging teachers to work on student confidence in school, sense of belonging, locus of control and peer relations, as well as their own relationships with the students. Finally, the research identifies some of the challenges involved, including system preoccupation with a highly stratified and limited measure of school performance, that is, academic achievement, performance outcomes and test-focused teaching.

Teachers

To succeed in a rapidly changing and increasingly complex world, it is vital that schools grow, develop, adapt and take charge of change so that they can control their own futures (Sweetland and Hoy 2000). Stoll *et al.* (2003) argue that teachers and schools that are able to take charge, to be empowered rather than be controlled by what is going on around them, have been shown to be more effective and improve more rapidly than schools that are not. Others have shown that teacher empowerment increases not only the quality of decisions, teachers' work lives, commitment and instructional practice (Somech 2002), but also students' academic achievement (Marks and Louis 1997).

Several studies document a strong link between collective teacher efficacy

(CTE), the shared beliefs of capability that the efforts of staff as a whole will have a positive effect on students, and differences in student achievement (Ross *et al.* 2004; Mawhinney *et al.* 2005). Goddard *et al.* (2004) have even demonstrated that the effects of CTE on student achievement were stronger than the direct link between socio-economic status (SES) and student achievement. Goddard (2002) also found that where teachers have the opportunity to influence important school decisions, they also tend to have stronger beliefs in the co-joint capability of their staff. Louis *et al.*'s (2005: 198, emphasis in original) research on teacher collective sense making in a time of increased regulation of the curriculum found that it 'was directly related to their willingness and propensity to change' and that it 'involved developing an understanding or interpretation of the meaning of *professional control and responsibility*'.

Mawhinney *et al.* (2005) recently sought to understand better how, under pressures of accountability, districts are fostering organizational learning in schools; as well as perceived conditions of professional learning, teachers' collective efficacy beliefs and student achievement. They found collective efficacy preceded professional learning communities. This finding increases the relevance of research on the stages of group (staff) development (Mulford *et al.* 2004). At the first or forming stage, group members are polite, avoid conflict, and are concerned about being accepted. At the second stage, storming, conflicts arise because of concerns about status, power and organization. The third stage, norming, sees more cohesion, openness, and willingness to share, but pressures to conform to the group (groupthink) may detract from the task at hand. Next comes the performing or work stage, which is characterized by increased task orientation and an open feedback. The final stage is transforming, in which the group does not just continue performing the same tasks well, but learns from feedback and, if necessary, changes the tasks and/or the methods. There can also be a dorming stage which allows a successful group to 'coast'. Dorming helps to prevent group and/or individual burnout. Finally, there is a mourning stage, which is triggered at any stage by the impending dissolution of the group. At this stage members reassert their independence from the group and start to disengage.

Teacher group effectiveness and productivity are related (Wheelan and Tilin 1999: 77); using a teacher survey and records of student grades, standardized test scores and degree of parental involvement, the authors found 'significant relationships between ... group development level and maths rank, reading rank and total achievement rank (a combination of maths and reading)'. Staff in schools classified as high in reading and total rank had significantly lower scores on conflict and significantly higher scores on trust and structure and work. In addition, those high on trust and structure and work also reported higher levels of parental involvement.

But expanding a team's social capital may not benefit all teachers. Blase and Blase (1999) argue that as schools become more collaborative, collegial and democratic, they become more political. Blackmore (1995) agrees, viewing discourses of collaboration as little more than rhetoric, given constraining practices of hierarchically organized education systems. O'Neill (2000: 19) maintains that while teacher collaboration is accepted as uncontroversial and likely to attract universal endorsement, in effect it may be employed by secondary school heads of department to get staff 'to do things they really don't want to do'. This is what Hargreaves (1991) termed 'contrived collegiality'. Achinstein (2002) warns that when teachers enact collaborative reforms in the name of 'community', what emerges is often conflict. But he also argues that conflict is central to an effective community. How teachers manage conflicts, whether they suppress or embrace their differences, may help define the community borders and ultimately the potential for organizational learning and change.

Johnson (2003) found over 85 per cent of teachers in his study reported working collaboratively in teams to 'some extent' or a 'great deal'. The perceived advantages of collaboration were seen to be increased support, morale and teacher learning. However, a minority of teachers were opposed to new teaming arrangements, claiming that the changes had led to increased workloads, decreased autonomy, and the emergence of competition between teams for resources, recognition and power. Johnson (2003: 349) concludes that: 'even with school reforms which seem benevolently "good" and almost universally accepted, it is likely that some groups and individuals will be silenced and marginalised, and that their professional standing will be compromised'.

Despite these challenges to bonding social capital in schools, research indicates that student performance is more variable within than between schools (OECD 2000). Given this finding, it makes sense to ensure that the practice of effective teachers is used to support and develop the work of others. A study of 24 UK schools belonging to the National College for School Leadership (NCSL) Network (Connor 2005) suggests four approaches that schools used to reduce variation, several of which include facets of bonding social capital:

- collecting, analysing, interpreting and using data;
- developing strategies that focus on teacher learning through, for example, the focused observation of specific aspects of practice;
- proposing reforms that relate curriculum more closely to student interests and learning preferences;
- focusing on the development of middle leaders and learning from the innovative practice of others in the school.

Part of within-school variation can, as the recent OECD (2005) report

Teachers Matter points out, create growing teacher shortages, some of which is caused by high turnover in the first few years in the job. Researchers have started to explore the reasons for high turnover. For example, Johnston (2003) has found that successful schools hire through an information-rich process that ensures a good match and purposefully engage new teachers in the culture and practices of the school, beginning with their first encounter and continuing in induction. The successful school also provides ongoing curricular and collegial support and acknowledgement.

The importance of bonding social capital for teachers has clearly been illustrated. Collective efficacy has even been shown to be precursor to a professional learning community. However, a number of factors have also been found to challenge the development of bonding social capital, such as professional autonomy, the inevitability of conflict, the fact that not everyone benefits, its use for political purposes, the stage of staff development and the possibility of groupthink, accountability press and a lack of school ownership or control over its actions. The type of school (high poverty, secondary) and the pressure of high stakes testing could also act as challenges.

Leaders
Research on effective school leadership (NCSL 2005a: 5), suggests the need for leaders to develop people and to be person-centred, 'putting a premium on professional relationships, and build trust and collaborative ways of working throughout the school'. Leithwood *et al.*'s (2004) review of the research literature in the field have found that leaders contribute to student learning indirectly, through their influence on other people or features of their organization. Thus their success will depend on their judicious choice of priorities. Identifying which knowledge, dispositions, or performances have a greater impact on student learning than others is an important task. It is clear in the growing number of national school leader standards that place a heavy emphasis on interpersonal skills.

Scribner *et al.* (2002) found that professional autonomy and attention to individual needs are necessary and salient conditions of strong professional communities, and that principals are indispensable arbiters of tensions that may arise when these priorities conflict. Marks and Printy (2004: 370) conclude that transformational leadership (building organizational capacity) was a necessary but insufficient condition for instructional leadership (individual and collective competence) but when 'transformational and shared instructional leadership coexist in an integrated form of leadership, the influence on school performance, measured by the quality of its pedagogy and the achievement of its students, is substantial'.

Confirming and building on these mainly North American reviews and research, evidence from other counties clearly demonstrates that leadership that makes a difference is both position based (principal) and distributive (administrative/leadership team and teachers) (Mulford *et al.* 2004). Agreeing with Leithwood, both are indirectly related to student outcomes. Organizational learning (OL) involving three sequential development stages (trusting and collaborative climate, shared and monitored mission, and taking initiatives and risks) supported by appropriate professional development is the important intervening variable between leadership and teacher work and then student outcomes. That is, leadership contributes to OL, which in turn influences what happens in the core business of the school – the teaching and learning. It influences the way students perceive teachers organize and conduct their instruction, and their educational interactions with, and expectations for, their students. Positive perceptions of teachers' work by pupils directly promotes participation in school, academic self-concept and engagement with school, both of which are related to academic achievement. School size is negatively, and socio-economic status and, especially, student home educational environment are positively linked to these relationships. Other research confirms this developmental sequence (see, for example, Mitchell and Sackney 1998; Mohr and Dichter 2001) and experience in the field of professional development also suggests that training in team skills and staff collaboration is connected with outcomes, including student achievement (Little 1982; Joyce and Showers 1995).

The above research clearly underscores the importance of school leaders for within-school bonding social capital. It also makes clear that bonding social capital is not the end of the matter for organizational learning or a professional learning community; it needs to be used for something, such as the mission of the school, curriculum and instruction. Other challenges to bonding social capital formation could be identified as the need to build staff capacity and competence, school size and socio-economic status, and student home educational environment.

Bridging social capital: among schools

Testing and attainment targets are limited tools for improvement, and must be supplemented by new strategies for supporting excellence and equity (NCSL 2005b: 7), and 'Networks [among schools] are perhaps the best way we have at present to create and support this expectation' (NCSL 2005b: 7). Leadbeater (2005: 6) argues that genuine reform 'will only become reality when schools become much more networked, collaborating not only with other schools, but with families, community groups and other public agencies'. But Leadbeater (2005: 22) also indicates that collaboration 'can be held back by regulation, inspection and funding regimes that encourage schools to think of themselves as autonomous, stand alone units'.

In a worldwide research study summarizing the findings from productive private sector network arrangements, Kanter (1994) identified three fundamental aspects of such alliances:

- they must yield benefits for the partners, but they must also have significance beyond corporate advantage;
- networks that partners ultimately deem successful involve collaboration;
- they cannot be 'controlled' by the formal system.

Similar results have recently been found by one of arguably the best funded and continuous school networks, The Networked Learning Communities (NLC) programme, with its hub at the UK's NCSL (see Jackson and Temperley, Chapter 4 in this book). Two NLC developers, Holmes and Johns-Shepherd (NCSL 2005b) have examined how school networks grow and change over time. Five key activities – courting, aligning, connecting, embedding, and re-focusing – were found to vary as the network developed from its early days, to an emerging, mature, and disengaged or renewed network. In the early days courting and aligning activities dominated and then, as the network emerged, the focus shifted to aligning and connecting. Courting involved getting people on board, building consensus and trust around a compelling idea and securing commitment. Aligning involved using the established trust to set parameters for collaboration, establishing working groups and securing resources, and connecting involved creating a critical mass of enthusiasts to participate fully in the network, modelling some of the processes, uniting the senior leaders around the purposes, and encouraging low-risk, quickly won activities to start.

The above research underscores the importance of bridging social capital. But, again, the advice is that the social capital constitutes the starting point, a necessary but insufficient condition for effective networks. There is a need to use it to develop priorities, a plan and a structure to sustain the network. Continuing challenges to networks include the hard work and commitment involved, the required base of relationships and shared values, naturally occurring variances such as changes in leaders, the shifting focus as networks develop, and external pressures.

Linking social capital: between the school and its community

While there is a long research tradition on school–community relations, it tends to be unidirectional, concentrating on what the community can do for the school, rather than being multidirectional. Yet schools play a vital role in strengthening linkages within their communities by providing opportunities for interaction and networking, which, in turn, contribute to the community's well-being and social cohesion. The close links between the survival and development of schools and their communities are demonstrated by a number of researchers (Jolly and Deloney 1996), who provide evidence, for example, that many rural communities have failed to remain viable after losing their school.

An Australian project (Kilpatrick *et al.* 2001) confirms this importance. The research examined the extent and nature of the contribution of rural schools to community development beyond educational results. Kilpatrick *et al.* (2001) found that rural school–community partnerships delivered a variety of positive outcomes for youth and for the community, such as improved environmental, cultural, recreational and economic outcomes. While these tangible outcomes are important to the sustainability of many small rural communities, the potentially more valuable outcome was increased individual and community capacity to influence their own futures.

Effective leadership for school–community partnerships was found to be a process that is typified by collective learning and teamwork – in other words, linking social capital. Twelve indicators, largely sequential in that later indicators build on earlier ones, characterize leadership for school–community partnerships:

- School principals are committed to fostering increased integration between school and community.
- School has in-depth knowledge of the community and resources available.
- School actively seeks opportunities to involve all sectors of the community, including boundary crossers, and those who would not normally have contact with the school.
- School has a high level of awareness of the value and importance to school–community partnerships of good public relations.
- School principals display a transformational leadership style which empowers others within the school and community and facilitates collective visioning.
- School and community have access to and use extensive internal and external networks.
- School and community share a vision for the future, centred on their youth.
- School and community are open to new ideas, willing to take risks and willing to mould opportunities to match their vision.
- School and community together play an active, meaningful and purposeful role in school decision-making.
- School and community value the skills of all in contributing to the learning of all.

- Leadership for school–community partnerships is seen as the collective responsibility of school and community.
- School and community both view the school as a learning centre for the whole community, which brings together physical, human and social capital resources.

Linking social capital results in a community's capacity to influence its own future (see also Mitchell and Sackney, Chapter 3 in this book). But, as with the bonding and bridging social capital, there are challenges. These challenges include moving from a looser structure and more informal relationships in the earlier stages to a tighter structure and more formalized relationships in later planning and delivery, the need for different leadership roles at different stages and for leadership to become increasingly distributed. As Henton *et al.* (1997) point out, it seems unlikely one person would be skilled in all roles.

The importance of and challenges to social capital

The research evidence reviewed in this chapter is clear in its support for all three forms of social capital. The outcomes are impressive, not the least of which being improved student engagement, academic performance and later life chances, improved teaching and learning, reduced within-school variation and retention of teachers in the profession, and increased individual and community capacity to influence their own futures.

But there are many challenges to overcome at the contextual, organizational and individual levels including the current accountability press, especially system preoccupation with a limited number of academic performance outcomes, the micro politics of schools such as contrived collegiality, groupthink and conflict avoidance, differences between policy development and its implementation, dedicated leadership, large, secondary, high poverty schools, and professional autonomy. Some of these challenges are summarized in Figure 12.1.

A way forward

Where do we take this research evidence on the importance of and challenges to social capital? I believe a way forward is to see the task of establishing professional learning communities as developmentally *starting* with the building of social capital (see Figure 12.1). A message arising from the research in this chapter is that those in schools must learn how to lose time in order to gain time. Awareness of, and skill development in group

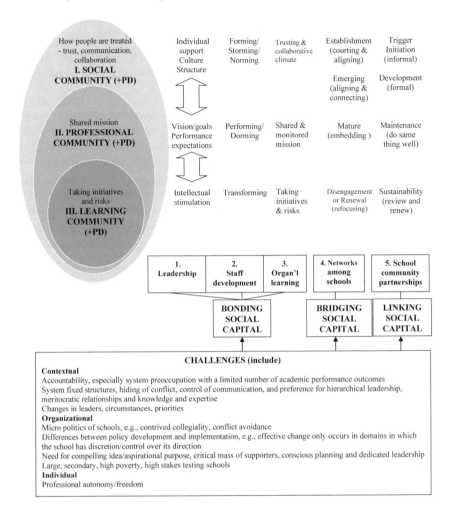

Figure 12.1   An integrated model of social capital and social professional learning communities

and organizational processes is a first step in any effective change. Instead of others trying to insert something into a school's (or community's) culture, the school, and especially its leadership, should first be trying to help that culture develop an awareness of and responsiveness to itself.

Development can be seen in findings regarding teacher collective efficacy preceding professional learning communities, the forming, storming, norming, performing, transforming and dorming stages of staff development (see column 2 in Figure 12.1), the trusting and collaborative climate, shared and monitored mission and taking initiatives and risks stages of organizational learning (column 3), the establishment, emerging, mature and disengagement or renewal stages of school networks (column 4), and the trigger, initiation, development, maintenance, and sustainability stages of school community partnerships (column 5). Elsewhere I have conceptualized the factors that make up school principal transformational leadership as sequential (Mulford 2003). Individual support, culture (including promoting an atmosphere of caring and trust among staff and setting the tone for respectful interaction with students) and structure (including participative decision-making, delegation and distributive leadership) precede vision and goals and performance expectations which, in turn, precede intellectual stimulation (column 1).

In brief, Figure 12.1 identifies three major, sequential and embedded elements in successful school reform. It takes the two elements in the definition of social capital, 'groups, networks, norms, and trust' and 'for productive purposes', and extends them to include a third element, learning. The first element in the sequence relates to the social community, how people communicate with and treat each other. Success is more likely where people act rather than are always reacting, are empowered, involved in decision-making through a transparent, facilitative and supportive structure, and are trusted, respected, encouraged, and valued (see oval I in Figure 12.1). It is likely to be a waste of time moving to the second element until this social community is established. The second element concerns a professional community. A professional community involves shared norms and values including valuing differences and diversity, a focus on implementation and continuous enhancement of quality learning for all students, de-privatization of practice, collaboration, and critical reflective dialogue, especially that based on performance data (oval II). But a professional community can be static, continuing to do the same or similar thing well. The final element relates to the presence of a capacity for change, learning and innovation, in other words, a professional learning community (oval III). In brief, and in order to better reflect this developmental sequence, I am talking about 'SPLCs', that is, social professional learning communities.

Each element of an SPLC, and each transition between them, can be facilitated by appropriate leadership and ongoing, optimistic, caring, nurturing professional development programmes. Also, each element is a prerequisite for the other – as the 'ovals-within-ovals' or 'eggs-within-eggs' diagram implies, they are embedded within each other with only the emphasis changing. For example, when learning is occurring there is still a need to revisit the social community and the professional community, especially where there has been a change of personnel and/or a new governmental direction announced.

Using this analysis of bonding, bridging and linking social capital to understand the importance of, challenges to and developmental nature of professional learning communities can assist in better translating the research into policy and practice. It can help us to:

- understand better and be able to take action on the intricacies involved in moving a school, or part of a school, from where it is now to becoming truly a place of ongoing excellence and equity without those in schools being 'bowled over' by the demands for change that surround them;
- target appropriate interventions to ensure more effective progression through the stages. In targeting interventions recognition will need to be given to the fact that it is a journey and that actions at one stage may be inappropriate, or even counterproductive, at another stage;
- support the position that a school will need to be evaluated differently depending on the stage it has reached.

Note

1   For example: www.socialcapitalgateway.org/.

References

Achinstein, B. (2002) Conflict amid community: the micropolitics of teacher collaboration, *Teachers College Record*, 104(3): 421–55.

Beatty, B. and Brew, C. (2005) Measuring student sense of connectedness with school: the development of an instrument for use in secondary schools, *Leading & Managing*, 11(2): 103–18.

Blackmore, J. (1995) Breaking out from a masculinist politics of education, in B. Limerick and R. Lingard (eds) *Change Forces: Probing the Depths of Educational Reform*. London: Falmer. pp. 123–34.

Blase, J. and Blase, J. (1999) Principals' instructional leadership and teacher development: teachers' perspectives, *Educational Administration Quarterly*, 35(3): 349–78.

Connor, C. (2005) Within-school variation. Unpublished paper. Nottingham: NCSL.

Feinstein, L. (2000) *The Relative Economic Importance of Academic, Psychological and Behavioural Attributes Developed in Childhood*. London: Centre for Economic Performance, London School of Economics and Political Science, University of London.

Field, J. (2005) *Social Capital and Lifelong Learning*. Bristol: The Policy Press.

Goddard, R. (2002) Collective efficacy and school organization: a multilevel analysis of teacher influence in schools, *Theory and Research in Educational Administration*, 1: 169–84.

Goddard, R., Hoy, W. and Woolfolk Hoy, A. (2004) Collective efficacy beliefs:

theoretical developments, empirical evidence, and future directions, *Educational Researcher*, 33(3): 1–13.

Grootaert, C., Narayan, D., Jones, V. and Woolcock, M. (2004) *Measuring Social Capital*, Working paper no. 18. Washington DC: World Bank.

Hargreaves, A. (1991) Contrived collegiality: the micropolitics of teacher collaboration, in J. Blase (ed.) *The Politics of Life in Schools*. Newbury Park, CA: Sage. pp. 65–78.

Henton, D., Melville, J. and Walesh, K. (1997) *Grassroots Leaders for a New Economy: How Civic Entrepreneurs Are Building Prosperous Communities*. San Francisco, CA: Jossey-Bass.

Hogan, D. and Donovan, C. (2005) The social outcomes of schooling: subjective agency among Tasmanian adolescents, *Leading & Managing*, 11(2): 84–102.

Johnson, B. (2003) Teacher collaboration: good for some, not so good for others, *Educational Studies*, 29(4): 337–50.

Jolly, D. and Deloney, P. (1996) Integrating Rural School and Community Development: an initial examination. Paper presented at the National Rural Education Association Annual Conference, San Antonio, Texas, 11–14 October.

Joyce, B. and Showers, B. (1995) *Student Achievement Through Staff Development: Fundamental of School Renewal* (2nd edn). New York: Longman.

Kanter, R. (1994) Collaborative advantage: the art of alliances, *Harvard Business Review*, July: 210–19.

Kilpatrick, S., Johns, S., Mulford, B., Falk, I. and Prescott, L. (2001) *More than Education: Leadership for Rural School–Community Partnerships*. Canberra: Rural Industries Research and Development Corporation. http://rirdc.gov.au/reports/HCC/02-055sum.html, accessed 3 October 2005.

Leadbeater, C. (2005) *The Shape of Things to Come*. London: DfES Innovation Unit. www.standards.dfes.gov.uk/innovation-unit, accessed 10 September 2005.

Leithwood, K., Louis, K.S., Anderson, S. and Wahlstrom, K. (2004) *Review of Research: How Leadership Influences Student Learning*. New York: Wallace Foundation.

Little, J.W. (1982) Norms of collegiality and experimentation: workplace conditions of school success, *American Educational Research Journal*, 19(3): 325–40.

Louis, K., Febey, K. and Schroeder, R. (2005) State-mandated accountability in high schools: teachers' interpretations of a new era, *Educational Evaluation and Policy Analysis*, 27(2): 177–204.

Marks, W. and Louis, K.S. (1997) Does teacher empowerment affect the classroom? The implications of teacher empowerment for instructional practice and student academic performance, *Educational Evaluation and Policy Analysis*, 19: 245–75.

Marks, H. and Printy, S. (2004) Principal leadership and school performance: an integration of transformational and instructional leadership, *Educational Administration Quarterly*, 39(3): 370–97.

Mawhinney, H., Hass, J. and Wood, C. (2005) Teachers' collective efficacy beliefs in professional learning communities, *Leading & Managing*, 11(2): 12–45.

Mitchell, C. and Sackney, L. (1998) Learning about organizational learning, in K. Leithwood and K. Louis (eds) *Organizational Learning in Schools*. Lisse: Swets and Zeitlinger. pp. 177–99.

Mohr, N. and Dichter, N. (2001) Building a learning organisation, *Phi Delta Kappan*, 82(10): 744–7.

Mulford, B. (2003) *School Leaders: Challenging Roles and Impact on Teacher and School Effectiveness*. Paris: Commissioned Paper by the Education and Training Policy Division, OECD, for the Activity 'Attracting, Developing and Retaining Effective Teachers'. www.oecd.org/dataoecd/61/61/2635399.pdf, accessed 16 July 2005.

Mulford, W., Silins, H. and Leithwood, K. (2004) *Educational Leadership for Organisational Learning and Improved Student Outcomes*. Dordrecht: Kluwer Academic.

National College for School Leadership (NCSL) (2005a) *Learning-centred Leadership: Towards Personalised Learning-centred Leadership*. Nottingham: National College for School Leadership.

National College for School Leadership (NCSL) (2005b) *Establishing a Network of Schools*. Cranfield: Network Learning Group, National College for School Leadership.

Organization for Economic Co-operation and Development (OECD) (2000) Programme for international student assessment (PISA). www.pisa.oecd.org, accessed 18 July 2005.

Organization for Economic Co-operation and Development (OECD) (2004) *Learning for Tomorrow's World: First results from PISA 2003*. Paris: OECD.

Organization for Economic Co-operation and Development (OECD) (2005) *Teachers Matter: Attracting, developing and retaining effective teachers*. Paris: OECD. www.oecd.org/document/52/0,2340,en_2649_33723_34991988_1_1_1_1,00.html, accessed 2 October 2005.

O'Neill, J. (2000) 'So that I can more or less get them to do things they really don't want to do'. Capturing the situational complexities of the secondary school head of department, *Journal of Educational Enquiry*, 1(1): 13–34.

Ross, J., Hogaboam, A. and Gray, P. (2004) Prior student achievement, collaborative school processes and collective teacher efficacy, *Leadership and Policy in Schools*, 3(3): 163–88.

Scribner, J., Hager, D. and Warne, T. (2002) The paradox of professional community: tales from two high schools, *Educational Administration Quarterly*, 38(1): 45–76.

Somech, A. (2002) Explicating the complexity of participative management: an investigation of multiple dimensions, *Educational Administration Quarterly* 38(3): 341–71.

Stoll, L., Fink, D. and Earl, L. (2003) *It's About Learning (And It's About Time)*. London: RoutledgeFalmer.

Sweetland, S. and Hoy, W. (2000) School characteristics and educational outcomes: towards an organisational model of student achievement in middle schools, *Educational Administration Quarterly*, 36(5): 703–29.

Wheelan, S. and Tilin, F. (1999) The relationship between faculty group development and school productivity, *Small Group Research*, 30(1): 59–81.

thirteen

Sustainable professional learning communities

Andy Hargreaves

The rise of professional learning communities

Every so often, and with increasing frequency, a new buzzword or buzz-phrase enters the educational lexicon: 'guided discovery,' 'total quality management,' 'emotional intelligence,' 'learning styles' and now 'professional learning communities.' With the passage of time, as fashions change, advocates age, policy shifts and practices become discredited, the buzzwords disappear and the system directs its attention elsewhere.

If history is a reliable teacher, then professional learning communities will recede from priority, just like most predecessors. But if we are lucky, perhaps, some of the substantial changes in teaching and learning and in professional practice that professional learning communities are bringing into being, will persist and even proliferate long after the label itself has faded.

Professional learning communities (PLCs) are, at this time, undoubtedly in the ascendant in educational policy and practice. Efforts to convert schools into PLCs (the abbreviation, like a nickname, itself being an indicator of increasing acceptance), are spreading rapidly throughout the English-speaking world. Drawing on the emerging evidence that professional learning communities have a systemic and positive effect on student learning outcomes (Louis and Marks 1998; McLaughlin and Talbert 2001; Anderson and Togneri 2002; Bolam *et al.* 2005), schools and systems are investing considerable energy in developing themselves as professional learning communities.

Best-selling books, guides and training programs not only raise awareness of the importance and impact of PLCs, but provide practitioners with concrete advice about how to create and sustain them (Dufour and Eaker 1998). Schools and districts are rebranding themselves as 'learning communities'; systems are encouraging and investing resources in developing them (Fullan 2007). The Canadian province of Alberta has even decided to make PLCs the law and has passed legislation to mandate them! In name or in nature, PLCs will be an educational force to be reckoned with for some years yet to come.

Professional learning communities at the crossroads

In principle, the idea of professional learning communities engenders broad support. It appeals to both Left and Right, to those who value process as well as those who care about the product, to those who demand hard evidence and those who value soft skills, to evidence as well as experience, relationships in addition to results. The inclusive appeal of ideas such as professional learning communities, like the very idea of community itself, can establish enthusiasm, attract adherents, and build initial commitment. But this very attractive inclusiveness can also be its undoing when planning is followed by implementation and impassioned rhetoric is converted into imperfect reality.

This chapter addresses the realities of professional learning communities and clarifies some choices of purpose and emphasis that are best established at the outset of PLCs, so they do not disappoint and divide communities when they begin to surface and expose underlying assumptions and expectations later on. Drawing on many years of research and improvement related to professional collaboration (e.g. Hargreaves 1994), and on specific efforts to design schools as learning organizations and professional learning communities (Giles and Hargreaves 2006), the chapter clarifies some of the ethical and political choices and challenges of creating and sustaining PLCs, and exposes unintended consequences that can, if they are not addressed, easily lead to professional disappointment and cynicism about improvement efforts, among those who are optimistically committed to their development.

Professional learning communities are at a crossroads. Their origins and early development were professionally and educationally promising. They brought teachers and others together to work collaboratively for the benefit of improved student learning and achievement. This collaboration suffused every part of school life instead of being supplemental to existing operations. Professional learning communities created structures, cultures and leadership that promoted rich conversations and stimulating, challenging, rewarding professional relationships among teachers, throughout the work and life of the school, about how best to improve the learning, lives and achievement of students.

These PLCs encompassed and encouraged attention to the full depth and breadth of student learning in all areas of the curriculum. And they drew on all kinds of inside and outside evidence, on multiple sources of data and new cultures of evidence-informed inquiry, in order to locate how best to improve the quality of that learning.

Becoming a professional learning community was a voluntary or invitational process – the result of members wanting to improve the learning of students and the work lives of teachers. In the best-case scenarios, ways were then devised to network these learning communities together in enlarged communities-of-communities which extended the capacity and range of learning and improvement even further, and kept schools moving forward.

In recent years, as the idea and implementation of PLCs has spread, the result (as is common in many cases where innovations are scaled-up) is that their original meaning is becoming diminished and their richness is being lost. The increasingly diluted and distorted character of professional communities is also being exacerbated by ideological and legislative emphases on only literacy and mathematics as the focus of improvement, and on tested achievement as the only ways to measure it.

From their promising early beginnings, so-called professional learning communities are increasingly turning into something else. Instead of being intelligently informed by evidence in deep and demanding cultures of trusted relationships that press for success, PLCs are turning into add-on teams that are driven by data in cultures of fear that demand instant results. Data-driven instruction ends up driving educators to distraction – away from the passion and enthusiasm for rich processes of teaching and learning in classrooms and enriched relationships with children, into a tunnel-vision focus on manipulating and improving test scores in literacy and mathematics by any quick fix available – more test preparation here, after-school classes there, concentrating on cells of children who fall just below the failure line somewhere else. All this does nothing to enhance the actual quality of teaching and learning.

Like the large Bay Area School Reform Collaborative (BASRC) cluster of professional learning communities in California evaluated by McLaughlin and Mitra (2003), the PLCs concentrate largely on literacy. Popular PLC advocates, Dufour and Eaker (1998), rightly argue that PLCs should be given a focus but, for political reasons, this focus is increasingly narrow, marginalizing all other areas of the curriculum like the environment, social studies or the arts. Demanding that PLCs be data driven ultimately leads most of them to concentrate only on mandated tests. The result is a process that is not inspirational or stimulating for the teachers trying to develop their schools as learning communities, but a treadmill poised on a precipice of failure, inadequacy and unwanted intervention.

In the overtested environment, PLCs are becoming instruments of technocratic surveillance and oppression, turning school staffrooms into Aspergers' factories, into what Richard Sennett (1998) calls 'turnstiles of transient teamwork' where the mathematicians or statisticians and technocrats are now defining, delineating and diminishing what student learning and teacher professionalism will become. As Naylor (2005) has noted, popular writers on and trainers in PLCs devote much of their attention to specifying goals, defining a focus, examining data and establishing teams, but they rarely critique dominant interpretations of what the focus should be, give much attention to the value of intuition in interpreting data, or concentrate on the need to develop strong cultures of trust, reciprocal engagement and mutual critique in a school.

If our classrooms are to prepare all our children with the range of knowledge and creativity that will give them opportunities to participate at the highest levels of the new knowledge economy, and if teachers' work is to be enriching and engaging enough to attract and retain the most capable adults who will make up the next generation of the profession, then we must halt the degeneration of PLCs into the corrupted communities, the faded facsimiles, the perverted inversions of what they once so inspirationally aspired to be. We must move beyond designing PLCs as mandated teams that generate instant gains in tested achievement, to something that is more educationally sound and professionally sustainable instead.

Sustainable learning communities

There are, fortunately, many examples of professional learning communities that are less slick and stilted, and much more sustainable in their purposes and processes (see, for example, Chapter 5 by Stoll and her colleagues in this volume).

Drawing on my own research on examples of professional learning communities in the USA and Canada (Hargreaves 2003; Giles and Hargreaves 2006), on a current evaluation of an initiative to network and support more than 230 underperforming secondary schools in England and Wales, in an effort to turn them into stronger learning communities (Hargreaves *et al.* 2006), and on an analysis of long-term leadership and sustainability in eight secondary schools (Hargreaves and Fink 2004; 2006), I will now set out seven principles of more sustainable professional learning communities.

1 Depth

Sustainable professional learning communities concentrate on what matters. They preserve, protect and promote achievement and success in deep and broad learning for all, in relationships of care for others.

Professional learning communities rely on organizational learning – the collective ability of people, in an organization, to learn their way out of trouble, and forward into the future (Mulford 1998; Louis 2006). One of the obstacles to effective organizational learning is fixation on things that narrow the range of thinking and possibilities for problem solving (Rusch 2005). For Peter Senge (1990), the originator of the idea of organizational learning, the flaw of fixation was a concentration on immediate events as special cases requiring individual solutions. But people can also fixate their collective efforts on initiatives, policies and priorities set by others rather than on improvement needs explored and determined by themselves.

The global moral panic of literacy reform has turned the justified need for a focus within PLCs into a dysfunctional fixation on tested literacy achievements. Governments are setting literacy as the overwhelming priority in many educational systems even where it is manifestly unwarranted (as in high-performing Ontario and Australia), largely as a way to seize control of the educational agenda in order to create what Mulford (1998) terms 'procedural illusions of effectiveness'.

Strong and sustainable PLCs do not allow themselves to become fixated on raising tested achievement scores, but also develop a strong focus on improving deep and broad learning beyond the basics. They engage in intelligent and ethical deliberations about what kind of learning counts as achievement. These deliberations include courageous questioning and even creative subversion of the mandates and measurement tools that diminish this deeper sense of achievement.

It is often thought that in failing or underperforming systems, attention needs to be focused on the basics, especially as measured by test scores. Even jurisdictions such as Ontario in Canada, which are among the highest performers in the world in literacy, still drive their reform agenda by taking the politically popular area of literacy as their focus (Fullan 2005). Yet Chris James and his colleagues' study of ten outstandingly successful primary schools serving disadvantaged communities in Wales reveals that while these schools pay proper attention to the basics of literacy and numeracy, they also extend far beyond these basics into an enriching, engaging and enjoyable curriculum that expands students' horizons and deepens their connections to their learning (James *et al.* 2006).

In this respect, strong and sustainable professional learning communities are also ethical learning communities (Campbell 2005). They are communities where teachers discuss and determine how to act in the face of instructional fixations with the excesses of testing – such as the lack of attention to deep literacy or creative writing in prescribed literacy programs that prioritize basic phonological awareness; the cultural bias of test items and whether teachers should interpret them for and mediate them to their students even though that might be illegal; or paying attention to the learning needs of second language students by communicating with them in their first language when test items, legislation and officially sanctioned research-based programs prohibit bilingual instruction (Sanchez 2006). Sustainable PLCs, in other words, are courageous and committed about putting learning before achievement, before testing, not vice versa.

2 Breadth

Sustainable professional learning communities develop and depend on shared learning and leadership for achievement and improvement.

Sustainable PLCs are not just bunches of teams that sit down and analyse data together after school is over. They are a way of life that changes the entire school culture as leaders come forward from every part of the school in communities that inquire into teaching and learning practice, then create improvements which benefit all students.

This entails two requirements. First, analysis and management of data concerning student learning and achievement need to be integrated technically and culturally into the ongoing life of the school. Data management needs a person in a designated position of responsibility within the school to manage and coordinate the vast and complex body of information that comprises the data system. This process also benefits from outside technical support that can help the PLC interpret the data intelligently (McLaughlin and Mitra 2003).

Reduced overload and improved effectiveness in analysing data to improve the quality of teaching and student learning also depend on the data being accessible and usable in real time, within the teaching and learning process, and not just in chosen or imposed, added on time, at the end of it.

Noumea Primary School in a highly disadvantaged part of Sydney, Australia, has provided one example of such an integrated data management program (Lewis and Caldwell 2005). The program (now being exported to national and state systems elsewhere) collects student achievement and behavioral data, along with teachers' comments on students' work and welfare information, which are entered on an ongoing basis into the database by laptop (in every classroom) rather than into teachers' notebooks or students' agendas. The data can then be disaggregated by teacher, class, age group or individual child, as well as by ethnicity and socioeconomic status. Teachers use the data routinely as part of their pedagogical and whole-school decision-making to diagnose and respond accurately and appropriately to increases in behavioral problems, for example.

Professional learning communities appear to work best when evidence-informed change is incorporated into regular cycles of planning, implementation, inquiry and review focused on learning (McLaughlin and Mitra 2003), that are reminiscent of the classic cycles of action research that are now becoming institutionalized as a part of school inspection and self-evaluation processes in the UK (OFSTED 2001). Although this planning and review process may look rather mechanistic as a school first emerges into a professional learning community, it works best when it evolves into a routine way in which the school and teachers operate – so that whenever a problem is experienced, the school's first response is not 'What do we do about this?' but 'What do we know about this?' (Hargreaves 2003).

All this means that secondly, as a way of life, sustainable PLCs attend to their 'soft' relational side as well as their 'hard' data-based side. Professional learning communities are at their strongest when they are supported by and thrive on cultural norms of *collegiality* (Little 1984; 1990; Nias *et al.* 1989; Rosenholtz; 1989; Hargreaves 1994; Lima 2001), *continuous improvement* (McLaughlin and Talbert 2001), *inquiry* (Cochran-Smith and Lytle 1993), and *professional dialogue* (Louis 2006).

The backbone of a strong and sustaining PLC is *trust*. The pursuit of improvement, management of change and rectification of under-performance all create difficult emotions of anxiety, fear, threat, and loss (Marris 1974). Confrontations with disturbing data that challenge people's sense of their own effectiveness magnify these feelings. Successful change efforts do not eliminate these difficult emotions and anxieties, but create a holding pattern for them so they do not become unbearable or flood the teacher so he or she is unable to cope (Heifetz and Linsky 2002). The heart of this holding pattern is a web of trust (Meier 2002).

Trust is an investment in one's own and others' reliability, predictability and good intentions. Unlike faith, trust is not blind and unconditional. 'Trust is hard earned and easily dissipated. It is valuable social capital and not to be squandered' (O'Neill 2002: 4).

Trust takes time and effort to build. It is an active process, established and reaffirmed through many small and repeated interactions. Single and spectacular moments of betrayal can undo months or years of building trust (Hargreaves 2002; 2003). Trust is both a moral commitment and acceptance of the other's good faith, as well as an emotional disposition of reduced anxiety, of ease and acceptance, that accompanies this suspension or expulsion of doubt.

In their study of Chicago elementary schools, Bryk and Schneider (2004) found that high-trust schools produced higher levels of student achievement. High trust among teachers and between teachers and others created a culture of belief in all children's capacity to learn; and a commitment to bring this learning to fruition.

Strong and sustainable PLCs are therefore characterized by strong cultures of trusted colleagues who value each other personally and professionally, who are committed to their students, who are willing to discuss and disagree about evidence and data that can inform them about how to improve their practices in ways that benefit their students – and who are willing to challenge one another's practice in doing so. Culture, trust and relationships are at the heart and soul of PLCs, and of all that will eventually sustain them.

3 Endurance

Sustainable professional learning communities last. They preserve and advance the most valuable aspects of learning and life over time, year after year, from one leader or change champion to the next.

Strong and sustainable PLCs cannot be rushed or forced. They can only be facilitated and fed. Professional learning communities take time. Like virtue or community in general, they cannot be mandated or legislated by imposed and overconfident design. They can only be built and developed through strengthened relationships.

While leadership of PLCs sometimes needs to convey and develop a sense of urgency about improvement, leaders who rush the work of PLCs will only meet with resistance and resentment later on. And leaders who guide the process too closely, imposing their own visions and having the school share them, will find that their efforts and achievements will not survive their departure and succession, since these efforts have been too dependent on, and closely controlled by, the leader's own decisions and desires (Hargreaves and Fink 2006).

Professional learning communities are vulnerable over time at moments of high teacher turnover or when key leaders leave. The early success of PLCs, like innovative schools in general, can be the incipient source of their subsequent undoing. As emerging teacher leaders rapidly develop their skill sets, they become noticed by leaders higher up in the system or they themselves seek opportunities and challenges elsewhere, and become ready to move on (Fink 2000). Their replacements can easily misinterpret the distinctive culture they are entering and, because they have not been part of that culture's history and its formation, their loyalty and commitment has to be actively encouraged; it cannot be assumed (Giles and Hargreaves 2006). So, it is important to renew the distinctive culture of a school as a professional community on a periodic basis, and especially at times of significant teacher turnover – through re-visioning and retreats.

Successful and sustainable PLCs hinge on having an outstanding and supportive school principal at the helm (Spillane 2006). Sustainable PLCs depend on there being stability and longevity of this high-quality senior leadership, over at least five years – as James and his colleagues found in their study of successful primary schools serving disadvantaged communities in Wales (James *et al.* 2006). And when the principal's tenure is over, a planned and smooth succession is essential and is prepared for long in advance in a culture that never becomes overly dependent on one leader, that actively and ongoingly incorporates open discussion about the school's emergent leadership needs as an integral part of its improvement planning, and that allows and encourages many other leaders to emerge and come forward in the school, creating big pools from which future successors might come (Hargreaves and Fink 2006).

In all this, it is vital that an incoming leader is sensitive to and appreciative of the achievement of an existing professional learning community, has entry strategies to understand it, and has a willingness to work with existing leadership in the school instead of imposing his or her own passion, plans and visions upon it.

4 Justice

Sustainable professional communities are not luxuries for teachers of the privileged but equal entitlements for all students, teachers and schools.

Strong and sustainable PLCs do not exaggerate inequities between rich and poor schools or districts, but they provide equal opportunities to learn, whether in conditions of affluence or of poverty.

According to McLaughlin and Talbert (2001), the flexibility and professional discretion that characterize professional learning communities tend to flourish in more affluent communities whose schools meet the measured standards and enjoy the freedom to explore beyond them (Baker and Foote 2006). Datnow *et al.* (2002) similarly found that US schools which adopted the more flexible and open-ended versions of Comprehensive School Reform tended to be located in more affluent districts.

Poorer districts, meanwhile, are more likely to adopt reform models of a more prescriptive, micromanaged nature – evident in a number of tightly scripted, widely adopted, and officially sanctioned literacy programs. These programs combine a *contractual* insistence on performance standards using prescribed classroom teaching techniques with a *cultural* emphasis on required teacher collaboration, intensive coaching and technical assistance, and closely monitored therapeutic sessions among implementers devoted to the disclosure and remediation of 'problems' (Hargreaves 2003). Despite benefits of short-term achievement gains, shifts in some teachers' beliefs about their students' abilities, and teacher confidence-building (Elmore and

Burney 1999), these more prescriptive and closely monitored interventions have serious weaknesses. Their achievement effects seem to plateau after only two to three years, they exert high collateral damage on other less structured and prescriptive areas of the curriculum such as arts and humanities, and they tend to promote patterns of teacher dependency on and fear of outside-in evidence and programs that are the antithesis of discretionary judgment in a professional learning community (Datnow *et al.* 2002; Earl *et al.* 2003; Manzo 2004). These approaches to data-driven, rather than evidence-informed improvement exhibit few of the qualities of authentic professional learning communities. Professional learning communities that stretch their teachers and their students, should therefore not be an elite indulgence in well-resourced communities, but an entitlement for communities of all kinds.

5 *Diversity*

Sustainable professional learning communities promote pedagogical diversity with other schools and among themselves and find ways to make this diversity work through purpose-centered leadership, effective networking and cross-pollination of practices as well as intelligent reference to data and evidence.

Strong and sustainable ecosystems are biodiverse. Weak ecosystems have a narrow range of genetic and species variations and have no resilience to bounce back when unexpected adversity strikes (Wilson and Peter 1988). In brains, cell systems, species and ecosystems, diversity is sustained through neural, genetic and environmental networks (Capra 1997). Human organizations work best when they are developed according to principles of natural design which promote diversity, adaptation and networking; not when they are based on mechanical models of standardization, alignment and singular prescribed practices (Hargreaves and Fink 2006). Paradoxically, it is advanced technology of digital communication that now makes it easier for organizations to mimic the networking and complexity of natural design (Castells 2001).

Strong and sustainable PLCs thereby abandon singular pedagogical prescriptions and standardized practices in favor of pedagogical diversity that is networked together to develop increased learning, validated by references to collective experience and outside evidence, and organized around a common and shared purpose.

Strong and sustainable PLCs are also connected to others around them. They learn from the outside as well as the inside (Bolam *et al.* 2005). They do not sequester themselves in splendid isolation; nor do they connect with other schools only through the 'missionary' work of passing on wisdom and insight to those who are less fortunate.

Strong PLCs, rather, network with other schools and institutions, consistently accessing other learning, challenging their own assumptions, and pushing themselves to even higher levels of performance. If they mentor other schools, they open themselves to learning from these schools as well as offering learning of their own. Strong PLCs share staff development with their peers, participate as learners alongside them, and resist the temptation merely to provide staff development for others.

6 Resourcefulness

Sustainable professional learning communities conserve and renew people's energy and resources. They are prudent and resourceful communities that waste neither their money nor their people.

The world is running out of gas (Goodstein 2004). In our hunger to consume more than we can produce, we are treating the planet as if it is a bottomless pit of energy. Before very long, if we do nothing, all the oil will be burned out. People are no different. We cannot treat our human resources as if they are bottomless pits of gas; we cannot press on relentlessly for more and more tested achievement by burning our teachers and leaders out.

At their best, PLCs operate like wind and solar power. They are sources of energy renewal – moving energy around through the system. Authentic learning of all kinds renews energy, enlivening the work lives of those who experience it. Thus, in one professional learning community within the Spencer Foundation study of secondary school change, teachers found themselves extending their passion for their own learning beyond their workplaces into their wider lives – writing novels, training to be massage therapists, volunteering on the stock exchange, consulting in the corporate world, and so on (Hargreaves and Fink 2004).

But when PLCs are merely devices for implementing external pressures for greater tested results, the frantic rush to produce the right numbers that will appease outside authorities, drains teachers' passion and energy, and eventually undermines the essential human resource on which sustainable educational improvement depends.

7 Conservation

Sustainable professional learning communities respect and build on the past in their quest to create a better future.

Strong and sustainable professional learning communities acknowledge (though they do not automatically endorse) the wisdom, memory, accumulated knowledge and resulting intuition of the school's most senior teachers. They do not privilege more formal and objective evidence over existing intuition, but devise ways for evidence and intuition to inform one another – as in the very best medical practice (Gawande 2003).

Professional learning communities learn from what the most experienced teachers in a school know and believe, even if this is sometimes expressed maladroitly. They see that in teacher resistance there is a frustration arising from unheard wisdom, and that nostalgic retreats to the past represent an official failure to acknowledge that past and those who are the bearers of it (Moore *et al.* 2006).

Sustainable professional learning communities learn from resistance to change. They invite resistors into the early stages of change, rather than approaching or expelling them as a very last resort. When they are contemplating changes, they undertake a change audit to determine what memories more veteran teachers have of changes they believe are similar, and to deliberate on what can be learned as a result.

Whenever possible, sustainable PLCs value all their members, young and old, enthusiastic and skeptical instead of prematurely expelling those who do not fit with the consequence that they go on to spoil someone else's aspiration to be a learning community, in another school elsewhere.

Conclusion

As professional learning communities are becoming more widespread, it is time to revisit and renew the core principles that make them successful and sustainable. A sustainable professional learning community is not a team of teachers meeting after an exhausting day at school, under the watching eye of a matriarchal or patriarchal school principal, to disaggregate data of tested achievement as a way to devise quick-fix increases in test scores.

Sustainable professional learning communities, rather, make deep and broad learning their priority. They put learning first – before achievement and testing – and get better achievement as a consequence. They distribute leadership widely and wisely in trusted and also challenging communities that are dedicated to improving learning and achievement. They do not depend on the parental authority figure of the school principal but plan for the succession of principals and change champions, creating a strong, resilient and distributed teacher culture that will smooth the path of succession events.

Sustainable professional learning communities are the entitlement of all students and schools, and they continue to grow and prosper the most when they are connected to other schools around them, in networked learning communities that spread across a system. Sustainable professional learning communities renew teachers' energy by invigorating their collective learning, instead of depleting it by using PLCs as tools to implement mandates from elsewhere. And sustainable professional learning communities work hard to acknowledge and build on the wisdom and experiences of all their members, not just existing enthusiasts – especially those who have worked in schools the longest.

References

Anderson, S. and Togneri, W. (2002) *Beyond Islands of Excellence: What Districts Can Do to Improve Instruction and Achievement in all Schools*. Washington, DC: Learning First Alliance.

Baker, M. and Foote, M. (2006) Changing spaces: urban school interrelationships and the impact of standards-based reform, *Educational Administration Quarterly*, 42(1): 90–123.

Bolam, R., McMahon, A., Stoll, L., Thomas, S., Wallace, M., Hawkey, K. and Greenwood, A. (2005) *Creating and Sustaining Effective Professional Learning Communities*. DfES Research Report RR637. University of Bristol.

Bryk, A.S. and Schneider, B.L. (2004) *Trust in Schools: A Core Resource for Improvement*. New York: Russell Sage Foundation Publications.

Campbell, E. (2005) Challenges in fostering ethical knowledge as professionalism within schools as teaching communities, *Journal of Educational Change*, 6(3): 207–26.

Capra, F. (1997) *The Web of Life: A New Synthesis of Mind and Matter*. London: HarperCollins.

Castells, M. (2001) *The Internet Galaxy: Reflections on the Internet, Business, and Society*. Oxford and New York: Oxford University Press.

Cochran-Smith, M. and Lytle, S.L. (1993) *Inside/Outside: Teacher Research and Knowledge*. New York: Teachers College Press.

Datnow, A., Hubbard, L. and Mehan, H. (2002) *Extending Educational Reform: From One School to Many*. London: Falmer/Routledge Press.

Dufour, R.E. and Eaker, R. (1998) *Professional Learning Communities at Work: Best Practices for Enhancing Student Achievement*. Bloomington, IN: National Educational Services.

Earl, L., Levin, B., Leithwood, K., Fullan, M. and Watson, N. (2003) *Watching and Learning* (vol. 3). London: Department for Education and Skills.

Elmore, R.F. and Burney, D. (1999) Investing in teacher learning: staff development and instructional improvement, in L. Darling-Hammond and G. Sykes (eds) *Teaching as the Learning Profession: Handbook of Policy and Practice*. San Francisco, CA: Jossey-Bass. pp. 236–91.

Fink, D. (2000) *Good School/Real School: The Life Cycle of an Innovative School*. New York: Teachers College Press.

Fullan, M. (2005) *Leadership and Sustainability: System Thinkers in Action*. Thousand Oaks, CA: Corwin Press.

Fullan, M. (2007) *Turnaround Leadership*. San Francisco, CA: Jossey-Bass/Wiley.

Gawande, A. (2003) *Complications: A Surgeon's Notes on an Imperfect Science*. New York: Picador.

Giles, C. and Hargreaves, A. (2006) The sustainability of innovative schools as learning organizations and professional learning communities during standardized reform, *Educational Administration Quarterly*, 42(1): 124–56.

Goodstein, D. (2004) *Out of Gas: The End of the Age of Oil*. New York: W.W. Norton.

Hargreaves, A. (1994) *Changing Teachers, Changing Times: Teachers' Work and Culture in the Postmodern Age* (Professional development and practice series). New York: Teachers College Press.

Hargreaves, A. (2002) Teaching and betrayal, *Teachers and Teaching: Theory and Practice*, 13(4): 393–407.

Hargreaves, A. (2003) *Teaching in the Knowledge Society: Education in the Age of Insecurity*. New York: Teachers College Press.

Hargreaves, A. and Fink, D. (2004) The seven principles of sustainable leadership, *Educational Leadership*, 61(7): 8–13.

Hargreaves, A. and Fink, D. (2006) *Sustainable Leadership*. San Francisco, CA: Jossey-Bass/Wiley.

Hargreaves, A., Shirley, D., Evans, M., Johnson, C. and Riseman, D. (2006) *The Long and the Short of Raising Achievement: Final Report of the Evaluation of the 'Raising Achievement, Transforming Learning' Project of the UK Specialist Schools and Academies Trust*. Chestnut Hill, MA: Boston College.

Heifetz, R.A. and Linsky, M. (2002) *Leadership on the Line: Staying Alive Through the Dangers of Learning*. Boston, MA: Harvard Business School Publishing.

James, C., Connolly, M., Dunning, G. and Elliott, T. (2006) *How Very Effective Primary Schools Work*. London: Sage.

Lewis, J. and Caldwell, B. (2005) Evidence based leadership, *The Educational Forum*, 69(2): 182–91.

Lima, J.A. (2001) Forgetting about friendship: using conflict in teacher communities as a lever for school change, *Journal of Educational Change*, 2(3): 97–122.

Little, J. (1984) Seductive images and organizational realities in professional development, *Teachers College Record*, 87(1): 84–102.

Little, J.W. (1990) The persistence of privacy: autonomy and initiative in teachers' professional relations, *Teachers College Record*, 91(4): 509–36.

Louis, K.S. (2006) *Organizing for School Change*. London: Taylor and Francis.

Louis, K.S. and Marks, H. (1998) Does professional community affect the classroom? Teachers' work and student work experiences in restructuring schools, *American Journal of Education*, 106(4): 532–75.

Manzo, K.K. (2004) Social studies losing out to reading and math, *Education Week*, 24(27): 1–16.

Marris, R. (1974) *Loss and Change*. London: Routledge and Kegan Paul.

McLaughlin, M. and Mitra, D. (2003) *The Cycle of Inquiry as the Engine of School Reform: Lessons from the Bay Area School Reform Collaborative*. Stanford, CA: Center for Research on the Context of Teaching.

McLaughlin, M. and Talbert, J. (2001) *Professional Communities and the Work of High School Teaching*. Chicago, IL: University of Chicago Press.

Meier, D. (2002) *In Schools We Trust*. Boston, MA: Beacon Press.

Moore, S., Goodson, I. and Hargreaves, A. (2006) Teacher nostalgia and the sustainability of reform: the generation and degeneration of teachers' missions, memory and meaning, *Educational Administration Quarterly*, 42(1): 42–61.

Mulford, W. (1998) Organizational learning and educational change, in A. Hargreaves, A. Lieberman, M. Fullan and D. Hopkins (eds) *International Handbook of Educational Change*. Dordrecht: Kluwer.

Naylor, C. (2005) *A Teacher Union's Collaborative Research Agenda and Strategies: One Way for Canadian Teacher Unions in Supporting Teachers' Professional Development*. Vancouver: British Columbia Teachers' Federation.

Nias, J., Southworth, G. and Yeomans, R. (1989) *Staff Relationships in the Primary School*. London: Cassells.

O'Neill, O. (2002) *A Question of Trust: The BBC Reith Lectures 2002*. Cambridge: Cambridge University Press.

Office for Standards in Education (OFSTED) (2001) *Inspecting New Developments in the Secondary Curriculum 11–16 with Guidance on Self-evaluation*. London: OFSTED.

Rosenholtz, S. (1989) *Teachers' Workplace*. New York: Longman.

Rusch, E. (2005) Institutional barriers to organizational learning in school systems: the power of silence, *Education Administration Quarterly*, 41(1): 83–120.

Sanchez, M. (2006) *Teachers' Experiences Implementing English-Only Legislation*. Boston, MA: Boston College.

Senge, P. (1990) *The Fifth Discipline: The Art and Practice of the Learning Organization*. New York: Doubleday.

Sennett, R. (1998) *The Corrosion of Character*. New York and London: W.W. Norton.

Spillane, J. (2006) *Distributed Leadership*. San Francisco, CA: Jossey-Bass.

Wilson, E.O. and Peter, F.M. (1988) *Biodiversity*. Washington, DC: National Academy Press.

Part 4

Afterword

From her rich experience of professional learning communities and related areas, in Chapter 14 Ann Lieberman reflects on some key messages. While acknowledging that challenges still lie ahead, she concludes that the orientation towards professional learning communities taken by the contributors in this book may provide new ways of thinking about and bringing about educational transformation that will significantly impact individuals, collectivities and whole systems.

fourteen

Professional learning communities: a reflection

Ann Lieberman

The concepts, practices and policies for developing and sustaining professional learning communities is slowly creeping into the literature on reform – not just in schools, but in other workplaces as well. Why is the idea so compelling at this time? Is it an important response to the pace of change and the difficulty of most schools to improve their practices? Is it because the idea of social relationships has finally been recognized as an important condition for the growth and nourishment of intellectual ideas? Is it an organizational form that is uniquely suited to flexibility, looseness and focus, and hence is more adaptable to a variety of different contexts? Is it because people have a greater need for community in this increasingly technological world that is increasingly private? Does Wenger (1998: 4) have it right when he states that: 'learning as social participation shapes not only what we do, but also who we are and how we interpret what we do'. For him learning communities become arenas for professional learning because the people imbue activities with shared meanings, develop a sense of belonging, and create new identities based, in part, on their relationships with one another.

Answers to these questions may help us see why the idea is so attractive and why examples of professional communities are cropping up in many disparate places in the world. We are beginning to understand that if we are going to deal with the pressures of globalization (changing demographics, changing work structures, technology and the way people relate to one another), we need new forms for organizing people; a new sense of focus and frame for how we look at the problems of reform and improvement; and relationships that are supportive and sustained over time. And we are getting clearer about what the impediments are and how people handle the very tensions and dilemmas that these communities create.

New forms of organizing

From a group of teachers organized to talk about and support their peers in learning more deeply about their teaching (Little and Horn, Chapter 6 in this volume) to the networked learning communities in the UK (Jackson and Temperley, Chapter 4 in this volume) to the National Writing Project which has local networks in every state in the USA tied to a National Network (Lieberman and Wood 2003), learning communities are forming that are loosely organized, build norms of colleagueship, start with a focus on teachers' practice and provide a variety of activities for involvement. The forms of organizing are not insignificant. These communities are often informal and voluntary. Groups are sometimes mixed in terms of role and subject area, and spread across geographic areas and defy conventional wisdom (groups must be organized by grade/year level or subject; principals and teachers cannot be in the same group, people need to be teaching in the same context). People can come together face to face, but can also talk and communicate online. Participants can be organized in one school, across schools, across countries and states. And we are even beginning to understand that these communities are helping to create contexts where people's capacities expand, their motivations to improve increase and their commitments to students become re-energized. Teachers who swore they would be teachers forever become principals practicing and honing their new-found knowledge gleaned from their professional learning community. Teachers get involved in a networked community and find that they are learning facilitation skills as well as helping other people go public with their practice. Teachers in the National Writing Project become principals or work in the district or the state, but they have internalized a new set of norms of participation, support and knowledge building. They take these new learnings to their new positions and the impact of their professional learning communities are felt in more systemic ways. None of this happens easily, but it is happening in many places that have had time enough to create and nurture these learning communities.

A new frame and focus for work

The professional learning communities described in the last few decades, frame the problem of learning and improving by *starting where the learners are* and rooting early discussions in going public with *their* practice. This idea is critical. The message is that what *you* know is important. Learning more can come from peers, research or knowledge that is generated together, but the starting point is one's own practice. This not only serves to dignify the participant's work, but it opens them up to their peers and to knowledge from others outside their context (see McLaughlin and Talbert, Chapter 11 in this volume). Teachers become experts one day and learners on the next. The shifting of roles appears to happen more naturally in learning communities (and more fitfully in formal organizations).

Supportive relationships over time

Learning communities intentionally build webs of relationships around the collective work of the participants. Where schools are organized for the most part for people to work as individuals in isolated environments, learning communities are organized as collectivities surrounding people with others who are often struggling with the same problems and frustrations regardless of grade, context or subject matter. These relationships and supportive conditions help people build trust and openly talk about what they know and what they need to know and create a foundation for inquiry into new ideas, new ways of thinking and being in their world. At the same time it enlarges people's world beyond their immediate context (see Mitchell and Sackney, and Stoll *et al.*, Chapters 3 and 5 respectively, in this volume). Sometimes the communities are so strong that the participants feel like their experiences and their new understandings are transformative. Their allegiances to one another become stronger and participants find themselves moving from solo performers to members of a supportive group – building a common language, a way of thinking about improvement and practices that help them deepen their work. Some are even motivated to take on leadership positions as a result of their participation in their learning communities.

Practices that promote learning communities

From our study of the National Writing Project we learned that there were practices that help insure norms and purposes, a sense of belonging and opportunities to shape professional identities. These practices involved: honoring teacher knowledge; situating learning in practice and relationships; providing multiple entry points into the community; promoting an inquiry stance; and sharing leadership as well as creating public forums for sharing, dialog and critique about the work. When participants were involved in sharing their practice, they felt ownership not only for their work but for their peers as well (Lieberman and Wood 2003). These are the kinds of practices that change people's views of learning, improving and participating as a way of succeeding in their work. They turn people to ideas, to communities, to each other as means of further enhancement of their work. They learn by participation in their communities, rather than being told what to do. Internalizing new ways of learning, we are told, is what stays with people as they grow and develop, yet we see that only a few venues encourage this kind of modeling. The practices of learning communities are more cooperative and more connected to exposing the complexities and problematic nature of teaching, and hence the commitment that teachers feel toward them. Their authentic life in all its complexities is grist for the communities' mill.

Continuing to learn about impediments and possibilities

The organization of many schools creates major impediments to the development of learning communities (see McLaughlin and Talbert, Chapter 11 in this volume), as does the press for school improvements that treat teachers, principals and parents as objects for improvement, rather than participants, leaders and organizers of reform efforts. People need time to engage with their peers. They need administrators (leaders) who understand the importance of colleagueship and how to structure ways of organizing for it.

Policy makers need to see that their goals for achieving high-quality schools (and teachers) can be accomplished when the participants are engaged in the real problems of teaching in a supportive environment over time. Quick fixes only serve to frustrate people and alienate them from the ultimate aim of learning over one's lifetime. Learning communities last when they take up the problems of their participants, when they stick to their core work, but provide for constant trouble shooting and problem solving. In other words, they need the stability of predictable ways of working, yet they need constantly to nuance and change, dependent on the growth and needs of the participants. Stability and change are in tension, yet they are the stuff of learning communities that sustain and continue to serve their participants.

The accruing knowledge about professional learning communities continues to whet people's appetite concerning the possibilities for engaging groups of people in helping shape these loose organizations that build agendas that are responsive to both individual and collective development. Little by little, researchers are helping provide evidence that learning communities make a real difference to students and their teachers. Maybe we have finally found the conceptual hook that can provide us with a new form and a new way of thinking about the transformation of schools, which in its way can affect individuals, collectivities and systems.

References

Lieberman, A. and Wood, D. (2003) *Inside the National Writing Project: Connecting Network Learning and Classroom Teaching*. New York: Teachers College Press.

Wenger, E. (1998) *Communities of Practice: Learning, Meaning, and Identity*. Cambridge: Cambridge University Press.

Index

UNDERSTANDING EDUCATIONAL LEADERSHIP
People, Power and Culture

Hugh Busher

This book shows how school leaders at all levels – from the most senior manager to the classroom teacher – can help to build learning communities through collaborating and negotiating with their colleagues, students and students' parents and carers, as well as with external agencies and local communities, to sustain and develop the enjoyment of successful learning among the members of a school. It looks at how positive cultures can be constructed that support inclusive and exciting teaching, enthusiastic teachers and engaged students, parents and carers.

Drawing on research, the book examines topics such as the nature of leadership, especially distributed and teacher leadership; the politics of education management; the construction of inclusive cultures in schools; school improvement; and the construction of collaborative and inclusive work groups. It uses a range of critical perspectives to examine processes of change and the relationships of people in school communities to each other and to their social, economic and policy contexts. The book argues that it is essential to develop inclusive education in order to promote student engagement, social justice and equity within formal education.

Understanding Educational Leadership is key reading for teachers, head-teachers, school leaders, policy makers, Education students and practitioners, and others who have an interest in improving schooling.

Contents: *List of figures, tables and vignettes – Preface – Considering schools as organisations and communities – Mediating the external policy contexts of schools – Where power lies within schools – School leaders as politicians: Governing in whose interests? – The heart of the matter: The moral dilemmas of working in educational settings – Creating cultures: Facilitating engagement – Leading and constructing the curriculum – Developing cultures of learning in subject areas – Strategies of success at middle leader level – Leading purposeful change in schools: People, power and culture – List of references – Index.*

2006   200pp
ISBN-13: 978 0 335 21717 5   (ISBN-10: 0 335 21717 6)   Paperback
ISBN-13: 978 0 335 21718 2   (ISBN-10: 0 335 21718 4)   Hardback

EVERY SCHOOL A GREAT SCHOOL
Realizing the Potential of System Leadership

David Hopkins

'Every school a great school' is not just a slogan, but an aspiration for the next stage of education reform, in which each student has the opportunity to reach their full potential.

The book argues that, for 'every school a great school' to become a reality, requires a move from individual school improvement efforts and short term objectives to a sustainable system-wide response that seeks to re-establish a balance between national prescription and schools leading reform.

Achieving this goal requires strategies that not only continue to raise standards, but also build capacity within the system. David Hopkins identifies four key educational 'drivers' that, if pursued, have the potential to deliver 'every school a great school':

- Personalized learning
- Professionalized teaching
- Networking and innovation
- Intelligent accountability

The author believes that it is the responsibility of system leaders to mould the four drivers to fit individual school contexts. It is this leadership that enables systemic reform to be generic in terms of overall strategy and specific in adapting to individual and particular situations.

Every School a Great School is inspirational reading for head teachers, senior leaders and managers, researchers, lecturers and those with a passionate interest in improving education for all.

Contents: *Introduction – PART 1 The context of system reform – Every school a great school – From large-scale change to system-wide reform – PART 2 The four drivers of system reform – Personalized learning – Professionalized teaching – Intelligent accountability – Networking and innovation – PART 3 Realizing the system leadership dividend – The power of system leadership – Moving system leadership to scale – Bibliography – Index.*

March 2007   216pp
ISBN-13: 978 0 335 22099 1 (ISBN-10: 0 335 22099 1) Paperback
ISBN-13: 978 0 335 22100 4 (ISBN-10: 0 335 22100 9) Hardback

D0951252

THE BEST ALL AROUND

A STORY OF SPORT

By

Rick & John Birk

BEST WISHES
INEZ + GENE

Rick Birk

ISBN no. 978-0-9819964-2-4

Library of Congress Categories: Sports. Sports Fiction.
Sports events. Coaching. Ball games.

This book is easily available at go5books.com

Dedication

For Jonathan: Your lifetime love of sport and your all-around athletic versatility are simply amazing—a victory of which the only reward is a strong sense of accomplishment. I commend you on your spirit.

Love,
Dad

Acknowledgments

Tom Birk

Brad Cooper (Cooper Design Studios)

Barry Marks

Michelle Pettit

Jordan Shoenhair

Tammy Townsend

What People Are Saying About
The Best All Around

"*The Best All Around* is a fascinating, inspiring, and motivating book. It is encouraging to see how two overworked accountants create love, passion, and excitement in their lives by merely doing what they are truly passionate about–sports. Who is the Best All Around Athlete? He or she may be hard to find in this specialized world of sports we now live in. The scenes in the book read so real that it feels that the reader is watching the grueling three-day competition live in the stadium. It is a must read for athletes, sport fans, and all those who want to step outside the box and take a risk to find what they are truly passionate about."

-Sabine Krieger, M.S., Northern Arizona University All-American, German heptathlon champion, three-year top-twenty world ranking

"Every serious athlete comes to realize how closely sports mirrors life— that narrowing human abilities too often compromises human potential. Birk captures this metaphor brilliantly."

-Gary Brasher, member of the 1976-77 Colorado Big-Eight Championship Orange Bowl team, former Arizona state director for the Fellowship of Christian Athletes, current ironman and tri-athlete

"*The Best All Around* is an intriguing, thought-provoking story that grabs hold of you and won't let go. It explores the often confusing, controversial definitions of not only sport but our roles in society as a whole. The likable, relatable characters take you on an entertaining and uplifting ride–well worth the lost hours of sleep because you can't put it down."

-David Bickel, former Arizona State University weightlifting All-American, six-time USATF Masters National Champion

What People Are Saying About
The Best All Around

"*The Best All Around* is not only a measure of an athlete's all around athletic ability, but more importantly, a tribute to the size of a person's heart."

-Chris Johnson - seven-time Arizona Golden Gloves champion, former professional welterweight boxer

"Birk, an Academy graduate, hits on some important subjects in sports, specialization, and dreams. In this story of a young accountant with unfinished business in his sports career, *The Best All Around* reaches out to athletes with lingering feelings many have experienced—wondering after many years what's left in the athletic tank? After reading *The Best All Around*, athletes and sports enthusiasts will realize competing never has to end. And in many instances, it can end gloriously."

-United States Sports Academy

"*The Best All Around* deserves a standing ovation... Clever... Witty... Brilliant... A warm, vivid appreciation of an idea and the ultimate sports competition... The book is a must read for all those who strive to do their best with drive, commitment, and determination in life and sport... I hope vast numbers will read Birk's book."

-Michael Philipp, physical-education teacher, coach–Scottsdale Unified School District

"A powerful and positive message about following your dreams. *The Best All Around* is an exciting and inspiring story that propels the reader along. I enjoyed rooting for Dan!"

-Michelle Pettit, Library Director - McGregor Public Library

PROLOGUE

For Those Who Not Only Dream
But
Work To Realize Their Dreams

In the distance stood the stadium—an image of hope. The early morning sun shone brightly on its vast concrete structure. Its tiers lofted high into the blue sky and stood out majestically, defying the limits of mortal men below. Was this a symbol of an athlete's uncompromising will or perhaps the hint of a marvelous opportunity that lay on the horizon?

CHAPTER

ONE

A car horn interrupted Dan Driver's thoughts. He glanced into the rear-view mirror and noticed the approaching vehicle. He flicked on his signal light and edged into the right lane as an ancient, high-finned Cadillac carrying three teenagers sped by. From behind more cars came up, zipping in, out, rumbling, whooshing past. 'MINIMUM SPEED 45,' flashed a sign on the freeway. Dan accelerated to sixty miles per hour and rejoined the group.

Dan turned on the radio to a loud, barking commercial. With his eyes still on the traffic, he found the scan button and quickly selected the next radio station with lively, upbeat music from the "Great Oldies" collection. Ahead, the freeway lit up with flashing taillights. Dan braked. The line slowed to a crawl, then to a halt. A beep came from behind. Dan glanced up at the mirror. A figure in an SUV gave Dan an impatient wave and drummed his fingers on his dashboard to some musical beat. As the adjacent lane cleared, the SUV swerved out and shot past, leaving Dan sitting and waiting. Dan looked to his right and spied the imposing stadium.

Dan glanced over to the teddy bear in the kiddy-seat to his right. Dan's braking had caused 'Cuddles' to move forward. Dan cracked a smile, reached over and lifted the slumping bear back up into a more dignified posture. He looked off for a moment, pondering. Then, once more, he fiddled with the radio. Another commercial. No decent music anywhere? Dan continued exploring, listening to options, until finally he caught an enthusiastic voice, "One of the most formidable and tireless ever to play the game, offense or defense! Talk about 'The Best All Around,' sports fans, this man *is* the genuine article! Let me repeat Morning Sports Report's top story. B.J. Billings, star outside linebacker and current NFL contract holdout, has signed as a 'free agent' with A.H. Adams. He will serve in the capacity of celebrity spokesperson for the accounting firm right here in our fair city. B.J., do what you think is right. Don't let the media push you around. We want you to play this year, but it's got to come from you. Our helmets go off to you, big hitter! Yes, fans, brawny B.J. led our gallant team through many a heroic struggle. Clowning aside, his career is all-over-the-field football; football the way the game was *meant* to be played. Remember that game against Kansas City in '06? Then the even more critical match-up against the Forty-Niners just last year, when big number 66's giant smack forced that runner to cough up the ball and the NFC championship? Or that 'purposeful collision,' as B.J. called it, against Green Bay back in '04? That hit so hard. Uh, *how* hard? So hard, fans, that—I swear—that poor runner broke another bone on the instant replay!"

Dan snapped off the radio. Once again traffic stalled. For five years, every morning was like this, inching along slowly. Dan reached down, retrieved his brown leather briefcase. This time the car's quick stop had pitched the case forward onto the floor. Dan grabbed the case, positioned it carefully beside Cuddles on the front seat. Dan viewed the case, with its old creases and worn, gold-engraved letters:

DAN DRIVER
TAX ACCOUNTANT I
A. H. ADAMS & ASSOCIATES
CAMELBACK CITY

Finally, the traffic started to move slowly, then soon with full momentum. He glanced briefly into the rearview mirror and spotted the receding walls of the stadium now in the shadows. It was barely 8 a.m. and already hot. Suddenly, Dan remembered the Weber audit report was due today!

Dan wiped sweat from his forehead. Crazy. Yes, crazy. Something was definitely missing. Something very vital, but…what? Dan had comfort, security, success, for all intent and purpose… the good life. Dan appeared to have the American dream.

But Dan Driver wanted something more.

In the Whitney Building's marbled lobby, 40 conservatively clad men and women milled around a single coffee machine. Most held styrofoam cups as they stood in subdued clusters of three, four, and five. It was exactly 8:26 a.m. They chatted in low, respectful monotones, as if awestruck by something beyond the foyer's broad oak door. Across the highly polished marble hallway was the brass plate:

A.H. ADAMS & ASSOCIATES

Everett Winchell, a Tax Accountant II with the firm, stood near the entrance, away from the others. He was a thin, meek, cerebral-appearing man in his late twenties, clutching two steamy cups of coffee, sipping from one. Like those of his coworkers, Ev appeared timid, but alert. He paused for a moment to enjoy the hot coffee. Without spilling, he lifted a finger, scratched an itch on his nose, and reset his tilting spectacles. He turned rigidly, as if on the brink of a nervous breakdown, to witness the buzz a few feet away.

"Yes, Sir, Mr. B.J., there'll be—quite an 'accounting' behind that oak door today!"

The remark incited a mild rash of chuckles, followed by a bashful hoisting of cups. The speaker, Nolton B. Nippers, Senior Tax Accountant II, smiled smugly as he glanced in the direction of the snickers. In his early forties, Nolton "Nips," as he was called, sported a swept-back, rooster-comb hairdo above a pair of dark-rimmed glasses. Behind the glasses his brown eyes held an eternally sad, cow-eyed expression belying all his zaniness. He continued to grin, flashing his baby-like teeth which soon vanished behind thin lips. Ev continued to stare off, his expression one of acute injustice, like that of a man who has just learned he has only six months to live.

Ev's face lit up as he spotted Dan. He walked over and handed his friend one of the steaming cups. "Cutting it close, aren't you? Quarterly audit day and all? Did your daughter Lori hide your breakfast cereal or something?"

Dan took the cup, and nodded a thank you. "I'm more into the waffles and syrup for breakfast right now. This morning, she asked me if we can all watch one of her special movies together tonight. I sure don't want to disappoint her. Half-way to work, I noticed she left her teddy bear in the car again. I guess she'll just have to grin and bear the day, like everybody else."

"Bear it?" Ev playfully repeated. He raised his eyebrows and nodded over at Nips.

For a short time the two men glanced around, sipping their coffee. Dan checked his watch. "8:28! What's the hold up? Sooner we get in, sooner we get started, right?"

"Mossey's rechecking the place," Ev replied. "He just announced that the cleaning crew is going over the premises once more, for the hundredth time. One final inspection!"

"One of the best football players ever? Coming to work for *us*? Figure that one out!" said a woman in a conservative blue suit, aiming to tantalize Nips.

The opportunity did not go unnoticed. "Figure?" said Nips. "So that means we'll be 'toeing the line'!"

"Aren't we always?" shouted another colleague.

At this remark Nips and his colleagues peered off and then exchanged glances, searching for the pun. "Uh, figure?" Nips said. "Mr. B.J. can come waltzing in here to the tune of two hundred big ones just to show his face. And if he smiles he gets—"

The others nodded their approval. "Imagine, two hundred grand for just a couple of ads? That's what a big name will fetch you," a tall, older woman added.

"'Big name'? Hey, try—Lebenausheinkowskielowitz— *that's* a big name!" added Nips.

Ev surveyed. "Can you believe these baaaa-ing sheep?" he confided to Dan. "The man makes us wait out here with our pencils and calculators and laptops? It's going to ruin your daughter's movie and my favorite night of *Seinfeld*, *Cheers*, and *Taxi* re-reruns." He took a sip, and made a long face. "Ridiculous!" he remarked.

"I caught some of the B.J. story on the radio on the drive in to work. Mossey must be a nervous wreck by now," said Dan.

"A.H. Senior himself is slated to show up, along with radio, TV, newspapers, the works. That's why the coffee's set up out here. It's actually for them later, not for us now. But we *are* allowed one cup each. You know why? Nips went to Mossey and told him that if we had to stand out here without our coffee there'd be—are you ready for this one? —'grounds' for employee dis-satisfaction!"

Ev looked disgusted at Dan, then both realized the humor and started to chuckle. "The man's sick," Ev declared. "Certifiably sick. And on audit day. I'm starting to do it! Six years in this Black Hole, insanity's creeping in. I don't want to end up like Nips over there. I'll fight it." Ev wiped his face. "It's August already. Today I *will* finally tell Mossey about that desk I want."

Conversations stopped. Everyone's eyes turned to face the large oak door. An older, dignified man with white hair emerged as the door swung open. Mitchell Mossey, Accounting Supervisor, cleared his throat dramatically. Quickly the employees fell into single file and began to enter. From somewhere came the sound of "Moooo-ooooo." Others took up the chorus. Mossey raised his bushy eyebrows high, scrutinized each passing figure to determine the culprit. He could not.

At once the mooing stopped. Two of the older accountants shuffled to the head of the line. Others parted to let them by. Mossey nodded. "Morning, Miller. Morning, Wells." After Miller and Wells entered the office, the general entry resumed. Men and women took their final sips and discarded their coffee cups into a plastic container beside the door. Each nodded civil good mornings to the white-haired supervisor. At once Mossey tapped Nolton B. Nippers on the shoulder. He directed Nips and those behind him to stop. Mossey bent over, lifted Nip's pants leg, to expose a super-bright psychedelic sock.

"There's one in every crowd," the supervisor uttered, without amusement.

"Uh, two, actually," said Nips. He drew his other pants leg up to reveal the matching sock. The supervisor just stared in amazement.

"Sir! Just to brighten up our day!"

Mossey's replied, You'll have your 'bright side' changed at once."

"Absolutely, sir," said Nips and moved through the line.

Ev and Dan approached. Mossey nodded. They nodded pleasantly in return. Ev cleared his throat. "Uh, Mr. Mossey, sir, about that desk you have stored away, the, um, dusty, old mahogany one, that—that I want?"

"It is 8:30, my man," declared Mossey.

"I—I really could really use that desk."

"Good sir, it's already 8:31. That desk, Mr. Winchell, is for inventory accountants, not tax accountants."

"But I am an accountant. Six years now, this month. And that desk has been sitting there in storage gathering lazy little lint bits for what, the last five?"

"The point precisely. Six years in inventories, but not in tax. Make do with the tax model you have."

"Sir, with all due respect—isn't that absurd?"

"Sir, again. You're not in inventories, you're in tax. It's now 8:32. Time means money. Money means time. There's the Weber audit to tackle. Speaking of 'tackle'," his face creased, then brightened. "Ah yes. Our big day!"

Mossey ducked inside. The closing door bumped Ev's arm, spilling coffee across his sleeve. Ev peeked shyly at the cup, at the sleeve, and finally at Dan. "Okay Dan, this time around you want to 'tackle' the first half while I 'special team' my way through the second? No, wait. This time, for once, Dan, let's be rational. Let's decide with all our God-given brains, insight, and talent."

"Meaning what?"

Ev fumbled sheepishly, brought out a coin. "Your call?" he said meekly.

They smiled. Ev flipped the coin, re-pocketed it, and shrugged. Dan opened the oak door. From the network of cubicles came a hum of business activity, the mild clicking of computer keys, subdued background voices, and additional directions from the passing Mossey. "It's Monday, good people. 8:33. Time to shake off the weekend lazies. Time to hone minds, wits, and pencils. Time to boot up."

From somewhere inside came a disgruntled remark, "Really… two hundred G's just to show up? Shows what a guy can look forward to. If he's a star!"

"Stars, Mr. Smith, are defined by stellar performances."

"Yes, sir."

Ev and Dan glanced at each other.

"Six years? Dan, I don't want to roll over and die like this! There's got to be a way out. Got to be. All or nothing. And don't *look* at me like that, Dan Driver. You could be next!"

CHAPTER
TWO

Dan shoved the stack of papers aside to find his family photo. He picked up the picture, gripped the frame, and stared hard at his face. He noticed his vacant eyes as he held hands with Lori, his precious four-year-old, as his beautiful wife Debra held two-year-old Jeff in her arms. Suddenly the heat of the morning became too oppressive, the mountain of work too much. Dan placed the photo on top of the pile of papers. He leaned back in his chair, clasped his hands behind his neck, and gazed off. Ev was right, absolutely right. Somehow, somewhere, there had to be a better way. There *had* to be.

"Here's one of the three reports you want," a voice said. "I can't help you with the others because I know nothing about that sub-area of tax accounting. Not that I'm helpless, but I have no choice but to 'help less' because I'm - 'helpless'."

Nolton B. Nippers entered Dan's cube and dropped the report on Dan's desk, as he carefully observed Dan. Dan viewed his playful eyes above the big smile.

"Thanks for the information, Nips. It's not you. I'm just preoccupied."

Nips persisted, "And did you see how Mossey jumped me because of my socks again?" He leaned close into Dan's face, whispered the words. "Attacking my God-given freedom of expression in front of everybody!"

Dan nodded, without his customary smile. Nips momentarily removed his thick lenses, rubbed his fingers over his weary eyes. "Okay, okay, Dan, work, work. Fine, fine. My eyes were once like an eagle's too, until I put in my years here. Twenty now, to be exact. You'll need glasses yourself soon enough, you'll see. You haven't passed the ten-year mark yet, but … wait, 'you'll see' that 'you can't see!'"

Dan stared at Nips, stared at what two decades in a place like this could do to a man. Nips gave a loose shrug. "Twenty years? I've seen 'em crack up. Strong men and women to start with."

And with his crazy laugh, Nips was gone.

The morning dragged. By 10:00, Dan began to look forward, almost eagerly, to one of Ev's regular interruptions, when the frail, little man would drop into Dan's cubicle, coffee mug in hand. Like Nips, Ev only wanted a chance to talk, to commiserate, to empathize or blow off steam. Dan found himself more than willing to listen to both.

Shortly after 10:30, Ev was at Dan's desk discussing, of all topics, the weather. "Heat can't last *that* much longer. I mean—the worst August we've ever had. Dan, remember I told you about April's Boston Marathon in all that heat sending more than eleven hundred runners to the medical tents for dehydration, cramps, heart ailments, you name it? Same thing's going to be happening here. Whew, I bet. I—"

His words broke off. He and Dan looked up. The two senior accountants, Miller and Wells walked past, mumbling to each other, leaving Dan and Ev looking at each other in disbelief.

Ev whispered somberly, as if on the brink of desperation. "Wells has been at this for thirty-four years, and Miller for thirty-two. Look at them, Dan! It's scary. Too scary!" He marched to the doorway, took pause, as if about to say something. Then he swallowed, shook his head, and, wordlessly, stalked off.

By 11:00, Dan's cubicle had become a sweatbox and left him wondering when the AC would be fixed. He looked around at the various piles of papers on his desk—all of them seemed as overwhelming as when he had started. It felt as if the last two hours' work had been for naught.

The PA system erupted with Mossey's voice, "AC technicians have been dispatched to fix the cooling system, and in the meantime, do your best to persevere!"

Dan momentarily leaned back, and surveyed the paperwork. At once he leaned forward and scribbled a figure—his monthly salary—on a pad. He divided the figure by 2,080 and multiplied by two to learn what the last two hours had financially brought him. He took in the result, and frowned. He wrote down his wife Deb's hourly salary and added to it her differential for the night shift. This, too, he doubled, and added it to his own. Impressive on paper? Perhaps, but from a practical, daily standpoint of paying off a thirty-year mortgage and raising two kids, it might—just might—suffice, if not for the exorbitant taxes! And yes, he worked in taxes. Then it struck him. He was an average man working in taxes and was being destroyed by taxes at the same time.

Did Deb, too, suffer these long, boring stretches? Was her work as a nurse every bit as unfulfilling? Dan envisioned the faces on the picture of Lori and Jeff grinning amusedly at him. Two faces not the least bit aware of the cost and worry of maintaining a home. Better to let them enjoy life now, when happiness comes easily. Yes, life should be ice cream, merry-go-rounds, and a button-eyed bear named Cuddles. It should be wonderful!

Dan sighed aloud. Today was not the first time his mind had drifted in this direction. A brief escape of sorts, his run-away thoughts always seemed to hit the same dead end. What else could any father, any loving, responsible parent do? The rhetorical question seemed to have no clear answers.

Outside the office, footsteps and muffled voices were heard as Mossey and Nips walked past the window. "Get that AC fixed, sir, and the sooner we will be those 'darned,' 'cold calculating' accountants you want us to be."

At once the footsteps stopped. Mossey peeked to Dan and nodded. Dan nodded back. The supervisor cleared his throat. "Nolton, your humor has come up a notch," he retorted. Soon the two were out of sight, leaving Dan once more to his thoughts.

11:40 a.m. Dan labored, tie off and draped across the back of his chair, shirt collar unbuttoned, his chin, throat, and forehead gleaming with perspiration. Sensing a presence, he peeked up. "Going to make ample headway by lunchtime when our new man arrives?"

"I sure hope to, sir. Looks like another evening session for me."

"I see. Well, young man, I'd appreciate it if you and the others would take a short timeout to greet our new employee in the lobby. In the proper attire, of course!" he added, with a nod. "That's why I'm making the rounds. Say ... 12:03?"

Dan nodded.

Mossey surveyed the desktop. "See what happens when you don't hop to it and get that first big jump? It was after 8:36 before you and Mr. Winchell got started. Idle hands do the devil's bidding." He cracked a smile. Behind his tough exterior, he liked Dan.

Dan thought for a moment, then spoke. "I know how preoccupied you are today with B.J. Billings coming in and all, sir, but that desk Mr. Winchell was asking about?"

Mossey eyed him. "You want a shot at it, too?"

Dan shook his head no. Mr. Mossey frowned. "You heard. The man's not qualified."

"But why stick him with a tiny desk? Look at the paperwork I've got here. He's got at least as much. Consider the efficiency, the elbowroom, the morale. From a cost-benefit standpoint—and isn't that how A.H. Adams always judges things anyway?—wouldn't it make sense?"

Mr. Mossey mulled. "'Stick him'? 'Plagued'? 'Elbowroom'? Where is this discussion coming from, Mr. Driver? We both know the score, do we not?"

"The score?"

"Yes, it's an inventory desk!" implored Mossey.

They looked at each other, less employer to employee than man to man. After a moment the supervisor peeked at his wristwatch. "Right," he nodded. "The score. To get ahead and stay ahead. To specialize. Look at B.J. Billings, he's a well-tutored, professional outside linebacker. Which is why I am forever on the backs of you people to narrow your scopes accordingly. To know more and more specifics, to know how to perform more and more that the world at large does not know or cannot perform and yet so desperately needs. Law, digital systems, virtual reality, biomedical engineering, genome tracking, laser surgery, state-of-the-art small-business tax accounting, just to name a few. That's the button-down world of success today, Mr. Driver. Define your snug little niche. Master it. Make the world beat a path to *you*. Another word for it? Survival." He nodded to the family photo atop Dan's desk. "If—you get my drift?"

Dan looked at him. "Sir," Dan implored, "specialties are fine, but what results? Some 'specialist' designs a car or overpass or building and ends up killing my family or me and I'll never know why. Some repairman twists a screw a quarter-notch on my water heater and charges me a hundred bucks. How do I know I'm being ripped off? I don't. Nuclear plants, pesticides, felons 'rehab-ed' enough to walk among our kids? This whole setup is wrong. It puts each of us completely at the mercy of other 'experts.'" Dan pushed a new run of perspiration off his chin and nodded up at the AC vent. "Mercy, all right," he said.

"What about you and your own special skill, small-business tax accounting? Doesn't that make you as 'guilty' as the rest of us?"

Dan shrugged. "It's called—feeding my family."

"Exactly right. And the sum of so many specializations and family-feeders is what we call—civilized society. Look at countries where it isn't happening. Want to bring your kids up there?"

"Of course not. But, sir, look at the sadder side of each individual in the network. You find experts in nuclear-particle theory or data-storage management unable to fasten their new Velcro shoes."

"Or people like Nips wearing socks 'fitting' for the occasion?" Mossey added.

"Yes, he's another case in point, sir. He came to me just this morning, a micro-business Senior Tax Accountant II— and a darn good one—unable to help me, a fellow-micro-business Tax Accountant I, because my 'sub-sub-area' was beyond the scope of his 'sub-sub-area.' If micro-business-tax accountants can't help other micro-business tax accountants, who can? What's *happening* to this world?"

"Well, Mr. Driver, this isn't Philosophy 101. Your Weber audit is due by the end of the day. Just remember, you're doing very well for yourself here. You're neat, quiet, punctual, a solid worker. You keep a low profile. You've passed the five-year mark and are up for Tax Accountant II. I like you. We like you. I even happen to enjoy your sporadic outbursts of spunk. It shows a healthy skepticism, a depth of vision. Now all you need is to finish that fourth part of the

CPA and secure your Masters Degree in Taxation. That will be the yellow-brick road to your golden future, Mr. Driver. Want my advice? Don't rock the boat. Don't even jiggle it."

Dan stared against the frosted wall of his cube. Beyond, figures moved in blurred, indistinct motions. Meanwhile, atop his desk sat the huge pile of paperwork.

"Sir, don't you ever feel cramped or confined, like something vital is missing, like a huge slice of life, excitement, or fresh air?"

"Mr. Driver, what 'freedom' could you want that we don't offer? Do tell me? I mean freedom that isn't outright fleeing into lazy irresponsibility? The Sixties are long over. Some fifty-odd years now. The hippies have shed their locks and come back to work. A Baby Boomer has already been President. Why? Because that's 'where it's at.' Look around. It's the only thing that's real." He took pause, again glanced at his watch. "So in precisely nineteen minutes, you'll be in the lobby with the rest, in proper attire?"

Dan nodded. "Absolutely."

The white-haired supervisor headed out, shaking his head slowly, the woes of the entire clueless world on his shoulders. "Of course, Mr. Driver, ultimately it is up to you. If you are so intent on 'beating the system,' who am I to stop you? In fact, I 'darn' well invite you to try."

"Folks—here he ISSSSSS!!!"

The announcement was made on the intercom system. The employees quickly gathered as requested. It was the time everyone had eagerly anticipated. Flashbulbs lit up the lobby. A host of newspaper and TV representatives joined the accountants to cover the special event. Some strained their necks and went up on tiptoes to catch sight of the object of attention. Towering some six-and-a-half feet tall and weighing more than 250 lbs., B.J. Billings was imposing not only for his size but his energetic, aggressive style. Mossey remained at his side, hard pressed to stay close while maintaining an aura of unassuming dignity. B.J.'s dimply, playful face, his bright red sport coat with its NFL logo and well-tailored slacks—these stood in dramatic contrast to the drab, conservative demeanors and dress of the others. As the crowd parted way, B.J. and Mossey cut through, B.J. lumbering with an air of suave, laid-back confidence, the other nodding about pleasantly, shaking hands with everyone. "Ladies, gentlemen—please! This *is* an accounting firm." The supervisor mouthed these words repeatedly, but with scant earnestness. He was unable to hide his grin. Reporters crowded up. "One more, B.J.? One more? One more of you and Mr.—Bossey, is it?"

At this *faux pas*, laughter burst forth not so much from the media as from the employees, who until this moment had seemed content to linger quietly, good-naturedly, on the edge of things. "Print that!" a timid voice in the group suggested, and a second burst of chuckles erupted.

Mossey smiled dryly, raised a reluctant hand against the request for a joint photo, yet he edged in beside B.J. nonetheless. He had little choice in the matter. B.J. had stopped before him and the crowd pressed in from all sides. As lenses took aim, Mossey reached up, felt B.J.'s bicep, and posed with an exaggerated grin. Amid cheers, laughter, and a scatter of applause, cameras rolled and bulbs snapped.

"Mr. Billings," inquired a reporter, "Is it true you're picking up several hundred grand just to show up here two days each week?"

"That figure, my dear sir, is a grossly inflated one," Mossey broke in.

B.J. leaned over. "It is?" he asked, loudly enough to be overheard. Again came laughter. B.J. lifted a hand and the laughter fell away. "No really. I'm here to contribute," he protested. "To the A.H. Adams team. Besides—my golf game needs a little work." More chuckles ensued and Mossey ushered dimply-faced B.J. to the entrance of the firm, B.J. grinning, high-fiving, shaking hands with everyone. B.J. shook Dan's hand and nodded cordially. After shaking hands with Ev, B.J. winced and wriggled his fingers painfully, as if the slender man's grip had injured him. "Real friendly crowd you got here," he said, with deadpan sincerity above the snickers and smiles.

As the door wedged open, Mitchell Mossey turned back to the crowd. "Ladies and gentlemen, just *how* friendly are we?"

On cue the employees let out with, "B.J.! B.J.! BEEE-JAYYYYY!"

"Yesiree, we're glad to have the man aboard. One of the world's best at what he does. We are honored, sir."

None of that 'sir' stuff, 'Mr. Bossey.' We're a team," quipped B.J.

Again came cheers, whistles, and more applause.

"Are you going to perform at A.H. Adams like you do on the field?" a voice shouted from the crowd.

"And how's that?"

"Rumor has it—you're so quick that you can be in two places at once. And able to throw with either hand?"

"Hey, me? I ain't no Spiderman. Only thing I might throw around here is a party. Only thing I'll pitch is your product. All to aid the cause."

"Yes, a man of tireless, go-getting, dedicated energy," Mossey announced.

A young reporter squirmed close. "Is it true that to do the ads here you're going to give up football this season?" he asked.

B.J.'s face twitched. He viewed the reporter, then rolled his eyes over to Mossey, who gave the questioner an absurd look and shook his head. "Look, as far as this season goes, I'm still negotiating," said B.J.. "That's the NFL side of the equation, that you guys know all about. But I'm here cuz I signed a contract to what—'ensconce' the reputation of A.H. and the group."

"Uh—enhance," corrected Mossey.

"Whatever. Besides, I'm twenty-nine. A young twenty-nine. There will be a few more falls before *this* dapper dude waddles out to some cow pasture."

"Especially since you're so used to playing with—

pigskins?"

This remark came from Nolton B. Nippers, who had wormed his way up to the front. He and B.J. faced each other, the Nips peering up like an amused rooster through dark-rimmed glasses, B.J. blinking down perplexedly. "Sure, B.J., wear your identity, like I wear mine!" Nips retreated a step and hoisted up a pants leg to reveal—the brightly colored sock. A bulb exploded. One nimble reporter had photographed the sock.

"Uh, *don't* print that," beseeched Mossey.

"Looney Tunes all over this place!" B.J. shook his head, turned and ducked through the doorway.

The crowd dispersed, but Dan and Ev remained. From inside came more cheers, claps, and renewed laughter. The oak door closed shut, muting the celebration.

Ev looked to Dan for a moment. "Sure, Dan, sure," Ev said, then. "Easy as pie. If you're a star."

Just as sluggishly as the morning, the afternoon crawled by. Not long after lunch Mossey offered a PA announcement thanking all the employees for their participation and enthusiasm. Dan labored on, tie removed, collar open, cuff buttons undone, sleeves rolled up. Then all at once the AC came on. Was this a coincidence or in honor of B.J.'s arrival? Dan took pause to enjoy the sensation of the cool air brushing across his arms, chest and face. Then, just as quickly and inexplicably, the flow of air stopped, and the room relapsed into its sticky August oppressiveness. Outside the hum of human activity grew lower, less persistent. Conversation slowed. Chuckles were more sporadic, more subdued. Dan was not the only one suffering.

Shortly after 3:00 Dan's concentration was interrupted. From an adjacent cubicle came a loud commotion. The cubicle, a uniquely handsome one, was far more of a private office than a cubicle. It had remained idle since it was vacated a half year earlier by a retired Vice President. Dan paused, laid down his pencil, and listened as the conversation floated across in bits and pieces:

"... our very utmost to make you as cozy as you can be, B.J.. We can't give you the VIP suite. Not yet, anyway. This is the best we've got. The flooring—that special artificial grass you requested—will be in by Friday. We, uh ... didn't think we'd be so lucky to have you so soon."

"... is kind of snug, this cubbyhole, but an okay place to stash my sports-blooper videos. Hey, Moss, I'll be the first to admit, at least to you. I do miss football—the hitting, the crowd, the mud, and especially the cheerleaders."

"Uh, right. But you'll find a high level of competition here, too," B.J., added Mossey. "Just a bit more glossed over by the guise of civilization and good manners, that's all. We are every bit as competitive."

The voices faded, overridden by the hum of the air conditioner. Dan's spirits rose. Then, just as quickly, the hum had gone. Dan clutched his head in his hands for a time, wiped his face, and resumed his work.

Dan continued to work. At once from the hallway came an odd sound of wood scraping, amid subdued mumbles. Then came more scraping, followed by a rash of workmen's voices calling to one another. Meanwhile, from the cubicle next door, Dan could hear Mossey's voice:

" Your charity work is most impressive, B.J.. Talk about building credibility with the public."

"Uh, right. Big Brothers? Make a Wish Foundation? United Way? I'm into *all* of them. Big time. Got to pay back, you know."

"Splendid, indeed. No more than a few hours a week. Just to show up and bolster morale. Our profession is by nature low-profile, but now we have the okay from the top to advertise. You're a big name. Enjoy its marketability. Clowning around's fine, but ..."

"No, really, Moss. I'm here to play the game."

"Yes, as the poet put it, 'Play the play,'" said Mossey. "And we'll expedite the entertainment center with that new 52-inch flat screen so you can catch all the latest highlights. It should be here the day after tomorrow."

"Great."

"Really, B.J.. We're grateful. I know our competition, B.H. Baker and his boys down the block, laid out the royal carpet, too, but how else can I put it? The better team won."

"The final gun hasn't sounded on that one," said B.J. "Well, we both know all about that. We'll just play it by ear these first few weeks."

"Your first TV commercial will grant you ample public

exposure for your charity work," Mossey promised.

More abrupt scrapings. A dull thump. Dan listened, all curiosity now.

"I asked you gentlemen to *carry* it. That's prize equipment, you know."

"Hey, this chair is comfy," said B.J.. "Sure tops the cold benches up in Buffalo Bills land!"

"And formerly a decathlon runner, too? Simply amazing, B.J.. No wonder you're so famous for being what? Ambidextrous? And in two places at once. Really."

Dan heard a chuckle, and turned. Ev was peeking in, empty mug in hand. Ev peeked at his watch, then offered a crisp salute. "Now hear this. Come dinnertime, I should have my half done. Hey, why the long face?"

"The heat, I guess," Dan said. "It's been slow going without the AC."

"Tell me about it," quipped Ev. "Well, they can't fix the AC because they can't find a fifty-dollar-an-hour specialist who can, right?"

"Who can get in touch with him?"

"The twenty-dollar-an-hour dispatcher, of course!" laughed Ev.

Dan gave a vacant nod. Behind Ev a figure leaned in. It was Widham, another Accountant I. "Hey, you figure-fudgers want in on tonight's pool? Rams and Lions. Should be a good one."

"Still the exhibition season," said Ev.

"Doesn't matter. Bet's a bet."

"Odds-makers put the Rams up by eight and a half."

"How do you know?"

"I know."

"That's right. You're the whiz who checks out that stuff every day. Can't get enough figures here, you go home, pore through the sports pages!"

"Absolutely," said Ev.

"Well, I wish I had the time to, Ev, but I've got a 'marathon' project of my own waiting in my office," said Widham. "Hey, you know all about marathons, don't you?"

"Four-ninety B.C. Darius and his fifty thousand Persians outnumber the Athenians four to one. At Marathon Bay the Athenians with their long spears rout the Persians, who retreat and prepare to attack undefended Athens. Phidippides— not even wearing Nikes, mind you—races the twenty-six miles to warn the city, falls over and dies from exhaustion. Athens is saved."

Widham looked at him. "Uh, right," he said. "But then, tell me, nowadays, when your city's not under assault, why do people run marathons? I mean, it's so much simpler to sit at a desk and chase down info on the Internet, right?"

Ev shrugged. "For a variety of reasons. Novices run marathons to lose weight, win a bet, promote a cause—breast cancer, leukemia—or to enjoy the sheer boost in self-esteem that comes with finishing. Another runner I know does it to experience Zen, a union of mind and body."

"Well, speaking of triumphing over numbers, and exhaustion—catch you guys later. Money is time. Time is money." Widham winked and departed.

Dan surveyed the piled papers on his desk. "Marathon is right," he said, quietly.

"I've got to head down to the file room and dig out some of the old Hamilton information—you know, from the old storage files," said Ev. "Talk about fossils and data-space management? Some of the old stuff hasn't even been transferred onto our new software yet. Probably won't get to it till tomorrow morning either. Remember, Dan, the key is patience. Like that Slovenian guy we were talking about, in 1997, he swims from Africa to Europe, across Gibraltar. In 2000, he does the entire length of the Danube, almost two thousand miles—in fifty-eight days. In 2001, he breaks the world non-stop swim record by doing over three hundred miles of the Danube in eighty-four hours. In 2002, the same guy swims the entire length of the Mississippi, nineteen hundred miles in sixty-eight days. Uh-huh, patience and perseverance. I'll bet you he could even survive the Weber account."

There came another thump from down the hall. "Sounds like Mossey's prize recruit is moving in, with everything from padded goalposts to a padded expense account," said Dan.

"Incredible," said Ev. "Understandable, though. A super-athlete appears, the whole world swoons. Just one more instance of the worship of sport. Hey, do you know that the Greeks stopped entire wars to take time out to hold the Olympics? A British and American sub broke through the ice at the South Pole for the two crews to what?— play a game of soccer. And remember back in June when I showed you the photos of this year's Western States Endurance Run, that hundred-mile nightmare of climbs and descents that drains every ounce out of its participants? The five Ironman races in the U.S., and sixteen in the world, take place every year with a capacity number of athletes and thousands of lookers-on? Who wants to swim two and a half miles, bike a hundred and twelve miles, then run a marathon—all in a seventeen-hour limit? CBS's Amazing Race pits teams against each other for a million-dollar prize. Let's face it, America's still in its long honeymoon with sport. This reminds me, Dan. You played all kinds of sports—baseball, football, basketball, golf, track—in high school and in college, right? Why don't you finagle yourself some kind of deal? I mean, you're not exactly thrilled to be here. What sane person could be?"

"Because I'm not an NFL right outside linebacker," said Dan.

"Yeah, speaking of which. You know, I did some checking. Back at Alabama— or was it Texas Tech?—the record's still muddy, with B.J. rumored to be equally adept with either hand. Yes, we've all heard the one about his being in two places at once. But, the ability to use either hand? No one can say. His specialty is the ability to stop anyone from finding out. He shook hands well enough." Ev flexed his wrist. "But you did play. Still do, right?"

"Football? Ev, that was seasons back. One wife, two kids, one big mortgage ago."

"Twenty-eight, nine? You're about the same age as B.J., too. And still work out, right?"

"Sure try to."

"What? Basketball? Running? And that boxing club over at the Y, too, huh?"

"Twice a week, you name it. Everything *but* a marathon."

"There I don't blame you," said Ev. "You know that marathoners—the real serious ones—run between a hundred and a hundred and fifty miles a week. Many like to train at high altitudes, so their blood can make more red cells that carry oxygen to their muscles. How do most of them end up? With terrible tendonitis, totaled achilles, deep-purple body parts, off-the-charts shin splints. Who's gonna welcome that, right? But the mental pain is *even* worse. Watching your body do the same thing for two hours plus, with each step pounding quadruple your body's weight from foot up against hip—it can drive you crazy. But, ironically, some great runners actually do perform better when they're in pain."

Dan smiled. "Which brings us back to what—A.H. Adams?"

Ev smiled. "No, they do it to bring us all up a notch. To push the envelope as far as they can, to do the best the species can do. To shatter that record—now two hours, five minutes. Dan, that's four minutes, forty-seven seconds a mile for 26.2 miles! Last year, would you believe, almost half a *million* Americans ran marathons. It just shows that our culture *is* in deep, deep love with sport."

Ev hoisted his empty mug toward B.J.'s office. "Sure, so here's to our own new *'draft choice.' May he 'tackle' our 'over-padded' accounts, keep us all 'on the* line.'" He winked impishly to Dan. "Probably against NFL rules, but I'm going to get me an inside scouting report."

Ev popped up his meager chest, flexed a minuscule bicep, and strutted off. Dan grinned, and returned to his work.

Moments later Dan glanced up, to again spy Ev's face. The face held a radically altered expression, one of sadness, betrayal, hurt. "Sure. So give *him* the desk!"

As Ev's footsteps receded, Dan heard, "So darned easy, if you're a *star* named B.J."

Dan sat idly at his desk. The stacks of paper had for the most part vanished. Another announcement promising that the AC would be on soon was followed by another hour of hot oppressiveness. Yet somehow a sudden, mysterious burst of energy lent Dan some headway. He had at least three hours yet to go, but he felt relieved, and immensely grateful.

Dan had accomplished a great deal this afternoon, but not so much from a desire to help A.H. Adams. The desire seemed to come from an anger festering somewhere within, from a source he could not exactly define. His five years here, his life, his hopes, and his spirit, were these being wasted?

Dan felt fortunate to have this fairly solid job, but was it a cop-out? Was there another way, or a better alternative? With a wife and two kids, could he take a chance? Dan loved Deb and the kids. He would never jeopardize their futures.

So, to provide for their well-being, Dan Driver, at the ripe old age of twenty-nine, had 'retired' to the pasture that B.J. had scoffed at. Was he destined to sit for years to come in this cubicle cell, punching plastic buttons and sifting through volumes of figures, while, just outside, the glorious seasons came and went? It was already August. Summer would soon be over and transition into another brilliant autumn. For many, a time synonymous with gridiron action. However, Dan would scarcely have noticed had not Widham stopped in to mention tonight's game.

Again came chatter from the newly occupied cube next door. "We'll shoot the first two ads in the stadium, where you feel more at home. The last one we'll do here, right in our own Whitney Building. Meanwhile, rest assured that we'll do our utmost to make you as happy as you can be, B.J.."

The phone rang, and Dan responded. "Sure, I can pick them up. Shouldn't be much longer. Figure six, six-thirty at the latest. I'll grab a bite on the way. Uh, Deb—love you."

"Love you too Dan."

Dan hung up, smiling. He surveyed the papers, rechecked his watch, and labored on.

From next door he heard, "As I said, formerly a decathlon athlete. B.J., that's absolutely incredible!"

Dan stared off now, daydreaming, as he tapped the soft, compromising end of his pencil on the edge of his desk. After a few minutes, he put down the pencil and picked up his family photo. He thought of another family picture taken more than twenty -five years earlier. It was a cherished picture of himself as a child, sitting on his father's lap, clutching an oversized baseball mitt.

He then recalled a Little League game, what—two long decades ago? Dan had snagged a hard liner at short, had raced across second, had whirled and tossed to third to catch the other runner by a step. A glorious triple play, the only one Dan had ever made.

Another memory surfaced. Dan recalled a football game he played as the quarterback against the Arrowhead Warhawks. He recalled in minute detail a specific play. Dan had pitched the ball and had turned to block the defensive end. The back had been hit immediately. The ball had squirted out, and up. Dan had caught it in mid-air and had whirled straight into a wall of defenders. The thud and power of that collision had rung in Dan's dreams for days. It was Dan's very first varsity play as a sophomore.

Next, Dan re-lived the state basketball semi-finals, in his junior year. With four seconds left in the game, the score was tied, 70-70. Dan had caught the inbound pass and swiftly passed to a teammate, who had put up a quick shot. The ball had hit the rim and bounced off. Amid a herd of leaping bodies, Dan had rebounded the ball awkwardly and tipped it in a split-second before the buzzer sounded. The ball had rolled around the rim, and finally had dropped through, leaving Dan mobbed by teammates, cheerleaders, fans, and even Coach Blank. Dan wondered. Where had his teammates gone? They had been so young and each had been full of innocent, hopeful energies. What had the world done to each of them?

Then Dan was back on the golf course. He vividly recalled that fine spring afternoon of the Suburban Conference finals, less than a week before graduation. That day Dan had lived up to his name of "Driver" all right, striking the ball smartly, accurately, off the tee. He had putted very well, too, to come in a shot over par on a difficult course and become the match medalist.

Moving on to football once again, Dan recalled standing next to Coach Sims beneath the football goalposts of the state university stadium. On the far end a lone kicker was practicing field goals. The stadium was mammoth, easily seating 60,000. Dan had seen games televised from there even as a child. As he actually stood on the field, barely a month after graduation from high school, he was awed by the echoing vastness and history of the facility. The grass so green, the sidelines so sharply defined, the rows on rows on rows of seats lofting up against the sky. Coach Sims had escorted Dan out onto the field for precisely this reason—to impress on him, up close and personal, the prestige of playing at State.

"You're a fine all-around athlete, son, no question about that." Dan had sensed the coming damper in the coach's words. The damper had come. "However, here at State we basically run. We recruit offensive linemen and big backs, especially three-backs. You aren't going to fit into our system unless you're willing to work in the I-formation and run the option. It calls for a nimble, specialized quarterback. You'll have to forego your flair for scrambling, passing, and razzle-dazzle that you've shown in your films. You'll have to work more on pivots, on those handoffs and close pitches on the plays I diagrammed. And as far as basketball or golf, I'm afraid they'd be out of the picture, too. We, at State, expect our players to participate in spring ball and our off-season weight program, to be football players first and foremost. You've got the talent to contribute as an I-formation QB. We'll offer you the full ride. The choice, of course, is yours. But remember—only one sport son."

Only forty-eight hours later, Dan stood with Coach Wiley in the Lakefield College Stadium. The seats were wooden bleachers with ancient coats of peeling paint. The capacity of the structure was barely 5,000. Yet, in seeming defiance of the reality around him, Wiley seemed proud. It was his particular philosophy of sport that he seemed so happy to confess. "Play two or three sports?" he grinned. "You must be one real ball of fire, Dan, but okay by me. Here at Lakefield we're no football factory. We are in a solid, competitive league, and that's why we're recruiting you. We can't match State money-wise. No, you may not get the ink and possible pro offers when you finish, but here you'll have fun. I'm no believer in tying people down to narrow, fixed positions. Especially young people, whom the world should encourage to expand and try new things. Look, we pull ahead in a game, we run. We fall behind, we pass. Beyond that simple strategy, I can't predict." Once again he had grinned almost apologetically. "And we will try to get that, uh, scoreboard fixed by September!"

Dan chose Lakefield. His senior year at Lakefield was an unforgettable one. On a crisp autumn evening the Lancers pulled out a hard-fought season finale. Coming from behind with a 60-yard touchdown pass with eight minutes to go, the Lancers were threatening again. With less than two minutes to go Dan called a quarterback option, with the trailer-back to follow. At first contact, as a forearm pad thrust rudely up into his ribs, Dan twisted, somehow pitched the ball, then met another stubborn wall crushing him earthward. Dan tucked in his head, slid, and tasted the cold, sweet dampness of the grass. An eruption of screams and cheers from beyond told him even before he could shift his eyes that Willy Gant, the trailer-back, had taken it in. Now it was 20-20.

Dan and Willy traded high-fives as they trotted their way back through the Lancers jogging out to set up the extra point. At the bench teammates cheered, and planted capes on the two as they reached the sideline and then turned, fingers crossed, to witness. The snap, set, kick: good! Lakefield by a point. "One forty-six, man," Willy mumbled, peering to the ancient, still unreliable scoreboard clock and stamping his feet against the cold ground. Dan grinned, then eyed him curiously. "You're not celebrating?" Dan asked.

"Like one forty-six in this dude's life," Willy said. He watched the defense take the field like inspired demons and prepare to kick off. "Hey, this is the last real contest I'm ever going to play in. I mean, where people suit up and it counts. Next year you and I'll be lucky to—"

The kick came, deep, lofty, end over end. The receiver who took it at the ten was met at the thirty by so many inspired Lancers, that the collision echoed into the stands.

"—to play in an industrial league somewhere."

Willy undid his helmet, glumly planted it on the bench. Another senior, Tim, stepped up beside Dan. Tim's nose was bleeding. "Way to go, Danny boy! One more 'W' for Coach Wiley! Way to go!" Tim, too, paused to look off for a time. "Sure, Dan, you got buckets and track left," he said, then. "But what about us?"

Six months later, on a beautiful afternoon in May, Dan learned what Willy, Tim, and the other gridiron seniors had faced that night. Dan along with Bob, a fellow-experimenter in the high-jump, were refining their approaches to the bar. Dan propped the crossbar up to six-four, a full two inches above his personal best, walked back to the starting line, closed his eyes, and began to envision his stepwise passage through the effort. It was then that the words came, and broke his line of thought.

"Dan—this one's for the yearbook!"

Dan opened his eyes and turned. The shutter clicked. For a moment Dan stood by, dazed by the camera, her smile, her presence.

"Catch you tonight?" Dan managed.

"If you're lucky," jabbed Debra.

"Like little kids," she teased. "Never willing to just step out of the sandbox, brush themselves off, and let go."

She shaded her eyes against the brilliantly setting sun, then peered off toward the bar. "An adult working so hard to try to jump over a stick lying across two others? Why? It mystifies me. Absolutely!"

"You've got to love it to do it," explained Bob. "It's a different kind of sport."

"More an Olympic event," said Dan.

She shook her head, and gave a parting wave. "Uh, right. Okay, tonight. Say—eight?" She strode off, smiling, her camera swinging from her waist.

Once again Dan lined up, took a deep breath.

"Dan, maybe she's right?" said Bob. "Track season ended last week. Going on six. And tomorrow is graduation."

"Just one more. To top these last two inches."

"Dan—none of this *counts* anymore."

Dan held up. As he considered, a cloud appeared, temporarily blocking the sun.

"Really, Dan. I'm a junior. You're a senior. Your eligibility's *gone*. On to bigger and better things—like marrying that chick?"

Bob turned and started for the gym, the cloud gone, the sun casting his long, thin shadow across the grass. Dan stood for a time. Only minutes later did he take the cue, step away, and accept that his career had passed.

Other than a few times in his mind, Dan Driver never performed that final jump. The image of that bar poised two inches higher than his previous best had hovered in his thoughts and dreams for years. Now, on this late Monday afternoon, at the accounting firm of A.H. Adams & Associates, Dan Driver wore precisely the expression he had shown some eight years before—a look of painful, inevitable recognition, of sadness following in the wake of unanticipated hurt. It seemed so long ago. Yet it also ... seemed like yesterday.

As if acknowledging his remoteness from the here and now, the voices from the adjoining cubicle sounded in Dan's ears as if from another world. Mossey mumbled a question. B.J. replied. And then their chat faded into a lackluster mumble, overridden by Dan's own thoughts.

Meanwhile, before him, awaiting his immediate attention, sat the rest of the Weber audit.

Dan peeked around, shook his head. "To heck with it," he blurted.

His eye roved once again to the family photo and the smiles of Debra, Lori, and little Jeff. "Sure, to heck with it," Dan said, nearly on the verge of desperation. "But—*how*?"

CHAPTER
THREE

Rush hour was over. It was cooler now, too. The glorious sunset would be visible for only moments more. Dan could see the huge stadium, and then, its massive shadow, receding in the rear view mirror. Through the open window came the nostalgic sounds of a distant clock: … five … six ... seven. The chimes stopped. Once again there sounded only the thump-hump, thump-hump, thump-hump of tires on concrete. The bewitching hour was at hand.

On impulse, Dan glanced back, but the stadium was gone.

The store lay nestled on a quiet corner of the elm-lined street. "DUNTOOT DRUG," read the sign. Dan pulled up and parked, removed a scrap of paper from his shirt pocket, and walked into the store.

Almost immediately Dan was confronted by a prominent toilet-tissue display. 'Charming Chafeless,' the banner proclaimed. On playful impulse Dan reached out, picked up a crinkly cellophane pack, and squeezed it.

"You know the rule, fool: 'Touch it, it's yours.'"

Dan turned. A stocky form was grinning at him from behind the counter.

"I'm after razors, toothpaste, and deodorant," Dan explained.

The owner proudly gestured Dan to a nearby aisle— to a sea of razors hanging from a blue-white checkerboard display marked 'FACIAL GROOMING AIDS: MALE.' He cleared his throat, thumbed at the display. "B.F. Duntoot at your service," he announced.

"Thanks," Dan said. He replaced the packet of tissue, and stepped over.

"Got your steel handles there, hollow handles below, twin blades, injectors over there—"

"Do you have 'Silky Skin'?" asked Dan.

"A little personal, aren't you?" said the druggist. "Oh," he said. He scanned the rack. "Would have to be fresh out of those," he said. "Plenty of others though. Triple blades, quadruple blades, steel, titanium, plastic."

"So what's—?" Dan stepped over and selected.

"That's for ladies. Unless—?" And he viewed Dan curiously.

"Oh," Dan said.

Dan returned to the men's rack, and selected. "Fine. I'll take these."

"You're not left-handed, are you?"

"You're kidding?" said Dan.

"Nowadays can't tell. All this 'progressive consumer merchandise'?" He took the pack of razors from Dan, dropped the pack into a plastic bag, and handed the bag over to Dan.

"Now where can I find the toothpaste?"

"Please! You do mean, sir—oral cleansers?" He gestured toward an adjacent aisle. Dan stepped over to a sign 'TOOTHPASTES' topping an equally mysterious display.

"Where's—just plain toothpaste?"

"Just plain—? No such thing." Duntoot walked around the counter, and joined Dan. "We have mints, fluorides, fluoride mints, whitening, brightening, plaque fighters, plaque preventers, each geared specifically toward... Call it progress. Pure, unadulterated progress. I don't know anymore. I just sell the stuff."

"You use any of these items yourself?" Dan asked.

"Uh-no."

"But still willing to hype the stuff?" Dan played.

"Hype but don't use? Yes, sir. In my case, no need." He pulled a pinkish upper denture out of his mouth, showing a gaping smile. "High-school football," he explained. "Homecoming game. We lost. But one good thing, our family dentist was in the crowd. He cheered all the way home."

"Still keep track of the game?"

"You kidding? All those no-name, odd-name, every-name defenses and even crazier formations: left, right, back, forth, front, center, up, down? Gets worse every year. You've got to master Belichick's book on strategy just to coach Pop Warner." He sized up Dan. "You look like the typical strapping halfback," he said then. "Ever play yourself?"

"Once," Dan said. "Not anymore." Dan reached out, from vague memory, selected, and slipped the tube into the bag.

"And the last item?"

"Right." Duntoot nodded, and led Dan to another wall overrun with colorfully packaged products. Dan scanned. "Look, all I want is a simple—And *what* is the difference between an anti-perspirant and a deodorant, anyway?"

The druggist winked. "One stops you from sweating. The other stops your close pals from learning the hard way that you've been sweating. Like that brand right by your head? It's just a short-term cover-up—a deodorant."

"No, really," he went on, as Dan surveyed. "A deodorant does not directly impede a bodily function. An anti-perspirant does. Pharmaceutically speaking, that is. Wanna know more, email your user-friendly FDA.

"Dry, extra-dry, spray, roll-on, specially formulated ... Why don't they divide them all up into exclusive use for the left arm and the right?"

Duntoot mulled. "Get to it first thing tomorrow," he smiled.

Dan reached out, selected a roll-on, dropped it into the bag.

At the counter Duntoot removed each item and rang up the sale, then replaced the items in the bag. He took the bag back, studied it, emptied it. He reached down and wedged the items into a smaller bag. He pointed to a code on the first bag's bottom. "See these numbers? They designate this bag as suitable for five or six normal-sized items. You picked three, so ..." With a grin he handed over the bag and its contents, complete with sales slip, to Dan.

"Geez! Isn't there *anything* in this world left for normal, general, all-around use anymore?" Dan asked.

"I'm ... not qualified to say." Duntoot paused, grinned, mulled the irony.

"Well, thanks for your help. Good night." Dan headed

out. As he passed the 'Charming Chafeless' display he playfully squeezed a roll—to incite Duntoot's mock groan and stamp. *"Don't* squeeze the—!" he called. "Yup, been warnin' people about that for over thirty years now."

Dan smiled. "Sorry. I just couldn't resist."

Dan's Taurus nosed carefully into the narrow left lane then pulled into the fast-food drive-through. Outside his car a huge, plastic, toothy chipmunk, clad in a plaid kilt and sporting two prominent sets of makeshift sideburn whiskers, grinned its eternally fixed grin. Just beside the intercom the car halted. The chipmunk's nose, a neon light, flashed brilliantly.

"Top 'a the evenin' to ye! How might Mighty Chip aid ye, fine sir?"

The radioed voice, a playful sound, came from far away.

Dan leaned over. "A hamburger, fries, and a shake," Dan said.

After a blast of static, the voice returned. "Hey, please—speak up? See, we forest animals don't always have twenty-twenty in our ears."

"A bur-ger. Frrr-ies. And a shake," Dan pronounced.

Then came a loud chomping, a faint sound of background laughter, a rude blast of static. Officially, the voice announced:

"We have the Brogue Burger, our onioned specialty. Not much to behold, but wow! It lingers. It waters ye fine eyes with fond memory of dear old Glasgow. So ye speaketh with a *touch* of brogue. Then, sire, we've the onionless, more tolerable Kiltburger. That's with a wee less dressing than usual. Not enough for culinary scandal, but an item you'll truly 'relish'. Both Bravehearted Hem and Hemless. Uh, 'Hem' means with lettuce. Oops, what? Wait a sec—we're out of the Hem."

Again came giggles, followed by an awkward fumbling, then, "Ah, finally good sire, our Bagpipe Special. It's enough to satisfy the hardiest of appetites. If you try to lift it by yourself, you're gonna need good health insurance—or a strong truss!"

Dan turned and said. "A Bagpipe Special."

"A gutsy choice, sire. With or without notes?"

"Notes?" inquired Dan.

"Why, *fries*, me Laddy."

"I'll take it. A Bagpipe. With notes. But easy on the B-flats."

"Very funny. What about the shake?"

"I'm afraid to ask," said Dan.

"We have a Brawny Bottle, a whole quart of your standard gooey sloppy fast-food-junkie shoot-up. Known to commoners as—a *malt*?"

"Fine. Vanilla."

A horn beeped. Now a line of other cars had pulled in behind. Unfazed, Chip went on. "How about our Kilarney Special: three *full* scoops of ice cream ..."

"No thank you." Dan broke in. "A Bagpipe with notes. A Brawny—vanilla."

The neon nose flashed on, teasingly, inches from Dan's own. Behind, a horn blared. "Oh-*kay* already!" called the chipmunk. Dan drove up to pay and receive his order. As he reached the window he was saluted by a trio of teens working inside. The one at the intercom pointed to his nametag—CHIP. His fellow-workers chuckled and gave Chip a round of applause. Chip nodded and flashed Dan a smile. Dan just shook his head, noting the irony. Chip wore a meshwork of metal braces—for his prominent buckteeth.

It was the typical, well-kept suburban family home. The lawn was manicured, the shrubs closely trimmed. The well-lit address "1005 DELTA DRIVE" sat perched in neat letters beside the front door. In the garage a steel-blue Ford Taurus sat close beside a light-blue Corolla. From the den came the familiar sound of late-summer America: " … and the snap. It's Burton up the middle. Oh, he's hit hard! He coughs up the ball. No, it looks like Detroit still has possession. But Burton appears hurt. A Detroit timeout now. We'll be back with more action right after this."

Dan sat, and settled cozily, in his favorite armchair, remote control in hand. On the floor just beyond him sat Lori, playing with a pile of toys. At once she looked up. "Commer-cial?" she said. "Commer-cial!" And she lifted her arms toward Dan.

"Right." Dan turned down the sound on the T.V., bent down and hoisted her up, planted a wet, playful kiss against her ear. She giggled, showed him a toy, a computerized gadget of knobs, buttons, and a glittery display window. Lori peered down, and grabbed the toy. At once she tossed it up, tried to catch it. Dan reached in and caught the toy, and examined it more closely. "Right. So just how are you supposed to play with this thing? By hooking it up to a computer?"

"Honey— you didn't get our regular toothpaste!"

Debra Driver peeked in from the kitchen, displaying the tube Dan had purchased and eyeing him in glum amusement. "Did you read this label?" she asked.

"I … glanced at it," Dan said sheepishly.

"Right." Her head vanished, re-emerged. "Oh, by the way, good news today. That last payment? I called and guess what? We owe only two hundred sixty-two thousand two hundred and ten dollars. Only twenty-six more years." Her face drew into a smirk, then vanished.

"Daddy, what's 'payment'?"

Dan turned on the volume, snuggled Lori in his arms. "Something we all have to make sooner or later, angel."

The sound of the game could be heard. ' ... hit hard after only a short gain. Quite a collision that time, Al. They're doing some hitting out there tonight.'

'Yes, those guys are trying to stay on that roster. Giving it their all.'

"Do you ever have to payment?"

"'Make a payment,' we say. Mommy and Daddy do every month. But you won't have to. Not for a long time."

"Why?"

"Cuz Mommy and Daddy are here to take care of you."

"Why?"

"Because Mommy and Daddy love you."

"Is Jeffy still up?" Dan asked.

"Jeffy's sleeping now—remember?" said Deb.

At once Dan secured Lori, pushed back her curls, clutched her, and lifted her high above his head. She giggled.

" ... Detroit's ball, third and one. Here's the call, the snap, and ... again it's up the middle. I really don't believe they made it. It's ... going to be close."

"Oh, Dan—how *could* you?" came from the kitchen.

Dan turned. Now she peeked in with a half-pout. Her protruding hand held the deodorant Dan had bought.

"I ... couldn't remember our regular brand. There were so many. I didn't want to be late."

"Okay, okay." Her head dropped dramatically.

"I mean—they all looked the same."

"And to hurry home for what? To watch grown men— physically, anyway—bounce full-speed off each other for— a stitched-up piece of pork?

Dan rolled his eyes. "You just don't understand it, that's all!"

"Really? And what about Lori watching grown men tackle each other?"

"She'll see a lot more of it next July. When Daddy tries out," added Dan.

"Next July dear old Dad's going to be traipsing off to football camp?"

"Maybe," Dan smiled. "Just maybe. Wildest dreams die

the hardest."

"Daddy plays lots of sports with us," added Lori.

"Which is another thing. Does Daddy take our little offspring to the museum or the circus on Saturdays or Sundays? Uh-uh. Daddy takes them to the YMCA. My own DNA, aged two and four, already confirmed 'Y' groupies!"

"They both can swim like fish. And when they get their full rides to college you'll feel that special glow that comes with being the proud parent of a successful 'Y' groupie. Just wait."

'The attempt will be from just inside the thirty-two. Here's the snap, set, kick, and the kick—is *blocked*! Here's Foley, Foley scooping up the ball, Foley going ... going ... now only one man to beat and ... he's going all the way. A Ram touchdown!'

Alex Foley, a Ram defensive back, had scooped up the blocked field goal and raced some sixty yards for a touchdown.

"No flags. We can assume it'll stand, Al. We're back to a tie game now. It looks like Martinez, the Lion kicker, is still down. Let's ... catch it on the replay."

"Well, regardless of the specifics of time and place, Mike, I've said it in the past and I'll say it again here tonight. A kicker has no business attempting a tackle like that. No business. Especially a pint-size kicker of field goals like Aldo Martinez. We featured him at the beginning of our show, you remember? He's very good at what he does. I just hope he hasn't been hurt too seriously."

'Okay, here it is again. The snap, the set, a good set. And… yes, there's the breakdown. The left end got in first, got a paw on it.. There's the pick-up by Foley– Martinez moving in front of him and – *oh*, what a shot he took! That lineman *rocked* him. Looks like … a shoulder. A kicker in the wrong place … at the wrong time!'

'And by intention. It's a sad commentary, indeed, an injury bordering on the self-inflicted. It's one aspect of an otherwise great game on which we don't like to dwell, but which, sadly, at times like this, we must. Martinez has no reason taking on a man like that, especially a man with a convoy of blockers in front of him. He's been hired by the Lions to kick field goals. That is what he should stick to. And it does look serious.'

'Understandable, though. Fourth quarter? Your own kick blocked right in front of you when you're up by only six?'

'The heat of the moment is no excuse. Football is a game of emotion, of free-flowing energy. That we all know. But out on that field Martinez has to be a realist. The Lions don't fork over top dollar to a man of his unique talent for him to jump in like he's on the hamburger squad. I could see a special-teams kamikaze risking a shot like that, but not—'

'And here's the kick. It's … good. Rams by one, Al.'

'—Aldo Martinez. He's not been hired to tackle. He's been hired to kick.'

Dan sat by. At once he burst out. "What *is* this? If the guy can't make a simple open-field tackle he should get his butt off the field!"

Lori peeked around and blinked. Hearing Dan's tone, she began to suck her thumb. "Daaaa-aan," came the call from the kitchen. "Dan, you do have our daughter in there with you!"

Lori removed her thumb from her mouth. "Butt," she pronounced, looking up at Dan.

Dan sighed, took a deep breath. He gave his daughter a big hug. "Sweetheart, remember—it's not good for you to suck your thumb," he said quietly.

"Butt," said Lori.

"But what?" Dan played.

Dan looked to his daughter, somewhat stunned.

"And a word you're going to forget about, too, right?" he said, hoisting her high over his head toward the ceiling. She giggled, reached down. With her still-moist thumb and fingers, she grasped his hair, hung on giggling now, as he swung her about the room and then all at once pulled her to him and gave her a big hug.

Minutes later St. Louis had kicked off. The Lions had run the ball back up to their own forty. In two plays they had gained only two yards. '... and eight to go? No doubt even the cheerleaders will be reading pass on this one. The set. The snap. And yes, he fades back. Here comes that famous pressure. There's the throw and—ooh—in and out of the hands of Crosby. He should have had the interception, Al.'

'That he should. But the man's no defensive back. He's a linebacker. And linebackers are schooled not in how to catch as much as in how to stop.'

Dan leaned forward, jutted his jaw. "Come *on!*" Dan said.

Debra stepped in, clad in her nurse's uniform. She would soon be leaving for work. "Lori, please put your toys away. And Jeffy's, too, okay? Daddy'll put you to bed in a minute."

"Ohhh ... kayyy."

"Good girl."

Dan got up, and stepped over to kiss and hug his wife. "Don't work too hard," he said with concern. "Try to take at least one long break."

"Sure. That's if the babies cooperate. Can't always predict what will happen when you work in the baby intensive-care unit." She smiled, went up on her tiptoes, and kissed him in return.

"I'll keep the home fires burning."

"I know. You always do."

They both stood there. It was this particular moment— his wife heading off for work at night like this—that Dan so detested. Their eyes met and locked momentarily. Then simply, wordlessly, they looked away.

Meanwhile, Lori had separated her own and her brother's massive pile of toys and was beginning to box them. There were baseball and football figures. There was an ice-skater, a gymnast, a ballerina among the assortment of dolls and doll clothes. There was a mini-computer and other educational toys, as well as stuffed animals, action heroes, and a tiny basketball hoop with a shiny white backboard.

"Nice job, Lori." Debra said. "I guess the afternoon preschool is teaching her something after all," Debra smiled.

Lori lifted Cuddles and planted him atop her box.

Again Dan kissed Debra and quickly headed for the kitchen.

Already the receiver was in Dan's hand. Quickly he punched the number. "Got to make a call. A call to a man. About a *contest.*"

"Just … tell me about it in the morning." she said. She took a deep breath, offered a final, puzzled glance. "Promise me you're not going to hop some bus to a 'training facility' and leave me and the kids behind."

"Uh-uh. Nothing like that! Something better. *Much* better! Something that … might require a little capital."

She watched him cradle the receiver impatiently between ear and shoulder, his fingers drumming nervously on the countertop.

"Whew!" she said as she turned and headed out.

CHAPTER
FOUR

The mainframe computer had an awesome yet reassuring hum. It epitomized the smooth, clinical whirl of effort to pack more into less, to plant the entire known world into one cyber-technical machine. It featured snugger storage and the retrieval of bits to bytes, all in the name of data-space management. This was the epicenter of the new millennium, this room—the precinct of computer storage.

"*Still* think the Lions should have punted. A couple yards to go? Up by six? They blew it."

"You're telling me? Hey, I might not be a systems analyst, but heck—I could have made *that* decision."

Beyond these two and several other pairs of technicians, Dan Driver sat huddled beside a bleary-eyed Ev. Ev gulped steaming black coffee, fighting to keep his eyes open, scanning the room, all the while squinting from the bright lights overhead.

"Like I say, Dan, these figures aren't all the ones we'll need," Ev offered. "But, along with the ones you've been keeping about yourself, they should serve as rough indicators of what to expect during the—'qualifying meet.'" I'm speaking of the broad range within which 'normal' human performances can fall. Later on down the road we can use this program for strategy during the actual three-day match. The one for all the marbles."

Ev sighed. He sipped once more, rubbed his achy eyes, rolled them sleepily back to Dan. "This software was the least of it, though. I was able to write it, subroutines and all, in about two hours. Once we get this debugging done, we'll be able to plug in the parameters for each sport and input the data and have our answers in a few seconds. Or should I say—nanoseconds?"

He gazed at the printout running efficiently by. Again he sipped. "God, Dan, I must have pored through at least eighty websites last night! Blew the dust off all my old classic books too. Friedman on sports statistics, Kretchmar on philosophy of sport, Hay on biomechanics, Fixx on running, Bench on baseball, George Allen and Gayle Sayers on football, Floyd Patterson and George Sullivan on boxing, Edward Dolan on bowling, Chris Evert on tennis, and Ray Carlson on wrestling. Even checked out Gary Aldrich and Rob Lasorsa on the shot put. Over forty sports. Can you believe? That best-seller you mentioned—Krzyzewski's *Leading With the Heart*—is great for motivation, but for each sport we've got to be specific. Whew! I, uh, finally crashed about four-thirty." His words had come amid wide blinks and deep shudders. All the while Dan stood by, beaming.

"Ev, about all this—you *do* feel like I do?"

"Six years-plus at A.H. Adams? Might as well be the Black Hole of Calcutta! Believe me; I welcome the chance. You know how much I keep up with all the stats, how everyone sees me as the company sports nut? I mean—that's why you asked me to come in with you on this idea, right?"

"It's more than that. You're—my best friend."

Ev hung his head in his hands, and sighed. "Thanks, Dan," he said. "Thanks."

"Thank *you*, said Dan. "I didn't mean for you to stay up all night researching."

"I was up anyway. Couldn't sleep. Again. But that's the beauty of the Net, right? Access to any place, at any time. And your enthusiasm—so catchy! So when I came down here to fetch the old Hamilton tape—" he pointed dramatically— "there, I thought why not try to run a draft of this, too." He took another long sip, shook his head. "Why Dan, why? Why *hasn't* someone come up with this idea before? It's simply the current popular theory of multiple intelligences, multiple energies—applied to sport. All around us we see reality TV, survival-of-the-fittest, superstar competitions, but nothing like this, that *really* puts it all together! I mean, millions of average Joes will side with us! *Millions!*"

Heads then turned.

"Uh, sorry guys," Ev interjected.

"You're talking sports again?" one technician grinned.

"Again?" said another. "How about—always?"

"A nut for what?" remarked another technician. "Games that teach violence and selfishness? Didn't some dad kill another parent over his kid's soccer game? You're frequently reading about riots breaking out among the spectators in the stands watching games. I mean—it's all over the news, right?"

"Got that right. Isn't 'fan' the root word of 'fanatic'?"

Ev took pause. "Sports… out of control? You guys got it all wrong. All hyped by the papers and TV. Take youth homicide and school killings, which the media loves to exploit. A kid today has about a one in three million chance of such happening—numbers way, way down from the past. Way, way down because of what sports really teaches—responsibility, self-esteem, discipline, effort, teamwork. Any coach will tell you that."

"A bunch of rich, spoiled, violent brats, if you ask me," one replied.

"Rich? Spoiled? Some are, I'll grant you that. Remember in baseball back in 1960, when Bill Veek ordered players' names put on their uniforms. That was the debut of the ME generation and specialization. But violence? Sports was much more violent in the past. How about the Aztec ritual, when the losing captain was torn apart? Before the Marquis of Queensberry Rules—the 1860s, I think it was—prizefighters fought with their bare knuckles. Until the 1870s baseball was played without gloves. Football? In 1822 the President of Yale forbade students from playing it. In the late 1800s players grew their hair long to protect their heads. The first helmets—leather, non-suspension—appeared only in the 1890s. Did it help? Maybe. In the 1905 college season eighteen players died—and well over a hundred suffered permanent injuries. Linking arms, punching, gouging, kicking—these were legal. In over a quarter of the games, mob brawls broke out. It was so bad that in that same year President Roosevelt—himself a hearty former Rough Rider—established the NCAA to regulate it, to make the gridiron less lethal. Did a huddle signal 'togetherness'? Uh-uh. It was devised so a deaf player could signal his teammates without the opponents catching on. So this stuff about modern sport being more violent is—garbage. The violence we see today on the field is the toned-down version. It used to be a lot *worse.*"

"So you're saying—sports builds character."

"Believe it! Every coach sees it happening every day before his eyes. Sports 'out of control'? Sports 'rage'? No way. The problems—anger, drunkenness, psychotic personalities, vicarious living through kids—are brought *to* the stadium, diamond, or court. Sorry, guys, but the research shows clearly that overall sports provides a great, enduring *benefit.*"

The technicians looked at each other, shrugged, and went back to work.

Ev leaned in close to Dan. "Sorry," he said, "but this thing we've got here—it's great! It's a protest against every weak-side linebacker who majored in third-and-six blitzing, every tax accountant with a micro-economics focus—against everybody who thinks life means bottling yourself up into one teeny piece of a sub-even-teenier-sub-piece. It's against knowing more and more about less and less. Sorry? No, I'm *not* sorry."

Again heads turned. Once more Ev confronted them, then turned back to Dan. He hoisted his mug sternly, ventured a sip, but found the mug empty. He planted the mug on top of a small ledge just behind him. "Spineless? Misguided? Chickens all?" Ev then high-strutted in a quick circle, like an agitated rooster. "Sure, so here I am, slinking in here to get this thing off the ground. Who's really the chicken? Me!" He flapped his arms in self-satire, extended his mockery into a mating dance.

Now the entire room paused to watch. One figure began to clap to the rhythm. Others joined in. Ev continued his dance, cluck-clucking in rhythm.

Then, just as swiftly, the clapping stopped. Everyone turned back to his work. Dan glanced over—to spy Mossey. Dan turned back to warn Ev.

Miraculously, Ev was already gone. The supervisor spied Dan, gave a no-nonsense nod, and stepped over. "You haven't seen our mutual pal Winchell, have you?" he asked.

Dan glimpsed the familiar mug perched atop the ledge. "Must be on break," Dan said, edging his arm up to cover the mug.

"As he seems to be so often these days," continued Mossey."

As Mossey viewed the room, Dan leaned fully back against the smooth pulsations of the computer, covering the coffee mug.

"I must let Winchell in on some news. We are obliged to borrow his chair. Not that the man's ever there to miss it. Tell him—if you do see him—that a replacement chair will be forthcoming. With, maybe, a replacement." He peered to Dan. "Driver, do level; how many cups of coffee does your cohort go through in a day—fifty?"

Dan considered. "Give or take ten."

"Doesn't it keep him awake?"

Dan smiled. "It helps."

"Obviously the man's wired. Way too wired." He shook his head almost sadly. "Have Winchell stop in and see me."

"Yes, sir. Will do."

The supervisor turned away. At once a spool of tape skittered across the floor and unrolled across his shoe tops. He took pause. Slowly, unamusedly, he tracked the tape back to its source—a meek form crouched at the far end of the machine amid the unraveling tape himself.

"Winchell—!"

"Sir, I'm a bit ... wrapped up right … ah, exactly right …now."

"In my office. *Now*!"

Mossey turned on his heel and stepped away. Moments later Ev freed himself of the tape. He stood up, brushed himself off, edged over. "'Wired' was right," he confided.

"Better wired than fired," Dan smiled.

"I-I sure hope so."

They watched the supervisor exit the room.

And Ev scooped up his empty mug and stalked out.

The end of the day found Ev in Dan's office. "... best and fairest we can ever hope to condense it down to," Ev explained. "Even though we're still waiting on that final printout, I was able to reduce it down through simple manual-digital-operational logic along with the preliminary printout."

"Meaning—?"

"Uh, with pencil and paper."

Dan smiled.

"So we what?—asked the computer to choose the fifteen all-around most popular sports that take strength, endurance, hand-eye coordination, intelligence, touch, stamina, and savvy. Okay, so I loaded over fifty in the computer. And, Dan, here they are, the fifteen most popular that together demand—as you, ex-athlete, and I, goofball computer analyst/sports buff, and our favorite mainframe perceive it— the most overall athletic versatility."

Ceremoniously he presented the sheet to Dan. "And sorry about that outburst downstairs. Guess it all just got to me. I was out of coffee. The only thing I could smell was freedom."

Dan scanned the sheet. "Bowling, pool, ping-pong, swimming, and golf? I'm surprised. *These* should set back the animals."

"As we discussed, Dan, sports is never solely strength. It's every bit as much brains, judgment, coordination, speed, quickness, touch, and endurance. No one who fails to perform well in *every one* of these fifteen has any right to pronounce himself a well-rounded athlete. And *certainly* no right to the title of 'The Best ALL Around.'" He thumbed to the adjoining cubicle. "Not even that super-steroided B.J.."

"What about horse-racing? auto-racing? bullfighting? martial arts?"

"Do they all call for intelligence, guts, coordination,

stamina? Sure. Cycling, dodge ball, you name it. Sure, *look* at Lance Armstrong and Ben Stiller. And, of course, there's sheer popularity. The sport played in more countries than any other in the world but not in the U.S.? Soccer. So we have to draw the line. Legend holds that the original Olympic flame was lit by the sun's rays reflected off a mirror. And the sacred flame burning at Zeus's altar during the games was reinstituted in the modern era—that's the 1924 games in Amsterdam. So I wanted the computer to select sports that are as natural—as uncontrived—as possible. I also took to heart your idea that performance is a product of energy, that it's only fair that the athlete provide his own power. So we omit all motors and gadgets."

"Right." Dan continued to scan the list. "... baseball, football, basketball, weight-lifting, track and field ..."

"You got it. All popular, natural, and energy-demanding. And who can claim any of these fifteen is 'better' than any other? Each has its own rules, demands, dangers, so we weight them equally. One hundred points apiece. For a total of fifteen hundred."

"Three-point-one mile run? quarter-mile? hundred-yard dash? We've sure got enough running events."

"Better believe it, Dan. It's like you say. The athlete should provide his own power. Research shows that we humans look like we do because of running. Our ability to run distances gave us an advantage over other primates in hunting and scavenging. We're the only primate good at it, thanks to a head designed not to overheat, peripheral vision so we don't trip and fall, shorter forearms that balance our upper and lower bodies, shock-absorber ligaments in our back. Even our larger rear ends provide stability. Yup, it all began with running."

Dan continued to scan. "… boxing … wrestling …"

"Right. After all, sport does reflect our hunting, scavenging, violent past. In our case today, controlled violence. So the computer has included some close, mix-it-up, one-on-one competition. Boxing is the most popular sport with filmmakers. The WWW makes a mockery out of what in ancient times was a very noble sport. I don't want this to turn into a media circus, but our mainframe chose them—boxing and wrestling."

"No, I agree. And you've got racquet sports."

"Right. Tennis, squash, racquetball, ping-pong, badminton. Each has its special demands. You know that badminton is now an Olympic sport? It premiered in 1992, before a billion spectators. Dominant countries include Indonesia, China, Malaysia, and Korea. It began back in India—was called 'poona,' I think. Anyway, British officers took the game back home with them in the late 1860s, when it debuted big-time at some duke's 'Badminton' estate. Now over eleven million Americans play it every year. It calls for extraordinary quickness, coordination, and conditioning. That shuttlecock can whiz by at over two hundred miles an hour. In high competition, players compete for about half the time as a Wimbledon final and yet run twice as much and take twice as many shots. So the computer included racquet games. Three, to be exact: tennis, racquetball and ping-pong."

"What about time? Not even Spiderman could get through all these in one session," inquired Dan.

"We take three sessions," replied Ev. "Three days, at five events per day. We call the YMCA, a local park, bowling lanes, a golf course, and maybe even a top stadium about rental policies—how, if, and when we can get them, the costs, and so on."

"Want me to start calling?" asked Dan.

"My first of two surprises today. It's a done deal. The contest is slated for the Labor Day weekend. That's only weeks off. Five sports in a local field house on Saturday: 'Indoor Day.' Five on Sunday at various venues: 'Mix-em-up Day.' The last five—Monday's grueling finale—at a stadium: 'Outdoor Day.' So what's left? To map out the logistics. The qualifiers in less than two weeks don't give us much time."

"Qualifiers?"

"It's the only way. You know, to run in the Boston Marathon you have to qualify in, I think, under three hours and fifty minutes? So, before anything else, we have to hold qualifying heats, to involve every athlete who's fit and interested. Just as the five rings in the Olympic flag represent the five inhabited continents, we'll be as democratic as possible. We've got to let everyone in who wants a fair shot."

"But how exactly do we judge them?"

"With the amount of people I anticipate showing up, I

put together a day of competition. There would be no way to incorporate boxing and tennis and all the other one-on-one competitions, so I devised a schedule that includes nine of the sports. These events can showcase their skills. In the end, the leader in points is our qualifier, our champ. Here's— the list, Dan."

Dan took the sheet and scanned it:

Station 1: Football – pass, catch, kick and punt

Station 2: Basketball – thirty shots at varying distances

Station 3: Golf – two par-four holes

Station 4: Bowling – one game

Station 5: Pool – two racks of balls

Station 6: Swimming – 50 meters, 200 meters

Station 7: Track – 400-meter, 100-meter, broad jump, shot put, high jump

Station 8: Weight lifting – bench press, clean and jerk, squat

Station 9: Cross-country – 3.1-mile race

"By letting them put up their numbers against each other and the computer program—that's, uh, the program I'm still waiting for—I can come up with all the variables. I'm also using a more private gauge—data from the only highly motivated sportsman I'm personally familiar with."

"Who is?"

Ev's smile broadened. "You, Dan. You. I always keep track of your numbers." He looked at him. "I—assume they're legit?"

Dan looked at him. "Legit," Dan said.

"Good. Running all the numbers through the program should tell us something, provide us some general benchmarks. So are you ready? Off to the park now. Then to the stadium."

"Stadium?"

"Uh, right. Camelback Stadium. Where do you think the 'Outdoor Day' venue will take place?"

"Stadium!" Dan repeated.

Ev nodded. "A pal of mine—you know, the guy I did that audit for last spring—got us the okay. The field's available until the first Dromedary home game."

"Whew," said Dan.

Once again Ev nodded to the schedule. "And you know what's really great, Dan? Everybody I've talked to is excited about this thing. I mean—*really excited.*"

"And your share of the money?"

"As we discussed, I … don't think there'll be a problem."

Dan shook his head, still stunned. "Ev, you're a genius," he said. "A certified genius."

"More like a disgruntled flunky. Time and again it's been shown that the 'genius' is not the mad scientist, the Rain Man or exotic bug-collector. It's the man or woman who can master the broadest diversity of pursuits. Evolutionary biologists assure me that real genius means the greatest ability to adapt to shifting environments and demands.

We're simply applying this universal notion to sport. Kind of what a utility player would be to baseball, this person would be to sports. You and I are out to show the world that the narrowly specialized micro-economic Tax Accountant or ten-million-bucks-a-year left-handed designated hitter is *not* the best. That true rarity out there somewhere who does it all the best, that—" he paused, struck happily—"'jock of all trades.' We're doing it not just for him or for ourselves, but for everyone. For all folks across the nation who have ever played their hearts out on a team or watched TV and wondered what athletic excellence really *means.* Uh-uh, I'm no genius, Dan. Far from it. But I am mad. *Plenty* mad! Mad at how this job—any job—seems to make me—us much smaller!"

Ev took up the sheets, slid them back into his briefcase. "Well ... shall we?"

The two started out. At the doorway they heard a faint commotion, and took pause. Miller and Wells shuffled by, mumbling to each other in subdued monotones. Dan and Ev stood silent for a moment, then traded glances. Then together they shook their heads and, without a word, headed out.

It was almost dusk. Several joggers ran the oval track. A team of soccer players booted their checkered ball across the inner green field. At one far end of the complex, beside the Century fence marking a baseball backstop, stood Dan and Ev. The complex included a small two-hole golf course for the staff and was situated only a short block from the YMCA.

"All of our initial events can be held within a few blocks," Ev explained. "This is where the track and field events can take place. And we will conclude the qualifier with the whole group or whoever is lucky to be left, running the 3.1-mile event. I'm just glad it isn't football season. With all the college games and concerts going on, we wouldn't have a prayer of getting this place." He assessed the sheet, peeked out onto the green football field. "No, the logistics aren't all that complicated, Dan. Like I said, we announce the contest and hold the qualifiers here two weeks from Saturday. After that, it's our champ against anyone brave enough to put up the cash. Fifty big ones. Put up or shut up." He paused, looked off for a moment. "But fifty grand? Whew!"

"Dan, you're right. We're right smack in the middle. We probably can't drop in at the local credit union and state our case. Or find a do-good philanthropist eager to help us out. If we were famous—like Bozo Billings or whoever—we could get the cash on just our signatures. But no, we're suburban white-collar. We're the chumps that pay the nation's bills and taxes, and get no recognition. Then we're made to feel guilty for having semi-cushy lives. Yup, we're just two of the millions smack dab in that middle-income bracket. The money? Might be tough. Real tough. But—"

Ev poked at his pie. Here in the diner, in the mellowness of evening, he spoke quietly but with high spirits and obvious determination. Since this morning, in fact, he had been like a man released from a prison cell to dream of liberties previously unimagined. "But," he said to Dan now, with an even more decisive air, "we'll do it. *Do it*. You and I *won't* give up."

"If we had to, we could lower the ante."

"Fifty K? It's a lot, sure. But to me it's worth it. Practically speaking, it's the icing on the cake we have to offer. What will legitimize this escapade is its stakes. This could have mighty implications, Dan. We might be responsible for creating a whole new American institution. Could we ever go halfway on that? So the stakes have to be high to begin with. To make sure that no athlete worth his salt will turn down the chance. Three days for fifty grand and loads of free ink? Who'd say no?"

"But he doesn't out-and-out win it."

"Not for the qualifiers. As you proposed, he competes in the qualifiers and claims the right to the title as our champion. Then when he or she defends the title successfully, he or she hauls in fifty big ones."

"And ... that first fifty?"

"Uh, right. After you phoned last night, I thought about it. Basically, the idea is yours. So I'm willing to chip in more— like thirty to your twenty. And hey, don't look at me like that. It's high time original thinking was rewarded. Your concept alone is worth the extra five. Look, I've got ten in the bank. If I have to, I can even peddle my trailer, my 'refurbished, furnished mobile living quarters'—for ten and borrow the rest from my brother. That's my share."

"You're going to borrow? And fall even deeper into the

trap?"

"'Fall even deeper'? Dan, I *am* even deeper in the trap. Today or tomorrow I can't go off on vacation, because I need my income to pay my bills. My ten in the bank I can't touch because it's a 'watershed'—insurance against some disaster—while each passing day *is* a disaster. If that doesn't define 'trap,' what does?"

"Well, I've got ten in a personal account," Dan said after a time. "Deb and I each do. I can crawl in deeper, too, I guess, and borrow the other ten. That's the absolute max, though. I sure don't want to drag Deb into it."

"Something on this scale? Dan, sooner or later you're going to have to."

"I-I know," Dan said, looking away. "I know."

"We have a choice? To make this thing fly—to put our money where our mouths are—will demand nothing less than a cashier's check: 'Fifty thousand and 00/100 dollars' to dump into that pot, winner take all. Uh, that's why we've got to keep this thing a secret a bit longer—to make sure the money's a go and that hopefully our athlete will win it at least this first time around."

Dan thought for a moment. He peeked around, and gave a slow, solemn nod.

"Scary, sure. But look." Ev held his hand out over the table. His outstretched fingers barely shook. "Dan, already this thing is working wonders! All day long I've felt great. I feel healthy. I'm finally doing something I love! The best thing about it all? It's not fake. It's us. *Our* chance to finally stand up and do something. So let's not sweat the money angle that much. It's going to happen. Hey, we're accountants, right?"

Dan pushed up, stretched, cupped a yawn. "Think I'll hit the gym real early tomorrow," he announced. "Now that the Weber project's done, I'll take a few vacation days away from Mossey and his henchmen. They owe me comp time anyway. Ev, let me tell you, putting up thirty grand for me, performance unseen, shows a lot of class. Or craziness."

Ev peeked up through his glasses. "Hit the gym? Trying to keep your weight down again, huh. Hey, after pie—especially à la mode—that's good."

Dan grinned. "Good? Ev, which of us do you think is going to defend that fat fifty?"

For a moment Ev blinked. "You mean—? Oh. Um, neither one of us," he said, then. "When you first brought the idea to me, another pal of mine put me in touch with someone who knows this 'android' who spends his entire life in the pool, in the ring, on the track, on the courts, you name it. I met him at lunch today. He told me in confidence that this contest would suit him perfectly. He's the best man for the job. Sure, in fairness he'll have to top everybody else in the qualifiers, but right now we could say he's—definitely a leading candidate."

Dan was taken aback. "Ev, you found us a—'general specialist'!"

"Dan, be realistic. This guy has extraordinary skills. The whole package."

85

"But wait. I always thought from the start that—that I would be the one who competed," insisted Dan.

"Dan? It's not so much you or me, it's the *contest*. And I'm sure not that *eager* to toss away thirty grand of my own. You should feel the same way about your twenty. Meet him. You'll understand."

"I swim. I run. I play tennis and buckets. I bowl. I even box once a week at the YMCA," said Dan. "And how many times have I told you there's always been something about my sports career that was unfinished!"

"Left incomplete? I know, Dan, I know. And so you're free to take off for weeks of intensive training. As in— starting this very minute? You took two weeks for your annual 'Griswold' family vacation just last month and now Mossey will be glad to give you a couple more? Be logical. You're viewing it too emotionally, Dan. The concept of this contest is great. But don't let it cost you your hard-earned savings *and* your job."

Ev shuffled through his papers, hauled out another sheet, passed the sheet over to Dan. "Take a look at what the computer spit out for a typical practice week. Who can handle such a regimen? Maybe not even this guy, who will be in the weight room for another—" he checked his watch— "thirty-seven minutes."

Dan scanned the sheet. "'Seven: racquetball with Smith. Eight: wrestling with Tims and Bilson. Tuesday a.m.: Eight: boxing with Evans. Nine: free-style swimming with Porter. Ten: tennis with LaPlace and Wickfield. Eleven: ...'"

"Right. From the moment he is crowned until the Labor Day events, our qualifier must adhere to a schedule like this. I went out and contacted all those 'specialist trainers' and explained what we were up to, and you know something? Every one of them volunteered his time. Billitt, you recall, won Golden Gloves middleweight two years back. Porter took three state meets in a row in the hundred-meter freestyle and coached Lincoln High to the 2004 state championship. LaPlace placed in the NCAA singles finals two years back and is now—when he's not out of town on tour—Dromedary Country Club's resident pro. The list goes on. They're all as turned on by our idea as you and I. Sure, and I'd love to coach this thing, too. But I'm a realist. I have to get up real early five mornings a week and earn my daily bread."

Dan returned the sheet to Ev. "Forget it. In two weeks this guy'll be in an ICU."

"Or *so* in shape—in *so* many ways—that no one'll even come close. And by the way, right now this guy is at the Armbuster Iron and Spa waiting for you, Dan. I told him you'd be by—a chance for you two to get acquainted. Once you meet him, you'll understand my point and leave the competition to the generalists with lots and lots of time."

Ev rose, and stood by for a moment. "Yup, Dan, I'm just so sick of specialists raking in all the bucks and glory. Sick sick *sick*." He ran his eyes slowly down the check. He removed his spectacles, rubbed wearily at his eyes. "Okay, you *did* have the à la mode and I *didn't* have …" At once he glanced over at Dan, and smiled. "This is an indication of things to come."

"And his name is—?" Dan said, without enthusiasm.

"'Rob Hogan. 'Rough and Ready' Rob Hogan. Meet him. You'll see."

"Sounds like one real All-American name."

"'All-American,' all right. Real *All*-American. He told me that his family's been running, jumping, tossing javelins, and making baskets for hundreds of years."

Ev grinned as if he were holding back an amusing secret that he would, just for now, keep to himself.

CHAPTER

FIVE

Ruff Hogan sweated. Ruff Hogan winced. Ruff Hogan mustered strength from deep, deep within and grunted intently between his teeth. The weight ascended above his bulging eyes, and paused. Carefully Ruff unlocked his arms. The bar descended, until the solid wheel at each end clanked onto the floor and the bar rested inches below his nose. "Thirty ... seven," Ruff announced.

He exhaled mightily. Once again he gripped the bar. He took a deep breath, expelled exactly half of it, and hoisted. "Thirty ... *eight*," he announced a moment later, again exhaling the words after the weight clanked down beyond his massive shoulders.

Then once more—grip, exhale, hoist, lower, and—"Thirty ... *nine*."

A shadow slid across Ruff's contorted face. He veered his head, glimpsed the form obstructing the light above. "Huh?" he grunted.

"Rob Hogan? Ruff?"

"Try to be." Once more slowly up, lock, unlock, slowly down, and—"*For*-ty."

Ruff released the bar and relaxed. "Try to be, friend. Try to be. Ruff, ruff!" he barked.

Laughter broke out among the group of lifters beyond the alcove. Ruff Hogan, a handsome Native American was their hero. And now Ruff, loose and likeable in his own right, shook from his arms the effects of this last series of lifts and extended a huge, taped, ham-like hand. "Yup, one happy camp we got here," he said. "You're Driver, right?"

Dan forced a smile. "Try to be," he replied, shaking the hand.

"Pardon the sweat, but it comes with the territory. Yeah, Little Man said you'd be by tonight." He resumed his exercise, counting cadence softly, staring off as he continued to converse. "Strange dude, that Winchell. Almost got himself a grudge, it seems."

"This—is for you." And Dan held the schedule sheet before his eyes.

The weight clanked. Ruff's brow furrowed. "You guys kidding? No, I guess not. I'll have to take out another truckload of life insurance. But I have played all these. All in the last few weeks, too. None from scratch. We went through that before, Little Man and me. Another week, I'll be at peak performance. In all of them."

Dan nodded neutrally. Ruff viewed him for a moment, then resumed his task. The weight lifted, held, clanked down. "Forty ... *two*," Ruff announced. "Hey, you two ... bean-counters really ... are serious ... about this gimmick, aren't you?" he managed, puffing copiously now.

"No gimmick, Ruff. The optimum input to produce the optimum output. The best possible performance from the best possible athlete."

"So Little Man says. Fifty grand? I can dig it!"

Dan's words lacked zeal. "You cash in not by winning but by defending. The first time, as our 'The Best All Around' champion, you collect the title and the right to defend it. Then every time you win after that, you collect a full fifty from whoever challenges you."

"We … went through … that, too," Ruff said, straining again. "Fifty grand for three days? Okay by me. Oompf!" he said. "Four ... tee ... *three*."

"How solid a golfer are you?"

"Usually under forty. Except in the snow. Then ... mid-forties?"

"Bowling?"

"Average one eighty-six."

"In the pool?"

"No Shamu, but I can handle myself. Hey—I am a Pisces. And weight-lifting? Don't ask." He spoke loudly. "Why do you think I'm here—FOR MY HEALTH?"

Others in the room sounded a chorus of groans and chuckles.

Ruff hoisted, held, lowered. "Forty ... *four*," he managed, still gritting.

"And you'll keep it all under your hat?"

"Sure. Winchell said you guys might need a few days more to scrape up the dough."

Suddenly there came a thump, a cry, an eruption of voices. Dan turned and stepped swiftly back out. On the floor a husky figure lay groaning, a huge barbell straddling his chest. One arm wheeled up in a vain attempt to re-grip the bar, then flopped back down.

Dan moved quickly. He edged over, positioned himself, gripped the bar, locked his knees, and hoisted. The barbell wouldn't budge. Clenching his teeth, Dan exerted himself mightily, lifted the barbell and waddled it off into the corner. The others convened around their comrade, who now sat up, tapped his chest, coughed, inhaled deeply, and exhaled in relief. "Anyone get the license number?" he said. He looked curiously up and over at Dan. "Uh, thanks," he said. "A lot."

"Glad it's not serious," said Dan.

Still dazed, the man offered his hand. Dan stepped over and shook it.

There came a pause. All present, including lifters and spotters and the man on the floor, looked to the weight, then to Dan.

"Any idea how much that particular chunk goes?" one asked.

"At least five hundred?" Dan smiled.

"Not that much under."

"And in a sport coat?" someone said. "Someone tell me I didn't see it."

"You mean? He—?" Ruff asked as he joined the group.

"The adrenalin factor," Dan said.

"Then lend me a quart a week from Saturday."

Amid the chuckles, Ruff nodded to Dan. "Look, tell Little Man I'm into his regimen. Sure, when I win and we can disprove all the doubters.

As Ruff stepped over and examined the weight, Dan caught a glimpse of the back of his T-shirt: "THE BEST ALL AROUND!!"

"There's, uh, much more to this, above and beyond the money," Dan said.

Ruff turned serious as well and replied, "Hey, look. I want to show all those clods out there that the usual 'jack-of-all-trades but master of none' garbage is just that—garbage. I've been around. I know. Pros or not—and I've met my share—I'm better. Not in what each does, but ALL AROUND." He jabbed an assertive thumb over his back. "You get it?"

Dan cracked a smile. "'Jock of All Trades' might be more catchy."

"'Jock of All Trades'? Cute. Sounds like something Little Man would think up."

"It is."

Ruff grinned easily. Dan smiled back. At once a gray-haired man broke through the others, and offered his hand.

"Uh, this-here's Lew," Ruff said.

Dan shook the man's hand.

"So you're Driver? Glad to finally meet you. This thing Ruff here's been talking about is legit?"

"Legit," Dan said.

There came a silence. The lifters looked to Ruff, to Dan, to Lew. At once Lew retook Dan's hand, hoisted it high. The others broke into grins and applause.

"Our way of saying you're now in our group," Ruff explained. "One good guy to have around."

"Thanks. Well, I've got to get back to the homestead."

Dan bumped fists with Lew, Ruff, and the others. "Good luck, Ruff," Dan said. "Doubt if you'll need it, but good luck. And by the way—make sure you keep this under your hat until we unveil the plan in a few days."

"I understand," replied Ruff.

"Wow," Dan said. "Guess you're a regular Jim Thorpe?"

"Try to be," grinned Ruff.

Then, amid a final chorus of nods and pats on the back, Dan was gone.

"So that's the other one," Lew said, looking off after Dan. "Seems serious enough. Sure ain't no typical button-down coat-and-tie type. This thing really *is* on the burner."

"The front burner. Little Man says the fifty G's will be in an account the Wednesday before Labor Day. They're not kidding." He looked to the barbell in the corner, then off after Dan. "Not if determination has anything to do with it."

"Then you guys wouldn't mind some hype? Like a little blurb in tomorrow morning's *Times*?"

"Always the reporter, huh, Lew. Look, give me a break. I promised them a few days."

"Getting cold feet, eh? Just maybe you're no Jim Thorpe after all."

Ruff glanced to him, then to the others witnessing this exchange.

"Hardly," Ruff said. "Hardly." He thought for a moment. At once his eyes glowed. His jaw jutted. "Fine by me, Lew," he said then. "Fine by me. Call in all the *Times* you want. *Chicago Tribune? Boston Globe?* Bill O'Reilly? Doctor Phil? *Be my guest.*"

Dan high-stepped gingerly through the near-darkness to avoid the toys. He peeked in at Jeffy, lying deep in slumber on one side, thumb in mouth, the tiny fingers of his other hand gripping the smooth edge of his favorite blanket. Dan removed the thumb, planted a kiss on his son's warm, smooth cheek, and tiptoed out. Next he peeked in at Lori, asleep with Cuddles. He kissed her too, gently, noiselessly, and ducked out. As he tiptoed down the hall, Dan smirked.

In the bedroom Dan laid his sport coat neatly across the back of a chair and undressed. The light of an adjacent streetlamp filtered mildly through the curtains. Less than an hour ago Dan had come home only to again see Deb go off to work. Dan had felt guilty, yes, immensely guilty. But then— just for stopping off at a gym? Again something ponderous, almost foreboding, seemed to hover, something Dan could not define, something so vastly unfair, unfair less to him than to Deb. And yes, unfair to the children as well.

In through the screen came a breeze, cool and refreshing, along with the high-pitched chorus of crickets. Deb was a gem, a real trooper, he thought. Forty hours a week at the hospital, working night-shift for over four years now, without complaint. And despite two pregnancies she was as beautiful as ever. Always smiling, chipper, always the playful one-upper. Dan was lucky. Too lucky.

He still hadn't told Deb of this new development. Simply, it was all so strange and exciting and happening so very fast and chocked full of unknowns that telling her would be awkward, to say the least. Early this morning when she had arrived home and asked about his behavior the night before and he had mentioned Ev and a "contest," yes, but he had spoken vaguely, remotely, stifling a not completely genuine yawn all the while. She had not bothered to probe. And just when guilt had welled up and he had felt that he should tell her, especially about the overwhelming factor of factors—the money—Jeffy had spilled his milk. When that mess had been cleaned up, well, Dan had been in no mood to create another.

So he had kept silent.

Dan sighed, drew back the covers, and crawled into bed. The single, light blanket he peeled away, and pulled the sheet up just over his chin. Just like being DOA, he thought oddly. At once he rolled over onto his side, pounded his pillow. There he lay. Then once again he turned onto his back and stared up onto the ceiling. Sweat broke out over his forehead and, after a few moments, trickled down one cheek. Dan thought of his job, of yesterday, of today's formidable volumes of paperwork and reference texts, of the hot, oppressive cubicle. To resume again tomorrow. Right on schedule. All at exactly 8:30. But just how many more tomorrows?

Dan ventured his hand up and removed the sheet. He rubbed the sweat away. There in the half-light, Dan Driver lay, wide-eyed, immobile, considering.

"FIFTY GRAND! CAN YOU QUALIFY?"

As Mitchell Mossey sat in B.J.'s office, he raised his bushy eyebrows and scanned the newspaper article once more. Wholly perplexed, he ran a pair of rigid fingers through his white hair. "Got to be a mistake of some sort," he pronounced. "*Got* to be."

B.J. shrugged. "Like I say, Mitch, I always keep up with the morning sports. And when I ran across this I knew I'd heard the names before."

"As have I. Both names. But certainly never in conjunction with a character like this! I just cannot imagine … Especially when they must lack assets to pull such a thing off. Why, I ask? Why be so eager to transfer your life into the debit column—and then let everyone read about it in the local *Times*? And this 'Ruff' fellow. Who's *he*? And why is he quoted as saying, 'I'm invincible.' A gym rat? Con man? Obviously!"

Again Mossey peered down onto the photo of the confidently grinning-out-at-him Ruff. Again his eyebrows rose. He took a deep breath, hauled out his handkerchief, blotted his face.

"Seems like you got yourself two of them entrumpeters on your staff."

"Entrepreneurs," corrected Mossey.

B.J. nodded. "Whatever. But hey, Moss, you got to admit. I mean, even with this state-of-the-art turf and now this goalpost freshly spray-painted around the door here, this place is … Well, I've been here a couple days now and this corporate I, II, and III stuff don't exactly spell Super Bowl."

"You'll get your 52-incher and DVD player soon enough. A deal's a deal."

Mitchell Mossey looked off. "To gamble fifty thousand dollars on some 'athlete'? Professional accountants, mind you? Adults specifically charged with the proper tracking and disposing of monies?" He shook his head. "Well, look, B.J.. We didn't see this item, did we. This is an accounting firm. Let's let their personal business remain ... well, personal. At least for now."

B.J. looked around. "Yeah, how much *can* a guy take before he flips out? That I always wondered about."

Mossey nodded to the item. "B.J.—we didn't *see* this. Right?" With that he exited the office.

B.J. stretched mightily, flexed his formidable biceps, pronounced the words under his breath. "Maybe you or A.H. Adams or the Man in the Moon didn't see it, but B.J. Billings sure did!"

'FIFTY GRAND! CAN YOU QUALIFY?'

Deb was on the phone to her mother and was eyeing Lori playing with her cereal across the kitchen table. In her lap she held her young son, her cell phone, and the morning's sports section. "—not taking anyone for a ride at all, Mother. No, he's not impulsive, not insane. And yes, I do thank you for calling me. Yes, I know. Fifty thousand's a lot of money. He did mention something about money just the other night, but we didn't have time to talk. I know he'll be giving me a perfectly logical explanation."

'FIFTY GRAND! CAN YOU QUALIFY?'

Phone to his ear, Ev sat awkwardly atop the old wooden chair. He took a long sip of coffee, swallowed, then leaned back against his desk once again to focus. He spoke quickly,

99

nervously.

"I don't know, Dan. I haven't the foggiest. It's like Pittsburgh stealing that player away from Philly back in the 1880s and being labeled the Pirates ever since? I feel like a victim, too. But victims don't just lie there. They get up. What? Probably have to go through with it as planned, that's what! Trial balloon no longer, Dan. The real deal!"

Ev grimaced, took another deep sip. "Yes, I know. Fair *is* fair. But I'm sitting on pins and needles, too." As Ev leaned back and readjusted the receiver to his ear, the chair creaked. "The guys brought the article to me first thing, along with the national and local papers. Nothing nationally yet, thank God! Why does everything have to be so complicated? Okay, I'll be by. Just … give me a minute?"

With a shaky hand Ev elevated the newspaper, held the item close before his eyes. "I know, I know. But with all this out in the open now, we might have to pull off something really dramatic. Hijack the company coffee fund? Embezzle the Weber account? No, Dan, I'm just kidding!"

Another day slipped by. **'FIFTY THOUSAND TO THE BEST! IS THIS FOR REAL?'** asked an above-the-fold item in Thursday's *Camelback Times* sports section. Since the name Everett Winchell was cited as the PR link to the contest, this same Everett Winchell found himself hounded not only on his home phone, but in his tiny mobile home and the lobby of his firm. At his home reporters convened as a curious, smirking group late Thursday afternoon and were supplied with hot coffee by Ev as they, in turn, pumped Mr. Winchell with questions. No, Alex Rodriguez would not be flying in to kick off the affair. Nor would the Supersonics, Bears, or Redwings. Ashley Simpson would not be warbling "The Star-Spangled Banner." Nor would Janet Jackson. The qualifiers? That would happen a week from Saturday at Riding Crop Park. Cost? The cost for each candidate would be a nominal five dollars and twenty cents, which Ev Winchell, in the spirit of good sportsmanship, would round down to five bucks even.

"Yes, ladies and gentlemen, this project is for real. Mr. Winchell does handle all PR about this program, unprecedented in the realm of sport—a protocol that *will* take place and may the best of all athletes win it. We can't officially begin the contest until our cashier's check for the full fifty is placed in escrow as part and parcel of these proceedings and is, of course, matched by an equal part and parcel from an equally determined, yet unknown challenger. Yes, ma'am, both checks to be deposited by Wednesday of the week before. That's … two weeks from today. By noon, I believe, yes. Uh, Caldwell & Caldwell. Ruff who? Ruff Hogan? Yes, he does looks like a possible candidate, but he must win the qualifiers. After all, this is a democracy. Fair is fair."

"So come one, come all. Come out; give it a try. Yes, I do agree with you there, ma'am. Oh, and one piece of advice for the qualifiers—be prepared!"

The reporters who met behind the handsome oak door of

the Whitley Building confronted an edgy, white-haired figure who, despite their entreaties, firmly but politely explained that A.H. Adams & Associates was a *business* firm. All discussion not pertinent to this firm's line of work transpire off the premises, thank you. And this same figure, undaunted in his pomp and dignity, would deny all knowledge of any 'contest,' shut the oak door, and disregard all additional requests. By Friday the press had reached a compromise of sorts. Ev Winchell would be fair game both in his trailer and right after work in the firm's parking lot. From 8:30 a.m. until he emerged, however, his time was not his own.

Another unforeseen dynamic emerged as well. While the media quickly grew fond of the timid, eccentric Ev, several could not help but doubt the legitimacy of his project and the money invested and even take pot shots at his resolve. Friday morning's *State Daily News* was a case in point. In the section devoted to local banter and opinions, sat a short editorial entitled 'Accountant Goes Way Out on Limb to Save Face.' Ev found himself toting a chip on his shoulder wherever he went—the interviews, his favorite diner (where the manager, an acquaintance for five years, for some reason now requested cash instead of his VISA), and especially at work, where he had felt isolated almost from the get-go. By the first weekend Ev had come to see himself as the butt of jokes. "Did you hear about the Ev 'Wind Up' doll? Wind it up, it does a jumping-jack, hands you its wallet, and rolls over." This one Ev overheard just outside his own cubicle. "Ev—the man who'd bet a thousand bucks on instant replay" was scrawled across the men's room wall.

Ev Winchell could easily have teetered and fallen. But Ev did not. Hide weakness, show strength, he recalled as an axiom of his copious sports reading, and stuck to this axiom like a bug to the gooey-est of flypaper. If anything, such mockery made him stronger, even more determined to triumph. He was taking the heat, yes, but now he was liking it. And when Friday evening's *Times* displayed a page-one sports-section item capped **'COUNTDOWN TO FIFTY GRAND!'** below a sketch of a small nerd with a plastic pocket protector and a rain cloud over his head, Ev simply chuckled and thought no more of it. No, the pressure of this contest would *not* get to Ev Winchell.

Likewise, it was by this same Friday night—less than twelve hours before the qualifying matches would begin— that Dan Driver and wife Debra came to a pact of sorts. It wasn't Dan's risking of his own ten thousand that Debra begrudged him; it was about his borrowing ten more on their credit card that she found distressing. Dan understood her concern and said that he would pay back every penny with a second job, but also told her that the contest was something he had to do for his sanity and self-respect. Knowing how responsible Dan had always been, Debra, still dazed by the whole idea, pressed no further.

And so the matter stood. Debra and Dan scrupulously kept their tightrope schedules, he working the days and she the nights, both spending their prescribed hours with the kids and with each other. But even when she was not home

Dan felt a tension, a hollow, near-dark ambience that hung through the house. Guilt? Fear? Resentment? All of these. Yet, the topic was one she did not speak of again. The contest would go on.

As time and again Dan reflected on this, he marveled. What a woman he had married. What a *gem* of a woman!

Slowly, gloriously, the sun lifted above Riding Crop Park. It was an hour after dawn, the debut of a gorgeous late-summer day, the day of the qualifiers. A sedan pulled into the parking lot slowly, a solitary color of blue beneath a gradually matching sky. The car drew to a halt. Ev ducked out, squinted around, stretched, then lumbered toward the path by the tree-lined entranceway. He checked his watch, yawned, then stepped over and sat back, knees drawn up, on a still-dewy wooden bench.

Minutes later a second car arrived. A man in a green grounds-keeper uniform emerged, and approached Ev, who by now was up and pacing apprehensively. He paused to shake his hand. Both men proceeded to enter the stadium.

Twenty minutes later Dan Driver, at the park's athletic complex, was crisscrossing a soccer field, checking the quality of the turf, measuring and re-measuring distances. At a faint cry he turned. Suddenly, out of the trees emerged a slim figure in bright red shorts, green-striped track shoes, and an old undershirt. Dan stared for a moment, then grinned.

"Merry Christmas," Dan joked.

A few yards away the figure paused, huffing. "Don't

laugh. With this kind of money riding on it, why not try? A bout of bubonic plague could knock out all the others. Then who'd we have? No one."

And with this Ev, who now had joined Dan, chuckled and moved into a brisk series of jumping-jacks. "Me too—just in case," he managed.

"You might just pull it off by default," Dan said, glancing around. "You did tell everyone nine, didn't you?"

Ev nodded.

"This morning, right?"

"Right. You read the paper. And I asked the refs to show up a good hour before the start." Ev checked his watch. "Well, we still have almost two hours. Maybe we're just jumping the gun ourselves?"

Then Ev, too, looked around. He glanced over to Dan.

"You don't think the whole civilized world would boycott us, do you?"

"Why not?" Dan replied. "We're out here boycotting the world!"

At 9:05 a.m. the sun was in full view. Already the air held an oppressiveness hinting a hot, sticky day. Vehicles crammed the lot. Figures filled the entranceway. Athletes, fans, boosters were everywhere. In the complex proper, the stands on each side of the soccer field were jammed to near capacity, while further groups of spectators stood, sat, or lounged off to each side.

From one edge of the field Dan and Ev watched the

figures arrive and get situated, the athletes shed their sweats and stretch. "Thought it was 9," Ev said, then. He wiped his brow in both relief and concern. "Gonna be heck to play out here today, too," he said. "Humidity can cut into performance like nothing else." Once more he surveyed the scene, and swallowed mightily. Already hundreds of competitors accompanied by friends and family had shown up. A Channel 4 live news truck was on hand as well.

"Well, Dan—here goes."

Ev took up a megaphone and stepped out onto the field. He stepped gingerly atop an orange crate and waved the megaphone. The sea of several hundred athletes and a group of referees, now a dozen, crowded in. Ev glanced timidly back over to Dan, took one more long breath, and began.

"Uh, my name is Ev Winchell. You, uh, no doubt know why I called this meeting?"

Chuckles broke out, then a solid round of applause. Ev turned Dan's way, more confident now, looked back across the up-turned faces, and resumed.

"First, let me welcome—wow!—all of you and your families and fans to what I think—win, lose, or draw—is going to be an unforgettable experience. We only ask that you do your best. Because we're looking for that very special athlete who is the best— THE BEST ALL AROUND."

Ev stared. In the very center of the group stood Ruff, brawny arms lifted high in triumph, 'JOCK OF ALL TRADES!' emblazoned in brilliant red across his T-shirt. Voices erupted. Other arms lifted. More outcries came forth.

"Okay, okay!" Ev raised a hand of his own now to quell the outbreak. There came another rash of chuckles, a harsh yell. Then the outbursts fell away.

"Good," Ev announced. "Glad to see you've all had your testosterone shots. Now, for the rules and procedures. You each paid your five dollars, signed your waiver, picked up and read your entry slip and schedule, which explains how and where we're going to run you through these nine stations. And don't forget—we all meet together for that last event—the 3.1 mile run. Right?"

"Riiiiight!" a chorus sounded.

"Great! Uh, my name's Ev and I approve this message! So let's *do* it. Entries one through fifty report to Station One, football. That's—check your maps—near the far goal over there. Numbers fifty-one to one hundred meet at the park, a block east of here, for the basketball competition...."

As Ev continued to call off the numbers and stations, the athletes began to move off in groups and assemble at their assigned posts. At once the fans in the stands, then the athletes as well, stood to offer a long, vigorous round of applause. Ev looked around, puzzled, openmouthed. These folks, for now, just now, were applauding—him.

"I'll be darned," he murmured to a ref who had moved up near him. "This is the first time in my life I have ever received any positive response for anything I have done athletically. People do care."

He offered a cordial wave to the crowd. "You're doing a super job, Winchell," said the ref. "But do you think the fifty

Gs has anything to do with it?"

"That's not the spirit *I* see out here," replied Ev.

Everywhere athletes were warming up vigorously, shouting, growling, pumping their fists, kicking, short-sprinting. The mood was electric.

Dan walked over to Ev and took off his warm-ups, to expose the entry number 407. "I've decided to compete with everyone else," he explained. "I want to show you that the stats I gave you were no fluke. Besides, I'm very curious just where I might end up."

"You're curious?" O.K." Ev said. "Uh, good luck."

Over at Station Seven the ref lifted the starting gun. The athletes froze, arms, legs, faces set rigidly. Then—pop!— off they went, scrambling past the row of media standing or kneeling along the track. Already by the first curve one competitor tumbled to the cinders. Twenty yards or farther a second pulled out, to nurse a severe limp. At the fifty-yard mark the exertion of a third fell into disgust, as he exited the track. "What a waste of five bucks!" he muttered into someone's microphone. His disgust would play out on the local news that night.

At Station One the athletes lined up with eagerness. The first to punt—a flabby, fifty-ish candidate with salt-and-pepper hair, a sharp nose, and an intense face, traded his card to the ref for the football. He rotated the ball's laces topside. "Fine," said the ref, nodding. "Off—that-away."

The man hung the ball out before him, grimaced his face

with extra effort, kicked—and missed. As he lay on his back peering up dazedly, another alert photographer pounced.

"Uh, that'll cost you points," the ref announced.

"Wait! One just for practice?" came the plea.

As the ref weighed the request, the line pitched forward. "Forget that. Football is a *contact* sport, you wusses," came a growl. The ref handed the ball to the candidate to try again. He connected. The ball rose, hung, and nosed down—all of eighteen yards. "I-I was trying for the corner," he protested, amid laughter. Glumly he watched the ref mark his card, then thumped his considerable paunch.

At Station Seven the crowd comprised not only hopefuls, but gapers and gawkers. For warming up here with the others was the voluptuous Diana Hansen, a former NCAA track-and-field standout and a fledgling starlet openly wooed by William Morris, United Artists, and MGM. Wowing the crowd was not only the lady's exquisite physical attributes, but her outfit—a skin-taut Wonder Woman suit, complete with magic bracelets. Fans of film and sport alike would follow her efforts throughout the day, rooting wildly her dazzling, gazelle-like performances and groaning and clicking their tongues in sympathy at the less lustrous ones. Now a football from the punting competition came rocketing down short yards away. A ref raced in, planted a marker where the ball had fallen. Diana looked to the ref, lifted her bracelets up before her eyes, and did a quick spin. The ref paused, gawked dizzily, and tripped over his own feet. The crowd roared.

By 11:30 Ev was forced to phone for more stand-by refs. By noon the stands and the field's entire rim were thronged with well-wishers. Meanwhile, the competition continued to take its toll. Populating the rows of bleachers, sidelines, and grass areas ringing the field were figures sitting down or hunched over, figures tending to pulled arm or leg muscles, sprained ankles, blistered feet. Over at Station Seven a gawky candidate ran toward the crossbar, leapt into the bar and landed on the mat right on top of the bar, bending it slightly. His miscue postponed the event for several minutes.

"This is turning into a madhouse," declared a ref witnessing with several others and Ev.

"Should we have used this regulation shot put?" asked another.

"Yes, it's important," said Ev. "But it demands a degree of skill that most of these athletes simply don't have. There are two major techniques—sidestepping to the front of the circle and releasing or rotating like a discus-thrower. I included it, but hope we don't see too many of these overzealous people ruining their arms.

A second ref peeked around. "Maybe we're just a bit too paranoid. I mean, look. No fights. No bad blood. Amazing, really!"

"It's still early," warned a third. "Going to be getting hot out here."

"Same at my station," reported a fourth. "Friendly, polite, but not too fit. Face it, most of these folks just should not be out here."

Ev shook his head. "Guys, this is America. Everyone who wants to gets a chance."

"But what can we expect from these—average athletes?"

"Not average," said Ev. "Not by any measure."

"So what *is* average?"

"Let's avoid 'average,'" said Ev. "Each one out here is unique. Each is part of the genetic lottery. Each has something personal to offer, something to resolve, something to win."

"And something to lose," grinned one ref.

"So how *do* you ever find out how each can do in all fifteen? I mean—"

"We don't. Not at this point. Boxing, wrestling, racquetball, baseball, tennis we couldn't schedule. We couldn't run each of these people through so many tests in one outing, especially where one-on-one competition is necessary. These nine stations reveal basic speed, strength, coordination, conditioning, and desire. Later we'll have the luxury to elaborate. Take that high jump—our first measurement of a more sophisticated skill. More than nine out of ten of these folks are failing to clear five and a half feet—against a world record of over one and a half times that."

"So what did you expect? A field of marathon runners and bungee jumpers?"

"At least two of these guys *are* marathon runners," said Ev. "Both did the Boston just last April. I greatly respect their running skills, but unfortunately neither can pump much iron, or smoothly swing a golf club—or swim a competitive lap."

At Station Three a chunky candidate swung with all his might. He missed the golf ball entirely, but the breeze that was created sent the ball a good three inches off the tee. "Get in the hole!" a fan called, to the laughter of the crowd.

In the billiard room and bowling alley, Stations Four and Five, the atmosphere was more subdued. With the air-conditioning, the players enjoyed a welcome break. Meanwhile, it was amazing that most of the athletes seemed to think that the harder he rolled the bowling ball the more pins were apt to fall. Diana shunned this rationale. Her softly hooked ball hit the pocket time and again, allowing her to rack up what would be the second-highest score of the day.

On the basketball court at Station Two, the competition was intense. Ruff had made a phenomenal twenty-one of thirty shots, before Dan edged him out with twenty-two.

Station Six lent the oddest incident of the day, as one of the better weight-lifters tried to use 'floaters' in the swimming competition. He was afraid of water, he claimed. Refusing to leap in without them, he was jeered by the crowd.

It was not long before the growing heat and frustration incited some less-than-happy competitors. As a group back at Station Seven dashed madly around the first turn, one slender runner found himself elbowed off the cinders by a brawny foe, who forged into the lead. The victim stood for a moment, red-faced, puffing, and then cut angrily across the field through two other stations to meet his group at its next turn. He leapt out, clutched the leader's shorts, and yanked. The abruptly bared candidate briefly fell out to retrieve both his shorts and his composure, only yards away from a smirking Diana. The crowd hooted.

Again at Station Seven, the high jump, voluptuous Diana got her chance. She bit for a pensive moment on her collagened lower lip, gathered herself, and bounded off. She reached the bar and, cleared it flawlessly, and drew a robust burst of applause. "Great style," said a man in line behind a muscular figured athlete. "Awesome," the other replied. "Ruff ruff!"

Dan was awaiting his turn for the next heat when a bevy of runners sped by. Dan stared. In the midst of the cluster was—Mr. Duntoot. The druggist spied Dan, and waved. "Hey, I can use the bucks, too," he managed. The main body rounded the curve and headed down the straightaway, leaving him and several others in its wake. Duntoot glanced back to Dan, offered a vacant, half-embarrassed shrug. Pale-faced, huffing, he lumbered after.

Ev surveyed the field. "A few of these folks I recognize from the society pages. They're dropping like flies. I tell you, Richie Rich may have time and money for private coaches and stainless-steel showers and Jacuzzis, but when it comes to raw stamina and that hang-in-there extra effort, he seems to fold. We're seeing it plainly, Dan. This contest *isn't* for the fair-weather athlete. But, on the other hand, none of the lesser-offs have the time, training, discipline, or diet. Just look around, Dan. We're one super-sized nation. Is our food 'faster' than we are?"

"If that's the case, why are so many world records being broken?" one of the refs asked.

Ev shrugged. "Good question. You're right, there are. A new shot-put record in 1990, and a new pole-vault record in '94. In '96 the javelin record was shattered— with a toss farther than a football field is long! And look at running. In 1866 the world record for the mile was what —four thirteen? By 1900 that record had scarcely budged. But today that same time marks a good high-school runner, while the record is thirty seconds faster. A new men's marathon record was set in 2003. In Carlsbad in 2004 Isabella Ochichi broke the women's 5K—a record re-set only two years earlier. And swimming? Michael Phelps's won eight golds in this summer's Olympics—right smack dab in Beijing. Ask me, it's better training prep. Runners race much faster today in training, have shorter workouts and longer periods of recovery, which lets them use oxygen more efficiently in races where it counts. Put another way, we have relatively few general athletes. They each put all their eggs in one or just a few baskets."

"So what's the ultimate result—a one-minute mile?"

"Hardly. Don't forget, before what—1967, it wasn't illegal even for Olympians to use drugs as performance-enhancers. And we are leveling off. The times of over two -thirds of track-and-field gold-medal-wins in 1988 would have won again in 2000. But some of those performances may even have involved drugs, too. But then, we can't forget genetic engineering. Right now scientists in California are creating 'marathon mice' able to run twice as far and twice as long as normal mice, just by injecting them with a gene that mimics exercise, builds muscles, and prevents obesity. If this works—whew—think what might be in store for us humans!"

For a moment the group was silent, watching one more candidate head glumly for the aid station. "So much for records," one of the refs said after a time.

"But if not the country club, or the ghetto, where's our physical genius going to come from?" another asked. "I mean, he—" He broke off his words. They all took pause to witness Diana cap off an easy win in the hundred-yard dash with a flash of her glittering bracelets. "Or she...?"

"I don't know. We're seeing some solid performances here in ones and twos. We've seen Diana. We've seen Tim Crenshaw, that local quarterback bound for Notre Dame, and Nancy Seaver, the state record-holder in the women's mile. Dan Driver is putting a good performance together and is making a late surge. They're all great in their own ways, but, just as the computer predicted, no single athlete seems able to put it all together."

Once again Dan spied Duntoot. The druggist was sprawled, gasping, on the grass apron beside the track. He winced, visibly. Then, with a slow, mighty effort, he pushed up. At once he saw Dan, and waved a cordial, if weary, wave. He then turned and limped away, out of the brilliant sunlight and into the shade of the pathway to the parking lot.

The hours passed. Heat and humidity took their toll. Weekend athletes exerted themselves to the utmost, but such efforts revealed them to be weekend athletes and no more. After the track and weight-lifting events, most would be showing the agony of the day. Frequent wheezes and coughs exposed the heavy smokers. One candidate had even toted along an oxygen bottle, but to no avail; within half an hour he had failed to clear the high jump set at a lowly four feet. Likewise at Station Eight, men and women alike—often huge, Olympus-like men and fit, sculpted women—would swagger up to the iron and then, after the obligatory hoists, would wink with confidence. But after an event such as golf, almost all of these same contenders would turn and walk off, deflated, even disgusted.

Yes, in general, the running and lifting took the greatest tolls. A pattern emerged. The strongest could not run; the swiftest could not lift. It was as if each particular skill checkmated the stellar feats of the other. In due time figures huge and small, brawny and lean, trudged the tree-lined trail out of the park side by side, silent, heads bowed, knowing their efforts would not carry the day. By 3 p.m. the once-packed entrance lot was showing an occasional vacancy. By 3:30 empty spaces around Dan's blue Taurus were beginning to appear. As entrants lined up for the final event, the 3.1mile race, the original group of 407 contenders was down to 114. Shortly after 3:45 a mighty cheer and round of applause erupted from the remaining crowd. Ninety-six athletes had finished all nine events and were now in the running for "The Best All-Around." Diana Hansen, track shoes in hand, limped off. She had finished all nine events, and had performed nearly as superbly as the action figure she resembled. The reaction from fans in the stands and field alike, from groupies, friends, family, and fellow-competitors, was prolonged and enthusiastic. As she paused to wave a general thank-you and took a pen to scrawl autographs for young admirers, the sounds of appreciation lifted even more. Ruff gawked, spellbound. "What a *doll*!" someone behind him breathed. "Got *that* right," Ruff said back.

By 5 p.m. the sun was well on its descent. Reporters, camera crews, station captains—all began to gather up their gear. Referees signed and handed in the candidates' score-sheets, shook hands heartily with Dan and Ev, and departed. At 5:15 the remaining spectators rose and headed towards the parking area. With the last of the sheets turned in now, Dan and Ev were ready to call it a day. On the way out they thanked the arriving groundskeepers, who offered some mock complaints about the task before them, of cleaning up so many bandage wrappers and empty water bottles. As the two headed to the parking lot, Ev marveled. "Not far off at all. Really, Dan, that software program we put together is something! I could have written in these figures myself! And that Hansen gal! Her numbers—whew!"

"I noticed we did have a fair sprinkling of women. How did they do?"

"I don't know yet. My guess is not too well. The above-average female can outdo the average male, but not the above-average male. The best males routinely outdo the best females. The male record mile is about three forty-three, the female four twelve and change. Pole vault? 6.1 meters to 4.8 meters. Triple jump? I believe, about 18 to 15 feet. The long jump is about 9 to 7.5 meters. The javelin, too, shows a wide disparity—about fifty percent farther for men. Some funny stuff here, too. In 1932 a Polish Olympian was the first ever to clock in under twelve seconds for the women's hundred meters. When she died in 1980, the autopsy showed she was—a male!"

Dan smiled, and shook his head. "Ruff did pull it off, then?"

"That'd be my guess. Did anyone beat him? Did anyone even come close? I peeked through most of the score sheets. Off the top of my head, I'd say Ruff won, but you know something Dan—*your* numbers were very impressive, too."

The two men vanished into the shadows down the trail. Behind them a solitary figure who had been witnessing all day long from a cozy lawn chair set back amid the coolness of a cluster of pines. After a time the figure rose to his full height, stretched a slow, mighty stretch. He removed his sunglasses, his cowboy hat, and wiped his dimpled face with the back of a thick forearm. Then, casually, he folded up the chair and its cushion, and lumbered off.

As he reached the field one of the crew happened to glance his way, and yelled. The others hurried over. "One for my kid?" said one, and the brawny figure grinned. "My grandkids?" said another, bending over to retrieve a crumpled score-sheet. "Me, too?" requested a third.

Before he left the man had scrawled his large, aggressive signature, B.J. Billings, across a dozen sheets. "Coming back to make headlines soon?" asked one man wielding a rake. "There's lots of ways to make headlines," he replied. "And fifty big reasons to 'play this rough character.'" This he added with a mischievous twinkle.

CHAPTER
SIX

The caption read 'ARE YOU WILLING TO PLAY RUFF?' It stood beneath the full-color photo of the wide-jawed man grinning out in supreme confidence. Ruff had made good on his claim and had outdistanced everyone in the qualifier. Dan and Ev restudied the photo and the accompanying article set on the front page of the *Times* Monday-morning sports section. "Okay okay, the secret's out. Ruff is our man. The world knows it. But now *this*?"

Once again Ev veered a grim face toward the door, as he gingerly shifted his position on the old wooden chair. "I tell you, Dan, this chair may be an ordeal in its own way, but at least I'm protesting. I won't ask him for another, but I'm ruining my darned pants with these doggone slivers I'm getting!" He pulled a thin piece of wood from his slacks, and flicked it into the wastebasket.

"Can't you just make do for now?" said Dan.

"I'd like to. But Mossey has dumped three more accounts on me today. None are moneymakers—none the least interesting. But I thought of a way to get even."

"Hide his key to the men's room?" said Dan.

"Better yet, lure his resident ape into our trap. Look, Mr. High-and-Mighty B.J. Billings is your alpha, ultra-competitive type, right? We goad him, but we don't breathe a word about any contest. He finds out—which he will—he's not going to let it slide. Uh-uh. Dan, think of it! A major sports figure like B.J. Billings wiped out by some unknown? Yup, a 'Ruff and Ready' victory over that clown! It'd turn the whole sports world upside down! Talk about building credibility! And hey—it'd sure give Mossey the fits!"

Dan viewed him for a time. "You really are on a vendetta," Dan said.

"Three more accounts today, Dan! What *should* I do? Send him a thank-you card?"

Dan nodded, continued his gaze. After a time Ev shrugged. "Okay okay, maybe I am a bit edgy. Just a bit. But Dan, tell me, isn't this pressure getting to *you*?"

It was a gorgeous Sunday morning. The mellow strains of the organ could still be heard as the congregation filed out of church. Among them were the Drivers. Once outside, Dan and Debra mingled with others and began to chat. A few minutes later, a small but feisty figure—Debra's mom—exited as well. She turned back, peered up at the steeple for a moment, and then joined Debra and Dan. "I stayed to say an extra prayer," she said. "For *all* of us."

She half-glanced at Dan as she said it, then with Debra and several others launched into a discussion of an upcoming potluck. Dan hoisted Jeffy up into his arms. At once, at Dan's side, Lori pointed. "Uncle Ev," she announced. "Daddy—Uncle Ev!"

Dan followed the tiny finger. Sure enough, just across the road, in the shadows of an elm tree, stood Ev. He noticed Dan's stare, and waved. Dan bundled his son tightly in his arms, told Lori to remain by Mom, and he walked over.

"You here, of all places! Willing even to pray for victory?"

Ev gazed off at the assembly. "As good a place as any to break the news," he said quietly. "Dan, I put in that ten I had saved. But my brother can only put up five. Heck, with three kids—two needing braces—he's lucky to afford that." Ev peered around forlornly, and shook his head. "But the real kicker is this. My real-estate agent just called. The trailer deal fell through. As of now I'm short. Like—fifteen thousand in all." He gave Dan a desperate look. He chewed his lip, and looked away.

"You found this out on a Sunday?"

"An hour ago. I asked Blogett, my real estate agent to call at any time if there was any problem. There was. Is. The buyers he had lined up decided to go another direction."

For a time, the two surveyed the churchgoers. Conversations on the lawn seemed animated, happy. At one point Debra gestured half-comically as she spoke, and flashed a smile. Lori was engaged in a chat with a little girl in a dress as white as her own.

"Dan, we can't let the world do this to us. We're so close to pulling it off. It's just that fifteen more is beyond me. We'll still go over to the stadium tonight, as planned. Uh, look. You dig up an extra five. I'll *get* ten. Promise."

Dan could only stare.

"Dan—we can't let the world just pass us by."

Without warning, Dan edged off the sidewalk, Jeffy tight in his arms, just in time to avoid a jogger racing by. "Careful—" Ev called, and the jogger, in headband and sweats with an ipod securely plugging his ears, unseeingly waved back. Dan and Ev stood and watched the man jog away.

Within the hour Dan was on the phone. "Dad, I really appreciate the favor. I know how difficult this is and I promise to get the money back to you very soon. My love to you and Mom."

Dan took a deep breath, and hung up. It was done. Almost immediately the slam of a car door was heard. A moment later Lori burst in followed by Debra toting a bag of groceries. "He's still asleep?" Debra said, and Dan nodded.

Just as Debra was placing the groceries on the counter, the bag gave way. Cans, boxes, and wrapped packages tumbled onto the floor. "Oh, boy!" she said. "Just washed the floor yesterday, of course." She and Dan worked together to pick up the scattered groceries. "And why are you so down?" she said. "Got your favorite here. Beef roast, browned potatoes, applesauce, veggies—the works. Uh, kiss me?"

As Dan obliged, she pulled back quickly to direct her attention to Lori. "Noooo," she said to Lori, busily feeding a candy bar to her bear. "No, none for your bear." She lifted Cuddles and made a wry, silly face. "Now *look* at him," she lamented, laying the bear out on the counter. She grabbed a paper towel, held it briefly under the faucet. "At least he won't be needing CPR." She wrung the towel out, applied it to the brown blotch marring Cuddles' wooly face. "Messes, messes everywhere. So what's next?"

She and Lori broke into giggles, as Dan stood somberly by.

As Deb finished putting away the groceries, Dan asked Lori to get her wiffle bat and ball.

"We'll be outside. Working on her swing," Dan said.

Late Sunday evening Ev and Dan met. "We'll have the final five events—uh, that's 'OUTDOOR DAY'—right here. The last of them, that six-event, mini-decathlon, I think you call it, will start there." Ev pointed to mid-field, and turned. He spoke more quietly. "Look, I appreciate what you're doing, Dan. I really, really do. Things are happening so fast and furious we have to make on-the-spot decisions just to keep up. Okay, we're still ten thousand short, but it's my problem. Leave it to me." He took in the stadium once more, scribbled a line of hieroglyphics across the sheet. "Cheer up," he said. "I mean, look what we've got here. This whole contest is programmed, debugged, accounted for."

"I've never pulled anything like this before," said Dan. "The fifteen I can repay in due time, with outside work. But our marriage—I sure don't want to jeopardize that."

Ev looked at Dan long and hard. "You know as well as I do what we do every day, week, month, year. By being so 'exactly right,' we 'turn financial liabilities into assets' for *other* people. But not this time. This time it's for us. Like I say, Dan, we both just keep plugging away till someone challenges and they will—and we can pocket that original fifty. You agree. I agree. Then you take your cute Snow White and kids out to some nice restaurant, pop open a bottle of the bubbly, and spring the news on them. Minus, of course, the price of dinners and bubbly and, ugh, the tax! Dan, she'll love you for it! Love? Huh! This time next year you'll probably be claiming additional deductions for a new set of twins!"

Dan shrugged as they viewed the far stadium entrance, when a head-banded figure in track gear appeared.

"So you really think it'll work," Dan said.

"Is Mossey anal-retentive? Does Nippers think the pun is mightier than the sword? Do our aged accountants Miller and Wells have seniority on Ben Franklin? Got to believe, Dan. Got to!"

For a short time, they gazed off. At the far edge of the track, a figure limbered up briefly, then reached into a duffel bag and fetched a football. He started jogging down the track, football in hand. Several grounds men noticed the figure, and warmly greeted him. The man stopped, waved in return, and peeked around. He spotted Dan and Ev, and gave a friendly wave.

"Who—" Dan and Ev offhandedly returned the gesture. All at once the figure became familiar.

"Holy Cow! All right! Told you, Dan! We simply let the gorilla snatch the bananas and run. See, *told* you. Nothing to freak out about. Nothing—"

B.J. stopped, set himself, then reared back and abruptly hurled the football—some eighty yards. He shook out his arm in disgust, as if the toss were sub-par. Then he leapt high, danced around, threw a vigorous barrage of punches at some imaginary foe. As the grounds-crew urged him on, he somersaulted cleverly, added a playful cartwheel. Then down the track he sprinted, his legs driving like pistons.

"Dan, I told you!"

Dan drove through the heat and humidity. The AC at work had finally been fixed. That helped. It seemed to be the only part of Dan Driver's life that was currently in good repair. A truck edged up behind, swung out, rumbled by, leaving Dan peeking off against the receding image of the stadium. The song on the radio gave way to a rhythm vastly different—a bold, inspiring fight song now, followed by an enthusiastic voice proclaiming, "Fans, welcome to Morning Sports Report. Today we—"

Dan turned the knob briskly leftward, leaving the radio in silence.

The contest was twelve days off. As Dan and Ev conferred in the privacy of Dan's cubicle, Ev's confidence seemed to vacillate. Offering a broad smile one moment, a frown the next, his mood reached higher peaks, lower valleys. At times his voice even flirted with despair. "A week from Wednesday." he mumbled again, for the third time. "By noon? Okay, ten from my savings, five from my brother, bless his heart! With your twenty and the extra five you just added, that's ... forty? Whew, forty thousand! But we need—fifty." He looked to Dan. "I mean, we're going to be shot down by our own rule of 'exactness'?"

"I'm up to the hilt already, Ev. It's got to come from you."

"Then, to heck with smart finances. I will just let my place go for a quick ten— furniture, coffeemaker, the works!"

Just outside Dan's cubicle there hunched a figure, listening. After this latest woeful exchange he pondered for a moment. Then he smirked a broad smirk, and quickly made his way down the hall.

All at once interrupting Ev's words were harsh thumps on the wall, followed by a loud, gruff boast. "Easily the Best ALL-Around in this cow town! Eight seasons tackling for power, glory, big bucks? *Easily!*"

Ev stood back. "Been going on long?" he asked Dan.

"Every fifteen minutes. Like clockwork. He's taking the bait all right. He didn't toss that pigskin halfway to the moon just to sprain his wrist."

"Like I said, Dan, the intelligent athlete wins. And the intelligent businessman wins, too."

"Definitely the best," came the boast now. "Definitely!"

"Intelligent athlete?" Ev mulled a moment more. "Like a ripe plum. High time we started turning up the heat!"

He stepped over, picked up Dan's wastebasket, and dumped its contents out behind Dan's desk. "Got to get me some Saran Wrap and a glass of water. A big glass. Wow, yeah, *what* a thirst!" He winked to the curious Dan and, basket in hands, strode out.

Ten minutes later the basket stood back beside Dan's desk, its brim overflowing with litter and crumpled papers. "Okay—places," Ev announced. Dan hunched over the basket. Ev gave a casual stretch, slid off the desktop, and stalked out.

Moments later Ev returned, with a huge, lumbering companion – B.J..

"We were hoping that maybe you could talk to Mossey about this. We don't have the clout. We've only been here … six years." Ev shrugged in embarrassment. "I mean, let's be honest. You're Mister Strong in every way around here." Dan offered a cordial nod, then shrugged in exasperation back down at the over-packed basket. Dan made an effort to shove the pile down to make more room, but could not.

"I'll see what I can do," B.J. replied, smirking.

He sized up the cubicle, shook his head. "Geez, you ordinary dudes are hurtin' for closet space. Hey, wait—is this is a closet?"

"And too much litter," Ev moaned. "Too much even to work. I mean, look at all that junk in there! One audit? Hey, if you can't help us out strength-wise, at least mention it to Old Mosshead. Please???"

"Mitch, you mean."

"Mitch," Dan said, with a wry smile.

"Nice slacks," Ev said now. "Latest fabric, huh?"

"Believe it. Breakin' 'em in for my first commercial at the stadium. Where I bumped into *you* dudes last night." He grinned privately, then scrutinized Ev. "Hey—you gotta be that Little Furniture Freak everybody's mouthin' about."

Ev then redirected B.J.'s eyes to Dan.

"Sorry. You guys are on your own." B.J. started to exit,

then took pause. He viewed the exasperated Dan once more. "'OK. Seems you two do have a real problem." He stepped up before the basket, hoisted one foot high. "This will help stamp out paperwork? Hut hut—" As Dan bent aside, B.J. stomped, hard— "*hut!*"

The papers gave way easily, too easily. B.J.'s expression went from amused triumph to sick surprise. He withdrew his leg—a leg laden with, coffee grounds, lettuce bits, old pizza and other garbage. From the knee down the fresh sheen of his slacks had been replaced by dull, oily slime.

"The grease from the pizza and the other garbage was starting to set. Oh, geez, B.J.! So sorry!"

B.J. looked around. For a moment he seemed on the verge of a genuine flare-up. Swiftly he regained control. "*Mister* Billings to you." He looked icily at Dan. "Munchkin here *and* you."

Ev pointed at B.J.'s leg. "Looks 'mossy' to me. Or is it 'mitchy'?"

B.J. eyed them. His dimples had vanished. "You guys are on my list," he said. "On my list." He turned, started out. "Oops," he said. He stepped back, gauged. "Hut hut—" He kicked the basket once, twice, in brisk field-goal fashion. The basket toppled, rolled down the hall. Water, soggy papers, dark grounds, pizza and lettuce bits littered the floor. "Kick's goooood!" B.J. yelled, raising his arms.

Dan and Ev watched him depart.

"Was this really necessary?" Dan asked after a time.

"Big-time necessary," Ev said. "For four reasons." He

counted the reasons out on his fingers. "First, to let you see first-hand how the intelligent athlete—in this case, the dude who snoops before he stomps—is going to win it. Second, to stop all my doggone worrying, as in 'comic relief'? Third, to prod that bellowing behemoth into entering—into getting on *our* list."

"He probably would have anyway."

"Probably, uh-huh. But now he's got a vengeance. Now he really *wants* to."

Dan looked at Ev. "That's only three reasons," Dan said.

Ev smirked, consulted his watch. He raised his hand to lend a cue, then, after a few seconds, brought it down. Sure enough, a fresh round of thumps resounded on B.J.'s office wall, followed by a few revitalized grumbles.

"That makes four," Ev said.

Late that night, with Deb at work, Dan rested in his favorite armchair. At ten-thirty p.m. the phone rang. It was Deb's mom, upset. The conversation was more like a lecture.

"—treat them like a wife, son and daughter. Take the responsibilities that come with being a husband and father. I've always liked you, Dan Driver, trusted you, *loved* you. But this time you've gone too far. It's all so selfish! It's hard for me to believe we even go to church together."

"Mom, listen."

"No, you listen. If she had been blessed with more good sense than patience, my Deb would have told you days ago to give up this loony notion about tossing away so much hard-earned money."

"Mom, I said I'm sorry. And I am. Very sorry. But now I'm into it. I've given my word. I have to see it through."

"And a reporter called. Here, of all places! Wanted me to explain how my son-in-law 'could come up with fifty.' He mentioned the word gambling. Thousands of dollars! Precious life savings to—to most family-minded people."

And with that the conversation ended.

After lying dormant for days, it came back now suddenly, and with a vengeance—the hollow, pounding tremor in Dan's stomach. Dan took a long, deep breath. Dan stared off, sick to his stomach.

CHAPTER
SEVEN

Dan negotiated through the heavy traffic. Predictably, traffic slowed to a crawl, and finally came to a halt. 'Yes, fans, a week from Saturday. The first kick-off leg of the three-day context. Who will challenge? Who will plunk fifty Gs on the line and announce to the world, "I'm the best!"? Morning Sports Report says lots of talkers, but for this one we need—a walker. So if you know of anyone who—'

An angry, sulking Dan snapped off the radio.

Slowly, stealthily the coat-rack protruded into the hallway, holding a wastebasket filled nearly to its brim with cold water. Within seconds the basket had been carefully maneuvered to a site just outside Dan's cubicle entrance.

Inside, Nolton B. Nippers was whispering in happy confidence. "Really, Dan, I'm like your appendix in this. You know, on your side. Get it—'on your side'? The right side, too. Hey, yeah—the 'credit' side! I mean, versus the left—er, wrong—side." With that Nips turned and headed out.

Dan heard a thump, a splash, then hollow gurgles. He hurried out to see Nips sprawled amid a puddle on the floor.

"Oh, my side," moaned Nips. "My - left side!" He peeked about in distress. Up and down the hallway faces were popping out. A dimpled faced man edged out of the office bordering Dan's own. Dan spied the face. The face belonged to B.J.. Its grin clouded, visibly. Dan helped Nips get to his feet. Dan shook his head, smirked, and returned to his work.

The A.H. Adams & Associates Grand Executive Conference Room was closed to all but the conferring executives of the firm. Now these executives—an even dozen, sat in heated discussion behind the formidable oak door marked PRIVATE. Nolton Nippers had simply edged up to the door and, near the floor, slipped it open a crack and wedged a pencil between door and frame. Then, he placed his ear gingerly to the crack to hear the voices slipping through.

"Out-and-out extortion, B.J. trying to drag us into this 'contest' of sorts. He's breaching the contract he signed, sir."

"But consider the publicity the contest will bring. Media equals message, does it not? We can use publicity. Isn't that why we brought him on board in the first place?"

"Exactly right."

"Exactly right," chorused the others.

"And when the papers and TV learn that this whole 'contest' is simply one group of A.H. Adams employees pitted against another? That Winchell and that who—Driver?—guy are backing one competitor and A.H. here the other. Why, it'll all be seen as one raw, crass ploy for sensationalism. One silly, clowning publicity stunt! Gentlemen, I warn you. It can backfire. May I remind you of my reservations about hiring the man, about even 'doing ads'? A high-rep firm such as our doesn't have to advertise. Over the top! Scandalous!"

"Whittle does have a point. But let me once again caution. The man's threatened to resign. To sign with our competitor,

B.H. Baker, if we don't allow him to participate."

"And that *would* be scandalous."

"So he does have us over the well-known barrel?"

"Exactly right."

"But hold on! What's *wrong* with publicity? It's not like we're going out onto the street corner and hawking. Isn't ad-making also known as—smart business?"

"If done shrewdly. But to publicly jeopardize fifty thousand dollars of a firm's assets to back a part-time, temporary employee in ... in some ridiculous 'contest'?"

"Accounts have risen dramatically in the short time he's been with us."

Now the eavesdropper, sporting his signature bright socks grinned in delight. He gave out with a long, silent whistle, then he switched ears in time to hear an elderly, dignified voice reply:

"Gentlemen, gentlemen, please. As President, I do suggest we stand back to allow this unique individual his day in court. Just who is he? Where is he coming from? B.J. Billings has been hired in a free and open market. Thanks to Mitchell here, we have snatched him out from under the very nose of our number-one rival, all in the dog-eat-dog world of competitive enterprise. Primitive man did it. Modern man does it. Future man will do it. And sport, B.J. Billings' own medium of expertise, is one of the more popular expressions of this process. It is a way to acknowledge what is a part of every creature's make-up. It might be camouflaged, as so often it is, but it will never go away. If we are to succeed in the world we live and compete in, we must look beyond the present. We must allow B.J. his adventure. Remember, be it on a field or behind a desk, what this all revolves around is competition. While our brand of it here at A.H. Adams is a subtler variety, his is hardly so. We deal, gentlemen, with an individual who no doubt has been programmed since birth for hard, driving, open-air struggle. I say let B.J. Billings do it!"

"But, sir, I ... I disagree."

"Wilkins, I admire your spirit of competitive enterprise. Too bad you're wrong."

"But, sir—doesn't the man's having signed our contract leave *us* with the upper hand?"

"Sinclair declares the obvious. But then again, I submit. Why be so anxious to play our trump card? We want to keep B.J. on our side, to win not the battle but the war. And, yes, our contract, if our legal team has advised me correctly, gives us exclusive rights to all the man's endorsements here in Camelback until which time he opts to sign his football contract. The man's no dummy. No dummy at all. So I say let B.J. Billings peruse the fine print for himself. Like the Prodigal Son, he'll return to the fold. And so, then, what does all this hubbub here today add up to? Precisely nothing. Mr. Mossey, you've been uncustomarily silent. Are you—ill?"

"And why do you so persist in nibbling on that finger, sir? We do have a cafeteria."

Now Nips pressed his ear snugly to the crack to catch the familiar voice.

"I'd best be frank, gentlemen," said Mossey. "He—Mr. Billings, that is—wouldn't sign unless his contract stipulated that, first, he do a charity pitch during each commercial and, second, that the parties involved consider his first thirty days with us a trial period. In light of Baker Brothers' mad scramble to sign him as well, I okayed both clauses to be included."

There came an eruption of shocked whispers, indignant mumbles. Nips stood at the door, shaking an ecstatic fist. Again he listened, as the familiar voice went on.

"So, gentlemen, in this case the proverbial barrel is the one he's, uh, got us over."

There was a brief silence. Then, "Got you over, maybe. I didn't agree to this!" was capped by a general chorus of "We didn't!"

"Uh, gentlemen—I did."

The reply, bearing a weight of resigned confession, ushered in another silence. Now Nips, still listening, hoisted his clasped hands so high in triumph that both his socks toppled down his legs. "Oops—talk about 'tumble dry'!" he murmured.

"Indeed, this does bring a whole new light to bear," said Blackstone.

"Indeed, it does," replied Mossey.

"Exactly right," interjected Marshall.

"Yes, Marshall. Exactly right," offered Mossey.

Marshall spoke very seriously. "As for you, Mr. Mossey, the proper—the only—way for you to atone would be to agree that any and all of the firm's funds directly involved in this agreement come from *you*."

"But gentlemen, I—I—"

"What do you say? You *won't*?"

There came a vigorous outbreak of howling and yipping. Nolton B. Nippers peered blissfully to the heavens, danced a joyful jig, grinned off in sheer, unabashed ecstasy.

Dan arrived home late. He retrieved and perused the mail—three bills and a fashion magazine—and began supper. Tonight the kids would be staying at Grandma's. He would be alone, as Deb was joining them for dinner and would head to work directly from there. Dan flipped on the TV, to some mindless sitcom. The louder the laugh track, the more his face fell. Within minutes he snapped off the TV, to his immense relief.

Dan took his time eating. Slowly he lifted forkfuls of reheated beef up to his mouth as he peered out the kitchen window onto the quiet lawn and the vacant swing set. The sun was setting. Shadows hung, thin and frail. Then the sun finally set. Over a scoop of ice cream Dan watched as the multi-green backyard shrubs faded into vague, colorless silhouettes, and then into darkness. Out in the yard a solitary cricket began to chirp. Dan got up from the table, stretched stiffly, and gazed about the kitchen.

After putting the dishes in the dishwasher and wiping off the table, Dan sat. After a time he retried the TV, this time encountering a Tuesday-night movie interrupted time and time again by commercials. Dan once again turned off the TV and simply sat.

The house felt hollow and vacant. Each rustle and creak echoed and re-echoed through the empty air and conjured forth other rustles and other creaks from forces unseen. Outside, the concert of chirpings grew oppressive. Dan felt compelled to shut the windows and retire to his room. Crickets? Dan had scarcely noticed them before.

Shortly after 9:30 the first call came. At the initial ring Dan twitched, and flicked open his eyes. By the second ring he had reached across the darkness and was fumbling. He felt for the phone, wrapped his fingers around it, lifted it to his ear. "Driver residence," he managed.

"Dad? This is ... Dad-dy?"

Dan sat up in an instant. "Yes, Daddy. Daddy loves you. How are you?"

"I know our number cuz you and Mommy say I should always know it in case if I get lost. Our address, too. One oh oh five Delta Drive."

"That's great, honey."

"I just wanted to tell you I love you and to sleep tight and not to let the bedbugs bite."

"Thanks, Lori. I love you, too. Sleep well. And give Jeff and Mom a kiss."

With that Dan smiled glumly, laced his hands behind his head, stared wearily up against the ceiling, and drifted off.

Sometime later in the night another ring interrupted Dan's sleep. In an instant Dan came awake, rolled over, groped, and there in the darkness snatched up the phone. "Honey? Honey—is that you?"

There came a pause. Then—"Dan, I do appreciate our closeness, but isn't this carrying it a bit too far?" said Ev.

"Oh. Hey, you realize it's ... What time is it?"

"High time, Dan. There's been, um, a development. A *major* development."

"You sold the trailer. We've got the fifty. All *right.*"

"Uh, no, it's … not that. Uh, look, can you make it over here right away?"

" Okay. Give me … twenty minutes."

"I'm not at home, Dan, I'm"-

"Where? Some psych ward?"

"Close. Dan, this is serious. I'm at the hospital. The one where Deb works. Sacred Heart. As in—emergency."

Immediately Dan drove to the hospital. He exited the elevator, sidestepped a figure hunched over a floor-buffing machine, and bee-lined for the desk. On the far side of the corridor Dan spied the familiar thin figure, pacing nervously, Styrofoam cup in hand. Dan hurried over.

"Right after it happened, he called me. I didn't know any other place to direct him, and I do know your wife works here, so—"

"Who? What?" said Dan.

A door cracked open. A nurse peeked out. "You can see him again now," she whispered.

"Thanks," Ev said solemnly.

"The shock was a bit much at first. He kept mumbling on and on. Something about 'fifty big ones.' The trauma's eased now. The sedatives have helped."

"Thanks," Ev said again.

They edged in. There before them, planted in a wheelchair, staring off forlornly, was Ruff. He failed to acknowledge either Ev or Dan. On his lap lay the schedule. His right index finger was in a heavily bandaged splint. Close by stood Lew, patting his shoulder consolingly.

"Not broken is it?" said Dan.

Ev folded his hands, and peered piously upward.

"I guess you could say it is, but Ruff claims it don't hurt him so much anymore," added Lew.

"Him? Try *me*. My job, my trailer, my brother's loan, my ego, my—"

"So how?" Dan broke in. "Wrestling? The shot put? A weight fell?"

Lew and Ev both shook their heads sadly, absurdly.

"*How?*"

"Ping pong! He tried to spike back a serve and rapped his finger on the edge of the table. Yup, fractured. Scratch one all-around best!"

Dan stood by, unbelievingly. "*Ping pong?*"

Ruff's lips moved now, slowly. "Crazy … simple paddle game," they said.

"One of our fifteen, Dan. As hazardous as the rest. Make that more hazardous," added Ev.

Ev stared off, struck again by the incredible irony of it

all.

"Table tennis. Too much, huh! Want this in the papers, too?" Lew asked. "Hey, sure. We got us one 'a them human-interest stories? I can see it now. 'Ping Pong Scratches King Kong.' I'll call 'em, fill 'em in."

"No," Ev said. "Absolutely *not.*"

"No?"

"No."

"Hold on! What about the public's right to know? Ain't there such a thing as fair and balanced?"

"No!"

"Hey, if I have to, I can get a court order. I—"

Lew's words trailed off. Poised close up before his eyes was the splint.

Ruff nodded to Lew, to Ev. The splint descended.

"So where does this all leave us?" Dan said.

"I just want to say how sorry I am and that I let you down." And, with this, Ruff turned away with a look of sadness.

Lew reached down, took the practice sheet from Ruff's lap. With grim ceremony he delivered it to Ev. "What he's so un-politely telling you guys is— you're on your own."

And Lew gave an empty, I'm-so-sorry shrug, and turned away. "I'm sorry," Ruff murmured.

A long moment passed. Then Ev and Dan wished Ruff the best of luck for a quick recovery, traded glances, and mutually turned and walked out. They spied a vacant alcove and ducked in. By a spacious, uncurtained window they sat down. For a time they stared out beyond, onto the glittering view of the city lights.

"Uh, nice night," Ev said, finally.

"Shining night," said Dan.

Ev fell silent. For another long moment the two stared out. Then abruptly Ev stood up and began to pace. "Okay, okay, it can happen. Bronco quarterback Brian Griese sprains an ankle when his dog runs over him—and not long after that trips and knocks himself out. A Kansas City royal starting catcher checks for traffic when crossing a street—and wrenches his back and lands for a month on the disabled list. Okay, okay, it can happen. But where does this one leave us? I'll tell you. First, the big-mouthed publicity—way too early for our schedule. Then the money—and we still need thousands. And now this? Right back to Square One, Dan. Without funds *or* a shining knight. We've got exactly ten days to come up with another player and ten grand—or two one-way economy bus tickets to southern Brazil."

Dan looked at him. "You're suggesting—we split?" Dan asked, then.

"Uh, no. About Brazil, I was just, um, kidding."

"We are running away, Ev. Counting on everyone but ourselves. I mean, whose idea was this thing, anyway?"

Ev suddenly brightened. "Hey? Could be—just could be—no one else'll even challenge? I mean, Ruff's numbers were splashed all over the papers. So just may ... be...?"

They turned to a commotion. The door to the room had opened. Lew was stepping out. He spoke briefly with the nurse and an orderly, hurried off toward a bank of phones.

"Of course, with big-mouth Paul Revere riding again, we will need a miracle."

Dan stared out. The yellow lights beckoned, seemed to wink.

"Ev, just where did I finish in the qualifiers?" asked Dan.

"Uh, you eked out second—a good seventy points behind Ruff." said Ev.

"Miracle?" Dan said. He spoke slowly. "Ev, I've got ... an idea. No—*the* idea. How it should have been all along." He gave Ev a long, steady glance. "That shining knight we both need? You're looking at him."

Ev stared. "You," Ev exclaimed. "You!"

"If you declare war, you'd better be willing and able to go out yourself and fight. Hasn't that been the trouble with too much? For too long? Besides, out of fairness, I am the next in line."

"Dan, you've seen those performances. This is no three-legged, picnic sack race. You'll risk your house, your marriage, your job, your ego! Dan, dreams are fine, but ... "

"It's not a dream. It's a goal. Unfinished business. I've got to have the guts to show I can do it. Or at least that I'm willing to try."

"Dan, you're talking fifty grand!"

"Don't you see? If Dan Driver and Ev Winchell, the guys who thought up this bizarre idea, go out and show they are Dan Driver ALL-Around Athlete—and, yes, Ev Winchell

ALL-Around Coach—it'll prove our point all the more. The way it *has* to be proved."

Ev looked to Dan as if viewing someone from another planet.

"Okay," Dan went on. "I can announce tomorrow that the contest will go on as planned but that one of the backers is pulling out. The contest will go on for twenty-five. My twenty-five. A couple days' work for all that free cash and PR? It'll still be enough to lure some top jocks."

Ev gulped, and peered off out the window.

"Another benefit? You'll be back in Mossey's fold. And he'll be glad to have you."

Still Ev peered off. His lower lip began to tremble.

"And I won't take it personally. We're friends. And always will be."

As Dan patted him on the shoulder, Ev nodded and looked around. At once he lifted the Styrofoam cup, timidly drained it of coffee.

"Nice night," he said after a time.

There came another long silence. Then—

Ev spoke. "I'd have to, uh, completely revise this, you understand? This, uh, schedule. I mean. For the next what? N-Nine days? And ... and ..."

"It's tacked up in every locker-room in America, Ev. You know it and I know it. 'When the going gets tough, the tough—' Well, I'll tell you what. I've got to get this thing moving. So just go home and sleep on it. Call me if you want to do it."

Dan gave a wink, turned, and headed off. Ev remained, mumbling. "So let's say I *do* go along with this? Let's just say I do. We can downplay Ruff's injury. Deny what's … really behind that splint. Logically, everyone'll think he's still our man. Logically, they'll be too chicken to put up the fee. Which means, logically, that we'll have to call it off due to lack of … of … competitors? Which means, just as logically, I have n-nothing to worry about? Which means—"

Ev watched Dan enter the elevator, watched the two halves of the elevator door smoothly, silently shut. "Show strength, hide weakness—the first principle of good coaching. What do leaders do in crises? Stay calm." He pondered a moment more, and bit his lip. Then—

"But *fifty thousand bucks*?!"

He first viewed her from behind, walking down the corridor in her scrubs and soft-soled shoes. As he caught up, she turned and paused. For a moment they simply looked at each other.

"Dan, what are you doing here?"

"Visiting an injured friend."

Quietly Dan explained the situation with Ruff.

"So what will you do for a replacement?"

"You're—looking at him."

He clutched her, hugged her close. Then abruptly he dropped his arms and stepped back. "Deb, I have to go through with it. It's a matter of word now. I *have* to."

She simply stared.

"Have to."

Saying it again, he felt awkward, then suddenly determined.

She viewed him for a moment. A visible shine came to her eyes. "Okay," she whispered. "Then—go for it. I believe in you." She leaned up and kissed him, then turned and walked off.

"Deb," he called after. "Deb—I love you!"

She turned, looked back briefly, nodded, and then broke into a brisk walk. She hurried down the corridor, turned the corner, and vanished.

"Ev, really, I'm glad you stopped by."

"Right. You, um, wanted to know my decision. Besides, I couldn't sleep," he replied.

"Thanks."

"If you're crawling way out on a limb, I might as well, too." said Ev. I'll try to have your complete schedule by tomorrow. You claim you're in shape, but fifteen different *kinds* of shape?"

Dan peeked at the kitchen clock. "It's four a.m. Ev, it *is* tomorrow. I'll call in to take some of that comp time they owe me."

"Right. Stay home and crash. Till noon, if you want to. Build up your energy. I'll handle things at the salt mine."

Dan nodded.

"Dan, try to look beyond it. Like you said, it's the long run that counts. You and Deb are way too tight to let this thing shake you up."

"It's … how she looked at me. She's never ever looked at me that way before."

Ev peered for a time down into his cup. At once he rose, stepped over to the sink, and dumped its contents. Dan stood, sheet in hand. "Should cut down on this stuff myself. Even the decaf." And he planted his cup next to Ev's in the sink.

"Uh-uh. Studies show it. Coffee ingested before an event can yield a far more alert, coordinated performance."

Dan yawned. "But you're right. At this point, shut-eye is the word."

They stepped towards the door.

"We'll give it everything we've got. Everything," said Dan.

At once the phone rang. The two men paused. Dan looked to Ev, picked up the receiver. "Hello?" he said.

"Dan, this is Nips. I've been trying to track you guys down all night!"

"It's 4:03 a.m. What's up? Did your socks turn white?"

"No, but your face will when you hear this. The head-honcho get-together yesterday? The firm decided *not* to back B.J.. They turned down his request. Just thought you'd want to know."

"Thanks," said Dan. He turned to Ev. "It's official," he announced. "B.J.'s out of the contest."

Ev stared. "What? No challenger? Which probably means no contest? Darn!" Ev peeked gratefully heavenward.

Dan turned back to the phone. "Thanks again, Nips," he

said.

"Not so fast. B.J.'s putting up his own money. Some twenty-five grand."

"But the ante is fifty. Sorry, rules are rules."

"Nice try, but too fast again. The firm voted to keep on B.J.'s 'good side.' So, they're putting up that other twenty-five out of—get this—Mossey's next few year-end bonuses!" Then came a crazy, loon-like laugh.

"You've got to be kidding."

"No kidding. See, bet your face *is* turning white. Should've caught a gander at Mossey's! Anyway, the fifty will be in escrow by next week. Just thought I'd call." Again he broke out in his shrill laugh.

Dan hung up. He turned to Ev. "Good news and bad news," he said.

"Oh, brother. Okay, the bad news first."

"The company is backing B.J.'s request. B.J. is in the contest."

Now Ev's face visibly paled. "And the good?"

Dan looked at him. "B.J. is in the contest."

They traded a long look. At once Dan broke into a mighty, anticipative grin. "Doggone," Dan said. "Doggone!"

Ev hauled back a chair. With a hand visibly trembling he ushered Dan into it. "Um, so it's on? On? Yes, I know it is late, just a wee bit late, but I don't have to leave right this minute. And where is that sheet? Here! Uh, you got coffee too, right? Plenty coffee?"

CHAPTER
EIGHT

After a day of plotting and a night of solid sleep, Dan Driver trained more vigorously than he had ever trained in his life. He got out of bed at 5:30. Between his exercises he ate five meals, precisely spaced. He retired each night at ten on the dot. Sport to sport, skill to skill, he labored, striving to absorb in both mind and body the unique demands of each, trying as he had never tried before to work himself into the upcoming contest's rhythms. He envisioned he was a dancer, a dancer like one of the famous Four Horsemen who made ballet meaningful on the gridiron. Yes, it all came more easily to him if he imagined himself a dancer mastering fifteen different routines, from the most intricate clockwork waltz to the let-it-all-hang-out lambada. Or he was an acrobat, straining to twist, prance, and spin against the stiffness and pull of his body. He was even a Japanese archer of Zen, a samurai swordsman thinking about the success in the moments before its actual execution.

At the end of the first day Dan was wholly stiff, spent, weary. This he traced to his lack of sleep two nights before and his grueling schedule. But another night's uninterrupted slumber and another day's grinding toil left Dan shocked to discover that his soreness had not abated, not in the least. And then a concern wholly unanticipated came to intrude on his thoughts and then his actions. Am I too old? He was a finely wrought specimen with a respectable athletic history. Was this same athleticism ancient history, deeds past and done with forever, without his knowing? Then the third full day had elapsed and the sacrilege had emerged even more, from the realm of the speculative to that of the all too possible. Daniel Jonathan Driver realized his body was not as resilient as it had been in his youthful college days. By the end of the afternoon even his pride seemed to have been breached. As Dan caught his breath in hotter, shorter bursts, the possibility turned into plausibility. By 6 p.m. his every muscle ached. His every pore fairly screamed for the relief offered by hot, pounding water and soothing ointments.

On one bizarre occasion on day three of training, Dan's legs had reached the limit of both pleasure and pain and had simply—gone numb. There his legs were—before him, exhausted, no amount of mental goading could convince them to budge. Dan carefully moved off the cinders and onto the adjacent grass. He remained motionless for several anxious moments, deliberating amid the unforeseen thought of mind over matter, this harsh separation of nerve from spirit. Again the thought was apparent. A muscle could be repaired, an ache rubbed away, a mind reinvigorated, but ... but youth?

Could one recapture youth? Would he, could he, ever be the athlete he once—he still thought—was? As Dan laid sprawled on the turf he considered. Just as swiftly hope, logic, and, yes, even energy rallied to his cause. Hadn't he just completed almost another three miles? Hadn't he embarked on this run after a grueling four hours in the gym? What's going on? Four hours? Three miles! Wouldn't this happen with any twenty-year-old as well?

Ev took off early. After Dan's concerned call, the two

had met. There in the cool shade of a maple grove in Riding Crop Park they had engaged in a candid chat.

Putting friendship aside, Ev pulled no punches. "Age twenty-nine? No escaping it, age does make a difference. Some athletes—gymnasts, swimmers, divers—mature almost out of the high chair. Didn't Joe Nuxhall of the Cincinnati Reds pitch his first major-league game at age fifteen? Others—distance runners, for example—might peak quite late. Still others just *do* it, age be darned. Ev cited the case of Johnny Kelley, the 'Runner of the Century' who ran sixty-one Boston Marathons, from 1928 until 1992. At age eighty-four, he covered the distance in under six hours. See? You've got a solid half-century on him!" Ev grinned.

In all, Dan's condition, like the contest itself, brought a harsh mix of mind and body. For some events Dan's physical versatility was far less than what he had assumed. But wasn't this to be expected? "Ask any American male what kind of shape he's in," Ev had put it. "If he doesn't presume far better than he is, then he isn't an American male!"

And in Dan's case there was a great counterbalance. Dan's opponent was not that lean in years either. What's more, there was the man's special skill and training. Did life as a professional outside linebacker grant B.J. the freedom to churn long laps through the pool, play leisurely hours of ping pong, invest more than twenty minutes or so working combinations on the heavy bag, bowl ten games a week? It boosted Dan's confidence greatly to realize that, NFL status notwithstanding, B.J.'s protocol was not tailored to this contest more than Dan's. As such a highly accomplished figure of sport, B.J. Billings, age 29, had been enticed into maintaining an arrogant public image that, in reality, prevented his becoming an all-around sportsman. There were his charities, public-service gigs, pep talks at schools, associations with a host of celebrities local and national, sports and other. Then, just like age, the factor of daily regimen regarding Dan versus B.J. was no real problem to fret about.

So, under the keen tutelage of Ev, Dan Driver's goal shifted. Rather than strive to resurrect the Dan Driver of a decade ago, Dan worked to surpass the conditioning and broad athletic abilities of B.J. Billings today. And, in time, the fruit of Ev's wisdom did sprout forth. While revisiting such a variety of athletic skills brought Dan a more general stiffness and weariness, his exercising so many parts of his body allowed him to limber up his complete self that much more quickly. Paying a high price at the start, but bucking the storm led to a faster, more welcome profit in both body and mind.

It was just after the third day—yes, early on the morning of the fourth—that Dan rose and stood by his bedside and felt it. The grogginess of slumber was lifting so much more swiftly! That nagging ache in the small of his back was gone! All at once Dan sensed the sheer joy of freedom from what had been a perpetual bone-wracking stiffness. This freedom, in turn, let him redirect his focus more purely when he found himself up for a rebound, against that same heavy bag, across the crest of the ball to deliver a top-spinning groundstroke. Yes, new life now was beginning. The gasping, dejected, tentative half-cripple had been shed. And as the fourth day ended and the euphoria remained, Dan, charting wholly new territory, could truly label it all a natural high, a re-embracing of his mind by his body and vice-versa and the two in concert readying to conquer whatever tracks, courts, or courses the world might present.

Put more simply, Dan Driver *was* getting into shape.

In close concert with Dan's physiology was the most vital ingredient of all, his mind. Fully aware of this immense variable—the memorable fight in the dog rather than the dog in the fight—Ev had constructed Dan's schedule to keep his mind focused to prevent boredom. Ev was keenly aware that Dan was walking a tightrope. Boredom notwithstanding, Dan's regimen had to offer enough routine to keep Dan aware of the particular demands of each sport and instill muscle remembrance. "Yes, repetition coaxes your system into feeding itself that oxygen which will prevent fatigue and injury and allow your mind and muscles to perform at peak levels," Ev explained. "For a wide-range, three-day performance, that's what a winner will have to have. While scientists have told us for years that flexing for as little as thirty seconds a day will cause a muscle to grow as fast as it can, that's not our aim. Remember the old isometrics? For this contest, Dan, you don't have to be any stronger than you are. Less is more. The goal is to make optimum use of the muscles and brain that you've already got. Teach them fifteen kinds of discipline. Teach them muscle memory." So, in the weight room Dan Driver labored more vigorously with less. He fortified his endurance through multiple repetitions instead of major lifts. Likewise, he trained the same for the other events.

Yet, the need for memory aside, Ev did not want to flirt with boredom. So he devised a clever compromise. Each day Dan would start off with an early run through the streets. Then, amid a slow, leisurely high-carb breakfast, he would relax. An hour later the sequences would begin. To the baseball diamond for a set of hitting and fielding, to the track for field events, to the driving range, to the basketball court for one-on-one up to 25 points, to the racquetball court for two brisk games, to the field for football maneuvers, to spar and wrestle two rounds and periods in the ring, to the pool for a 200-meter swim, to the tennis court for a short set, to the rec center to shoot pool and bowl, and to the weight room for not just a few impressive repetitions with one or two huge weights, but various exercises with many.

Each day, each hour, came to be a mystery. Dan never know what he would be engaging in next. Each evening, after having studied Dan's performances for the recent day, Ev would hand Dan an envelope of folded slips for tomorrow, a specially designed schedule, hour to hour, at Riding Crop Park's vast athletic complex or at the nearby Y. "Other than stiffness—a desire to return to normalcy—your body has no prejudices," Ev put it. "For a contest demanding so much diversity in mind and body, spontaneity is the key. It's all-important that we simulate the real contest in your practices. It's called 'winning the moment.' Each moment. To a wide range of activities the body, if it has to, can and will adapt. That we've seen. So now let's make the mind match up."

Moreover, this mind-over-matter protocol came to involve an unforeseen mutual feedback. Dan performing as he always knew he could with such a variety of sports built up not just his body, but his confidence. And his confidence, in turn, urged him to push his body even more. Not knowing which specific skill he would be called on to perform each coming hour prompted Dan to pour more energy and concentration into each task at hand. It surprised him to realize that he could seemingly expend all his energy on one task, and yet, after even a brief rest period, his performance in a subsequent one would not be so compromised. Winning the moment now came to mean—winning the *moments*.

Thanks to the wisdom of Ev, neither boredom nor expectation nor fatigue came to impede Dan's progress. It was all a mind game. Dan knew it. Ev knew it. Ev knew that Dan knew it. There was no deception. None at all. And since it all went mainly unsaid, taken through faith in science by Ev and through trust and friendship by Dan, this protocol fused their relationship all the more. The two were becoming that entity so vital to any athletic success—coach and player, a *team*.

One afternoon Dan was free-styling in the pool when suddenly his upper limbs began to deliver punches. Amid his rhythmic strokes through the water, Dan's left hand had jabbed the surface and his right had complemented with a pair of vigorous crosses. The gesture promptly sent Dan gasping and groping amid a blurry, airless world of bubbles and chlorine. Dan shot back up to the surface, less worried than curious, took several deep breaths, and soon fell back into the rhythm of his stroke. For some mysterious reason beyond his own will, the complex circuitry in Dan's brain had triggered such a reaction. How? Why? The body is, ultimately, a mystery. Ev tried to explain. "Don't forget, you had boxing practice just the hour before. Call it a 'muscle memory remnant' or 'physiological dyslexia.' But as he pondered further, Ev could only look away, as mystified as Dan. "Just so you don't do the backstroke against the heavy bag!" he smirked.

Ev prided himself in his coaching, which was based more on knowledge than experience. "In sport you never know what's going to happen," he advised. "So neither should you in training. Apply mind, body, and soul to what you're doing now, because, let's face it, it's the only thing you can be sure of. Once again—Win the moment!

Ev tried hard to break the routine. One evening he was holding the heavy bag for Dan. Dan's energies were tapering off into a weary crab-crawl of punches just as Ev rotated the bag to reveal a scrawled caricature of Mossey's face. Dan could not help but grin. From somewhere within an extra burst of energy burgeoned forth to allow the stenciled brows and nose of Mossey to receive three, four, five solid blows. Yes, the unforeseen was used as a force to quickly convert emotion into renewed energy!

In body, mind, and even in spirit, Dan Driver, even if not by express intention, was recouping the Dan of a decade ago. Moreover, Dan was supplementing his younger notions with a far more mature philosophy of sport. This habitual participation in all fifteen events revealed a basic truth— athletics is a metaphor for life, a stand-in for life's wide adventure. You plan. You prepare. You execute. This most often decides the result.

Now Dan's conviction was more profound. Any such activity he engaged in linked to a greater something and solidified the hopes and dreams of not only Dan Driver Ex-Athlete/Accountant, but the entire race. No wonder all cultures have sports, he thought. No wonder the Olympics are thousands of years old. What one athlete might reap, all humanity could lay claim to, rejoice in, define itself by. The prospect of widening the bounds and imaginations of not only himself, but also people everywhere—represented the real glory of sport.

With each forehand stroke, each elbow jumper, each leap over the bar, each forward plunge and spiral pass, Dan Driver was returning from a near-comatose stage of life.

It was Sunday evening and the end of day four. Dan topped the concrete steps and lifted his arms high in wearied triumph. Below, beyond, lay the city. Dan breathed in a deep, intoxicating scent and grinned. Here on the steps, with the city glittering below, it seemed too much like *Rocky*. Still euphoric, Dan took pause. But this was no parody. This was for real.

Dan's eyes took in the huge sky. Off, on, winked the star, off, on, at its own particular rhythm. Just how long have those stars been up there? He wondered. The star was evidence of an energetic something vital and boundless—like Dan himself.

CHAPTER

NINE

E v squeezed the phone, peered in near-despair against his frosted Plexiglas cubical. "I know. But one of us has to mind the store. Better me than you, obviously." he said but failed to detect the figure lurking just outside his entrance.

"You saw it, too—*USA Today*? National news? Uh-uh. Didn't mention anyone else, just a short piece on Ruff. No, nothing about his injury. Anyway, I'm letting it all go—bed, favorite coffeemaker, the whole works—for ten. They offered cash. Thirty days and I'm out. No, he can't do it. My own brother! I hope the publicity didn't scare him off! It still leaves us with five short. Hate to have the whole house of cards come tumbling down cuz of a measly five. All our talk about how only when we become part of something bigger than ourselves do we finally become whole. How about a hole in my *pocket*! Yes, yes, I believe it, too, Dan, but ... there's the question of control. How to get that five? Maybe I could take a collection? Borrow off the guys? They do seem to be behind us. Unofficially anyway. Problem is, they're all as mortgaged to the hilt as we are. Huh! Maybe your end of this bargain is easier than mine?"

Ev picked another splinter out of his slacks. He stood up, glared down at the wooden chair. "Yeah—safer, too." He flicked the splinter into the wastebasket. "Speaking of safe, remember what we discussed about moods? Those studies suggesting that too much exercise can breed euphoria—euphoria that's fine now but might prompt downswings later. Right, that body-moving-toward-equilibrium thing. Be careful, Dan. Don't overdo it. Even the pros can over-train. I don't want to end up coaching some manic-depressive. Oh, and yesterday's numbers, the latest printout shows you..."

Ev cradled the phone, hauled out the sheet, chatted on. A figure outside his cubicle smirked a broad, knowing smirk and walked away.

A few minutes later a shadow slipped across Ev's desk: It was Mossey's.

"Oh. Hello, sir," he offered.

"You wouldn't happen to know why Mr. Driver requested so much compensatory time off, would you?"

"Sick, I guess."

"Then why not take sick days?"

"Probably too loyal an employee for that."

"Sick? From what?" Mitchell Mossey rubbed his chin. "Speaking of which, Mr. Winchell, it's high time you stepped into my office again. For a review of your performance of late. Say—" and he consulted his watch—"in niner minutes?"

"Nine-er minutes. Yes, sir."

And off he strutted, Ev looking after.

"I okayed your contract. I stuck my neck out. And now I'm on the hot seat. So I'm asking you again, B.J.—stay out."

B.J. smiled, "Yeah, I did hear that the twenty-five they're tossing in comes from you, Mr. Mossey. And now they want you to—how'd they say it?—'take the greater initiative and save the firm even more money.' All the penny-pinching around here as it is, how you going to do that?"

"I'll find ways."

B.J. mulled for a moment. "Funny how this world works, ain't it, Mitch?"

"Yes. *Very* funny."

Mossey shook his head. "You've ... memorized both of your scripts?"

"Could do 'em in my sleep," replied B.J.. "As a matter a fact, last night I *did*."

Mossey sighed, shook his head, rubbed his achy eyes. "Sorry B.J.. Perhaps I am coming down too much on everyone today. But when you get out there before the whole TV world, I want you to do your absolute best."

"Hey, Moss Man, don't worry. I'm hyped."

"Yes, yes. I'm sure you are." Now Mossey turned to a figure appearing in the doorway. "Ah yes, Winchell. Do come in."

Ev edged up before the desk.

"You do know Mr. Billings, of course."

"We've ... met," said Ev.

"Right. One big, happy A.H. family," B.J. said.

Ev looked to Mossey, to B.J.. "Big, anyway," he said.

Mossey leaned back in the plush leather chair, steepled his fingers, chose his words carefully. "Winchell, I'll ... be blunt. We want no more shenanigans. We're an accounting firm, not a playground. I don't claim to be privy to all the sad particulars of this absurd 'contest' or whatever you've cooked up. Nor do I care. My interests lie in your playing ball with us, the firm who signs your paycheck. I've known for a time of Driver's independent streak. And I suspect he's lured you into it. If I may venture to guess, you are not the best-equipped individual to say no. But now we're all going to help you stand up to him. Here—" and he passed to Ev a slip of paper—"is a figure you might find enlightening. Your new rate of pay. As Tax Accountant III."

Ev took the slip, glanced at it. "I'll be blunt, Winchell. It's called salvaging a career." Mossey squinted out against the stark brilliance of the sunlight beyond. "Yours."

"Lotta that 'salvaging career' stuff going on 'round here today, huh."

B.J. grinned.

There came a prolonged silence. "You're right," Ev said. "Maybe this whole idea is asinine."

"So? We *are* getting through to you?" added Mossey.

"I mean, how could anyone—even B.J. here, who sits around all day just like your garden-variety, bump-on-a-log accountant—how could he ever hope to top a true ALL-around like Ruff Hogan? You're right. The idea is absurd!"

Mossey's face creased. "Nice try, Winchell. But B.J. here's not going to be in any contest."

"That's bad. Real bad. Ruff will take it personally. He likes people who chicken out even less than losers, who at least show up. But Ruff's one thing, B.J. here on a good day probably couldn't even beat—say, Miller or Wells."

Ev made this remark by leaning across Mossey's desk and laying the slip back on its polished top. With the same

169

motion he pressed the button activating the PA speaker. "Because the *intelligent* athlete wins," he said.

B.J. flexed his biceps, preened his body. "Eleven percent body fat," he boasted.

"Right. And all between your ears." And Ev broke off a snicker.

Now B.J., fully aware of Ev's draw-out tactics, had had enough. "Look, Pip-Squeak, whether I'm in your two-bit contest is *my* business. If you have the guts to go ahead and run it, that is." He rose to his full height, towering over Ev, and glowered down. "As far as Hogan goes, I'd run him into the ground. He at least might show up. Out of ignorance. But Miller and Wells? Two weak-livered, kowtowing, sweet-smelling accountants? I'd beat them both—and you—left-handed. Don't take it personal, but your profession's really wimpy. Want my true opinion, it *sucks*!"

Ev began to back away. "All talk, no action? Convince me—Dumbo."

B.J. assumed a linebacker's ready stance, body rigid, hands on knees. "Hut hut!" he called, and lunged.

Ev retreated hastily, and stuck out his tongue. As he stalked off he listened to the playfully blistering tirade tossed after him amplified by the PA system through the halls. "*Mister* Billings to you, chump! No wuss who never got his eye blackened—yet, anyway—is gonna tell *me*! Hey, just like you yourself put it, Mitch ol' buddy—that Pip-Squeak is still only a Tax Accountant II, right?

"Uh, exactly right. But, B.J., maybe we... "

Another mock barrage erupted, capped by an outburst of growls. All along the hallway faces were popping out from their cubicles, curious, wide-eyed, openmouthed. Ev ducked into his cubicle, hiked up his slacks, retook his position atop the old chair, and went back to his work.

"—pencil-pushing peons don't know Bo Diddly *squat* about surviving where it really counts, in the trenches! Forearm shivers? eye gouges? leg sweeps? helmets to the chin? Lemme tell you about some of the ... Hey, Moss Man, you remember Carlyle, that NFC ex-tight end with the limp? Lemme tell you how he got that."

By now a general commotion had broken out. A host of white shirts and blouses moved by outside, venturing in mass toward the supervisor's office. Ev took pause, shook his head. "Yup," he mumbled. "The *intelligent* athlete—he'll win it every time."

Ev's work was growing increasingly tiresome, especially with three more accounts. Meanwhile, on the inside, he was pondering issues far more weighty than the current status of this one. When the voice hailed him, he glanced up and set down his calculator in visible relief.

"All work and no play makes Ev a dull boy." said Nips. "Heard about you thumbing your nose at that raise. We all thought you and Driver were both about to wave bye-bye to A.H. through your rear-view mirrors. Then pow!—a raise?"

Ev smiled. "Helps to have 'connections,'" he played.

"Yup, that was something! Mossey having to stand up

and apologize to the whole firm, even the cleaning staff? And assuring all of us that he'll personally take the initiative to raise morale and save the firm even more money. Heck, so why should I stay here? Bigwigs are all off watching him do his ads. Think I'll sneak over, too. He peeked at his watch and reflected. "You know, almost twenty-five years in this town, and I've never even been to the stadium."

"That right?" Ev asked, taking up his calculator to compute a near-final tally.

At once Ev stared up. "Stadium—!" Now Ev, too, consulted his watch. He hauled a sheet out of his desk and scanned the contents. "Right!" he said, and peered off in distress.

"You want to go too?" said Nips.

"Right. *Exactly* right. " Ev stood up, groped for his sport coat, nodded quickly to the dumbstruck Nips, and scurried out.

Mitchell Mossey and the entire team of A.H. Adams & Associates executives—Wendell C. Whittle, Richard M. Wilkins, Samuel L. Sinclair, Bertrand O. Blackstone, Thomas F. Marshall II—stood by at the stadium. While every member of the higher-ups was present—including Archibald Huntley Adams himself—none had much to say. The group was content merely to stand by, hands in pockets, observing, gawking. Their understanding of the world of film had apparently tied their tongues. Authority figures in their own right, they found themselves entranced by ruddy-faced

Carnegie Bombe, whose bobbing goatee, boldly assertive voice, impatient gestures to his underlings made him the very model of esteemed directorship. Or—had it been the recent glitch back at the firm that rendered everyone cautiously mum? For any of these reasons, the group stood quietly on the sideline, witnessing less in interest than in awe.

From one shadowed corner of the stadium Ev emerged, running after Dan, who in a jogging outfit, was on the verge of launching into a series of short sprints. "Psst! Daa-aan-"

Dan turned in time to see Ev's urgent gesture toward the group of technicians, cables, and cameras venturing out toward the center of the field.

"Holy—"

"Right. The whole 'Adams family.' They spot us out here, we'll be filing for unemployment. Now, how do we get you out? Ev looked around. "Not *my* way in," he said as he nodded toward a side gate, now blocked. "Somehow we'll just have to— sneak by."

A panel truck flashing a flamboyant BOMBE PRODUCTIONS logo came rolling along the grass apron skirting the track. 'If it's fine cinema, it's a BOMBE,' read the sub-logo. Dan looked to Ev and Ev looked to Dan. A moment later both had slipped in beside the vehicle. As the truck rolled toward the massive front gate, they both blew sighs of relief. Then—

"No, no—over *here*!"

The truck halted. At mid-field the director was gesturing impatiently. The vehicle abruptly moved on an altered course.

"Okay, okay, people, run those last lines off that master. Bring that overhead down a tad more. Not that much—he's a tall fella. There." With an quick motion, Carnegie Bombe gestured to his crew. "So let's go-oooh, people! Money is time, time is money. Mr. Billings, can you handle your lines?"

"In my sleep," replied B.J..

The truck pulled up close, drew to a halt. Bombe gestured to the witnessing entourage, who had edged up curiously. Then he stood back, made a square with his thumbs and forefingers, and squinted professionally through them. B.J. stood boldly in the foreground, the truck on an angle behind. In the far background sat the goalpost, in front of the lofting bank of end-zone seats.

"Move that truck just out of the frame. Uh, good. Cards ready? Everyone? Places. Places, and quiet on the set."

As A.H. and the others backed around and stood by, Bombe tugged one more time on his goatee. "Ok, people. Ready, and…"

Behind the truck Dan and Ev remained frozen. "Geez," Ev murmured. "Six long years and it's come down to this?" Sick-faced, he ventured a peek around the fender.

"Action!"

The clap stick sounded. B.J. took a final survey of his cue card, and grinned out.

"How ya'll doing,' fans? B.J. Billings, Footballer here, for A.H. Adams and Associates. You've all seen me do my thing on a clean, flat field like this one, with a rule book and the sidelines marked clearly in white. Where nothing unforeseen can intrude."

From somewhere off-camera a football arrived, stamped with brilliant green dollar signs. B.J. caught the ball, feigned surprise. "Well—almost nothing," he said with a wink. "But a business owner's life is not always so uncomplicated. With all the new tax codes every year, you sure don't want to step offside or out of bounds. You want to make your plays work. So recruit us, A.H. Adams, to step in and do the blocking for you." He tossed the ball away. "Are you tired of passing up tax savings, running up tax debts? Folks, why not let our All-Star lineup join yours for some concrete—" and he thumbed toward the pillars looming behind—"All-Pro financial advice. To reach your—" and he nodded back to the end zone—"business goal. A.H. Adams and Associates. More than just 'exactly right' for you. Oh, and don't forget, folks, this fall give to your favorite charity."

With a wide smile, B.J. grinned out to the camera triumphantly.

"Okay, and ... cut. Not bad. Not bad at all," replied Bombe.

'Not bad'? Why, it's fine. Just fine," said Mossey.

Carnegie Bombe peeked back, blinked. "EX-cuse me?" he said, to Mossey who had edged in closer.

"It looked great, sir. I do commend you on your professionalism."

"And you're—?"

"Mitchell Mossey, Supervisor II. The firm's charged me with this project."

"Charged *you*." With a smirk Bombe shook the other's extended hand.

"Caught some background action," the photographer reported. "Want the second take from right here?"

Bombe looked at Mossey, then to an aide holding his cup of hot herbal tea. He reached over, took the cup, indulged in a thin, eye-narrowing sip, passed the cup back. "So you're the one in charge?"

"Exactly right. Out to get the best product at the lowest price."

"Aren't we all!"

"Yes. Yes, we are, so I—"

"Go on. No, please—"

"—suggest that we do no more takes than we really need, good sir."

"Meaning?"

"If you strike gold the first time, why keep digging? Besides, don't we want as natural a product as possible? Won't multiple takes ruin that?" And Mossey lent a dignified smile.

"Wow! You've … studied film."

"I'm no expert, but I am more than a mere buff. I visited Universal Studios a few years back. And I've toured what they say is the original house of the Munsters. I took my grandkids to see all three *Lord of the Rings*."

"That so?" said Bombe, seemingly unimpressed. "Good

sir, you yourself have said it. Time is money, money is time. I concur. I mean, why turn an asset into a liability?"

Mossey grinned back to his colleagues. "Ask me, fine as is."

Bombe looked at B.J., who shrugged. "Hey, dudes. Split the uprights by me."

Bombe, his assistant, and the photographer traded looks. "Okay," Bombe said. "A wrap. Into the can. On—the famous 'Steven,' is it?—Spielberg say-so!"

Once again his voice became that of the booming professional. "Commercial Two. A.H Adams. Western motif. Time *is* money. Let's set up, people."

The others nodded, made ready. B.J. stepped in, peeled off his sport coat, slipped into a cowboy vest and grabbed the offered gun-belt and holsters as a young woman went up on her tiptoes to plant a white ten-gallon hat on his head. He walked back to his mark, shoved his thumbs loosely into his belt, peered at the new cards, and nodded. "Hut-hut any time now, partners," he announced.

"Fine. Places, everyone. Quiet. Quiet on the set. Ready, and—*action*!" barked the Director.

The clap stick sounded. B.J. winked, broke into an exaggerated drawl. "Folks, like these wide open spaces on this-here field all have to be patched up an' smoothed out before they can accommodate everyone from running backs to wide receivers, like sure can leave one plumb lots of room for improvement. Buckaroo B.J. here, for A.H. Adams and his fine folk. Pesky tax problems popping up like prairie dogs to damage your business turf? Why not mozey on over our way. Thirty-five years as a firm, with a posse of trouble-shooting employees to serve you in *any* financial capacity. Partners, send them pesky tax varmints to the Deep Six. Make them keep their heads lower than Death Valley—lower than our prices! First sign 'a trouble, call A.H. an' his boys. He'll stampede them nasty critters out of town. Make 'dog gone' mean 'dog gone.' A.H. Adams an' Associates. Exactly right—for you. And folks—*don't* forget your favorite charity."

"And ... cut."

With this, several of the onlookers broke into applause. Yells erupted.

"Marvelous, B.J.! Marvelous. B.J., it's ... like you've got a double personality. Where did you learn that accent?"

"What ak-sent?" B.J. played. And he winked privately to Mossey.

"So this one's a keeper, too?" Bombe asked.

B.J. grinned. "Right down the middle."

"Marvelous job. As they say—smack 'into the can'? On my say-so.'"

Mossey edged in, smiled broadly, offered B.J. a jaunty high-five. "Fine job," he said. "First time, every time. Knew it would pay off to have you on board."

"Did you catch that background action again?" asked the photographer.

Mossey followed her finger toward the vast vacancy of end-zone seats. A trio of what appeared from a distance to be groundskeepers were stepping away. "Ask me, others in the background just makes it appear more natural. Time is money. Money is time. This is an accounting firm." he said.

The photographer smirked. The assistant grinned, handed Bombe his tea.

Bombe took a long sip, winced, and shrugged. "Oh-kayyy. Wrap. On his say-so." Deftly he again tugged at his goatee, and started off. "Besides, I've got to get back anyway." He glanced back to Mossey, gave one more semi-temperamental look, and stalked away.

"You've hurt his feelings," said the technician.

"Questioned his artistic integrity," said the camerawoman.

"Saved A.H. Adams a *bundle*," countered Mossey.

They all watched as Bombe strode off.

"Guess he is one of them artistic types," B.J. said.

"Be that as it may," Mossey consulted his watch. "Time for us to get back, too. Gentlemen and, uh, lady—it's been a real pleasure." He flashed a parting grin to all and nodded to B.J.. "First time, every time," he marveled. He ushered B.J. through the crowd, patted him on the shoulder. "Yesiree, B.J.—you, me, A.H. Adams—we're a *real* team."

Then Mossey himself felt a clap on the back. He paused, turned. The well-respected A.H. Adams himself was extending congratulations. Mossey stood, basking in the glow. At once he managed to clear his throat. "Why, I, uh, do thank you, sir," he said.

Then off toward the exit gate Mitchell Mossey strode,

beaming immodestly, B.J. at his side, the entire entourage in tow behind. The world was a beautiful place.

Inside Nolton B. Nippers' cubicle sounded mumbles, subdued and yet marked by an unmistakable sense of awe. "Best darned figures you'll ever see in this place, B.J.! Hey, these are last month's. Talk about a 'top rated firm'?"

"Doggone know it, Nips-Pips or whatever. You know, the more I look at these, the more I dig it.

"Glad these come out monthly instead of quarterly, huh."

The two men traded snickers. There came the faint turn of a page, a new round of appreciative whistles.

Mitchell Mossey, listening from outside the cube, nodded his approval and then resumed his trek down the hall. As he walked he thought to himself, 'Tops in the NFL? A natural before a camera? Now an interest in, of all things, accounting? Mossey, you've landed yourself one blue-chip prospect! Mossey, you're a genius!'

The deep-green turf lent a natural hue to B.J.'s office. A new DVD player accompanied the latest model 52-inch screen. A spacious poster of a dimply, grinning, gap-toothed linebacker hung snugly on one wall. Each side of the doorframe was decorated in a candy-cane motif, like a holiday goalpost, with an equally candy-caned crossbar above.

Mossey was on the phone. B.J. lounged on the posh leather

couch. "No, really. More comp time? Sure, as much as you need. We do owe it to you after all the extra hours you've put in over the last few weeks. Personal issues? Pressures of the job? You don't have to tell me. Yes, Winchell mentioned, but I'm glad you called. Till … a week from Tuesday, right after the Labor Day break. Right. See you then. Goodbye, Mister Driver."

Mossey hung up, turned to a figure who had just entered the room. "You must be Tim Teeler, our resident lion-tamer?"

Mr. Teeler grinned, and shook hands firmly. B.J. stood by, arms folded. "Right," said Teeler. "It's now up to me, as B.J.'s new coach, to make sure our guy here is tops. Not in just one or two sports, but in all fifteen."

"Fine. Well, B.J., I guess I have now been persuaded,'" said Mossey. "It's official. You don't have to call your 'twin brother' or 'twin grandma' to compete. And now I understand the 'Ruff' fellow's been nixed from action? In fact, I'll tell you what. Why not let me in on more of the action. Officially I am putting up that twenty-five, right? So how about—say, another fifteen? To make it an even forty."

B.J. peeked over at him. "Nice of you," B.J. smiled. "Real nice."

"No, really. I insist. It'll show how much I really *am* committed to this company. It's important to maintain such a climate of confidence, if for no more reason than morale. Plus it means all the less you'll have to toss in yourself. I'll tell you what, if you win—that's assuming there even is a match—I get my forty back and ten more, thanks to Winchell, Driver, and their unknown assassin. You put up only ten of your own and collect it back with forty more. Then you have the right to defend the title and win fifty more each time after or just take the money and run. How's that deal sound?"

B.J. nodded his approval.

Mossey pulled out and uncapped a fountain pen. Slowly, carefully, he filled out a check, and scrawled his signature across the bottom. Ceremoniously he blew the ink dry, handed B.J. the check. "So here's another fifteen. With Mister Teeler here as my witness. Really, B.J., take it. If I've learned one thing in my thirty-one seasons, it's if there's money to be made, *make* it."

B.J. shrugged, pinched the check between a stubby thumb and forefinger. "Sounds like a possibility," he said, the irony of all this becoming apparent. He folded the check in half, tucked it into his shirt pocket.

'You two get acquainted, I'll be right back," said Mossey.

With that, Mossey ducked out. Moments later he returned with Ev.

"This is Mr. Teeler, B.J.'s trainer-coach. This is, uh, the Mister Winchell we've been talking about. The one with the, uh, contest."

"Hello," said Ev.

"Hello," said Teeler. Neither extended a hand.

"As for your request for a few days off, Winchell, I'm afraid it's a no-go. You or Driver has to hold the fort—

'preserve the world of tax,' as we say?"

"Fine, sir." Ev seemed resigned. "I thought you would say no."

The others traded curious glances.

"And we all know about Ruff being 'rough' no more," Mossey continued. "Ping pong can be dangerous!"

"'Ruff'? 'Rough' who?" said Ev.

Mossey lifted a newspaper item up before Ev's face. "This Ruff. The Ruff mentioned in this article here with you."

"Oh—that Ruff." Ev looked down at the sheet of paper he had brought with him. Now he scanned it more carefully.

"Yes, this Ruff. And now you and Driver need a few days to beat the bushes for a new boy. Is that it?"

"We've already found one."

"Really?"

"Really!"

Ev leaned forward, planted the sheet of paper on B.J.'s desk. Without a further word he nodded to them all, turned, and headed out. As he did, B.J. with a sly foot nudged the wastebasket into Ev's path.

"Like who?" the supervisor inquired.

Ev stopped and turned. "No comment," he replied. He sidestepped the basket gracefully, and proceeded out. "Big but dumb," he said, quietly. "Really dumb."

"What the dickens is the meaning of this?" Mossey called out. "Win-chell!"

Ev's head peeked back in. "'Darned' if I'll tell, sir," he

said.

"Not that—*this*!"

He held up the sheet Ev had deposited on his desk.

Ev edged back in, stared at the sheet, took a deep breath. A deep sadness showed in his eyes. "It's ... my resignation, sir. So it looks like it's goodbye."

Head down, with visible trembles, Ev turned and departed once more, leaving the others staring after him.

Ev entered his cubicle to pack after going for a brief walk to think things over. Shortly after, Mossey, Nips, and even B.J. had come in to see him. Each had asked him to reconsider. Mossey had spoken kindly, almost cordially. B.J. gave Ev a fraternal pat on the shoulder and acknowledged having "no hard feelings, nothin' the least bit personal against you, Ev." Taken aback by this attention, seemingly sincere, Ev balked. He had accepted their urgings to reconsider, yes, and had again wandered out onto the spacious company grounds to think. He surveyed the freshly cut grass, the manicured flowers, the smooth, worn tiles of the walkway, the marble fountain bubbling out front, the cars whizzing by on the familiar avenue beyond. And in the end he considered this: Ev was, if anything, set even more firmly on his course. A.H. Adams really did not want him any longer; even more significantly—he did not want them. There would be a mutual parting of the ways, a healthy division for the growth and benefit of each. Some six years of accumulated seniority ... would come to an end. Alas, so be it. He, Everett B.

Winchell, would be packing his items and leaving as soon as he could. This was the price of free play in the modern world.

It was while stowing away his favorite items that Ev spied it. Had he somehow missed it before? There it sat on the corner of his desk. He examined the document—a cashier's check. He looked at the payee—'Ev Winchell'—and the amount—"Five thousand and———no/100 dollars." He rubbed his eyes. Then, still in disbelief, he lifted the check and examined it. It was authentic. He pinched the check tightly between his fingers, held it up once more against the lights. Legit! Trembling visibly now, he made a mad grope for the phone.

At once he paused. Quickly he hauled out, unfolded, and consulted his copy of Dan's schedule. "'*Dog*gone." he mumbled. He took a long, gulp of coffee, draining the cup. Then for a moment he sat, drumming his fingers atop his desk, staring, wide-mouthed, still, at the check, which, like the key to a jail cell, lay just a few short inches away.

Nolton B. Nippers was dry-mouthed, bone-weary. "Figures *schmigures*," he muttered. As he rounded the corner he encountered Frank Detra, an audit clerk.

"Hey, you hear?" quipped Detra.

Nips viewed him oddly. "Hear what?"

"About that weird contest. Guess who's going be in it—Driver! Can you *imagine*?"

"Oh," said Nips.

"But can you believe? One of us—a *jock*?"

Nips shrugged. "Driver, huh," he said. "That *is* the craziest one I've heard around here. I'll … believe it when I see it."

On the phone with Dan, Ev spoke. "Absolutely sure you didn't tell anyone? Well, then, who? And why? No, I don't know. Right, the whole five. A cashier's check. As in payer/benefactor untraceable. What do you mean maybe we shouldn't? Dan, do you realize? Now it is official. All systems are *go*!"

CHAPTER
TEN

L ate Wednesday morning, an hour before the noon deadline, the entire $50,000 was deposited. Each and every penny. Dan contributed his personal ten and the fifteen he had borrowed. Ev chipped in his personal ten and another ten from the hasty sale of his mobile home. This, with the final five so mysteriously donated, did it. With scant ceremony Mr. Everett Winchell, in a sharply pressed, conservative blue suit, slightly frayed striped tie, and slightly trembling demeanor, strolled in and deposited the money and then, without so much as a single quip, walked out. A $50,000 cashier's check now lay in the capable hands of Caldwell and Caldwell, Trustees. Upon accepting the money, Caldwell and Caldwell, Trustees, as per arrangement, informed the media. Within the hour reporters from radio, TV, and the newspapers converged.

Also within the hour, as per arrangement, Mr. Mitchell Mossey, flanked by Mr. B.J. Billings, arrived at Caldwell and Caldwell with a cashier's check of his own. "One hundred thousand in this kitty?" a reporter put to B.J.. "How does it feel to have a tenth of a mil riding on your performance?" As the supervisor stood by with a frozen smile, B.J. lent an easy shrug. "Just like back in my rookie year," he grinned. "'except this time my agent ain't going to take so much of it." At this, a third figure, I. O. "Homer" Eushystropolos, a former NFL player now turned sports agent seen lately around town with B.J., excused himself to fetch a soft drink.

A second hand shot up—already the proceedings had evolved into a makeshift press conference. "B.J., do you worry or suspect that you might be too specialized for this thing?" the reporter asked. "I mean, your opponent's camp just may have an argument."

A silence fell. This had been the topic to shun. B.J. mulled for a moment. "Well, the shrinks say fear comes from intelligence, right?" he replied.

"Then, sir, you must be fearful!" quipped the reporter.

B.J. gave him a puzzled look. "Uh, no," he played. "Not in the least."

With the media all laughing and B.J. standing by beaming confidently to them, Mossey vacantly shook his head.

B.J. lifted a ham-like hand. The laughter ebbed. "No, really. I got no worries." He frowned. "Hey, maybe I should be worried—I mean, about not having any worries? But I'll tell you what I do have to worry about. I mean, who-the-Sam Adams will I be up against?"

There came mumbles of agreement. B.J. had broached the other topic weighing on everybody's mind. Today's powwow was unfortunately and embarrassingly one-sided. "Where *is* that little blue-suited man?" came the general cry. "And where—who—is his athlete?"

But the fact did remain. Mr. Everett Winchell had deliberately chosen not to court publicity, not to bask, even for so fleeting a moment as destiny might allow, in the spotlight. Was it fear? Or cunning? Or—perish the notion—had he foreseen this whole gathering as nothing more than a sham? This last suggestion surfaced in a bland murmur put forth by a *Times* reporter. Suddenly CEO Canby Caldwell stood up. He held the two checks out before the assembly. "Good folks—these look deceptive to you?" His gesture incited applause, whereby the inquirer shrugged and mumbled a confession of error.

But if not from fear, superior strategy, or the good sense to elude public humiliation, then just what? Did Winchell have a sure-fire ace up his sleeve? Maybe some wizardly DNA blend of Roger Federer, Bret Favre, LeBron James, and Spider-man himself would be dropping in to compete? Winchell's mood on delivering the money? Calm, confident, cerebral, Canby described. Oh, yes, and a bit apologetic. And come to think of it now, even a bit sad. Aces up his sleeve? Mr. Caldwell predicted—none.

Then this whole contest was ... a death wish? Some bizarre, compulsive need to commit suicide on the public altar? To this Caldwell shook his head. "Uh-uh," he said.

"Maybe just a clever pressure tactic," someone else posed, at which B.J. scoffed. "Pressure? Ain't gonna work with me. In my business you fight pressure head on. No easy detours to a ball-carrier. Besides, got me an ace up my sleeve as well. Make that two, actually." Once again he grinned, slyly. "Uh, but to get back to this Winchell guy—one elusive dude indeed."

With this, the same perplexed silence hung over the assembly. In time another hand wormed up. "This Winchell, if cornered, he'd have a statement?" someone asked. "Probably will right after the contest. If he even shows," B.J. replied. "Look, all you dudes are digging *way too deep.*

Winchell's simply out practicing what'll soon become his permanent lifestyle—hiding."

Amid the laughter Canby lifted a warning hand. "Ladies and gentlemen, B.J. is probably right. This is not *The Bachelor*. Let's not make a cult of this man!" He pushed back a sleeve to reveal a handsome Rolex. "Good folks, we appreciate your interest. We thank you for coming."

The assembly broke up, with B.J., Mossey, and Homer vanishing into the web of offices in the back and the others venturing out into the parking lot amid baffled murmurs.

"Who *is* that Masked Man?" So posed an anchorwoman on the local evening news. "If you're watching, please call in!"

The media would not gloss over the obvious absence of Mr. Everett B. Winchell. Here in one corner, an NFL star. Here in the other, zilch.

But meanwhile, beyond these and other explanations, a cry persisted. Who, where, when, what—yes, even why—*is* the Masked Man? Why *does* he wear his mask? Late Thursday evening two reporters found Ev Winchell just outside a local coffee shop and cornered him into a comment, yes, but concerning the identity of his champion he remained mum. A blind wall? Apparently. The city, state, and even certain observant quarters of the nation would hold its collective breath until 8 a.m. Saturday, when the Masked Man, Woman, or Alien would trot out and this bizarre, unprecedented venture of ventures would begin.

Thoroughly beat, Dan trudged down the avenue. A vehicle approached from behind. He turned once again, backpedaled, stuck out his thumb. Dan had finished his prescribed jog. Now it remained for him only to return to a hot, steamy shower and solid night's sleep.

A vehicle slowed, an old car with one burned-out headlamp. The car veered over, drew to a halt. Dan eyed the car for a moment, then edged closer.

"Young feller—wanna hop in or not?"

The driver was an older man with a white beard and cowboy hat. Dan nodded, and ducked in. The car rumbled off.

"Thanks," Dan said. "Just trying to get across town. Almost got run over a couple times. Tell you, some of these—"

Dan took pause. The old man sat by. In his hand he held a pistol.

"Oh, no," Dan said.

The finger twitched. A stream of water squirted onto Dan's neck and chest. The old man shook his head, half bewildered, half irate. He blew on the plastic barrel. "Try to warn you young pups about 'hitchin,' but do you listen? Noooo. So a scare's the next best thing!"

Dan peered wryly out the window, chewing his lip.

"If I would have been a real psycho and this-here woulda been a real pistol with real live rounds, you'd a been in real trouble."

Dan looked at him, caught his curious gaze. "You might

have missed," Dan said, forcing a smile.

"NRA groupie?" Dan said after a time.

"Lifetime member."

"When people use guns to make a point, they usually don't have a solid point to begin with," Dan said. "But again—thanks for stopping."

"No problem. Could use some company. Where you off to?"

Twenty minutes later the car swung to the curb and drew to a halt. The chat had been mostly one-sided. "Really. They all do damage, but you still ain't gonna top the destructibility of a .357," the old man, Jim Stockwell, explained. "A .357's all she wrote."

Dan ducked out, poked his head back through the open window. "Thanks again, " Dan said. "Really."

"Don't you forget, anything you wanna know 'bout guns—anything—don't be afraid to ask. Guns and gun safety is my business. Keep that range card and number I gave you handy, too. Just in case."

"In case," Dan smiled. "I hear anyone needs a gunslinger, I'll call you!"

"Appreciate it. And don't—" a thin stream of water shot out of the dark and struck Dan's nose— "hitch. Oops. Hey now, don't turn ornery again!"

Dan glared back, half-amused, half-angry.

"Just tryin' to cool you down some. Remember—no more 'hitchin'!"

"I won't," said Dan.

The car rumbled off into the night.

Finally home at last, Dan exited the glare of the streetlight and slipped into the shadows. Past the lilac hedge, along the walk, beneath the trellis. Dan lightly opened the door. He edged in. He spied Deb asleep on the couch.

He kissed her, generously. "You didn't miss me?" he said.

"Jury's still out," she said, hiding a smirk. "But after your call, maybe a little. Maybe." She nodded toward the hallway, and drew a finger to her lips.

"Kids asleep?" he whispered, and she nodded. "It's contagious for some of us when it gets late. Those of us on schedules, I mean."

"Deb—"

She reflected. Then, thinking it better left unsaid, she left the room. "Oh—what time in the morning?" she asked, turning back.

He held up six fingers.

"It's a good thing I'm off the next three nights."

She walked down the hallway to the linen closet, and a moment later returned. "For you," she announced. She shot-putted a huge, white terrycloth towel his way. "Use the shower over here. It won't wake them."

The room lay hushed. Outside a car passed by. Dan and Deb fell fast asleep. Moments later a shadow bobbed slowly up, then slipped across Dan Driver's face. Against Dan's cheek came to rest the wooly, button-eyed form. Dan mumbled, fumbled, then tossed. The bear toppled away. A pair of tiny, patient hands propped the bear up again, this time more snugly, just under Dan's chin. The small face closed on Dan's own, and on his forehead she planted a kiss. Then quietly the figure climbed down, and departed.

Over the rooftop, eaves, and shrubs, the sun burst gloriously. Thin shadows draped the lawn. Inside, in the kitchen, Deb and her mother were having a chat. "His choice, yes, but yours, too, dear. I'm from the old school. You should never have…"

"Mother. I am over twenty-one. I happen to be *married* to Dan."

"So you'll just let him go off and—?"

"Mom—I *love* him."

It was Friday morning, in less than twenty-four hours the contest would begin. Dan had slept in, until nearly nine. Then he and Ev had retired to a quiet cafe on the south edge of town. "Not too much," Ev advised now, as Dan hailed the waitress for a refill. Dan shrugged and withdrew his cup.

"Heart problems or something?" the waitress asked.

"You might say that." Ev glanced onto his twin sunny-side-up eggs and bacon strips, then back over to Dan. "Nothing that won't be cleared up by this weekend, though."

"That's good." The waitress topped off Ev's cup, winked, and strode away.

"Nice gal," Ev said quietly. "Real nice." He took a slow munch of toast. "And so how do you feel? Still stiff? Sore?"

"Not really. Almost wish it would begin right this minute.

Maybe I should be worrying."

"You peaked too soon? I doubt it. But maybe we'll have you do a bit less today than we planned. Why dull the knife?"

Three men at the counter were staring. One of them rose and sauntered over. He wore an Ohio State sweatshirt.

"Hey—go, Buckeyes." Ev smiled.

"Hey, you are—"

"Are—?"

"*Are.*"

Ev shook the extended hand. "Uh, right. Look—just don't tell everyone?"

"Whole north side of town's out looking for you."

"So I've heard."

The man gestured back to his friends. "It *is*!" He padded Ev on the shoulder. "Nice to meet you. You ever dig yourself up that ringer?"

"Why? You want to try?"

"No way. Tell you what, though. You don't have enough for your meal, me and the guys'll throw in. Really."

"Thanks, but we're okay. Just wish us luck. That we *can* use."

"We?" He looked curiously over at Dan. "You mean—?"

"Me," Ev amended. "I mean me. I can use the luck."

"No, the guys and me, we thought we'd help out cuz—" He glanced back to his pals, his grin broadening—"they find out who you are, these folks probably ain't gonna even take your check." He smirked. "No, really. Good luck. Takes a lot to put so much on the line." He lent Ev another pat on the back. "One real gutsy man here. Take care of him," he said to Dan.

"I'll do my best," Dan said. "Thanks."

The three paid their bill. With final nods, they ducked out.

Ev gulped the last of his coffee. "Ready?" he said. "On me. Cash, of course."

Dan stood by as Ev paid. Then the two ducked back out into the sunshine. "Going to be a long day," Dan said. "The lull before the storm."

"Okay?" Ev had thumbed two quarters into the metal stand, and now he bent to retrieve the morning *Times*. He scanned the front page. "Unemployment's down," he said. "Inflation, too."

"And—?" Dan reached out a hand.

"Whew—another earthquake! This time in Turkey."

"Ev—?"

Dan's fingers remained extended.

Ev gave a casual shrug, folded the paper. "Uh, okay. I can get back to it at the motel. We'll head on over to the gym in a while. If you want to. Remember, though—just a light loosen-up."

Ev yawned, offered the paper absently over to Dan.

Dan took the paper, unfolded it. On the right side of the front page, just below the fold, he spied:

'THREE-DAY COMPETITION BEGINS TOMORROW.'

'All-Pro Superstar B.J. Billings to face—WHO?'

Dan scanned the item. "You ... did see this, right?"

Ev looked at him, nodded. "Should be 'whom,'" he said.

Dan read on. "Televised, too, huh." He continued to read. "One thing about problems," he said after a time. "To solve them, you have to face them. Squarely."

He refolded the paper, handed it back to Ev.

"Uh, right. Get to it later."

Then Ev could hold back no longer.

"Holy—! The *front* page? On *TV*! Holy—Holy *cow*!"

CHAPTER
ELEVEN

A beautiful dawn, the sun scarcely up but the sky already assuming a bold, buoyant blue. Outside sounded the chirpings of birds. The rhythmic drip of brewing coffee could be heard. Quickly she broke out of her thoughts, yawned, and stretched. Then she got up, stepped over, and poured herself a steaming cup.

Deb heard the front door. Soon her mother appeared, nodded a good morning, fetched a cup and poured herself some coffee. Slowly she blew across the lip of the cup. The steam dissipated.

Both women sat down at the breakfast table, and gazed out the window. For a while neither spoke.

"Nice day," her mother offered after a time.

"Beautiful day," Debra concurred.

"Uh-huh."

"I ... I know what you're thinking," Debra said, then, after a time.

"Look, honey," said Gram. "A man should feel perfectly free to take all the chances he wants—but not with his wife and children. However, these ... are unique circumstances. I believe that Dan wants what's best for everyone. No matter what happens on TV, let's make this a win-win situation. It's your—our—job to support him till the end."

Deb starred at her mother in disbelief.

Her mother's face twitched. "Really," she said.

"Mom—I really appreciate you."

"No, Deb, I admire you—how much you believe and trust in Dan."

"Mommy—it's here!" The voice from the living room was followed by a quick, light pouncing of feet, a creaking open and thumping shut of the front door. Moments later Lori burst in, the *Times* in her arms. "Morning, Mom! Morning, Grandma!" She gave them each a quick kiss and handed over the paper.

"Honey—thank you." Debra unfolded the paper, turned to the local section, peered through. She scanned the classifieds. She even perused "Women's Forum," peering at the ads and at several of the recipes. Then she took a deep breath, and readied herself. She turned to the sports section, and searched the page curiously.

She laid the paper out atop the table, to display the page-one heading to all:

'THREE-DAY COMPETITION BEGINS TODAY!'

INDOOR DAY

The sign before the gymnasium proclaimed it. The hour hand stood just slightly left of 8:00. Above the milling and commotion around Court Three came the slap and thump of a racquetball—slap, thump, slap, thump. B.J. Billings was warming up. In the partially glassed-in balcony above B.J.'s head, the seats were filled. A.H. Adams, his two senior vice-presidents, and Mitchell Mossey occupied front-row center, the Supervisor glancing around with both a snobbish, refined air and a nervous smile. A multitude of other bigwigs and local celebs occupied seats to the sides and behind. Nearly all fidgeted in happy, curious anticipation. Many exchanged feverish whispers. All the while, just below, B.J. struck the rubber ball again and again, lazily, casually, as if in the midst of some ho-hum, time-killing chore. At once he lifted a palm, caught the ball, turned back, and grinned up. For at one corner of the makeshift gallery, in a row below the TV camera, a face had appeared above a clipboard packed with notes. "Hey Teel, I'm feeling fine." He cupped a yawn, then gave the ball a mighty whack, causing it to zing and reverberate.

A buzzer sounded. B.J. fetched the ball as it skittered near his feet and retired into the corner beneath his coach. He stood, waiting. It was now exactly 8:00.

From outside there came a growing hubbub—mumbles, shouts, an outbreak of applause. Spectators in the gallery stood up to let a figure make his way through to the other corner of the balcony, a figure with spectacled face and frail torso clutching a clipboard heaping full of notes.

"Hey, 'Chairman of the 'Bored'—I'm waiting!" B.J. called. "So where's the incredible Mister X? Or should I call him—Mister Why?"

The door of the court popped open. A figure ducked in, racquet in hand. B.J. stared for a moment, then returned the figure's nod with one of his own. From the gallery above came stares, then audible gasps. Heads leaned forward as the figure—Dan Driver—stepped into the adjacent part of the court and began to limber up.

"Well, your money!" B.J. said.

With this, Mitchell Mossey stood up and dramatically cleared his throat. The concern etching his face had fallen away. As he beheld the two players, their coaches, and the packed gallery of media and fans, he displayed far more than his usual neutral civility. He genuinely smiled.

The PA announcer then spoke. "Ladies and gentlemen, welcome to 'Indoor Day,' the first five events of our three-day contest. And so at last here we have them, yes. Ladies and gentlemen, may we hear it for our two competitors—Daniel J. Driver and B.J. Billings."

The gallery stood and broke into vigorous applause. Flashbulbs exploded. Video cameras followed every move. "To the victor goes every spoil," Mossey threw in. "All the hard-fought spoils!" He lent Dan a stern smirk. To the others he grinned.

B.J. turned an eye toward Dan. "So enough of the festivities, huh, pal?"

"Right. Enough." Dan stepped forward. To another burst of flashbulbs and a polite and then enthusiastic rerun of applause, the two men shook hands.

Now the gallery reseated itself, amid a hum of excitement. Beside Mossey a referee stood up and faced the camera, the crowd. "Ladies and gentlemen, our first event is racquetball. The contenders will play a total of one hundred points, each receiving the same number of points he wins on the court. A short halftime will occur when the points won by both competitors total fifty. Should either contestant be unable to complete this or any subsequent event, he will cede his opponent the entire hundred points for each event forfeited. Serving the first five points of the match will be the challenger Billings. Receiving will be Driver. Gentlemen—?"

B.J. grinned. "Challenger?" He and Dan shared a high-five and assumed their positions. The competition was finally underway.

B.J. served, a high, spinning ball. Dan returned the serve likewise, with ample height and spin. Dan was ready. He had ducked in early to warm up in a less obtrusive court in a distant section of the complex. Dan won the first point easily. B.J. served again. Dan returned the serve deep into the corner, but B.J. reached back with his racquet, slapped the ball against the back wall, and then stood firm as Dan tried to dart around him to retrieve it: 1-1.

And so it went. A pattern soon became apparent. His huge form camping out at center court and dominating the action, B.J. was virtually immovable. When Dan placed balls to the sides, B.J.'s reach often compensated for his position in the middle. Stubbornly he stood, bending left, bending right, leaping high, smashing vicious overheads to put even Dan's wall-hugging lobs away. While Dan's serves continually coaxed B.J. from the center, the big man would inevitably gravitate back and there remain, an obstinate pillar of granite, forcing Dan into attempting the most difficult of drop shots or skidding his returns along the side walls.

After the fiftieth point had been played—a drawn-out struggle which B.J. won with a diving swipe—the buzzer sounded. The gallery burst into applause. The two men retired to their corners to catch their breaths and towel off and confer with their coaches. Dan had taken a brief lead, but B.J. had caught up and edged ahead, with Dan hanging on doggedly. The last ten points had been evenly split. B.J. was ahead, 27-23.

"Great to be back into it, Teel." B.J. buried his face in the towel and came up, hair disheveled, wide dimples, grinning. "I mean, for the big, easy bucks?"

"Guy's quick though. Have to give him that. Keep camped out in mid-court like we figured and you'll be fine. Kinda hard to chase a piece a rubber around Mount McKinley."

B.J. passed the heavy terrycloth towel back up. "Question— Can the dude hold out? Answer—Uh-uh. Gimme time, I'll put 'em away. In a nice, friendly sort of way. Fifty thousand smackeroonies for *this*? Youuu-eeeee!" he called, and his supporters in the gallery echoed his glee.

The other corner's mood was markedly different. "Not the easiest way to wake up in the morning," Dan puffed. Already he was sweating, his face flushed, the front of his jersey blotted in sweat.

"You woke up? That implies sleep—which *I* didn't get one wink of." Ev nodded to the scoreboard up behind the gaping faces. "And by the looks of that, neither did you. Dan, we've got fifty more to divvy up. Bear down and slowly but surely destroy this over-bloated lunatic. Racquetball's a game of speed and scramble, sure, but it's also one of prediction. That ball's a glob of fiscal trends, right? Study it now, predict where it'll end up later. Then position yourself there. Like he's doing."

"Like he's—?"

"Believe it. Linebackers tackle runners not where they are, but where they will be. That's what he's feeding off of. Use our profession's principles to do the same. I know he's only slightly smaller than the Wrigley Building, but try to coax him out of the center. His middle-linebacking is forcing you to beat yourself with low-percentage shots. Take a tip from Wimbledon. As in—hit to the backhand and rush the net for a drop shot."

"In racquetball?"

"In racquetball. Principles of one sport can always translate into another and give you insights you've never had before. It's think-on-your-feet creativity. Remember— 'Win the moment.'"

The buzzer sounded. "Predict and position. Drop shots will do," Dan repeated to himself. He strode out, got ready to serve, as B.J. lumbered into position. The gallery grew hushed. Heads bent forward. Dan served. The second half was under way.

After giving three quick points, Dan served and charged up in front of B.J.. There he dropped a weak shot low off the front wall. The baiting worked. Thereafter when B.J. would lunge up to return, Dan would slide into the gap behind him in the middle of the court, hit a deep shot, and operate from the center.

With this tactic in place, the match proceeded on virtually even terms. The match provided some exciting points and the crowd responded on each occasion. The final point—a long-fought sequence which incited the gallery into shouts and screams and ended with a freak spin of the ball off the frame of B.J.'s racquet into one corner—going to B.J..

Amid prolonged applause, the two men retired to their corners. Now B.J., too, was soaked with sweat. His face was ruddy, his chest heaving. But his grin was a grin of triumph. The two men raised their hands to the gallery, amid whistles and cheers, Ev and Teeler joining in with the others.

"All Pro?" said Dan. "No wonder. Guy's quick!"

"You drew him out of the center and still he adapted. Flexible. All-Pro, right, but not ALL AROUND. That huge reach of his will help in some sports but not others. Come ping pong, you can jam him, Dan. We've learned a lot here. A lot." Ev gave a nod and returned to his notes.

Now an official PA announcement proclaimed the score. B.J. had won the racquetball competition, 52 to 48. There came cheers, followed by a run of applause. "So that's where you've been every morning and afternoon?" a blissfully clapping Mossey grinned down at Dan.

"Just one of fifteen places," Ev called back.

"Sixteen'll be the poorhouse," quipped a figure to Mossey's right.

Meanwhile, the TV announcer had taken up the cue. "The most amazing quickness we've seen in quite some time. His size, moves, grace, reactions—all point to B.J. Billings as the most adept, All-Pro, All-Around."

"Hey—aren't you guys supposed to be neutral?" called

Ev. "Ever hear of fair and balanced?" He turned back to Dan. "Fourteen more," he confided. "Just remember, best ALL around. First one to reach seven fifty. A long way to go." He reached down, shook Dan's hand. "You did well. Real well. You're ... closer than I thought you'd be."

And at this remark, followed by a cryptic wink, Dan could only peer up and around at the hubbub as those in the gallery rose and grinning, backslapping, and elated, filed out.

The ball thundered down the alley, and collided. There came a mighty whacking of wood, a ponderous, echoing silence.

"Darn—!"

The seven and ten pins stood stubbornly.

"Looks like my Granny's teeth," Ev said, referring to the pin alignment. "Should really hurt him this frame."

B.J. retrieved his ball, and lined up. His ball sped down the alley, clipped the outer edge of the seven pin, but failed to pick up the spare.

"Told you. It's all going to his head. Power means little in this game. At least today."

"Today?" said Dan.

"Right. Back in the 1800's bowling balls were wooden, weighed about twenty-five pounds each, and had no finger-holes. Back then it was obviously a man's sport. But today? Today it's no longer a power game. Today the key is— smart mixing."

Dan hoisted his ball, carefully inserted his fingers. "You don't have to tell me," he said. "We've gone through the fundamentals so many times."

Ev peeked his way. "Okay. I guess I'm still ... a bit nervous."

"You are?"

Dan stepped up to the alley, stood poised, motionless, concentrating. Then gracefully he bowled, coaxing the ball into a gentle curve into the pocket for a strike.

So the bowling went. Dan took ample time between rolls, slowly and patiently gauging his posture, his approach. He managed a share of strikes, even made a few difficult spares. At one point, after temporarily losing the pocket and watching three successive rolls fail to contact the head pin, Dan calmed down and took Ev's advice, re-gauging his aim through the marks on the alley and spot-bowling his way back into the center.

Quickly it grew apparent that bowling was not one of B.J. Billings' favorite pastimes. Through the entire first two games he seemed content just to hurtle the ball powerfully down the alley and stand by and grin with fists high at the smashing and scattering of pins. By the end of the second game, Teeler called a timeout and whispered some harsh advice. B.J. nodded, took up his ball, and in sulking assent bowled more meekly. His first effort, off the side of his hand, displayed a great overabundance of sidespin, the ball languishing its way down the alley so leisurely that it made gentle, clapping contact with the pins and toppled only four. "Bit slower than that?" B.J. called, with fake concern. B.J. grinned. The lethargic, marbled ball moved like the spinning-in-slo-mo planet Saturn, before the oddly brief, near-noiseless collision and weak topple of just four pins. The camera caught it all, and displayed B.J.'s antic not once or twice, but three times and was re-played in genuine slow motion on the local Nightly Sports Round-Up.

Hype, hand size, and evil eyes notwithstanding, the event showed clearly that Dan was the far better bowler. His meticulous size-up and delivery, his patient adaptation to situations as they arose, and, of course, his experience— his average was a shade under one eighty—all paid off. Twice during the match Dan was able to string together three strikes in a row. Each time Ev would howl, "That's a turkey!" and do a strut, flapping his arms like wings. The second time this brought a big hand from the gallery. Yet, by some astonishingly fortunate toppling of pins B.J. managed to keep it close. The final frame, which saw B.J. snag a spare and Dan topple an even more difficult one, was capped by a solid round of applause.

Together the players and coaches turned and nodded to the crowd. B.J. grabbed a towel, draped it in mocking self-condemnation over his head. "Told you," Ev confided to Dan. "Told you. You're now winning. ALL around, right? Fifteen different happy faces!"

And as the score was posted—'B.J. 43, Dan 57'—the announcer conveyed in a tone notably flat—"has caught up and passed B.J. Billings—for the moment anyway—with the pool contest slated for one o'clock over at West Hall." Ev took in Dan, B.J., Teeler, the crowd, all the popping cameras, and beamed. The expression, as contagious as unanticipated, prompted Dan to beam in return.

"Again—best of one hundred. Call the ball *and* the pocket. Gentlemen, good luck."

The ref retreated. The two players stepped around the table, chalking and re-chalking their cue sticks. Dan nodded to B.J.. B.J. shrugged, leaned intently into the table, and poised his stick. At once Teeler broke in with a harsh whisper. "Careful. He wants you to set him up. Go for a safety instead."

"Cool. So where's the end zone and the ball-carrier?"

"Come on, B.J., you're taking this way too lightly. A pool safety. A tactical delay."

"Like tricks are for kids? Like I got lunch waiting?" He lumbered over, gauged the triangular mass, aimed his stick, and whacked a mighty whack which sent balls scurrying at odd angles all across the table. Miraculously, the ball B.J. had called happened to fall in, right where he had predicted. The crowd cheered and laughed.

"Hey! Ok! That *is* the one I called, right?"

B.J. next aligned a relatively easy shot and promptly missed.

Again, as with the bowling, Dan operated patiently, coolly. He lined up each shot, took proper note of the angle, and slowly, smoothly, poked the cue stick into motion, with ample follow-through. "Easy ... easy ... now," Ev mumbled throughout. "That other attribute of the veteran athlete—patience. Remember, for this one you imagine yourself driving an overloaded nitroglycerine truck along a bumpy road at midnight. A physicist's game of angles. A diamond-cutter's finesse."

While Dan concentrated and played methodically, B.J. seemed content to settle on an unorthodox, seemingly self-defeating strategy. Throughout the match he ribbed Teeler, the gallery, his own efforts. On one occasion he took pause to examine his cue stick with round, curious eyes and then utter loudly enough to be overheard—"Hit with the *skinny* end? No wonder!" On another he jabbed with the stick so hastily that the cue ball spun off into the air, banged down onto the green felt, and rolled into a pocket. "Scratch," the ref called. B.J. viewed him oddly. "Fleas again, huh?" he quipped, then stepped over and obliged by extending a hand to scratch the man's back. The ref ignored the gesture and handed Dan the cue ball to place, as B.J. stood by with a greatly hurt look. Yet another time, after Teeler chided him for playing with so little caution, B.J. took a long survey of the table, and grinned. "Impatience or whatever killed the kitty." he posed. He licked his shoulder, knuckles, fingertips. He mewed daintily out to the crowd. "Not *this* cool cat," he added, with a wink.

While B.J.'s clownings and quips incited their share of giggles and even awe among the bystanders, they served an agenda less obvious. Much like recognizing, reacting, and destroying the variations of a pro-set offense, B.J. was swift to spy the advantages offered by the table and direct his shots accordingly, sending balls bounding, skittering, rolling in directions seemingly random. This strategy of defensive play masked by such seeming carelessness worked well. While pool was hardly B.J.'s forte, Dan rarely found himself with an easy shot—or, if so, a shot that by all unfair coincidence would involve more difficult, unmanageable successive shots in the midst of an increasing bottle-up. Even more important, this strategy, cloaked so craftily behind the dry, offhand clicks of the balls, invited Dan to think that weighing against him was not just B.J. but fate itself. The shot of the match came when Dan called a combo involving two balls and, remarkably, the shot dropped in the corner pocket. By the time the event drew to its end, the hallmark of each man was sheer concentration. B.J.'s playful, prankish, offhand manner was a total contradict to his soaked shirt, shiny hair, and gleaming forehead.

Out of what truly appeared to be a bad hand after bad hand dealt Dan's way, the finale found each man's score at forty-nine balls. Two remained. B.J. leaned to Teeler. "I'll take 'em both on banks. Like a safety blitz. Dump the dude's morale, dump him."

B.J. mulled for a moment, then shook his head. He bent forward, drew back his stick slowly, and aimed. At once he blinked, took pause. Then he stood up and slipped his cue stick behind his back for a trick shot. He aimed, tapped. The white ball thumped the far side of the table, bounced back, making feeble contact. The nudged ball came to rest at the pocket's edge.

Dan bent, lined up the shot, stroked lightly, and sank the ball. His second shot demonstrated equal dexterity. The target ball plopped into the pocket.

Dan acknowledged the applause, then stepped over and re-inserted his cue stick into the vertical rack on the wall. He walked over to Ev, who merely nodded.

"Hey," Dan smiled. "We pulled it out, right?"

"'Dan? I, uh, projected you'd be up by … a lot more than two," Ev said. He peered across at B.J.. "Look at that. Putting on one happy face. But beneath that grin, look out. He's a master defensive strategist. Wants us to think we're beating ourselves and so bye-bye confidence! Dan, stand back and consider that these are the indoor sports and he's staying so close. Need I say more?"

The scoreboard flashed the totals—'B.J. 49, Dan 51.' A tightlipped Teeler exited with his player. "Funny thing about playing with morale," he muttered to B.J.. "Can boomerang. Big time."

B.J. slapped his shoulder and grinned. He peeked into a camera, all innocence, made a cynical, pouting face, and finished his antic with a loud mee-ooww! "Only if you let it," he voiced. Then, under his breath—"Only if you let it."

As with the three earlier events, ping-pong involved the contestants vying for a share of a hundred points. With the cameras readied and the makeshift gallery crammed, both players took their positions. The two coaches offered last-minute counsel and encouragements, and backed away. B.J. licked the tip of his finger, then held it to the wind. Dan smirked, and got ready.

Dan served. B.J. swatted the ball off the table. Three times in a row Dan's serve spurred this strange, uncoordinated, galvanic response. Eyes began to narrow, jaws to drop. The gallery grew alive with mumbles. Then Dan's fourth serve provoked a tremendous swipe that sent the white plastic hissing by Dan's right ear.

"Oops—sorry!" B.J. called again, studying his paddle as if it were defective.

Again Dan served. This time B.J. returned a solid rap to the far corner. "Ah— *now* I've got it," he grinned.

From here on the two played evenly, neither building any wide lead. At the halfway point a loose, happy, and confident Dan, leading 27 to 23, stepped back over to Ev. "Bit of intimidation there at first? That's gone," he said. "A little stiffness here, too. But the nervousness? Huh. The throttle's open."

"The nervousness indicates how much your body is willing to give. You've got that lead, Dan, so pour it on. Keep in mind that on occasions B.J. seems just a little too far from the table. A short shot might play nicely. Remember, 'Indoor Day' is supposed to belong to us pencil-pushers."

In the other corner B.J. was his usual self, leaning to the gallery comically, courting the reporters. "These-here dinky sports?" he said loudly to Teeler. "Like who cares?"

Teeler leaned up to his ear. "We care," he declared. "You're gonna blow this show cuz of some macho complex!"

The ref summoned the players. B.J. looked past Teeler's reprimand, strolled out to the table, swung his paddle through a series of smooth and then vicious practice swings as Dan took up position. The ref handed B.J. the ball.

B.J. winked to Teeler. Then he served, wildly. Dan ducked. The ball sped by. "Darn!" B.J. said, all astonishment. B.J. served again, just as erratically, into the net. The ball spun away, dropped onto the floor. "Oops—single fault?"

The next point was, from the fans' viewpoint, the best of the match. Each player returned the ball three times, each time with more velocity. Now with each point B.J. seemed to edge back a bit farther, giving Dan his cue. Dan obliged, and cut at B.J.'s next return for the little dink shot Ev had suggested. The shot barely cleared the net. In an effort to reach the ball, B.J. lunged forward, losing his balance and landing atop the table, collapsing it and sending wood fragments everywhere. The crowd responded with laughter and amazement. B.J. pushed to his feet. "What a hit!" he yelled.

A replacement table then had to be moved in to finish the match. After the ref checked B.J.'s condition and cautioned each player not to touch the table, the match resumed.

Dan returned B.J.'s serve. With barely an effort B.J. slightly hoisted the end of the table high with one hand and scooped up the still-bounding ball with the other, to the crowd's oohs and aahs. "Oops. Oh, yeah. Sorry, almost forgot." With a huge smirk, B.J. lowered the table. Again he served, this time at Dan directly. Dan bent away, but not before the ball grazed his cheek.

"Hey—" Dan yelled back.

B.J. served, this time, legitimately. Dan smacked the ball toward B.J.'s leering face. Immediately Ev broke in, his hands hoisted into a T. "Timeout," he said. The ref stepped up. As he and B.J. had a private word, Ev ushered Dan away.

"Why not?" Dan protested. "I'm up a bundle anyway, right?"

"Because it's a psyche-out. And you're falling for it. Dan, ping-pong is not a game of force. "Tell *him* that," Dan countered.

"Dissension? That's just what he's after! The only benefit he can get out of this sport—and you let him. Besides, the time for force will be in ... about forty minutes."

"Okay by me," muttered Dan.

B.J. was standing at the other end of the table, surveying the ball oddly now, as if it were defective. Again B.J. served—once again at Dan's face. Dan ducked. There came a heavy silence, then a chorus of boos. "Come on, B.J.!" someone urged. "Play!" Others took up the cry. "Twenty-three serving thirty-one," barked the ref. B.J. took pause, peeked sheepishly around. "Folks, I'm so sorry. I'm just getting hyped for the next event."

"You mean – the, uh, boxing?"

Teeler pronounced the words as affectedly as B.J., and

B.J. beamed. "Yup, the, uh, *boxing*. And so what's all this about a dude having to hand over the entire hundred points— hey, this whole contest—if he can't finish? Like, say, he gets knocked out."

B.J. winked evilly back to Teeler, grinned over to Ev, to Dan.

"Uh, that's why I did put the boxing in as the day's last event," Ev mumbled in quiet confession. "Just, um, in case?"

Dan looked at him, looked at B.J.. "Fine by me," Dan said. "Fine by me."

The ping-pong match concluded with Dan the winner by a score of 51-49. No points were added or deducted for the damaged table. With this event done, there was a thirty-minute break before the athletes would meet for the boxing match.

The punch came solidly, with unanticipated force through Dan's half-canted glove, and struck just below his eye. Immediately a bell was clanging, echoing close and then buoying its clangs to Dan's ear as if from far away. Then the shock subsided. Strength returned to Dan's legs. As he stepped dizzily toward his corner he heard, above the remote ringing in his ears—

"You see them punches? A hoax? No way!"

"So much energy out there! You'd swear B.J. had the whole morning *off*!"

"Wait till he gets to *his* sports!"

"Looks like he has," mumbled Dan.

Dan slumped down onto the stool. A towel slipped damply across his neck and face. He popped open an eye. Through the leather headgear he viewed Ev and the two helpers. A hand groped for, removed Dan's mouthpiece, and immersed it into an unseen bucket below. From somewhere another hand blotted his cheekbone. Then a third—a hand he traced to Ev—smeared thick fingerfuls of grease across his nose and unwittingly over one eye. "You rocked him with that cross," Ev's voice said. "Ever since that one, he's stayed away. At least till the end of the round."

"Where'd he learn to box left-handed?"

"I don't know, Dan. Guy's got ... quite a special bag of tricks."

Dan nodded. Meanwhile, Ev was pondering. "Had the morning off?" He looked over at B.J., blinking curiously. "Holy—?" he said, then, staring.

"Tell me he just collapsed," said Dan.

Ev looked around. "Adjustments in sports aren't unusual, they're usual," he recited. "But this? This is ridiculous!" He leaned to one of the helpers, spoke into his ear. The man viewed him oddly. "You heard me," Ev insisted. "I'm serious. *Do* it."

Dan watched the man duck below the ropes and descend off the apron into the crowd. The towel came again now, less numb, more soothing, against Dan's face. Warm sensations pulsed through his being. His head was beginning to clear.

"Right now I'd call it even," Ev said. "That last punch

of his more than grazed.   When—or, *if*—you're hit hard, be quick to duck in, clinch, and catch your breath. Oxygen can do wonders for consciousness. And if—or *when*—you can, work inside his reach." He slipped the mouth piece back into Dan's mouth. "As far as getting caught on the ropes— don't! He's untrained, undisciplined, and unorthodox. And, yup, even a southpaw now, too. A boxer that can cause big problems."

The bell rang. As Dan rose off the stool, he spied Deb standing behind the last row of seats. He shook out his arms, stalked toward ring center. From the other corner B.J. approached. There came a rising well of cheers and applause.

Dan threw a jab, danced away, lunged in, threw a double jab. B.J. retreated and, without any preliminary jab, tossed a spectacular roundhouse right. Dan slid easily beneath, delivered another crisp jab and then a straight right hand that cut between B.J.'s gloves and thudded onto his neck. B.J. backed off, mimicking a slow, laborious moonwalk, and then fell into a surprisingly adept imitation of the Ali Shuffle. The crowd gawked, laughed, urged him on. Dan pursued. Two well-timed jabs shifted B.J.'s grin into a look of cautious surprise. He turned, confronted Dan, backed away just in time to avoid Dan's right-hand follow-up.

Then, as abruptly, B.J. shifted tactics. He clenched his teeth and simply barged into Dan, robotically. Both men pummeled each other at close quarters, Dan giving the better of it. B.J. lifted his spliced forearms. Dan persisted.

A lunging jab snapped B.J.'s head back. B.J. turned, tucked his chin against his neck, flailed his arms like pistons. Dan backpedaled, found himself against the ropes, bent and whirled just beyond a fist, which caught the bottom of his left elbow and drove against his ribs. Dan spun away, gained the center of the ring once more, caught Ev's mutter—"Yes, get out and stay out of that corner."

B.J. stood red-faced, puffing. For the rest of the round he stayed away, content to rely on his reach. When Dan ducked in and faked an attack, B.J. tossed out several countering jabs, but for the most part chose not to follow them up. For some curious reason he hung back, peering intently out at Dan between the leathery bulk of head gear, over the top of his gloves, gauging, blinking, as if trying to figure Dan out. Toward the end of the round it was Dan who was on the offensive, providing a disjointed series of jabs and crosses against B.J.'s gloves and forearms. Yet, Dan had difficulty breaking through. Long adept at fending off 300-pound blockers, B.J. seemed equally adept at compromising Dan's blows and keeping the bout a defensive struggle. Stubbornly he set his gloves straight out before his face or cocked back his left and then his right hand menacingly. Now even Dan's deception failed to incite a clumsily tossed right hand which would allow a counterpunch. When the bell clanged, the two were locked in a clinch, a result of Dan's tossing an ill-aimed right hand and pressing forward in spite of both men's fatigue. As B.J. turned and wheeled for his corner, a bizarre event took place. B.J.'s skull bumped squarely against Dan's nose and forehead. Both men continued for their corners, gasping.

As Dan slumped, he felt a slow trickle down the bridge of his nose. There came a familiar taste, warm and tinny. "I don't care. Purple is fine," Ev was mumbling to the aide who had returned. Ev planted a tiny bottle beside the stool, then ministered to Dan. "Hold—perfectly still," he directed, and applied a compress to Dan's face.

"I kill myself leading with my nose and you fool around with—?"

"It's dye, Dan. I'll explain later. Look, if I've counted right, this is the last round. Before it ends, you've got to usher him into this corner. I don't care how—just do it."

"So now it's dancing lessons?"

"Just *do* it."

"A Nike ad?"

"Dan —"

Dan peeked oddly up at Ev, then down and away from the harsh glare of the lights. The bell clanged. Dan peered across, spied the huge bulk rising slowly off the stool. "You're doing great," Ev threw after. "Keep it up. Looks like he's almost out of gas." Dan rose. The crowd broke into shrieks and cheers. The ref stepped in. "Round Five. Final round," he announced, and motioned both fighters to approach and touch gloves.

Dan obliged, nodded to B.J., then backed off and resumed his stance. Dan moved in, threw two quick jabs, a sharp right. B.J. seemed content to keep his distance. The head-butt was having—a reverse effect? All at once B.J. began to inhale in huge, openmouthed gulps, his gloves poised loosely before him. Dan darted in, threw a body shot, bent away from a weak right jab which missed his cheek. B.J. backed off, peered at the laces of one of his gloves and then, as if preoccupied, nodded over to the ref. Then suddenly, in a move unanticipated by Dan or anyone else, B.J. threw an erratic, rocking left. Interrupting Dan's vision was a bright blue flash. His face numbed. Then, as he instinctively retreated amid a new onset of pulsations, his equilibrium returned. His back met the ropes, rebounded rudely, sagged back against them. Now B.J. was wading in, pummeling eagerly, a frenzied windmill. Dan bobbed, twisted, lifted his gloves to cover his face. Dan leaned back against the flexing cords, edged over, felt the cold sturdiness of the ring post marking his corner. Now, amid a barrage of stinging punches, B.J. was closing and closing fast. Dan countered with a brisk uppercut, set himself, and managed a solid right to the chest, which momentarily froze B.J..

As Dan's head began to clear, he viewed Ev. "Good work," Ev called. "Got it." He heard another familiar voice—"Come *on*, Dan!"—which seemed to be that of Deb. Suddenly another punch grazed Dan's cheek. Dan wheeled, sagged forward against the bulky, shifting form before him. "Break!" came a voice from faraway. From somewhere a striped arm slipped in to intercede. Dan turned, gasping, beheld once more Ev's image—now a face of concern. At once the face dipped away. As quickly, in its place, a sign popped up, and revealed the scrawled features of—Mitchell Mossey. Dan sucked a long, thin breath. Through a rain of punches he got off one blind jab and then another, meeting stiff, wheeling resistance. He threw a hard right, into a force just as rigid. At once the punches stopped. Dan peeked over, glimpsed once again the picture propped on a pole short inches beyond his vision. Dan ducked, wheeled away, broke toward the center of the ring. "Thought we might need that boost," he heard from behind.

"Thirty seconds," came a call. Dan peeked around. Everywhere figures stood, roaring, exhorting.

B.J. lunged in. Dan would not retreat. B.J. threw a wheeling, roundhouse left. A knockout was on his mind. Dan blocked the punch, and countered. B.J. shoved Dan. Dan shoved back. Amid a tangle of arms, gloves, and elbows the two men clinched, a dull ache began to assert itself over Dan's right eye. Pain pulsed in his forehead. Again came the warm, tinny dripping off his nose and into his mouth. Dan pulled back, and stared. B.J.'s chin was caked with red.

"Ten seconds!"

They eyed each other oddly, awkwardly, as if unaware of what to do next. At once B.J. launched one more haymaker. Dan bent aside, and wheeled as B.J. barged past. As B.J. stood stubbornly, Dan moved in with three straight, right-hand body shots. Then the two had fallen against each other, half-clinching, half-flailing. From somewhere erupted a series of clangs, then a mighty burst of shouts, whistles, and applause.

"Nice fight. *Both* you guys." The ref slipped in, split the two men apart. "Heck of a performance, Driver!" came a voice beyond the apron. Dan lifted a glove in weary salute, then wandered back and slumped onto the stool. Ev ducked through the ropes into the ring. "Day One is history?" he grinned. "Proud of you, guy! Real proud!"

Dan burrowed his face into the towel. "Thanks," he mumbled. Dan withdrew the towel, glimpsed the shiny red blotches and smears. Dan peered up. Across the ring he saw B.J., set in the same bent-down, weary posture, his chin rimmed in red. At once the two men caught each other's eye. Dan smiled an absurd smirk, and received one in return.

Card in hand, the announcer stepped out. The room fell into silence. "Ladies and gentlemen, based on an even one-hundred-point system, with judges Talbert and Johnson marking totals of thirty-three each and referee Hansen thirty-four, we have a decision: Talbert: 18, 15. Johnson, 18, 15. Hansen: 17, 17. The winner, 53 to 47, is—B.J. BILLLLL-ings!"

Matching the whistles and cheers was a outburst of boos. Ev laid a second towel across Dan's shoulder. "Olympically, purely as a boxer, you won it, Dan. You won it hands down. But in America? Here it's the haymakers—the brawlers—who impress." He peeked to his clipboard, rechecked some figures, nodded up happily. "All rii-ight!" he smiled.

"But—I *lost*."

"Dan, it's the best ALL-around. Who cares about a single battle when—"

Now on a nearby screen, along with the announcement, came the official posting of the day's competition:

'INDOOR DAY TOTALS: B.J. BILLINGS 246.00. DAN DRIVER 254.00.'

"—We're in the middle of a war!"

Ev blotted more blood from the bridge of Dan's nose. Dan winced at the sting. "Sure," Dan said. "Easy for the general to say."

Dan lounged in the shower for a full thirty minutes. Then he hobbled out and blotted himself dry. Slowly he dressed. His nose and forehead had stopped bleeding, but his right eye was still swollen. The hot, steamy water had eased the aches away. At least for now.

Dan simply sat, then, in shirt and trousers, his hair slicked with moisture. From an adjoining section of the locker-room sounded voices, occasional bouts of merry laughter.

Ev stopped his pacing. Once more he cocked his head to listen. "It's because they still can't believe you can do it. *Will* do it. That's why," he said. "It'll just make the victory all the sweeter."

From the rows of lockers a solitary figure emerged, and stepped over. "My name's James," he announced. "Don James." He looked to them both. "Mind if I … have a word?"

"You're—a life-insurance salesman?" Dan smiled.

"A reporter. Channel 4. Like to do a piece on you guys. Your side of all of this."

As they shook hands, Ev winked. "Couldn't even get near B.J., huh?"

James shrugged. "Okay, so I am a new guy on the block. But I'm more the human-interest type anyway. There's a tremendous story here. I mean, with what you guys were doing. You know how many people I talked to out there today who were on your side?" He looked at Dan for a long moment. "And I was one of them."

Ev shrugged. "How about tomorrow? Right now we've … Well, that forehead may need some work."

James nodded. "There's what—a hundred and eight stitches on a baseball? Looks like Dan here's got a good start. So about time you guys called it off?"

Ev looked at him. "Called what off?" he said.

James viewed them curiously. "You mean—he's going to continue? You're not throwing in?"

"What are you—?"

"The guys over there were saying"…

Ev took a deep breath. "Like who's ahead at this point?" he said.

James looked at Dan. "Right. But … you're confident you can complete it?"

"Complete it? How about—*win* it."

"Really?"

"Really. But also let me say—and this is for the record—B.J. Billings may well turn out to be twice the man everyone thinks he is. And *still* we'll win. That you can quote me on."

James looked at Ev oddly. "Wow!" he said. He thought for a moment. "I know B.J.'s doing a spot live tomorrow evening over at Channel Twelve. You know—Rod Perry's show. I'd love to get both you guys on as a simulcast, but … Okay, how about an interview live? On Night Spot? Tomorrow night? Ten-fifteen. We'll come out to your house, Dan. That is—if you're still breathing?"

Ev unwrapped a fresh band-aid. Carefully he applied it above Dan's right eye. Then he took another bandage the same size and pasted it just above Dan's undamaged left eye.

"Both eyes?" asked James.

Ev peeked over. "Hides weakness," he recited. "By morning B.J. will probably forget which side of Dan he hit."

"Hopefully I will, too," said Dan.

James looked at the two bandages. "Ingenious," he smiled.

Ev stood back. Then he unwrapped yet a third bandage and applied it above his own left eye. "To show how much *I* feel it, too," he said. "To show that head-butt was taken by both of us— by the team." He looked to James, and nodded. "Tomorrow night. 10:15," he said quietly. Then, "You're on."

"Hey, it could make you guys celebs!" added James.

Ev looked at him. "No thanks," he said. "No publicity stunt, please. Just a chance to tell it, like it is. That's all we want."

"Really?"

"Really. The *contest* is more important than Dan or me."

"You are serious."

"We are," said Ev.

"Yes we are," said Dan.

James smiled. "Okay," he said. "You guys certainly *are* the real thing."

"We're sure trying to be. Tomorrow. 10:15 p.m. Dan's house."

"I thank you, gentlemen."

CHAPTER
TWELVE

Debra sat in the kitchen and peered out as the hedges gradually revealed themselves in the growing light. Soon the sun was lifting visibly. Shadows began to assert themselves. Then came the peep and twitter of birds. It was Sunday, 5:30 a.m. Debra was up already, on the phone with her mother.

"Right. I am really worried about Dan."

"He's—okay?" inquired her mother.

"He sustained some bad cuts. I re-bandaged him last night. There could be some internal issues as well. He keeps saying that he's fine. Right. He's still asleep. Look, Mom, can you take the kids again? I … want to be with him all day."

A pause, then—"Absolutely, honey."

'MASKED MAN UNMASKED'

Nipps propped the article with its **'WHO? Not Any More!'** subheading up before his large eyes. He spoke into the receiver frantically. "I don't care what Mossey said! You, me, we all saw TV yesterday! I don't care what all you guys thought. He's *in* it. And, hey—he's *ahead*. We're going! All of us! Pass the word! Right—everybody in your area! Beltram, Detra, Dibbell, Sims, Seymour, Tims, Walkenstein, Wallace … The whole alphabetical she—*he*-bang!"

MIX-'EM-UP DAY

The sign on the wrought iron gate read Camelback Country Club. Then came the sharp swat of a driver. The ball lofted in a high, smooth arc and bounded down some thirty yards short of the pin. B.J. nodded graciously to the polite applause, and returned the club to his caddy.

It was then Dan's turn. He studied the fairway a moment more. Then, after a few more practice swings, addressed the ball, and teed off—a smooth, solid *whaaack* that sent the ball lofting higher and scooting farther than B.J.'s and suggested the chance for a birdie. There came deep, long whistles of appreciation, followed by sustained if subdued applause. Perhaps it was the early hour, the sport's traditional civility, or was it the more cautious, calculating manner of play? For whatever reason, the witnesses here today were far more temperate than those of yesterday. Likewise, the two contenders, sporting prominent facial bandages, began by exhibiting somewhat less zeal for the task at hand. Each made a point of avoiding the other's eyes. Each exhibited a mood best labeled as grim determination. Each, mentally, was digging in.

As with the bowling, it soon became evident—embarrassingly so—that golf was not one of B.J. Billings' strong suits. The success of his first drive notwithstanding, as the entourage advanced through holes two and three, then four and five, B.J.'s game grew defined by the various, frustrating faults of the amateur. B.J. sliced shots, over-tapped putts, played in far too much of a hurry. "Oops! At this rate I'll never make CEO. Golf? I could play me three hundred and thirty-six holes a month—right-handed—and it wouldn't do me no good," he quipped with visible, irritation as he blew an easy two-foot putt on the fifth-hole.

"That's not what you told us yesterday at breakfast," a *Times* reporter teased, edging up curiously.

B.J. took pause to glance oddly at the man. "Yester—? Oh, yeah," he fumbled. "Yeah, so I, uh, did. Hey, golf is one of my favorites!"

What's more, B.J. elected to golf left-handed. Moderate of mood as they were, this strategy sent a buzz through fans and media alike. Could this contender afford to clown his way through an entire event? But as the match proceeded, the buzzes and whispers grew in another direction. Even as a southpaw, B.J. was not that bad a duffer after all. Hadn't his first drive from the southpaw stance raised eyebrows all around? The rumors were right. A truly ambidextrous athlete.

Ev turned to Dan. "Wow," he said "then, the next event will tell us even more." Beyond this he would not elaborate. Even when Dan coaxed him about what he meant, he gave only a cryptic nod.

It was on the eighth fairway that B.J. sliced his tee shot far off the manicured grass and into the rough. His somewhat spray-and-pray approach had, again, gotten the best of him. After a short search he and his caddy came upon the ball— nestled snugly amid the gnarled roots of an oak tree.

"Any ideas how we duff our way out of this one?" B.J. muttered.

"With a large axe?" quipped the caddy.

The caddy peeked toward the group of fans walking up

behind. No one— certainly no golf official—was around. Privately he winked at B.J., then made an unauthorized field-goal kick, as if to send the ball onto the fairway proper.

B.J. looked at the lad, looked around. It was true. For this one odd, incredible moment nobody *was* watching.

Then B.J. spoke, harshly. "That might be in the interest of PR, or of B.J. Billings, but it sure as heck ain't in the interest of sport."

"Aw heck, man. No one'll ever *know*," said the young caddy.

"*I'll* know." B.J. glanced around. "You know that man in the moon. You wanna be joinin' 'him?'"

"Uh, not particularly."

B.J. fished a twenty-dollar bill out of his slacks. He wadded up the bill, flipped it to the caddy. "Here. Go fetch yerself a lie-detector test. And set them clubs *down* right now."

And for the rest of the event—some ten holes—B.J. toted his own bag, withdrew and prepared his own clubs, his caddy nowhere to be seen. The added physical burden was easily offset by the firmer step and more upbeat feeling the decision had given him. When on the ninth green a reporter finally asked B.J. why he was carrying his gear—had his caddy seen fit to abscond with a souvenir ball?—B.J. simply smiled. "Price of knighthood in this-here modern world," he replied. But not even when urged would he elaborate. However, more than once B.J. was heard complaining that a three-hundred-yard drive counted for the same number of strokes as a two-foot putt.

The sun rose higher, hotter. The sky assumed a deep, healthy blue. By mid-morning a vigorous breeze flushed the trees. Large oaks, maples, and fragrance-laden pines bucked loftily, handsomely, along the fairway. Over all lingered the lush smell of fresh cut grass. It was all a serene backdrop, which added to the competition. Indeed, the competition seemed to have ended holes ago. Long before the two parties and the onlookers in their wake had paraded themselves off the course and had walked the quaint flagstone path to the clubhouse, just who was the better golfer was no longer in doubt. Deftly eluding the hazards of sand, water, and yesterday's aches and pains, Dan had negotiated the 18 hole par-72 course with a very respectable 76. Dan's best shot of the day came on the par-four 4th hole. Thirty feet off the green, he pulled out a wedge and holed the ball for a birdie. B.J. managed a whopping 124. His best moment appeared to be when his long drive on the third hole, slicing way out of bounds, miraculously hit a tree and with a loud thud bounced back into the fairway to roll just ahead of Dan's effort, to the roar of the crowd. Total strokes had been converted into a hundred-point system. Due to golf's procedure that low score wins, each man had received the score of the other. Short moments after the last ball had dropped, the word had gone out. The result was sobering, even astounding: B.J. 38, Dan 62.

Now already some of the crowd, including the media, were beginning to query—even shift—their affiliations.

"*All*-around? Now I see it. Those Driver and Winchell guys aren't so dumb after all." At the clubhouse bar this sentiment was voiced more than once.

In like measure, there was delight. "Way to DRIVE-Driver!" elated a wide-eyed figure who, escorting a group of his own, had caught up with the general procession leaving the eighteenth tee grinning amiably at his pun. His coworkers were relaxed. Their demeanors had gone from timid, unbelieving curiosity to hopeful contemplation. Could such a thing *really be happening*?

"Way to go!" Ev agreed, and patted Dan on the back as they departed the clubhouse to prepare for the next venue. "Now for a quick stop at Wimbledon and really pour it on."

In B.J.'s quarters, the attitude was markedly different. "Too bad the highest score don't take it in this one," Teeler scolded. "We'd be renting our tuxes for the victory dance."

"It don't?" played B.J.. And he grinned.

Quickly Dan rushed the net. He had guessed right. B.J.'s attempt at a passing shot, easily anticipated and not well executed, had sent the ball floating. Dan positioned himself, waited, and blocked the ball with a careful, composed, textbook follow-through. The ball angled sharply across the opposing service area, landing far out of B.J.'s reach.

"Picture perfect," Ev called. "Attaboy!"

"Fifteen-forty," the PA system sounded.

B.J. sauntered over into the deuce court, and served. The ball slapped hard against the net.

"Second serve!" the linesman called.

"Who invented nets anyway?" B.J. asked. "Dude sure knew how to ruin a fun game!"

He took pause, rubbed his face, hiked his sweatpants, gathered himself, and served. This time the ball traveled more slowly, and again smacked the net.

"Game, Driver. 6-4, first set, Driver," the announcement echoed.

The two players retired to their benches.

"Don't shed tears for the klutz," Ev declared. "Serving's as much a part of it as anything else. Besides, he's highlighting his inadequacy again so you'll let down your guard. Six-four is not an overwhelming win."

Dan peeked over to B.J. and his coaches. "That's Nick Bollettieri! At least give the guy credit for bringing in a big-timer."

"By the way, Dan, you see what I see? or don't see?"

Dan peered across, and shrugged.

"B.J.'s right calf? As in—the dye is gone?" exclaimed Ev.

"Probably washed off. Hey, just what *is* all your concern about dye, anyway?"

Ev continued to study B.J.. After a time he turned to Dan. "Ah, yes, tennis. Okay. Tennis, too, is a game of position. You're doing fine, but when you end up hitting so often to his forehand, you set him up."

"But is he right or left-handed?"

"See which hand he's holding the racquet in. Hit to the

other side!"

"Got it," Dan smiled, crowding in more closely as Ev hauled out his notes.

As Ev mapped out his second-set tactics, Dan's rival did the same. The mood was glum. "You sure ain't no Andy Roddick out there," Teeler said. "Ever been served a tennis ball before?"

"Just once. At a dinner," grinned B.J.. "Really," he insisted. "Fraternity prank. Don't laugh. That darned fuzz catches in your teeth. Anyway, I'm no Wimpy Wussy Wimbledon or Mister Forest Hills or whoever and I know it. So I'm into a little intimidation. These candy sports? That's why I'm playing this one left-handed, too. I'll do this to coax him in—then clean his clock when we get to my games."

"Right, B.J.. Look, you can't rally from the baseline with this guy, so just do your thing. Nick here gave you your basic strategy—hit the ball deep and attack. Return his serve deep to his backhand, rush the net, rely on your wingspan. Remember racquetball? Now let's do it."

The linesman summoned. The players took their places. After missing his first serve, Dan offered a slow spinner. B.J. returned the ball deep to the backhand, and charged. Dan struck back—an oddly weak, slow-lofting lob—and approached. B.J. reached high, swung. The ball smashed viciously at Dan's feet, giving him no opportunity of return.

"Hey—it does work," B.J. called, with a grin.

And so the second set went. It quickly grew obvious that B.J., again, was less intent on hitting winners than on rattling

Dan. To compensate, Dan retreated to his own baseline and aimed the ball sharply toward the corners.

The most amazing point of the match came when B.J. dribbled a shot just over the net and Dan raced in to make the shoestring return. At once both men found themselves facing each other at close quarters. Dan's return barely cleared the net. B.J. gauged its bounce and swung his racquet mightily—to send the ball caroming off Dan's bandaged forehead. The incident prompted an official timeout, during which Ev stepped out to remove the one bandage and apply another, all the while B.J. protesting his innocence, palms up beseechingly, heeding a warning from the linesman.

After Dan signaled his readiness, the match resumed. Now just as important was the activity outside the lines. By the middle of the second set some two dozen more colleagues had arrived to join Nippers and his group. From high in the stands the group cheered Dan on enthusiastically, but then, as a rather pale but stern-faced Mossey returned to rejoin his own entourage, they fell silent.

As with bowling and golf, Dan was clearly the better player, but B.J. managed to hold his own. After his warning B.J. shelved his aggressive tactics and several times elicited oohs and aahs from the crowd for some solid, well-placed shots. By the end of the second set, however, Dan's first serves were zooming in to catch the back edge of the service square with unnerving pace and regularity. B.J. could only stand deep behind the baseline and look on, all hopes quashed for rushing the net. The match ended with Dan serving not one but a pair of aces to claim the set, 6-4. Dan had won both sets with relative ease. As Ev's scoring system was the ratio of games won, Dan and B.J. divided the 100 points 60 to 40.

As they gathered their equipment and exited the court, Dan and Ev were silent. What could they say? From a broader point of view, Dan had played a fine round of golf and some equally impressive tennis, yes, but in these "clubhouse" sports everyone expected that Dan *would* outdo his foe. Dan had claimed the alley, links, and court, yes, but the overwhelming question was whether Dan had won by *enough*? To this, Ev could only pore for the hundredth time through the collection of squiggled hieroglyphics which now arrayed his clipboard and shrug. "I can look to past performances in individual sports, Dan, and from that predict. But, to forecast the results for a mix of them all? Simply, there's never been a contest on this broad a scale. What we're doing here is—breaking new ground. Peering at the unknown."

B.J. and Teeler were equally reflective. Somehow the zest and zaniness, which had marked B.J.'s antics most of the day, had ceased. Like his spectacled counterpart, Teeler spent long moments scribbling notes, studying the facilities, the wind, the bold, unbroken sky, the other candidate's odds and ends. For some reason, by this, the middle of the second day and midpoint of the competition, both parties had opted to trade open, energetic, chompings at the bit for a cool calculation. Ev and Teeler had become like two patient boxers, probing in the early rounds each other's strengths and weaknesses, seeking gaps and biding time for … the opportunity to pounce. While Ev seemed able to hide this slow but building pressure, his counterpart was not. "You and your 'intimidation,'" Teeler muttered audibly to B.J. as the tennis totals were flashed to a considerable burst of fanfare. "*Told* you to listen. Yup, all started when you went out hot-dogging on your own yesterday with that safety."

"Safety? Whattaya mean? The football's tomorrow, right?"

At the oddly blinking B.J., Teeler stared and shook his head.

"I meant pool safety," Teeler exclaimed. "Geez, it's hard to keep you straight."

A reporter edged in. "You sure B.J.'s okay? Got his bell rung? The boxing?"

Overhearing, B.J. retorted, "Hey, lady—I look un-okay?"

"No, B.J.. Um, not at all."

B.J. thumped his chest. "Just a bit too much sugar poured into my cereal this morning. Hey, don't forget—I am ambidextrous. Heh heh."

Ev had been a close witness to this exchange. Now as he watched the two men duck away, the one mumbling and gesturing to the hulking other, he gave a deep nod. "Punch-drunk as my calculator finger," he said. "Now I'm almost *sure* of it.

"Sure of *what*?" Dan insisted.

Ev continued to stare. "You know, Babe Ruth could toss two baseballs parallel to each other—all the way from the mound to home plate?"

"Meaning—"

"Meaning now I've really got my suspicions about what's happening out here."

"Like *what*?" Dan said.

But Ev fell silent, and offered only an empty shrug.

B.J. dug in his cleats, and waited. The pitch came.

"Steee-rike!" called the umpire.

The pitch, a juicy fastball, had come humming right down the pipe, but B.J. had been looking elsewhere. Even now, moments after the call, he stared off. For moving cozily down into her seat in the first row along the third-base line was Diana Hansen with Ruff standing by gallantly, before assuming a seat himself. B.J. shook his head, turned to the pitcher, dug in. The pitch came. He swung the massive wooden bat left-handedly—*whaack!*—sending the ball smartly up and over the right-field fence. He peeked over to Diana, and grinned. The grin froze. Before his eyes stood the splinted finger. And from just behind the finger its possessor stared out. Was Ruff taunting him? B.J. couldn't tell. B.J. looked away, took a long, deep breath, and re-concentrated on baseball.

In one of the dugouts sat Dan and Ev.

"That last one must've gone four hundred feet." Ev still shaded his eyes and stared after.

"The pitcher's sure giving him some fat ones to hit. "

"You mean, like baseball used to be," said Ev. "Back in

the mid-1800s the batter told the pitcher where he wanted the ball to come, and the pitcher obliged. Can you believe it? Of course, back then bunting was deemed ungentlemanly." He watched B.J. hit another solid ball and strut about arrogantly in the batter's box. "And the bases used to be stakes or posts arranged in a 'U.' Today it's shaped like a diamond—that is why we don't call it a baseball U."

"Speaking of? I sure wish homers weren't so stressed in this thing. Singles? Doubles? Bunts? Walks? Baseball savvy? Aren't they part of baseball? Do long-ball hitters end up with the most RBIs, highest batting averages, MVP tallies? No way!"

"Again the American love of the spectacular. But don't grumble, Dan. Just mention it to the jerk who designed this set-up."

"I'd sure like to," quipped Dan.

"You're, um, looking at him."

The two men viewed each other, then smiled.

There came a ripple of applause. B.J. had finished hitting and was retiring to his dugout. Dan rose, bat in hand. "Well, here goes." He stepped up out into the sunshine and strode toward home plate, to applause. The pitcher hung back until Dan had taken a few practice swings. "Play baaawwll!" came the call. Dan moved close to the plate, and dug in.

The sequence began. Out of twenty-five pitches, Dan socked three out of the park. Many other swings were solid base hits—more than several bounded energetically to the fence—but, yes, the scoring arrangement placed a top-heavy weight on home runs and total bases. In time Dan tossed the bat away and retreated to the dugout. "Sorry," came the murmur. "Next time I'll ... um, restructure this part."

"*What* next time?" mumbled Dan.

Now B.J. and Dan were timed running the bases. They each took two trips around the diamond and were allowed to keep the best score. Then came a five-minute break. Again came the summons—"Play baaawwll!"

The final part of the competition would begin. Gloves in hands, B.J. and Dan trotted into left field. There they took turns casually fielding fly balls, line drives, and ground balls. Then the warm-up ended. Dan edged off to the sideline. Working first at short stop and then in left field now, B.J. retrieved twenty batted balls, attempting to catch them on flies or field them on bounces and complete the task by hurling each to a designated base. Poised on the first and third-base lines, two judges gauged each effort for smoothness, speed, and accuracy. While B.J.'s arm—his left arm, no less—was powerful and some of his throws surprisingly precise, he dropped several routine fly balls and bobbled several ground balls as well.

The crowd responded accordingly. "Linebacker hands!" one fan heckled from the foul-line area. "*He* sure couldn't work for All State!" sneered another. Hoots erupted.

B.J. took it all in stride. His final retrieval from the outfield and toss was a fine piece of work. He had fetched the ball with a bare hand on one hop at the 320-foot line in left-center and flung it sharply, accurately, to the bag at second.

Then off he sprinted, grinning, to stand just outside the foul line and glare up and around in mock fury at the chuckling, chiding fans as Dan trotted by.

If anything, B.J.'s final feat proved an inspiration, for Dan played virtually flawless defensive baseball. He cleanly fielded every ball hit. His throws to the bases were quick and accurate. He capped his performance to a large round of applause, and joined B.J.. Together the two men trotted in to home plate, removed their caps, bowed to further acclaim, and retired.

As B.J. ducked in under the apron of the dugout, he tossed his glove across the bench. "Never *could* snag passes," he said. "Especially with my hands taped."

"Ain't taped now, good buddy!" came a call from above. B.J. retreated a step and gawked up, to incite a fresh outburst of chuckles and cheers. Teeler peeked out as well. "Like your mouth should be," B.J. yelled out.

Howls erupted. B.J. edged back out into the bright sun, and faced the fans. He grinned around cordially, tipped his hat again, and winked. His gesture converted the howls into cheers and applause.

"Just gotta know how to handle 'em," he mumbled to Teeler as the two ducked back in. "Got a crowd on your back? Hey, that's strike one to begin with."

In the other dugout stood Ev, deeply vexed. "Okay okay, I decided not to include so much defense because of the variables—spins, bad hops, poor infield or outfield grounds, sun, night, lighting—that can make fair judging so hard. The way that guy catches, in hindsight, I wish I would have made it all defense!"

Now there came a general commotion. Dan and Ev peeked out. Above the center-field fence the scoreboard was flashing: 'B.J. 47. DAN 53.' For a time the two men stood by, wordlessly, until the commotion had abated and the crowd had started to file out. "That's the breaks," Dan said. "One of my favorite sports of all—and I barely win it."

Dan stepped right, left, faked a jump shot, then dribbled around B.J. for the left-hand lay-up. "Make it, take it, right?" Dan said. The ref nodded, and awarded him the ball. Dan retreated across the three-point line, then turned and dribbled in. Just beyond the free-throw line B.J. edged up, his long arms sweeping vigorously when Dan stopped his progress. Dan faked left, forward, then leaned back and released a soft jump shot that swished the net.

Already 4-0. And still B.J. had yet to touch the ball.

On his third possession, Dan's short jumper thumped off the rim and into B.J.'s waiting fingers. B.J. dribbled awkwardly, with his left hand, back across the three-point line. Then abruptly he turned and, still spinning, threw up the ball—which struck the backboard and dropped through the net. B.J. took the ball at the top of the key, dribbled in, faked a shoulder, then drove straight into Dan, who, arms high, stood his ground. Both men toppled. As they regained their feet, the bandage hung half-unpeeled off Dan's forehead. And Dan's nose was bleeding.

Ev barged onto the court. "Flagrant! That goon oughta be disqualified!"

The ref motioned Ev away. Ev persisted. Slowly the ref's hands made the sign of a timeout. "Perhaps ... we can negotiate?" Ev protested, and turned away, still grumbling, to attend to Dan.

"Much as I love this game, fouls are fouls." Dan gave a sullen look around. "That one was obvious."

"Right, Dan. It was. But too often. That's not what sport is."

To Dan's questioning gaze Ev smiled, thinly. "In basketball, especially—with all the guarding and dribbling—it's not what you do but the illusion of what you do. What it *seems* to be. If it looks like a foul, it'll be called. No high-jumper in human history's ever been able to stay off the ground for more than a second, yet we think —no doubt due to so much slo-mo—that athletes can glide or soar. Sports are deceptive. What one witness swears is the truth, another witness often does not even see."

"Then why go ballistic about that call?" asked Dan.

"Just ... to keep him honest. Better, to make him lean in our direction. Sure, we'll get a payback call now. Just wait."

The ref summoned both players back onto the court and awarded Dan two free throws. Dan blotted his eyebrow, concentrated, and sank his first attempt but missed the second badly. B.J. scooped up the rebound, dribbled casually away, then suddenly reversed course and burst past Dan, who stood by, still blinking. B.J. put up a lay-up, and scored.

And so the basketball went. Dan's far greater experience made him the better ball-handler and shooter, but B.J.'s skin-tight defense, height, and reach—as well as the effects of his early charge—helped even the odds. Only short minutes after the collision Ev had to call a timeout to stop the blood streaming down Dan's nose and forehead. When play resumed, Dan, reaching deep, turned it on. Two fine moves left B.J. groping air, and made for easy lay-ups. Just after Dan's second shot dropped through, a buzzer sounded. The crowd rose, applauded heartily. Nips gleefully nudged his colleagues and flashed Dan a firm thumbs-up. Dan returned the gesture, trotted over to Ev, and grinned.

"About time I started hitting," Dan said. "You see those first easy ones I missed?"

"Your forehead doesn't bother you, does it?"

"Not right now. But my eyes? That collision? I'm seeing two B.J.s out there."

Ev nodded. "Me, too," he said. He wiped his spectacles off, carefully reset them on his nose. Dan took a deep breath, pumped a fist. "Guy doesn't know a thing about sealing the baseline or defending the fade-away. Lay-ups and short jumpers are all I'll need. No reason to even try from downtown. Now I'm back into it, Ev. Second half I'll just pour it on."

Ev studied Dan. "You're ... sure you're feeling okay?" he asked.

"Sure. Why?"

"That buzzer—I hope you heard it? Dan, that was the

end of the basketball competition. We just hit a hundred. In … thirty-five minutes we hit the pool."

Dan could only look to Ev, to the empty court, to the crowd—yes, the crowd filing out now and taking time to peer up at the scoreboard flashing the news— 'B.J. 49. DAN 51.'

Dan was stunned. "Are you kidding me?" he said. "How? But … how?"

Dan stood at the water's edge, a referee behind him. At the far end of the pool Ev, Teeler, and many spectators stood congregated. At once there were cheers, shouts, shrill whistles, then general bursts of laughter. A tall, husky figure cut through the crowd and then emerged, in a tight black Speedo and bright, floral-patterned swim cap. Casually B.J. loped the length of the pool, nodded cordially to Dan, and took his position in the lane adjacent. "Okay, so I don't wanna ruin my blow-dry," he called back against the hoots. "Next one who laughs, I'll break his face. How's that?"

From all around came unruly shrieks and wolf whistles.

A figure stepped forward, microphone in hand. The crowd fell silent.

"This is the last event of the day. The first of our two races here this afternoon will be the fifty-meter freestyle. Gentlemen, are you ready?"

Dan nodded. B.J. shrugged. The ref lifted the gun. The two edged up, coiled into final, frozen stances. There came a hollow *POP*! The two men leapt.

Dan churned furiously, and broke out ahead. B.J. drew even, then fell back. Dan upped his intensity, scarcely daring to breathe, converting throbbing bursts of adrenaline as best he could into a series of swift, rhythmic, strokes. Soon the tile bobbed close, closer. Dan lunged, touched, took a great, ecstatic gulp of air, and then turned back in glad relief. But B.J. was nowhere. Dan glanced back to the wall, spied the floral cap. "You. *Barely*," came Ev's voice from above. "Thirty point nine."

The scoreboard flashed the score. Dan had won, yes— but by less than a second.

The two climbed out of the pool, shook out their arms, and slowly padded back toward their original positions at poolside. "I ain't no shark," B.J. quipped. He spied Diana. "Of *any* kind," he said. "I can do maybe fifty yards through this fish stuff, and that's it. Closest thing was that mud bath in Green Bay back in the late Nineties. Nope, finning is not my game. I'm a Taurus. This here cap's to cut friction. But I, uh, do hope to make a big splash with my fans."

The crowd offered more cheers and applause. One cow-eyed spectator, Nips, groaned audibly.

After a ten-minute break, Dan and B.J. were summoned back to the starting line. Again, both assumed their positions. The announcer began. "Ladies and gentlemen, the second half of the swimming competition, the two-hundred-meter free style. Gentlemen, are you ready?"

B.J. peeked around, gave Dan a thumbs up and grinned.

Again the two men edged up, and froze. The ref raised

the gun— *POP*!

Instead of churning rapidly, each struck the water, surfaced, and fell into a slow, steady pace. Smooth, rhythmic, energy-saving locomotion was the key. True to his word, B.J. was no long-distance wiz. In time he lagged, considerably, even to the point that the more persistently stroking Dan passed him in mid-pool going in the other direction. As Dan drew near and passed, B.J. lifted his head and spit a copious mouthful of water across the rope against Dan's cheek. The crowd roared. On Dan's next pass B.J. lifted his upper half high above the surface and trod water with his palms, like a huge, flippery walrus. He emitted a loud bellow. The crowd responded with laughter.

"Piece 'a cake, this one," Ev smiled, kneeling at the pool's edge and looking back to a young cameraman. "Piece 'a cake."

Suddenly, an erratic wall of water had dashed up across the apron to sweep Ev's coffee out of his hand and into the pool. For a moment the Styrofoam cup and diffusing black liquid lay on the top, then receded, in slow-mo suspension. At once from the depths a face approached, white, whiter, hugely grinning, snapping at the cup and pushing it back toward the surface. Then off, away, paddling zestily, still submerged, was B.J.. This evening all three local channels would air the unique video which an amateur had alertly caught on camera. Each channel, by no coincidence, presented the clip with an audio background from *Jaws*.

Put simply, B.J.'s antics revealed that swimming was not

his forte. He was hardly constructed like the classic swimmer of lean, lithe muscle and limb. His figure was anything but unknotted. He had not had enough time in the short prep period to establish a comfortable personal pace—much less a protocol—for a swim of any duration. And his clowning zeal, which had masked his clever defensive strategies in earlier events did pay a scant dividend. Most often Dan was not even aware of where B.J. was.

Ultimately, inevitably, Dan touched in long before B.J.. Dan frog-kicked easily to the side of the pool, ascended the ladder and clambered out, shrouded himself in a towel handed him by Ev. To a hefty round of applause he padded off to the locker-room. At the locker-room door, Deb was waiting with a big hug and kiss. She told him she would see him at home after his dinner with Ev.

"Two thirty-one. Great time!" Ev delighted. He started after Dan, then held up. He smiled impishly, stepped back to poolside, and knelt. In due time the thrashing, gasping form touched in. "I, uh, think he's gone somewhere off that away," Ev announced, thumbing after Dan. "Something about going out to dinner? So by now he's ... probably into dessert?" He checked his watch. "Yes, it still is ... September?"

B.J. ducked under the surface. A moment later he surfaced with his reply—a swift spurt of water that doused Ev's spectacles. Ev backed away, removed the glasses, wiped them clean. "And you owe me one-half cup of coffee," he called, pointing. "With sugar and two lumps."

"I'll get you all the lumps you want right here," said B.J.

removing his floral cap.

As the scoreboard flashed the two contestants' raw times for each race, Junior Accountant II Buford Bertram, poised beside Nips, dug out his pocket calculator and went to work. After a bout of swift, deft pecking on its plastic face, he found his answer. "Darn!" he called, frowning, and met Nips's curious eyes. "Oops! For swimming the ratio is—the inverse?"

Nips and the others exchanged glances, nodded obvious yeses. Bertram went back to work. At once Nips spied the executive entourage filing out, faces neutral, and Mossey's as solemn and white as paper. "'In … verse'?" he mumbled.

Now Bertram had recomputed. His scream of *yahooo* came just as the scoreboard flashed 'B.J., 44.5. Dan, 55.5.' Applause broke out, then waned. The crowd held back now, in anxious wait. The figures vanished. Seconds later new ones appeared. 'TWO DAY TOTALS— B.J. BILLINGS, 464.5. DAN DRIVER, 535.5.'

Now the cheers echoed robustly, above sustained applause. In marked contrast to twenty-four hours before, a bevy of reporters accosted Ev. One posed a question, inaudible amid the bustle, and thrust her mike into Ev's face. A second leveled a camera. Ev peeked around, gave an affected shrug. "Ladies, gents, sorry. Uh, I don't know where Dan is. Probably grew tired of waiting for his opponent to finish. Can you blame him?"

Then the half-playful tone shifted into earnest appeal. "No, really, ladies and gentlemen. You want a statement?

Please tell everyone to—or if this is on right now, will all you folks out there please—tune in to our interview? Tonight. Ten-fifteen. Channel 4. Thanks."

"Ten-fifteen. Channel 4," the reporter said. She and the others watched as Ev gave a perky thumbs-up and then vanished into the locker-room. "Now there's a man with a purpose," she said.

"Huh! More like a man with a porpoise! Driver could play for the Marlins or the Dolphins! Hey—how about the Manta Rays?"

This outburst came from near-by. The reporters glanced over to a smiling face sporting a pair of cow eyes and rooster-comb hair. "You guys want to interview me?" Nips said.

The reporter clicked her mike off. "Why would we want to do that?" she said.

The cow-eyes glittered, danced. "Oh, I don't know. Just for the 'halibut'?"

Dan and Ev sat huddled in a dark, secluded corner of the restaurant. While Ev poked emptily at his food, Dan, though bruised and bandaged, showed improved spirits. At one point Dan even threw a playful punch toward his sirloin. "Maybe I should be laying this thing over my eye?" he grinned.

In the time they had been sitting here—half an hour at most—several fans had come over to request autographs and wish Dan luck. To each Dan had vowed to do his best and had cited the interview scheduled later. Each had promised to watch.

"The word *is* getting out." Dan said after fans six and seven, with freshly penned autographs in hand, had walked off to their tables. "My headache is finally going, too. How about that computer? All set to dump its figures?"

Now, finally, Dan leaned across and asked: "So what *is* with the long face Ev?"

Ev cut off a dainty chunk of potato, slid it through a pool of butter. "535.5 to 464.5? Not bad. Not bad at all. If it were to end right now." Ev popped the chunk into his mouth, chewed roundly, swallowed. "Coffee's not bad either," he said. He took a leisurely if neutral sip. "Needs a third lump though." And he obliged.

Dan looked at him. "The battles are won, the war's won. Isn't that how it goes?"

Ev planted his cup down carefully. "Battles won, okay. The first two battles. But the war?" Now he looked over. "No, I've never been one to think that ignorance would help. So maybe I should drop it on you right now rather than during our nightly chalk talk. Besides, you could use the extra sleep. Dan, these figures we've been projecting—the minimum you'll need to pull this thing off?"

"Deep-six them, right Ev?"

"Deep-six is exactly right. 535.5 to 464.5? Our model predicts you at 543.7. That's—eight-point-two more points than you *do* have." He lopped off another chunk of potato. "That's, um, why I've been so quiet," he confessed.

Dan placed down his knife and fork, looked long at him.

"Sorry, Dan. You know my motto: 'Always tell the truth.' The athlete learns far more from reality than from illusion. And far more from defeat than from victory. Right?"

"But I'm *winning*."

"Against the computer, you're not."

Dan continued to stare across the table at him.

"We've got to face the facts, Dan. That pace we predicted would keep you in the lead, but you've slipped slightly below it. The baseball and basketball, especially. We thought you'd pick up a bit more there. The program predicts that, overall, those five events tomorrow are—going to be his."

Dan picked up his silverware, resumed his meal.

"By a lot?" Dan asked after a time.

Ev nodded. "A lot."

"So I'll just follow what some software program says I must. Is that it?"

"If we live in a predetermined universe, Dan—and many of us believe we do—computers are a lot closer to 'right' than we care to admit. Chillingly close. But we've talked about that before."

"If we do. If. A man can't escape what lies ahead? What a machine claims lies ahead?"

"I don't know, Dan. It's been argued for centuries. Machines today are no smarter than those yesterday. And I'll grant you, their only intelligence is what we humans give them. But we can't deny it. As predictors, machines are faster and more sophisticated. *Is* that intelligence?"

"You tell me, Ev. All I know is I'm beating a guy—not

losing to a computer."

"I hope you're right. It could be the old GIGO—'garbage in, garbage out.' If we haven't accounted for all the variables, the system *will* be in error."

"Variables? You bet," Dan said. "You bet."

"Well, I know over-analysis can only make an athlete— and his coach—even more tired than they are, so we'll leave it at that. For now. But I've also got to say that when a sports contest is close, it usually means each opponent is letting the other pace him. That's what he's been doing, Dan. He's crafty at just staying near enough in your events so that he can pull it out in his."

Another patron stepped over and shook hands heartily with Dan and Ev. Ev took the offered napkin, he and Dan both signed it and handed the napkin back. The man nodded a neutral thank-you and returned to his family. There he handed the napkin to a beaming boy, apparently his son.

"Ev, I will dig down deep and win the *war*," Dan said.

Ev nodded. "I know you will," he said. "You will step it up a notch when the going gets tough. And trust me, tomorrow it will. Count on it. Tomorrow you'll be competing against a lot more than a machine. I want you to put on 'the look'—the same game face you had on a moments earlier today.

"The look?" asked Dan.

"Right. The face of an athlete that comes not from the outside but the inside."

Dan thought about it. "Amen," Dan said. "Amen."

CHAPTER
THIRTEEN

Rod Perry was candid. "Can't say I'm surprised by the man's overall lead at all." B.J. was quick to interject, "Look, let me say this to each and every one of you out there that Dan Driver is a fine athlete. I greatly respect his courage, his ability. Above all, I respect what he's trying to do. So many sports call for a range of skills the great majority of us don't own. Take bowling, swimming, tennis. What do *I* know about *them*? Zilch. And five more tomorrow that, yes, I do happen to know a little about. Anyway, to conquer all this 'sport diversity' stuff, I've tossed in a trick of my own. Or make that two."

It was 6:25 p.m. While Dan and Ev were at dinner, B.J. Billings was the special guest of well-known local TV sportscaster Rod Perry. Perry had posed a few questions to B.J. and B.J. had responded with civility. Now, some ten minutes into the interview, B.J. had leaned his eager, earnest, dimpled face forward to announce his goal—to defeat Dan Driver and claim himself 'The Best ALL-Around.' He had faced the camera directly, to speak with deep conviction.

"Trick? Tricks? What sort? More amazing ambidextrous performances?"

B.J. leaned casually back.

"This time tomorrow, you'll see. The world will see. Talk the talk? Walk the walk? Yup, Rod, I've decided, in my own special way, to make Dan Driver's task twice as tough—to push that man to his max."

"You seem very committed. But dare I ask, B.J., are you as confident now as you were yesterday morning, at the kickoff to this all?"

"Believe me I am. I'm a believer. I'd like to see this contest go big-time every bit as much as those two, Driver and Winchell. Just as any athlete across the nation, amateur or pro, would. Yup, I'm from a blue-collar Texas town. I relate to where those two are coming from, what they're saying. I really do."

"It's reported that more than ten thousand fans watched today's competition—more than double yesterday's attendance. And that doesn't include the figures for TV. Tomorrow? The finale? The stadium? By all forecasts, it should be a popular place to be."

"I'll be there. I urge every one of you fans out there watching to join me."

"Seven-fifty is the magic number. Realistically, B.J. — Think you'll catch up?"

"Like the rabbit did to the tortoise."

"But, B.J., the rabbit didn't catch the tortoise."

"That rabbit? He wasn't properly motivated. This one is!"

Perry smiled. "You don't have to tell us."

"I could moonwalk to victory if I had to. Hey, that's not a bad idea," B.J. mused. "I mean, gravity's a lot weaker up there.

"On the moon," grinned Perry.

"Right. Sure make everybody lighten up. And ain't this what it's all about?"

"Well, looking purely at the numbers, there's little doubt.

Tomorrow should be your day. You an ex-decathlon athlete and the whole affair culminating with six track events.

"That's—a mini-decathlon," B.J. added. He grinned. "Oh, hey—you mind if I, uh, break in with a personal message?"

"Be our guest."

B.J. looked directly into the camera, grinned out, tapped a thumb solidly against his NFL sweatshirt. "Diana, this Bud—I mean me—is for you. Keep showing up. But come by yourself. Give that Ruff character you've been using as an excuse to see me a quick exit. Your chance will come."

He glanced awkwardly back over at Perry. "That's my message," he said.

"And a wonderful one. No doubt to some aspiring athlete out there who'll want his—or is it her?—chance to excel, too?"

B.J. smiled. "Sort of like that," he said.

"Also tomorrow, another sport you just might happen to know a little about."

"Football, you mean. Yeah, just a little."

"A little. Well, we all wish you luck." The two men leaned across and clasped hands. "Folks, our very own B.J. Billings, All-Pro linebacker. All Everything. A guy with every reason to believe that by our next interview twenty-four hours from now, he'll be a richer, happier, more 'ALL-around' man. B.J., we do thank you. We'll let you head home for some well-deserved sleep. This is Rod Perry, Channel 12, live and exclusive here with B.J. Billings. All of you watching out there, keep up those exercises. And tune in tomorrow to see

B.J.."

After Deb applied fresh bandages, Dan lay exhausted on the couch. He and Ev had returned from dinner after their brief strategy session. Now Dan had begun to nod off. The interviewer and crew would not arrive for another two hours, so Deb and Ev let Dan sleep. He would need the energy tomorrow. He would need every *ounce* of energy he could muster. Deb was in the kitchen with Lori. Jeff was already down for the night.

The den clock precisely showed 10:15. "Thirty seconds," called the producer. The two figures sat rigidly on the couch, the artificial lights spilling brilliantly down across their fixed faces.

"And ... and ... The producer signaled with a descending finger. The reporter spoke in a tone hushed, earnest, as if in the presence of something truly momentous.

"Ladies and gentlemen, sports reporter Don James here. I'm coming to you tonight from the quiet, modest, suburban home of Mr. Dan Driver, a man who has made quite a bit of noise of late. By now most of you know that Dan is the 'Mystery Man' who has come out of virtually nowhere to build quite an impressive lead over B.J. Billings in this contest taking our city and state by storm this long holiday weekend. With Dan tonight is Ev Winchell, like Dan a local tax accountant and a man currently doubling—very well, by all accounts—as Dan's coach. 'The Best ALL Around,' their joint brainchild designed to discover the truly most gifted athlete, is enticing them to risk a substantial amount of hard-earned cash—fifty thousand dollars, to be exact. Gentlemen, we welcome both of you to 'Night Spot.' First, let me ask it. *Why* such a contest?"

Dan and Ev traded glances.

"He's the athlete, the doer. So I've got to contribute, too." With this, Ev cleared his throat, shifted for a moment, peered anxiously into the camera, and began:

"This, um, whole thing, Don, is, um, a p-protest. A protest against a trend not just in sports but in our world as a whole. Virtually every sports celebrity today is so because ... because he or she has mastered one sub-sub-area of competition and that area alone. Specialization infects all sport. Why were the Olympic games established? Why have they endured for thousands of years? To celebrate success in a *diversity* of sports, in that same country that invented democracy. I don't wish to slight today's fine athletes, but what this means is that while they specialize and do their narrower and narrower thing the rest of us—the overwhelming rest with jobs, families, mortgages, and broader interests—must be content to sit home and watch. The Super Bowl? World Series? NBA finals? This is what athletics has come to. Hundreds do and millions watch."

"Is there a precedent for your idea?" James asked. "I mean, things like this just don't come out of the blue. Or do they? Where did ... "

Ev nodded, and took pause. He had begun with visible nervousness, but toward the end his statement had taken on tones bold and decisive—tones tinged with protest themselves. Ev paused a moment more and went on:

"To be honest, Don, this is from frustration. And the idea is far more Dan's than mine. I guess, if we had to, we could compare it to what many viewers out there know to be the theory of multiple intelligences—social, spatial, musical, poetic, even athletic—so popular with mind researchers today. We've taken the 'athletic' brand of intelligence and defined genius as the ability to excel in the broadest possible way."

Ev took a deep breath and went on.

"The superstar specialists may be fun for us all to watch. However, today's hallmark—specialization—not only makes us less and less aware of the big picture of the world we live in, but brings a fear of judging who or what is right. Look around. For most of us, life is a bye. Our citizen groups, our families, even our churches—we're afraid to speak out or act on any issue before we get the 'go-ahead from the experts.' *Do* I control my world or *don't* I? Dan and I want to break out of that.

Ev exhaled a long breath, and peeked over to Dan.

"Uh, I'm in full agreement," Dan said, with a smile.

Ev nodded earnestly now. "But where this especially impacts us is in our kids. Even coaches like to let a kid play only one position on a team. It makes managing and winning easier. But when a kid begins to specialize, look at what he loses. A big kid in fifth grade will, of course, play center in basketball. He'll never learn guard skills. When he reaches high school and the other kids— the dribblers and outside shooters—catch up to him in size, he'll be a relic, a fossil, a monument to fifth-grade sports. Similarly, the kid stuck in right field who never pitches or plays shortstop will not develop, either. Make a pitcher a catcher for a while, he'll understand pitching more. Wasn't Babe Ruth—a truly great hitter—a pitcher? What is better is to play a kid at five or six positions. He'll come to understand the game. Mentally and physically, Don, the kid who plays multiple positions simply develops multiple skills. And we want to extend that notion to more sports, and then to life itself."

"What he means, Don, is that the eventual winner of this contest is not one man or one woman but *all* of us," Dan put in. "That single, legitimate 'Best All Around'? He or she may even be looking in right now, doubtless an unknown. Let's face it, who today gets credit for doing *many* things well?"

"I see your point," said James. "When I think of my own job, it makes sense." He glanced off at one of the technicians, who flashed a hearty thumbs-up in assent. James grinned, nodded deeply. "About time someone gave credit where credit is due," he added.

"Better yet, put it where the rubber meets the road—on the field," said Ev. "But we would like to honor all sports. It was just over a century ago—yes, the late 1800's—that sports as we now know it came to be. In 1875 the first annual Kentucky Derby was run at Churchill Downs. In 1876—the same year as the famous Custer Massacre—the National League was born. The following year saw the first Wimbledon competition—purely an amateur event back then. The year after saw the first annual White House Easter Egg Roll begun by President Hayes. In 1891, a man named James Naismith invented his weird 'hoops' game—as a pastime to keep students busy between football and baseball seasons. Since 1894 the Stanley Cup has been with us, and 1895 saw the invention of volleyball. In 1896 the first modern Olympic games were held in Athens, then four years later— the turn of the new century—in Paris. So we think a centennial— wow, now a millennial—statement honoring all sport, for all time, is extremely fitting."

James nodded. "Uh, right," he said. "I can tell that you're far more than just an enthusiast."

As Ev nodded, James assumed a graver expression. "Now to your problems Dan. Apparently you are in an exhausted physical condition—and one of those bandages, I'm told, hides a nasty cut. You feel strong enough to compete tomorrow? We've all seen that collision many times on replay, and …"

"I've seen the replays. I hold no grudge." Dan lifted a pair of fingers, tapped both bandages gingerly. "As far as I'm concerned, it was just an unfortunate slip."

"One of several 'slips,'" threw in Ev.

At this odd remark, both Dan and Jim eyed Ev curiously.

"Okay. Now's not the time to elaborate," Ev said. "But let me say that Dan here is competing fair and square. And he's going to win it the same way. Strength, agility, stamina—

and above all, desire—Dan's got 'em in spades. And Dan's got—" Now Ev reached down off the side of the couch and brought up a wooly form—family support. "Dan—from your daughter."

And with due ceremony Ev deposited Cuddles into the surprised Dan's arms.

Dan clutched the bear, peeked out. "Uh, what can I say? Some folks put pennies in their shoes. Others put dollars in banks. I … hug this little guy."

James looked at Dan, then at Ev. "Now I do understand why there's no 'I' in 'team,'" he smiled.

"Right. But … there sure is one in 'family.'" Dan leaned forward, peered into the camera. "Where your family goes, you go," he said. "And where your family should go, you should go first. No matter what the cost."

"And speaking of family, we wish to thank all our supporters." Now Ev, too, peered earnestly into the lens. "Nips, Detra, all you other hard-working A.H. guys and gals out there—thanks."

James smirked broadly. "Which brings us, gentlemen, to the final topic— money. I'll be frank. There's been criticism. Don't you think that pricing this contest out of the average Joe's ballpark—and fifty thousand G's does just that—lets only the rich athlete participate?"

"Don, we're accountants. Ev and I are realistic. We know the ways of the dismal science. We put a solid price on to draw serious contenders."

"Realistic in this way," Ev elaborated. "A cheap

investment would be a meaningless one. That's exactly what Dan and I learned a few weeks back in the qualifiers, where the fees we charged—a nominal five bucks per entry to cover facility rentals and refs—brought in far too many weekend athletes. Don, over *four hundred* showed up. Yes, this is a democracy. Yes, we wanted to be fair to all. But we were mighty lucky not to see a stroke or heart attack. Let me put it this way. Would you take time out and train like crazy and then endure three even crazier, grueling days of what Dan is going through right now for some pat on the back or tin cup? But, yes, we admit that the money aspect does bother us. We are open to suggestion. If anyone out there has any idea how to make this thing easier or fairer, please let us know."

The producer then signaled.

"I hope any and all of you folks looking in will. So there you have it, fans. Dan Driver and Ev Winchell, local celebrities of late. Gentlemen, I thank you for sharing your time with us tonight. Dan, you've certainly got your work cut out for you tomorrow. And Ev—best of luck in the coach's box. Don James, Channel 4 News, reporting live for Sunday's 'Night Spot' from the cozy den of a man who—yesterday a relative nobody—tomorrow night, if dreams still do come true, will be a truly richer, truly more blessed, truly 'ALL-around' superstar. Tomorrow's sequence at Camelback Stadium, capped by the mini-decathlon, will be carried in its entirety here on Channel 4, starting at 8 a.m., with cut-ins both local and national. We hope you'll all be looking in—or, even better, heading out to the stadium for yourselves.

Sports fans, good night."

The camera pulled back. The building notes of a victory march as the smiling face of Don James receded into a broader shot beside Ev and Dan, and then the screen flashed onto the image of a small, button-eyed bear.

CHAPTER
FOURTEEN

The sun had lifted like a huge, bold globe, casting the structure's long, mighty shadow to the west. Already the sky was a healthy blue. The air was sparkling, clear. The stadium lay empty, awaiting the day.

Dan was already off, having bid his family good-bye. Deb would join him as soon as Grandma arrived. Lori lifted up the box of Special K; slowly she tilted the box until a heaping amount of flakes slid into her bowl.

"Honey, put some back. Please."

"Yeeee-esss, Mommy."

"Whew." Debra peered outside. A solitary robin hopped across the lawn, then vaulted again like a long-jumper behind a hedge. Another bird—a meadowlark—swooped in smoothly, then high-stepped about, flicking its wings, preening. Deb pressed her nose onto the cool pane, viewed a lightening patch of sky. This is getting to be a habit, she thought. But today would be … the last day. And then what?

She took a meditative sip of coffee, turned to a rustle behind.

"Hi, Grandma," said Lori.

"Morning, Sweetheart."

"Good morning Mom," said Deb.

"Hi, Honey," answered Grandma. "Thank you for the call last night. The interview was great, but Dan really looked beat up. I hope he'll be all right."

"He seemed better this morning, but you know—he doesn't complain much. And you know, Mom, a few days ago I found that book Dan had lent to Ev—the one by that famous basketball coach from Duke called *Leading With the Heart*. I … took some time to go through it."

"And?"

"And, yes. I do think I better understand where Dan's coming from, just what it all means. Men *are* one crazy species, but—"

"You know Deb, I hate to say it, but taking chances can be mighty dangerous in today's world."

"That it can. But it can also be—no, Mother, it *is*—the most rewarding thing of all."

Grandma and Deb stood side by side before the kitchen window. Grandma lifted a hand, placed it gently on Deb's shoulder. "Uh-huh. It's going to be a beautiful day. I just know it."

OUTDOOR DAY

It was nearly 8 a.m. Already thousands of people had passed through the turnstiles beside the huge poster set above the opposing action photos of B.J. emerging shark-like from the depths and of Dan throwing a punch.

"On locally, sure, but I'd much rather be out here to see this," said one fan. "All across the state, too," said his pal. "Heard it be might even be mentioned on Monday Night Football. Would you believe it—*our* contest?"

Parading into the stadium in a steady line was a cross-section of many people. Even before 7:30 a harried Mr. Duntoot had arrived, to point proudly at the photo of Dan, thumbs-down the photo of B.J., and then punt an invisible football and grin privately to a middle-aged pal.

A few minutes later, a group of young people clad in Chompy McBurger outfits gestured mockingly at the stadium menu displayed at one of its fast-food counters. "Talk about your hot dogs—plenty of them out here today," quipped Chip, the drive-in comedian. Close behind, Coaches Wiley and Sims moved through, nodding absorbedly, anticipation lighting their faces. In their wake stepped a considerable contingent of bulky ex-footballers, ex-teammates of Dan, to include tailback Willy Gant, clad in a handsome letter jacket. Moments later, striding through the entrance was filmmaker Carnegie Bombe, flanked by his assistants. At first view of the playing field, Bombe strutted out into the sunlight, and there among the seats framed the view professionally with his hands and lent several intellectual remarks.

At exactly 7:50 Mitchell Mossey and party sauntered through, to a section of choice seats reserved on the fifty-yard-line. There they sat, biding casually as the minutes ticked. The supervisor engaged in idle chat and once threw back his white hair and offhandedly shrugged his shoulders, but as he gestured to make a point about the fine view they all had of the scoreboard not a few noticed that his fingers were crossed, rigidly. Not far behind, bobbing above the crowd was Ruff Hogan, proudly escorting Diana Hansen. As they passed through the turnstile the crowd gawked, grew hushed, parted respectfully. Ruff lent Diana a playful poke in the side with his splinted finger. She giggled, poked him back. They made a lovely pair, these two. Nor could the crowd easily close ranks behind them, for in their wake hulked Lew and the entire membership of the Armbuster Iron and Spa, a squad of two dozen super-burly individuals, including two women, each walking more side to side than forward, staring around with jaws clenched and eyes keen and focused.

Not far behind moved a rather tall group of men in their late twenties, nearly a dozen, led through the turnstiles by another tall, thin figure, Coach Blank. Dan's high-school basketball team had convened to cheer him on. Just behind Coach Blank and his former players walked a couple obviously impressed by the huge facility. It was the first time that 'Bart' Bartholomew Winchell, Ev's brother, and wife Beverly had ever set foot in a professional stadium. Now the two took pause to gawk about, both overwhelmed by the sheer grandeur of the site and the buzzing enthusiasm of the crowd. Short and slender like his brother, Bart smiled easily but exhibited a marked tenseness. Was it the gene pool? Or was it a symptom of his keen appreciation for what would be happening here today?

At exactly 7:58 some forty figures hastened through, toting banners, signs, and other paraphernalia. "Told you! Told you!" a poking, urging Nips in his rooster-comb hairdo exalted as they convened before the photo of Dan. He cast a scoffing finger at the photo beside. "*He'll* be overtaxed today!" came the quip, inciting chuckles. Yet a glimpse at their signs and banners—'B.J.'LL BEE 2 MUCH 2 BARE!' and 'THIS JOCK'S NO JOKE!' printed on a cutout of B.J.'s grinning profile—showed precisely the opposite sentiment.

What was up? Had these A.H. faithful endured a sharp, solid talking-to and had swung their loyalties back? They had simply recognized the powers that be. Was some ruse in the making? Perhaps so, for A.H. Adams himself, grinning in exuberant anticipation now led his group out under the sunlight and down to yet another reserved section at the fifty-yard-line—a site just above and behind the executive entourage.

Ev smiled as Dan's family approached. Ev stepped over to greet them, taking in Jeffy's tiny t-shirt with its blue-lettered logo 'I LUV MY DADA.' Between Deb and her mother Lori edged out. 'ME, TOO,' her shirt read, in letters softly pink.

A local high-school marching band high-stepped smartly in one end zone. They had already serenaded the crowd for fifteen minutes and now they engaged in crisp, mark-time wait as a trio of twirlers performed preliminaries on the equally deep, green turf of the field beyond. At once cheers erupted. The scoreboard was flashing. A moment later the PA system broke out, first in fits and starts of static, then in an echoing ring, finally in bold, near-smooth intonation. "*Wel* ... come ... *sports* ... fans." With this the announcer launched into his scripted prelude.

Then, on cue, the music and prelude fell away. A collection of referees marched smartly, single-file, out to mid-field. As the announcer gave the introductions, each took a step forward to a ripple of polite applause and a burst of playful boos. Then the refs retired to the sidelines, to gather in a final collective huddle.

In the tunnel behind the east end zone stood Dan and Ev. A courier peeked in. "Two minutes," he announced. "Quite a crowd. Filling up fast. They're saying already twenty thousand."

A long, quiet moment passed. At once Dan and Ev traded glances.

"Crunch time," Ev said. "For a very special athlete. And, I hope, his special coach. The world's waiting for us."

Dan stared off. Now the band in the far end zone had re-erupted, this time into a spirited fight song. From above, from beyond, from all around sounded yells, whistles, and cheers.

Dan smiled.

"That's the spirit," said Ev. "This may be his house, sure, and game day's not the time for speechmaking, but let me say one thing. Remember how carefully we've gone through it all. The skills each event calls for, the probable times and performances, the pacing. You've had your two bowls of cereal. I've had my gallon of Maalox. You know. I know. He knows. Every one of those screaming thousands out there knows that public worship or not, *he's* the challenger, Dan. He's behind. He's got to push *you* off the mountain. Pressure's on *him*." He wiped his already moist forehead, took a deep gulp, re-scanned his thick-sheaved clipboard. "If it comes to any real crisis out there, just relax. Remember how easily 'team-think' can slip away into 'me-think.' It happened to him yesterday. Let's not let it happen to us today. And anger? Let's not use that as a divider but as a unifier. Let's not help him."

Dan nodded.

"And as far as you not being able to sleep much last night—who can blame you?—there's an upside as well. You know that Slovenian bicyclist we were talking about who won that three-thousand-mile race? For months beforehand, to prepare, he denied himself sleep for intervals of two days at a time."

"His lack of sleep *helped* him?"

"It did, yes."

"How?'

"It prevented him from hallucinating during the race."

"Great, I'll keep that in mind!"

The two men smiled. Dan extended his hand. Ev met the gesture halfway, then withdrew. "Uh, right after?" he suggested. "Let's save it for—the victory?"

Dan smiled again. "For the victory," Dan agreed.

In the west tunnel B.J. Billings stood beside Coach Teeler and his aides. The courier had come and gone. The press had snapped parting shots and had departed for the stands. Teeler slapped B.J. on the back, loosely. "Won't even have to break a sweat out there, big guy. Fifty big ones waiting. You—did get enough sleep last night?"

B.J. grinned. "Plenty."

As the last note was played the band marched off the field and infiltrated the stands. From end zone to end zone the grassy field appeared conspicuously vacant. The crowd fell hushed. A silence lingered—heavy, anticipative, electric.

At once a referee stalked smartly out onto the center of the field. He took pause, blew a single shrill blast on his whistle, gestured to each end zone. "Ladies and gentlemen—our two contestants," shrilled the PA announcer. "Let's give a big, rousing hand to—Dan Driver and B.J. Billllll-lings!"

There came an explosion of cheers and applause. The band broke into "You've Got To Be a Football Hero." From the tunnel just beyond each end zone the two parties emerged. Fans in the front rows, then gradually fans up, up to the very nosebleed section, came to their feet. On a signal from Nips, one group—the A.H. Adams employees—rose in unison and hoisted signs. To the refs convened on the cinder track craning their necks to peer up at the resulting clamor, the signs were loyally, adamantly pro-A.H. 'B.J. ALL THE WEIGH!' urged one. 'THE BEST DEPARTMENT IS BILLINGS!' and 'BILLINGS? MUCH MORE THAN A COWTOWN!' proclaimed others. Bosses and execs in the front row peered back and grinned genially.

But soon a far mightier cheer of amusement erupted from vaster numbers farther up. For when the backs of these same signs were freshly unveiled now, they told of a radically opposing sentiment. 'Go DANNNN' and 'RACE, DRIVER!' exhorted two. 'DAN'LL CONQUER BY ALL ACCOUNTS!' promised a third. 'B.J. = BIG JOKE!' taunted yet another.

Indeed, to the greater number of fans and photographers present it appeared that the entire firm of A.H. Adams and Associates—its front-row echelon of golden parachutists included—was solidly behind Dan. Nips stood up to wild applause and boldly uncloaked and hoisted a huge, psychedelically hued sign shaped like a giant sock. 'SOCK IT TO 'EM, B.J.!,' its one side urged. To those vaster numbers behind he revealed the cutout's more flamboyant backside— 'DE-FEET 'EM, DAN!'

Next, Nips blew up and released a two-tiered balloon shaped like Dan's head crowned by laurel leaves of victory and a gilded scale. 'KEEP WEIGH A-HEAD, DAN!' it implored. Hilariously, volleyball-style, the balloon was tapped employee to employee, to finally bump its merry way down to the front row, where it rolled over and met stony silence. Next, Nips distributed a cluster of brilliant pennants. 'DANNY—How about a GREAT Accounting?' read one crafted like a grate. 'FIGURE FIRMLY ON DAN—THE WELL-ROUNDED BEST!' proclaimed another contoured as a curvaceous torso. Amid its applause for the two athletes and their coaches, the crowd hooted, whistled, and grinned with delight.

The two parties had convened at the fifty-yard-line to trade handshakes and stand by wordlessly. Chat would have been impossible. The hubbub was overwhelming. Finally the clamor began to subside. The band stopped its wild oompahs and chaotic blares. The PA system broke out again. "Gentlemen, yes, good luck! Ladies and gentlemen, our first event of the day will be—the 3.1 mile run."

The two groups left the field for the sidelines beside the cinder track. Now Dan and B.J. shed their sweats, high-stepped about and whirled their arms for a few moments, then took position. A figure sauntered over, poised the starting pistol. Dan glanced up, smiled and stared.

He rolled his eyes, grinned impishly. "Why the look? Ain't loaded," Stockwell said. "Nope, don't pay me a heckuva lot, but it is my field. Uh—you guys ready?"

Stockwell raised the gun, clenched his teeth, and fired.

The two started off. For a time the urgings went on, then ebbed, and ultimately transformed into a sequence of rhythmic claps instigated by a wildly grinning figure with a rooster-comb hairdo. At once all around Nips low mooing erupted, capped by bursts of jolly laughter. Meanwhile, on the track, B.J. assumed the early lead, with Dan dropping some ten yards back and hanging on.

Of the thousands bearing witness and of the many, many more thousands watching via the modern miracle of TV, there was one who kept his eye especially fixed on B.J.. Ever since Dan and B.J. had shed their sweats for the event, Ev had been scrutinizing the back of B.J.'s right calf. Now as the two runners rounded the curve and entered the straightaway to finish the initial lap, he had ample chance to view from short yards away. The huge form trotting by left him mumbling—"There? Tireless energy? All-P-Pro? Ambi—? No *wonder* he pulled it off! But how could I ever prove—?" Ev then gave a reassuring thumbs-up to the second runner trotting past. "Can't be," he mumbled again, denying the evidence plainly before his eyes.

By the end of lap four B.J. Billings was starting to fade.

Simply, line-backing was not distance-running and, whether to intimidate or by sheer, proud mistake, B.J. had set far too swift a pace. As he, between gasps, gave an unfaltering thumbs-up, Dan swung out and, to a considerable burst of applause, took the lead. B.J. ran along doggedly behind and then, in a burst of stubborn energy, shot by Dan. The crowd roared. As the two rounded the curve and gained the straightaway, Nips began to wave his sign vigorously, directly in Dan's vision. As Dan crossed the original starting line, he grinned over at Nips and hoisted a fist. Nips stood open-mouthed, enthralled.

By the first turn of lap seven, roughly the halfway point, B.J. was fading badly. Dan kept up the pace, and saw his lead steadily widen. In time the clapping stopped. The crowd sat back, squinted at the sun, the shade, the cooler dark of the tunnels, the wind-whipped flags at the structure's crest. Applause built again as a hard-blowing Dan crossed the line at 19:14—some six minutes ahead of his rival.

A few seconds after B.J.'s finish, the scoreboard flashed. The accountants laid aside their graphics, fished out their calculators. They punched, peered, and then broke out jubilantly. Meanwhile B.J., head hanging down, was panting, hands cupped on his knees, confiding to a somber Teeler. "Okay okay, my pre-season regimen—them windsprints and nothing but—don't cut it here. Football's where I make my bucks, running east and west. So now I'm supposed to be a wide receiver?"

The scores flashed. On the inverse, hundred-point-share

system, Dan had won handily, 56.5 to 43.5.

Teeler shrugged. "It's like we figured. Let him kill himself for a few piddly points. Yours'll be here soon enough. Big guy, we're right on course."

And B.J., his gasps subsiding now, grinned up in spite. "Exactly right," he winked.

"Think that goofy cluster of steroids is going to pull this one out? Huh!"

With this, Ruff Hogan pointed his splinted finger toward the weights assembled at field center. Diana, too, stared and moved closer to Ruff.

On the sideline the men and their coaches conferred. "Okay, Dan, we both know what you can do here. But just keep it close," Ev advised. "Don't try anything dramatic, like lifting the Northern Hemisphere? Hernias can cut into our plan big time."

Dan nodded, and strode out. He began the first series, the best of a trio of bench presses, and managed a hoist of three hundred and five pounds. B.J. countered with a lift of some eighty pounds more. Dan increased his second lift to three-fifteen. B.J. upped his to four-twenty. When Dan went to three-twenty five, hoisted, and held it to a slight wobble, B.J. increased his own to four-forty, with a final straining, tooth-gritting effort inciting a burst of enthusiastic oohs and aahs and an explosion of flashbulbs. The two men shook out their arms, hands, legs, and walked about.

Next was the squat lift. B.J. approached the bar, made

ready. Suddenly the accountants' section erupted into screams, whoops, mad applause—so much so that B.J. stood back as one ref blew his whistle and gestured the group to calm down.

His effort was in vain. The noise persisted. For along the track two slender figures were displaying bright red blazers. The front of one blazer read 'B,' the other 'J.' Now the executive group rose to welcome them warmly.

The pair climbed up and found seats. "Hot one," Miller remarked. "Sure is," said Wells. Together they removed their blazers—which spurred the group behind to break out into a renewed clamor. For the backs of their shirts read, respectively, 'GO!' and 'DAN!' Now the two craned their necks. "Mossey suggested we do it," confided Miller to his fellow-workers. "The fronts, he means," quipped Wells. "Obviously," said Miller. "Obviously," said Wells.

The competition resumed. For his best effort B.J. managed an even six hundred pounds, Dan about a hundred and thirty pounds less. After another five-minute break the men moved on to the triad's finale, the dead lift. Here B.J. topped Dan's high of five hundred and fifty pounds with a tremendous, face-straining hoist of seven hundred and ten pounds, an effort which drew the most enthusiastic reaction of the day. And when the score was flashed—B.J. 56.9. Dan 43.1.—B.J. strutted about with hands clenched high in triumph. "So I just made up for that distance run. That's all we're after at this point, right?"

Teeler gave a happy nod. "Right on schedule, big guy.

Right on schedule."

Dan and B.J. stood in football gear. Dan had been first to enter from the tunnel. He trotted to field center clad in a uniform from Lakefield boasting his college number, 16. Two groups gave him an especially warm welcome— the workers at A.H. Adams, who now were beginning to receive more than a few icy stares from the executives just below, and former and current coaches and players of the Lakefield Boosters Club—now over two hundred strong. Only when Dan had come to stand at the fifty-yard line and drop the arm he had used in greeting had the groups lent one final burst of cheers and retaken their seats.

With the entry of number 66, the entire stadium had virtually rocked. Fans of all persuasions had come to their feet to whistle, clap, whoop, shriek, stamp with delight. Ripple upon ripple of applause echoed as B.J. jogged easily out into the sunlight and then onto end zone. Then with a frolicking impulse, he leapt up and wrapped his fingers around the crossbar, there to hang, monkey-like, for a long, unnerving moment before dropping into a playful, madcap somersault and finishing off by running in place and growling loudly. The announcer had been equally unreserved:

'—even kicked field goals his first year in college, folks, so we expect a truly inspired gridiron performance from everybody's professional out here today! Again, how about a very warm welcome. Folks—give it up for our very own BEEE-JAYYYY BILLLL-INGS!'

With this the entire structure shook—screams, cheers,

whistles, shrieks—even Dan at mid-field applauding along with the rest, followed by a massive, collective retaking of seats amid happy mumbles of anticipation.

Football in hand, a ref strode out. After Dan and B.J. shook hands at field center, he gestured to Dan to face one goal. He tossed Dan the ball, blew his whistle, and signaled for Dan to start.

Dan gauged, then punted. The ball lofted as a high spiral, hung for a time, and descended just short of the ten. B.J. punted, equally adeptly. Both men's second efforts were likewise virtually the same. Dan's third effort drew a chorus of groans. He shanked the ball out of bounds near the thirty.

B.J. took the ball, concentrated, kicked—a lazy, lofting effort, which rose higher and higher, seemingly floated for a moment, and spun down like an angry rocket shell deep behind the end zone. "Nice kick," Dan called. B.J. turned, bowed nobly. "Oughta see how I do with my *left* foot," he grinned.

Next, the referee placed the ball on the forty. A wiry athlete in shorts trotted out from the sidelines. He gripped the ball off the turf. "Side!" he called, and Dan, set like a receiver on the makeshift line of scrimmage, raced off to the man's "Hut!" Ten yards down the field Dan cut sharply for the sidelines. The pass came without so much as a wobble and smacked onto Dan's outstretched hands. Dan cushioned the ball gently, pulled it into his body, and turned up field, to applause.

B.J. lined up—"Side!... Hut!"—and did the same. Each man ran nine pass patterns—sides, mids, hooks—and then capped his performance with a fly pattern. Dan managed to snare eight passes. One thrown slightly behind him he juggled and lost out of bounds. B.J. caught six. While two struck him in the hands and caromed away, his spectacular, one-handed grab of a poorly thrown ball earned him redemption in the eyes of crowd and judges alike.

In the third phase of the football event, a corps of receivers lined up on each side to run the prescribed pass patterns. Another athlete trotted out, ball in hand. He hiked the ball to Dan and B.J., who each threw a series of passes. "This thing is getting kinda close. Think I'll stick with my right hand." B.J. announced. While Dan hit every receiver but one, B.J. tossed the ball hard, far too hard, and in one case even down onto the turf. When one receiver dropped a hard-flung pass, B.J. protested comically, and was awarded the point. But as a quarterback, Dan did markedly better. It was during the fourth and final phase of the football event— field-goal kicking—that B.J. came to show his amazingly broad talent. Again using his right leg, B.J. kicked four successive field goals—from the 10-, 20-, 30-, and 40-yard lines. A final attempt from the forty-five cleared the crossbar with room to spare, but sliced just left of the upright. "Four for five!" the announcer exclaimed after the feat. "B.J., forget linebacking! From now on, you're our Dromedaries' kicker!"

Dan also kicked well, hitting from the 10, 20, and 30 yard lines but falling short on his final two efforts. To applause,

Dan trotted to the sidelines, where Ev stopped nibbling his thumbnail long enough to clap him on the shoulder pad. For a long moment Dan stared at the ground, in silent wait. At once Ev gave a dejected cry—"Oh, boy!" Dan followed his finger to the scoreboard—'B.J. 55.20. Dan 44.80.'

Then, finally, it happened. The mounting pressure of today, yesterday, the day before, the week preceding finally overtook both coaches. "Ten measly points!" Teeler gawked, incredulously. "This guy's a football pro! *All-Pro!*"

He hurled down his clipboard, stomped on it.

Ev leaned in. "No, cuz you've got too measly a player," he mocked.

"Measly," Ev repeated. "Meeeee—"

"We want a recount! A re-contest! A re-do of this whole setup! Being a football player's a lot more than—" and he gestured effeminately—"pass, punt, and kick!" He glared at Ev. "And what do you mean 'measly' - measly!"

"Okay? Then how about—weasly!"

Their faces hung a foot apart, jaws clenched, eyes snapping.

"This thing *is* purposely biased against football!"

"Hold your cloppy Clydesdales, Pigskin Breath! You agreed! In writing! And so what about baseball? Walks, line drives, double plays? How many double-play balls, curves, and change-ups did that super-size goof of yours have a chance to flub? How many?"

"Head-on tackling? *Real* crunch time? Defensive alignments? Covering the second back out on the option pass?" continued Teeler.

"Court sense in basketball? Like not charging? Mirroring the offense? Dribbling, the art of passing or faking, posting up? The old Dean Smith Four Corners? The McGuire Marquette Wheel?" retorted Ev.

"And that stuff you're always feeding *your* pencil-pushing clown! Coffee my percolator! Caramel Gatorade laced with steroids! Il-legal!" Teeler turned to the referees, beseeching. "We WIN!"

"Speaking of caramel, your *brain*—"

The two squared off, then mutually lunged. Teeler bent back, swung at Ev's nose. Ev ducked, and tackled Teeler. The two met in an awkward spin, and toppled to the ground. A whistle erupted shrilly. A trio of striped shirts waded in. One stepped back, threw a yellow flag. Another groped for the assailants. The third retreated, waved his arms. "Uh, time *out*." he called. Now at the scuffling and rolling, a sea of whistles erupted. "Gentlemen, *gentlemen*!" the trio of refs called, waving their arms briskly. "TIME OUT!"

The crowd was roaring as the two were separated. Dan ran over and grabbed Ev. B.J. picked up Teeler. The two gave each other a scornful look as the crowd continued to cheer.

CHAPTER
FIFTEEN

In the center of the field stood the ring, complete with a thick mat, heavy-gauge ropes, and two still-puffing wrestlers. The gong sounded. Again the crowd came alive. The two men left their corners for this, the second period of the wrestling competition.

After an interval of slow, calculated circling, B.J. attacked. In a sudden, quick burst he grabbed Dan, hoisted him up off the mat, flung him down, and leapt cat-like. Just in time Dan rolled out and regained his feet. Again B.J. charged, this time pausing just short of contact to unleash a leg-sweep toward Dan's knees. Dan avoided the blow, and lunged. The two toppled, spinning, as the ref, whistle tight in his teeth, dropped to his knees and watched for the pin. Although B.J. lay atop him, Dan managed to roll onto his stomach. There he rested. The ref signaled two points—a takedown—for B.J.. The points registered on the board, to cheers, groans, applause.

For a moment the two men simply lay there, gasping. At once Dan slowly, steadily hunched his spine up, regained his knees, and commenced to crab-crawl, with B.J.'s full weight atop. B.J. bore down, twisting Dan's shoulders, trying to turn Dan onto his back again. Dan struggled, kicked mightily, and broke free. The ref signaled a one-point escape. Immediately B.J. closed. Dan turned, and met B.J. obliquely. Again the two collapsed in a heap, each bustling for the advantage.

The gong sounded. The ref ducked in, and broke them apart. Slowly each rolled away, regained his feet, and trudged wearily, gasping, hands on hips, back to their corners.

Sporting a second bandage of his own now—this one across his nose—Ev surveyed Dan with concern. "Dan, where we're going now you just can't shove into any computer." With a cool sponge he blotted the sweat from Dan's eyes and face. "It's here that some athletes have it. Most don't. But the Best ALL Around? He *has* to have it."

Dan looked to him.

"Guts," Ev said.

Dan stood, head tilted back, mouth open, gulping. Dan lowered his gaze and peered across—to encounter a similarly gasping B.J.. At once Dan caught B.J.'s eyes. The eyes showed a gauging perplexity, and swung away. Dan smirked.

The gong sounded. The two rose, shook their arms, stepped out and slowly circled each other in this, the third and final period. Yells, cheers, pleas erupted. Dan faked a rush. B.J. backed off nimbly, then did the same. At once B.J., still retreating, glanced to the crowd. He paused, moved ritually down into a lineman's three-point stance, loudly panted cadence—"Hut! ... Hut!"—and charged. Dan leaned forward. The two collided, and tumbled. Dan rose to a knee, then twisted away.

In a flash B.J. was atop, shoving. Dan pinched his shoulders into his chest, bridged his neck, bent to one side, and came back up on one knee, gulped a huge mouthful of air, steeled himself, and twisted. To his surprise he met no resistance. He scrambled up, peered about warily. Then the attack descended, from behind. Dan whirled to meet it, tumbled stomach-down onto the mat, and once more found himself crab-walking with the full weight of B.J. atop him. Amid all the faraway commotion Dan heard—"it goes, that big lead of Driver's, and we may now have a brand *new.*"

Dan pushed his face onto the mat, gathered himself, shoved—and again met log-like resistance. With a mighty effort Dan managed to lift the bulk away, and spun out. A point, the ref motioned, to cheers. B.J. backed off. "Two points for one? My kinda trade. Any day," he gasped. "Third down? Time for a blitz! Hut!" He barged in.

This time Dan caught the brunt of B.J.'s leading shoulder, toppled backwards, and managed to turn onto his side just as the weight descended. Dan shoved, vainly. Dan steeled himself, shoved again. B.J.'s weight scarcely budged. "Nice afternoon, ain't it?" came a mumble in Dan's ear. Dan peered about, spied a niche of daylight, and with a quick, mighty effort twisted up, out, and broke free. The ref signaled a point. "Depends how—you look at it," Dan said. Again came the bark—"Hut!" Again the two collided, whirled, then fell. This time Dan gripped B.J.'s wrist, shoved it toward the other, pushed both wrists into B.J.'s stomach and leaned onto them, driving with his legs. B.J. adeptly rolled over onto a shoulder, shedding Dan. Dan somersaulted onto his stomach, felt the weight crash down. Dan twisted up onto one elbow, steadied himself, and readied to break free.

Then, oddly, the weight had lifted. Dan sprang up, spun around, beheld B.J. a few feet away, bent over, puffing, hands on knees. Dan prepared to spring, then spied the ref's interceding hand. From all around came shrieks, yells. Dan glanced over to spy a neutral-faced Ev.

The gong had sounded? But—?

Dan turned, trudged toward his corner. At once Dan paused and glanced back. Teeler, with a spacious grin despite the bandage on his nose, was tossing a towel over B.J.'s head. No, thought Dan. Oh, no …

Dan turned, reached his corner, hung his arms limply across the ropes, as the PA system announced:

"—has *done* it! *Has* caught up and even taken a slight lead from what all day long and only moments ago seemed an insurmountable Driver lead! Big guy, way to go! And Dan—hang in there best you can!"

Ev was staring toward the scoreboard. Gasping, Dan did the same. Amid a mighty burst of cheers and equally audible wails of disbelief, the wrestling figures flashed—'B.J., 80. DAN, 20.' A sign shaped like a giant sock rose feebly across Dan's vision, hovered for a moment, and swung down. From somewhere sounded a jazzy version of "The Impossible Dream." Once again Dan sensed the run of warm fluid down his nose, caught the familiar tinny taste. "No—let me," Ev said and applied the towel gingerly.

Dan peeked across. B.J.'s nose, too, displayed a conspicuous red trickle. At once B.J. stood up, wiped a forearm across his face and waved huskily to the crowd. Beside him Teeler hoisted his fist and in wild delight, to the yells and cheers, brandished a cell phone.

Through Dan's temple raced a mighty throb. His vision

blurred. He edged a hand up and there, above his right eye, felt a burn. From somewhere came a voice, too brash not to be overheard:

"Yeah, big fellow, so now finish it! Victory dinner? Right. I'm callin' in our reservations *right* now."

"What's the score now? It's—??"

"Billings, 700.10. Driver, 699.90."

The two men conferred with their coaches. The upcoming race would mark the first leg of the mini-decathlon, the contest's conclusion. The six mini-events would be each man's last chance to reach deep down and generate a supreme effort.

"—with each of the events worth roughly sixteen and two-thirds points. The first will be the mile run. O.K. gentlemen."

The parties approached the starting line. "The beginning of the end," Ev said, more composed now. He scanned the crowd, feigned a casual shrug. "Or the end of the beginning?" Then all at once he fell into a bout of anxious fidgetings all over again. "You guys sure don't give much of a breather between events," he called to a referee. "My man might have been injured in the last bout."

"*Might* have been?" Teeler laughed.

"We all know the rules," the referee replied. "Both parties signed on."

"Uh, right. B-But—?"

The ref looked to Dan. Dan shook his head no.

"Okay already!" Ev said. "Sorry I … brought it up!"

The two men edged up to the starting line. At once the familiar figure appeared, pistol in hand. He aimed the shiny barrel up into the sky. He looked to Dan. Dan was taking in long, thin breaths and rubbing at one severely swollen cheekbone.

"So ready ... aim ..."

Click—

B.J. started briskly off down the track, then drew to a halt.

"Oops! This-here, um, thing ain't properly loaded." Stockwell peeked about curiously, blew lightly on the barrel, and motioned. "Uh, young feller—you wanna trot back, try again?" he called, fishing for a cartridge.

Back at the starting line, B.J. waved Teeler off. Once again Stockwell, now prepared, hoisted the pistol. "*Ready*—" He waved the barrel. The ref backed off.

As the two men stood poised, Stockwell leaned into Dan's ear. "You owe me one, huh?" he mumbled, with a wink.

"*Get* set—!"

The gun discharged. Both runners trotted off.

The runners rounded the first curve neck and neck. Each invited the other to set the pace and cut the wind. At the start Dan took the initiative and moved in front. B.J. swung into position just behind. After a time, Dan slowed the pace considerably, and swung out wide. As they completed the first lap they were neck and neck. On the first straightaway of lap three B.J. forged ahead, Dan hanging in behind. Three times during this single lap the lead changed, with neither runner enjoying as much as a two-meter edge.

When the pair crossed the line to start the final lap, Dan made his move. On the first turn he burst ahead, to open a five, ten, and then fifteen-meter lead. On the straightaway B.J. caught him, inched ahead. Dan bent forward, pumped furiously, drew even, and then passed B.J.. Dan began his kick in earnest now, pounding furiously. By the time the two men reached the final curve, Dan had forged ahead considerably.

"Five thirty-five," Ev called, as Dan sped by.

Several moments later B.J. barged by, and came to a huffing, puffing halt.

"He won? Who cares?" Teeler blurted. "What's the margin?"

The cheering ebbed. All heads swung to the scoreboard, flashing a bizarre series of numbers. The accountants, standing en masse, punched their calculators. They arrived at a tally and stood by, openmouthed. At once, on a signal from Nips, a new sign lifted skyward, 'DAN'S THE MAN.' The scoreboard told it. 'B.J. 7.92. Dan 8.75.' Dan Driver had retaken the lead by a 708.65 to 708.02 margin.

Teeler glanced anxiously to his notes, then to Dan. "The guy's surging, B.J.! He sure didn't forget his breakfast!"

Ev was grinning. "Just like Steve Prefontaine. You looked like one heck of a miler out there," he beamed. He patted Dan on the back.

Dan nodded, gulped in more copious drafts of air, and

grinned. For this moment, just this moment, life was good.

The shot-put event would allow three tosses. On his first two tries Dan performed well, but each time his rival heaved it slightly farther, seemingly content just to outdo Dan's effort with his own. Dan's third attempt was a solid one, almost 40 feet. Then came B.J.'s final chance. For a moment he weighed the heavy sphere in his hands. Then carefully he poised himself, took a slow, graceful wind-up, and hurled—a mighty toss. The sphere thudded down just as B.J. recovered his balance and lifted his arms in triumph, to a substantial ovation from the stands. His attempt had surpassed Dan's by nearly 20 feet.

The scoreboard posted each man's best effort. Immediately the accountants hauled out their calculators. Sitting beside Nips, Burford Bertram obtained his result and let loose with a mighty cheer. At once he paused, to confront the sea of somber eyes around. "Oops! This one *isn't* inverse scoring?" He re-pecked the plastic buttons, emitted a groan, to the wiser nods of the others. Nips poked him with the tip of the huge sock sign. "It's the grand total that counts," he said.

The converted scores flashed— 'B.J. 10.16. DAN 6.51.'

On the field Dan and Ev traded silent glances, then looked away.

The TV announcer offered his own take. "Looks like Driver's going to need all the help he can get, Fred. The air out here's finally beginning to clear. B.J.'s now up by three points and needs only what—thirty-two more to win it?"

"But, Tim, you have to agree. We're seeing one real rock-'em, sock-'em competition."

"All we hoped for and more. Much more. Perhaps the very ultimate in reality shows. A lot of back-and-forth, shocked fans, too. Until that wrestling disaster, Driver had kept it close, had even built a lead. How about you? Impressed as I am?"

"Impressed is the word. B.J. we don't question. He's always been a sports maniac. He's a man who lives in the limelight. But Driver? Driver's been hiding under a bushel far too long. If you take the time to trace his career, which I did, you can now understand. Anyway, two real dedicated can-doers out there.'

"A prediction at this point?"

"Thrills."

"Beyond that?"

"These guys? Anybody's guess. *Anything* can happen. But I'll stick with B.J.. He's a known commodity. Tons of pressure now, too. But the kind a veteran's used to. My money's on him."

"Well, fans, there you have it. My own view? I'll hold off. Let's get back to the next event."

"Hundred yards? Easy pickin's. Way you two Supermen are high-tailin' it through these events, you might even get there faster than a bullet," said Stockwell.

Dan crouched, balanced himself, peeked skyward.

"Make it happen?" he mumbled. Then—"No. Just give me the chance to make it happen."

POP! The two men sped off. As the precious seconds unwound, Dan grabbed a slight lead, accelerating all the while—this run would be one increasing kick—and saw the figure stubbornly occupying the corner of his vision fall away. The tape loomed. Dan extended his chest, peered gratefully upward, glanced down—and was stunned. Already the tape was bounding aside. The huge figure had barged through to snag the race by a hair.

"Ten-eight even!" Teeler called. "Got the Slice on ice. Let's goooo!"

The two men jogged to a halt yards beyond the finish line. B.J. smirked Dan's way, then, between gasps, replied loudly enough for all to overhear. "Hundred yards? I've run that a few thousand times. Chasing down fast backs from behind. Supposedly fast."

The scores then flashed, B.J. 8.36 and Dan 8.30.

"—that everybody's favorite big man now needs less than twenty-four points to win it!" sounded the PA. The crowd burst out with an equally lively response.

"So much for prayer," Dan mumbled. "A man really is all alone out here, isn't he?"

Ev clapped him on the back, lent a solemn nod. "Dan, you know it, I know it, we all know it. God helps those who help themselves."

Dan approached the bar, planted his foot, and elevated

smoothly, effortlessly. He cleared the high jump bar with several inches to spare, kicking his back foot high on his finish. He landed lightly on his back, gazing up. "Five ten!" the ref called. Amid the vigorous general applause, Ev lent a cautious thumbs-up.

With the bar set at five four B.J. poised himself, took a deep breath, and raced off. He planted his foot, elevated his body up, up—and at once lost both balance and velocity and onto the piled mats in a heap, taking the bar with him. There he lay, disheveled, amid an outburst of shrieks, cheers, hoots, and laughter.

After a time B.J. edged up. He brushed himself off, took in the crowd, and grinned. "Unfriendly 'bar' scene down here all right," he called as he moved off to make room for Dan. "Best 'a three? I'll get the hang. You clowns just watch!"

At Dan's request the bar was raised four inches, to six feet two. Dan readied himself, then raced down the runway, wheeled smoothly up and over. The effort, eclipsing his first in both height and grace, drew an enthusiastic response. As Dan trotted back he gave an all-yours gesture to B.J., who nodded and made ready.

Despite his last miss, B.J. motioned the refs to raise the bar another two inches, to an even five feet six. He set himself, focused earnestly for a moment, then dashed off. He planted his foot, lofted up and up and somehow, for all his clumsy, aw-shucks, offhanded style, managed to clear the bar grazing it slightly and thump down onto the mats below.

There he lay, grinning up dazedly, ecstatically, as the crowd roared. At the wholly unanticipated feat, several sections—prominent among them being the A.H. Adams front-row entourage—stood up and applauded wildly. Still grinning, B.J. regained his feet, brushed himself off, and lumbered back toward the starting line. As he approached, he matched Dan's all-yours gesture with one of his own.

The crowd hooted its delight. "Nice jump," Dan said above the noise.

"Thanks," B.J. replied.

Now would come each man's final effort. At Dan's request, the bar was raised an additional two inches, to six four. Dan had waited a long, long time for this jump. Remembering his college days, he mumbled to himself. "I mean, this one really counts."

Dan steadied himself, took a deep breath, expelled exactly half of it, and dashed off, another smooth, flawless jump. For a moment Dan lay atop the cool mats, savoring the applause, grinning up as elatedly as B.J. had a moment before.

Now the crowd grew hushed. With the bar set at five feet eight inches, B.J. took his place. At once he exploded, and thundered down the track. Again he lost his footing as he tried to plant his left foot, and ran right through the bar, taking it down with him as he tumbled.

"Name's Humpty. As in *Dump*-ty!" he called back.

The laughter crested, then fell away. As B.J. stood by with a loose shrug, all eyes swung away. The raw numbers appeared first, before the conversions. Dan's last effort had topped B.J.'s best, 6'4" to 5'6".

The accountants bent to their work. One by one, they grew perplexed. They pecked, stared, re-pecked. "Round off or not?" came the mounting grumble. "How far do we *carry* this?"

Teeler and Ev viewed the scoreboard with the same question.

"Just round off to eight apiece," Teeler suggested.

"In a pigskin's ear!" Ev replied.

The scoreboard flashed, granting Dan a score of 8.92 to B.J.'s 7.75. Ev gave a so-take-that nod to Teeler. His triumph was blunted almost at once, however, by the announcement. "Folks, B.J. now needs less than sixteen points to win it all!"

The next event, the second-to-last in track and field, was the broad jump. Each man was allowed three jumps, the best to count. B.J. waved to the crowd as he took his place on the runway. He moved his arms back and forth as he readied himself. Finally he took a deep breath and took off. He reached the line in mid-sprint, planted his left foot, and leaped.

"Fault!" called a ref. B.J. had stepped on the line. The attempt was void.

Next up was Dan. He started a few feet farther back than B.J. in order to gain more speed. Dan, too, took a deep breath, let it out, and dashed to a point just short of the white tape and took off, hit the sand and fell forward.

"Jump is good," called one official. Others ran to get

his mark where his back foot had touched. It was a solid jump—17' 6". One could tell. Dan's attempt had been much smoother and better rehearsed. His approach speed and arm motion while in the air had greatly aided his effort.

On his second jump, B.J. improved to 12' 9". He smiled as he rose from the sand. He winked to the crowd. Dan's second did not improve in length. Nor did his third. B.J.'s final attempt, his best, came in at 14' 6".

With the jumps completed, everyone gazed to the board. The score flashed— 9.12 for Dan, 7.55 for B.J..

A huge ovation for Dan erupted.

The scoreboard flashed off. Within seconds it came back on, now to display the cumulative scores:

Billings 741.84

Driver   741.50

Ev set down his clipboard, gasped, reset his spectacles, pasted the drooping bandage back on his face. Once again he took in the scoreboard. "M-My God!" he said. "It's— all going to—?" He fought another shudder. He spied his counterpart, likewise with bandaged face, staring just as attentively in the same direction.

Both had come to perceive that in all probability this, the quarter mile and final leg of the mini-decathlon, would decide the contest.

Already it was late afternoon. Already a moon was perched in plain view, full and whitish. Already now, too, thousands in the crowd and many more thousands in their homes, realizing the gravity of it all, fell silent as Dan, B.J., and their coaches marched toward the starting line.

"—closer than *anyone* could ever have predicted," said a TV commentator. His words were quiet, subdued. "Ladies and gentlemen, can you *believe*? This upcoming run is going to determine the vict—the whole ball of wax?!"

"Right," added his companion. "With B.J. in the lead, Driver will not only have to win but win by ... Well, it all depends on Dan's time and B.J.'s time—on that all-important divvying-up of the sixteen and two-thirds points. Or is it sixteen point six six six ... ?" His voice trailed off, ironically.

Dan and B.J. high-stepped about, took deep breaths, wind-milled their arms to loosen nerves and muscles. Each assumed his starting position, and then stared quietly down the track. At once Dan turned. "Either way, B.J., it's been one heck of an experience," Dan said.

"You got it," said B.J..

The two shook hands. To this mutual display of sportsmanship the crowd responded with a solid round of applause and, then, as the hands unclasped and the men turned away and made ready, a buzzing undercurrent came alive. Stockwell was sauntering over, pistol in hand. B.J. winked at Ev and said, "Either way, glad I could help you guys get this thing off the ground. Toss in my share."

"Your share?" said Ev.

"Sure. Who do you think gave you guys that extra five?" B.J. nodded up at the moon. "That grinning dude up there? 'Course, my motives ain't purely unselfish. I win now—and I will—I get back my five plus lots, lots more. Yaaaa-hooo!"

Ev suppressed a sudden twinge in his neck. He looked off sickishly, then—"Okay, why not let it all out B.J.? What about that mark?" He jabbed his finger toward B.J.'s calf.

B.J. twisted back, peeked down. "What mark?" he said.

"That one! Geez! Anyway Dan, you pull it out and we'll make this ulcer of mine a permanent fixture. We'll spend all our time promoting. Maybe even write a book about it."

Ev extended a shaky hand to Dan, then reneged. "Oops— forgot. Not to be too hasty." He walked a few feet down the track. At once he held up Cuddles. "We'll both be waiting for you," he said.

"You guys going to hoof it or have a gabfest?"

Stockwell ducked in. He blew on the barrel, swung it down the track. The refs backed off. "Okay. One lap. Quarter mile. *All* the marbles. *On* your mark. *Get* set—"

Both men froze, eyes fixed, jaws jutting.

"Yes," called Ev. "The look! Dan, you've got it! You've—"

POP! Amid a mighty eruption of cheers, both men sprinted off. The first curve they rounded neck and neck, both gasping. As they came out of the turn Dan forged in front. B.J. caught up, ran evenly, stride for stride, edged ahead ... a foot ... a yard. But on the straightaway Dan caught up. Then along the straightaway ... toward the turn ... into the turn ... turning ... turning ... through the turn ... and now in plain sight the finish line ... and ... neck and neck still, neither man ceding an inch ... then B.J. copping the slightest lead by poking his head just beyond Dan's own. Dan bent forward, pumped furiously, sucked in mighty, rhythmic gulps of air. He glimpsed the shoulder of B.J.'s jersey as once more the big man edged ahead. Then there, just beyond the shoulder, the tape, the finish line, Dan spied it—the button-eyed bear bobbing energetically before the efforts of a frantic, exhorting Ev.

Dan dug down, accelerated into a final kick, fast, faster ... as the buttoned face bobbed close, closer ... the jersey hung stubbornly abreast, then ... receded out of Dan's vision. Now Ev was leaping. Cuddles was leaping. From everywhere around sounded shouts, shrieks, screams. Dan thrust his head forward, nosed the tape, launched himself across, and collapsed onto the cinders beyond and rolled over onto his back and, gasping, peered up. B.J. flew by, hurdling him skillfully.

Dan reached his feet, brushed the cinders off his elbows and knees. Already heads were swinging en masse toward the scoreboard. "A shade over fifty seconds," came a voice. "So it's—?"

Dan shuddered, peered about. The world had ... become stuck in time. A wordless Ev, a B.J. with hands on knees, gasping, an immobile Teeler, the bank of refs—all had faces poised off, away. Just off the track Ruff and Diana were staring away, openmouthed, Ruff's jaw as rigid as his finger. Mossey and his entourage, Nips and his pals—all were likewise frozen in a limbo, faces set, the huge sock sign for the moment tilted, motionless, its message forgotten. Then the rows and rows behind—the thousands on thousands, on their feet, staring. At once Dan glimpsed at the only face besides his own not fixed toward the scoreboard—Cuddles, with his button-eyed smile.

The scoreboard flashed. There came several isolated yells, then a return of the hushed, collective silence. Raw numbers appeared: 8.41 for Dan, 8.25 for B.J.. Nips and his pals broke into action. The other faces remained astonished. Bertram was the first to arrive at a figure. He stared, incredulous. His jaw twitched. His eyes bugged. But he dared not respond.

The figures on the scoreboard vanished. Moments later the new numbers flashed forth:

'FINAL TALLY: B.J. BILLINGS, 750.09. DAN DRIVER, 749.91.'

B.J. had won it—by .18 hundreths of a point.

The stadium exploded. As Nips and the others sat back, numb, openmouthed, the execs in front of them leapt up, hugged one another, tossed their fists skyward, yelled and whistled. Then, seat by seat, row by row, section by section, the crowd in its vast entirety stood up, broke into applause, and then, directed by the gleeful Mossey now in the front row, rocked back and forth on its collective feet. "B.J.! B.J.! B.J.!"

Dan stared for a time at the scoreboard. Still dazed, he turned away, and spied B.J.. B.J. shrugged a good-natured shrug, stepped over, extended a hand and a pat on the back.

"Fair and square," said Dan, grasping the hand. "Congratulations."

"Great game! They call you 'Driver'? I see why. Congratulations to you."

"Thanks."

"No, really. Right through the uprights, dude—*really*."

Dan blinked. There was something odd in B.J.'s grin, and even more in his wink. "Folks want to be a part of something bigger than themselves," B.J. recited. "Only when you become part of something bigger than yourself you become whole. We pushed you and you didn't fold."

Ev broke in, embraced Dan immodestly. "Win or lose, good job!" Then in sudden, awkward apology he backed off, to reset his spectacles and regain his breath.

"Furniture Man—"

B.J. gripped Ev's still trembling hand. "Congrats to you, too. But, dude—you gotta cut down on that *coffee*."

"Uh, right," Ev said, backing away, his dejection now starting to show.

Now, suddenly, it had became pandemonium. Reporters, well-wishers, fans pressed in. Teeler nodded to Ev. Ev nodded to Teeler. Civilly, before the cameras, the two shook hands. Half the crowd broke out in wild celebration, the other half stood stunned. It was sinking in now. Ruff sat by neutrally, splint perched up at the scoreboard, Diana's gentle hand on his shoulder. The lifters around him stood up, stretched, and began a slow trek down toward the field. On their way they passed Mossey still blissfully patting backs and shaking hands, even high-fiving the esteemed A.H. himself. Yes, and now Nips and the others, disappointed still, shunning one another's eyes, rose as well and trudged down toward the field. Up in Section 22 Coach Wiley lent an empty shrug, took out a crisp $50 bill from his shirt pocket, and handed the bill over to a grinning Coach Sims. Just below, the group of ex-Lakefield athletes filed down, stepping slowly, heads bowed. In Section 61 Chip and pals still sat, their Chompy hats tilted slightly over their eyes.

So it went. Half the crowd was celebratory, the other half sullen. The stands began to slowly empty and fans spilled over the finish line and then the entire field, engulfing both B.J. and Dan.

In a milling sea of humanity, a single figure remained seated. High up against the sky, perched in the topmost row, grinning down on all the commotion, he sat, with his huge, white face covered by a cowboy hat and sunglasses. He witnessed as B.J. Billings broke into further antics—now flexing his muscles to a reporter. He witnessed as Ev Winchell quietly nodded and shook hands, and then took a moment to stare off amid a careful blotting of his nose and forehead. He witnessed, too, as an attractive woman holding a little boy with a little girl in tow stood patiently by and was greeted by Dan, who embraced all three. This family was inundated by a cluster of reporters and a sea of well-wishers. Away from the main hubbub, Ev hugged his brother and sister-in-law. The figure in a stylish cowboy hat and ultra-cool wrap-around sun glasses had witnessed all.

Now he stood, some six-and-a-half-feet tall, and peered off onto the sky. He spoke quietly to himself.,

"Be a standout in all fifteen? Who am I—we—trying to kid? I'm pretty good at it. Darned good at it. Proud of it. Darned proud of it. Football? It pays my bills. B.J. pulled it out. Or did he? Don't really matter. Driver made himself one real wacky run for his money, and now this thing is off the ground. Never dreamed it would be this popular and get such attention. I knew I couldn't cut the mustard during training—I lacked the all-around skills. Gotta hand it to them two, Driver and Winchell. Sure do hope their scheme catches on. Guys like them make life worth living. When it comes to finding that 'physical genius' or whatever—and, ah, find the dude or dudette who really can do it all—no use keepin' *that* a secret any longer. Right?" He flashed a reinvigorated, deeply dimpled grin. "Heck, could even be—you."

He rolled his eyes down. Casually he stretched. Once more he took in the sea of humanity below.

"Anyway, I was mighty glad to fly in and partake in the competition along with my twin B.J.. Or, hey—I'm B.J. and he's P.J.? Well, don't really matter. That was our secret."

Again he grinned, and shook his head. "But now it's time. Time I head down, tell 'em all the truth. You jest watch. *This'll* cause one real hub-bubba! Heh heh!"

Now step-by-step, row-by-row, he made his descent, moving loosely, hands in pockets, grinning all the while. He reached the playing field and removed his sunglasses and ten-gallon hat and entered the crowd and stepped up to high-five and embrace his brother. Then with his brother at his side, he shook hands with a stunned Dan Driver and an equally openmouthed and then yes-yes-I-*told*-you-so rapidly nodding Ev Winchell .... He amusedly lifted a pants leg to expose a dark spot on his right calf and then posed on the finish-line for a official photo-op beside his equally grinning twin ... Heads swiveled. Cameras flashed.

At once a *shot* rang out. The crowd fell back. Mr. Stockwell strode up, pistol high. "I would like everyone's attention. Now!" He faced the twins directly. "I—we *all*—reckon you two got a mighty lotta explaining to do."

Officials, media and most of the large multitude, dumbstruck all, edged in. Realizing now, some found themselves overtaken by sheer delight. Others were outright dismayed. Most simply gawked.

B.J. reluctantly took the microphone and began to speak. As acknowledgement of B.J.'s confession and Dan's victory became evident, color began to refill Ev's face. He raised his arm. He took the mike. "Um, ladies and gentlemen, I guess this—this means that Dan and I *are* your winners."

Bulbs popped and shutters clicked and cameras rolled to enshrine the event. Ev and Dan finally shook hands.

Nips and his pals edged up. Nearly berserk with excitement, Nips stared at the twins, gawked for a moment at the uncanny similarity of their features, and then thumbed at B.J..

As the truth of the matter leaked out, the crowd grew jubilant. Duntoot's fist shot skyward in joy. Ruff hauled down his right arm, splint and all, and more politely elevated his left. Diana smiled at him and reached over and hoisted his hand even higher. A truly pale-faced Mitchell Mossey craned his neck. Not far from the smiling Nips a sign now came into view— 'DAN NIPS B.J.!'

Nearby, Coach Sims retrieved the $50-dollar bill from his pocket. With bittersweet amusement he kissed the bill goodbye and re-deposited it with another onto the palm of Coach Wiley who nodded his approval.

Down on the field Chip and pals peeked at their watches, pinched the creases back into their plaid outfits, and made for the parking lot. "I've got it!" Chip blurted. "McCONTEST burger! *That's* what we'll call it!" He witnessed the milling crowd on the field around him. "Twin patties, a side of un-relished pickles, and fifteen different, mind-blowing ingredients! Wow!"

Happy commotion reigned. "No, no, the money's the least of it. See, the main idea behind all this…" Ev was compelled to take pause, avert his eyes from the reporters and his brother, and exhale in unabashed, shuddering relief. Stockwell patted Lori lightly on the head, blew gleefully on his pistol barrel. "If your dad can run like that? Why'd he ever ask me for a ride?" Just beyond stood Duntoot. He and Dan spied each other. Dan nodded. The druggist smirked. Dan smiled. Just beyond Bombe was framing the scene with a thin, square box of fingers and thumbs. "I've got first rights," Bombe called with zest in his voice.

The crowd pressed in at the finish line. Surrounded by former teammates, coaches, and the full Armbuster group, Dan shook hands all around. B.J. and P.J. grinned, shaking hands, laughing the whole thing off.

Dan Driver cradled his son, hugged his daughter, his wife, and even his mother-in-law. Dan did a final, celebratory high-five with Ev.

Epilogue

The stadium lay silent. Overhead sat the moon, white, bold, biding. At this same magic hour thousands of TV sets across the city and state and millions across the nation displayed the flashing, familiar sequence—an exciting half of Monday Night Football. The half ended, yielding way to a barrage of commercials. At last the halftime pageantry arrived.

As cooler wisps of early autumn slipped through the stadium and played amid the sections of empty tiers, there sounded on these same sets across city, town, and land the voice of Mike Tirico, a voice which in its own particular way could best pay homage to what had happened here:

"An understandably popular contest inaugurated this weekend in an American city, ladies and gentlemen. A curious concept, some might say. And an even more curious turn of events to send it all up to our studio tonight and into national prominence by the madcap antics of Dromedary linebacker B.J.—or is it P.J.?— Billings.

We must all certainly applaud the gallant efforts of Mr. Dan Driver. I have already heard from my dear friend and former colleague, John Madden. He has already concluded that Dan Driver would be a likely candidate for indoctrination on his infamous Horse Trailer.

This three-day competition captured the hearts and minds of fans everywhere. For this, more than anything yet devised in athletics, gives the quiet little guy or gal who can do a

317

great many things quite right—that bland 'All-Madden On The Inside' of each one of us who isn't so bland or little after all—a chance to enjoy public recognition.

Sports fans, this contest permits us to search America's heart—the small towns and metropolises, back roads and inner cities, playgrounds and professional stadiums—to find that most uniquely adapted individual, the non-specialized athlete who can do it all. Just who down the road will end up with all the marbles we've yet to determine, but you out there—whoever, wherever you might be—as one man in love with sport, we salute you. Yes, Dan Driver—'The Best ALL Around'—wear your title and wear it proudly. I, John, our entire staff, all of America—we salute you."